Converging Empires

ANDREA GEIGER

Converging Empires

Citizens and Subjects in the
North Pacific Borderlands, 1867–1945

The University of North Carolina Press *Chapel Hill*

Set in Arno Pro by Westchester Publishing Services
Manufactured in the United States of America

The University of North Carolina Press has been a member of the
Green Press Initiative since 2003.

Library of Congress Cataloging-in-Publication Data
Names: Geiger, Andrea A. E., author.
Title: Converging empires : citizens and subjects in the north Pacific borderlands,
     1867-1945 / Andrea Geiger.
Other titles: David J. Weber series in the new borderlands history.
Description: Chapel Hill : University of North Carolina Press, [2022] | Series: The David J.
     Weber series in the new borderlands history | Includes bibliographical references and index.
Identifiers: LCCN 2021054799 | ISBN 9781469659275 (cloth ; alk. paper) | ISBN 9781469641140
     (paperback ; alk. paper) | ISBN 9781469667843 (ebook)
Subjects: LCSH: Alaska Natives—Legal status, laws, etc. | Indigenous peoples—Legal status,
     laws, etc.—Canada. | Foreign workers, Japanese—Legal status, laws, etc.—Canadian-
     American Border Region. | Alaska—History—1867-1959. | Canadian-American Border
     Region—History—19th century. | Canadian-American Border Region—History—
     20th century. | Canadian-American Border Region—Race relations. | British Columbia—
     History. | United States—Foreign relations. | Japan—Colonies—Boundaries.
Classification: LCC F908 .G45 2021 | DDC 979.8/03—dc23/eng/20211206
LC record available at https://lccn.loc.gov/2021054799

Cover illustration: Detail of a photo of Mount St. Elias, Alaska, from the south, with men and
sled, 1906 (U.S. Geological Survey, Professional Paper 45, Library ID ric00539).

For Lawrence Roland Fast

Contents

Illustrations and Maps

Acknowledgments

This book is rooted in two long-standing areas of interest, one in Japanese history and the history of Japanese immigrants in North America and the other in Aboriginal law and in Indigenous history.[1] If I were to trace the origin of my own interest in the Meiji era and the decades that led up to the outbreak of the Second World War, I would have to go back to the stories that our calligraphy teacher told about his wartime experiences in Manchuria at the Japanese school my sister and I attended in Hiroshima. My interest in Aboriginal law was precipitated by courses offered by Ralph Johnson and Gregory Hicks at the University of Washington School of Law, and only deepened during my time as a reservation attorney for the Confederated Tribes of the Colville Reservation in northeastern Washington State. Michael Taylor, who later became a chief justice of the Colville Tribal Court of Appeals, helped me to better understand the real impact that federal law has had on the lives of Indigenous people in the United States and Canada over time. The same is true of the members of the Colville Tribes with whom I had the good fortune to work, including some whose ancestral territories span the U.S.-Canada border.

I have benefited greatly from the rich body of work produced by the many borders and borderlands historians, too numerous to name, who have thought deeply about the borders that transect North America and, in particular, the southwestern borderlands through which the U.S.-Mexico border now cuts. The same is true of scholars in the other fields my work engages. I owe a particularly deep debt of gratitude, all these years later, to the historians at the University of Washington who taught and inspired me to turn to history, particularly Richard White, John Findlay, Chuck Bergquist, Moonho Jung, and Ken Pyle.

My thanks as well to Chris Rogers and to my editors at the University of North Carolina Press, including Chuck Grench, Debbie Gershenowitz, Ben Johnson, and Andy Graybill for their warm support. Colleagues at Simon Fraser University who provided welcome insights and sage advice at critical moments include Janice Matsumura, Luke Clossey, Ilya Vinkovetsky, Sonja Luehrmann, Jay Taylor, Mary-Ellen Kelm, Mark Leier, and Alan McMillan. I am also grateful to Patty Limerick, Merry Ovnick, Eiichiro Azuma, Samuel

Truett, Michel Hogue, Lissa Wadewitz, and John Lutz, among many others, for their interest in my work and for understanding why it matters that we try to tell the more complicated stories.

I owe a deep debt of gratitude to the many archivists and librarians who went out of their way to assist me in archives around the North Pacific Rim, including the Yukon Archives in Whitehorse, Yukon Territory; the BC Archives in Victoria, B.C.; the Asian Library and the Rare Books and Special Collections Division of the University of British Columbia Library and the UBC Archives in Vancouver, B.C.; the Alaska State Archives and the Alaska State Library in Juneau, Alaska; and the National Diet Library in Tokyo, Japan. Linda Kawamoto Reid at the Nikkei National Museum and Archives in Burnaby, B.C.; Jean Eiers-Page at the Prince Rupert City and Regional Archives in Prince Rupert, B.C.; Nathalie Macfarlane at the Haida Gwaii Museum at K̲ay Llnagaay, and local historian Neil Carey, also in Haida Gwaii, were all unfailingly generous in sharing their knowledge and insights regarding the historical experience of Japanese immigrants and Indigenous people along the northern coast of British Columbia and across the Dixon Entrance. In Alaska, I was fortunate to have the opportunity to work with the generous and knowledgable archivists at the U.S. National Archives and Records Administration in Anchorage, Alaska, during the last two weeks before the facility was shut down. I am also grateful to Seizo Oka, director of the Japanese American History Archives in San Francisco, who generously shared a copy of his translation of *Zaibeinihonjinshi* (History of Japanese in America), a work over a thousand pages in length published in 1940. Translations prepared by Masaki Watanabe, in turn, made it possible both to test my own reading of certain Japanese-language sources and to review material I would not have had time to translate myself. The financial support of Canada's Social Sciences and Humanities Research Council and Simon Fraser University was invaluable in making it possible for me to spend the time needed in the archives. As always, the staff of the interlibrary loan department at the Simon Fraser University Library went the extra mile to track down materials throughout North America and across the Pacific Ocean in Japan that it would not otherwise have been possible to access.

Brief excerpts from some chapters were incorporated into articles on related topics and are republished here with the permission of the original publishers: "Disentangling Law and History: Nikkei Challenges to Race-Based Exclusion from British Columbia's Coastal Fisheries, 1920–2007," *Southern California Quarterly*, vol. 100, no. 3 (Fall 2018); "Haida Gwaii as North Pacific Borderland, Ikeda Mine as Alternative West: 1906–1910," *Pacific Northwest*

Quarterly, vol. 108, no. 4 (Fall 2017); and "Reframing Race and Place: Locating Japanese Immigrants in Relation to Indigenous Peoples in the North American West, 1880–1940," *Southern California Quarterly*, vol. 96, no. 3 (2014). Jonathan Fast made it possible to include a cartoon first published nearly a century ago, and Bill Nelson prepared the original maps. Both add a dimension to this book that it would otherwise lack.

While in the archives in Juneau, I happened upon the story of a young Japanese American woman with ties to Alaska named Kay Mikami who, after the war, settled on the East Coast, where she taught third grade.[2] I was one of her students. I had no idea at the time that my family would move to Japan and that I would attend a Japanese school there just a few years later or that the history of Japanese immigrants in North America would become a focus of my research. I am sure she would have enjoyed knowing that this was what one of her students went on to do and am only sorry that I did not have a chance to tell her as much during her lifetime.

As always, I am grateful to all family and friends, among them my sisters, Sarah and Vanessa, whose affection and support continue to sustain me. To all, I return their affection in full measure. My research for this book began in earnest when Lawrence and I drove north through British Columbia's mountainous interior and along the Alaska Highway to Whitehorse in winter nearly a decade ago, just the first of many adventures on which we embarked. He has been there every step of the way, and it is to him that this book is dedicated.

Note on Terminology

The names assigned to both places and people over time can tell us a great deal both about the history of colonization and about the perspectives and attitudes of differing groups of people at any given time. Left unexamined, certain names have the power to distort our understanding of the past. As historians of empire and colonization note, the renaming of Indigenous spaces lay at the very heart of the colonial endeavor and the erasure of the continuing presence of Indigenous people within a colonial framework.[1] Always a challenge, particularly in the context of a story as complex and multifaceted as that told here, is determining what name is best utilized for a given place or people at a particular time. The island group that lies off the coast of what is now British Columbia long known to the Haida people as Haida Gwaii (X̱aayda Gwayy'), for example, was renamed Queen Charlotte's Islands by British explorers and referred to as the Queen Charlotte Islands by British colonial authorities for over two centuries, even as the Japanese Canadian fishers active along the coast prior to World War II knew them as Kuichi Airan.[2] Generally, I have chosen to use the name for a given place that is most revealing of its time and that gives us the greatest insight into the attitudes or perspectives of the actors under discussion, while always remaining cognizant that the vast majority of this borderlands region remained Indigenous space, even as it was incorporated within the boundaries of what are now Alaska, British Columbia, and the Yukon Territory.

I make an exception where I discuss the geography of a given area and, for clarity, use the place-name most familiar to current readers, for example, Hokkaido for what is now regarded as the northernmost of Japan's four major islands even though it remains Ainu Moshir in the eyes of the Ainu people, whose territory it was long before it was formally incorporated within the boundaries of the Japanese nation state in 1869.[3] For the same reason, other than in direct quotations or where I paraphrase the words of a historical figure, I use the current spelling of the names of towns in Alaska, British Columbia, and the Yukon, for example, Whitehorse instead of White Horse and Skagway instead of Skaguay. I use "the states" to refer to the Lower 48 (as many Alaskans do even today), given that it serves as a useful reminder of Alaska's status as a territory during the prewar and wartime period.[4]

Although my primary geographical focus is the region along the north Pacific coast of North America where the national borders established by Canada and the United States during the second half of the nineteenth century cut across the traditional territories of Indigenous peoples, including areas that now also lie within the borders of British Columbia, the Yukon, and Alaska, I also follow Japanese migrants and Indigenous people along the entire length of that coast to the westernmost edge of the continent and, at times, across the North Pacific Rim to Japan or south across the forty-ninth parallel. When a general referent to the entire borderlands region that is my primary focus is required—and to resist the notion that its incorporation into the United States and Canada was inevitable—I use "north Pacific coast." Because writing across national borders makes it necessary to engage different forms of usage, I capitalize "Indigenous," "Aboriginal," and "First Nation" as is the custom in Canada, much as it is the custom in the United States to capitalize "Alaska Native." I avoid the use of "Indian" except where it appears in a quotation or as part of a title, as, for example, in what continues to be named the Indian Act in Canada.

Wherever possible, in referring to Indigenous groups and communities, who organize and identify themselves in a wide variety of ways, I provide the name preferred today by members of the group or community in question in parentheses or an endnote, in addition to the names used by settlers or others in the original source, given that historical documents often do not reflect these preferences.[5]

While it is customary to list family names first in Japan, many Japanese immigrants in North America adopted the Western custom of listing their given name first. The same is true of Japanese authors writing for English-speaking audiences, whereas authors of Japanese-language works follow the Japanese custom. In citing the work of a Japanese author, I generally follow the order utilized in the original source. In many instances, subsequent references make clear what a given individual's family name is; where this is unclear, I add a note to clarify this the first time an author's name is mentioned.[6]

Both English- and Japanese-language sources dating from the prewar period tended, for different reasons, to refer to all people of Japanese ancestry as Japanese regardless of their status as citizens or subjects of the United States or Canada.[7] I use the term *nikkei* [日系] ("of Japanese origin or ancestry") or *nikkeijin* [日系人] (person/people of Japanese ancestry) where a general referent to people of Japanese ancestry on both sides of the U.S.-Canada border is needed, given that these terms can include Japanese nationals, naturalized or North American–born citizens of Japanese descent, and their descendants.

As used in Japanese, these are simple descriptors, in contrast to the anglicized proper noun "Nikkei," which works to create those of Japanese ancestry as a separate category of people that share inherent characteristics.[8] The same is true of the terms *issei, nisei,* and *sansei,* which, in Japanese—the language most familiar to prewar Japanese immigrants—simply refer to first, second, and third generation and can also apply to immigrants from other parts of the world. This avoids giving these terms a level of emphasis they do not have in Japanese, which does not distinguish between capital and lowercase letters.

In cases where differentiating among *nikkeijin* based on their status as citizens or subjects of a particular nation is germane to the topic at hand, I distinguish Japanese Americans and Japanese Canadians from Japanese subjects. I also distinguish immigrants and migrants to differentiate—to the degree that it is possible to do so—between individuals entering Canada or the United States with the intention of settling permanently and members of more mobile populations primarily interested in responding to the demand for labor.

There has been considerable debate through the years regarding the appropriate term to use for the forced removal of people of Japanese ancestry from the coast and the camps where a great majority were forcibly detained based solely on ancestry alone in both the United States and Canada. "Evacuation" and "relocation," euphemisms employed by the governments of both countries, obscure the injustice and suffering that Japanese Americans and Japanese Canadians endured as a result of that uprooting. I refer to the sites where they were detained as detention camps following the practice of both the Nikkei National Museum in Burnaby, British Columbia, and Denshō: The Japanese American Legacy Project in Seattle, Washington.[9] While "detention" also does not take full account of the conditions in the camps or the failure of both governments to afford the detainees due process, it recognizes that their removal from the coast was not an action undertaken by either nation for the benefit of those forcibly confined in places far from their homes during the Second World War, as the euphemisms employed by both governments implied.

Introduction

Along the northwestern edge of North America, where the continent meets and extends out into the North Pacific Ocean, lies an area that was long omitted or deliberately obscured on early European maps because its contours were unknown to those who drew them.[1] Located, at various times, at the farthest edges of the Russian, British, Spanish, and American empires, the rocky coast of the continent gives way to a series of islands that reach across the North Pacific to connect it to Asia. Along the shores of what are now the Alaska panhandle and British Columbia, a series of archipelagos protects much of the mainland from the direct impact of the great waves that have made the journey across the Pacific Ocean. Made up of hundreds of densely forested islands and misty, interconnected channels carved into the landscape by glacial retreat, these archipelagos are home to ecologically rich and strikingly beautiful landscapes that extend from what is now the Washington coast to the Gulf of Alaska.[2] Further west, the cedar, pine and fir-covered islands of southeast Alaska and British Columbia give way to a rockier and more austere landscape marked by glaciers that tie land to sea along Alaska's southern coast. At the end of the Alaskan peninsula, the Aleutian island chain stretches further westward still, dividing the Pacific Ocean from the Bering Sea and linking the continent of North America to the Kamchatka Peninsula. The Kuril Islands, in turn, extend south and west to connect the Kamchatka Peninsula to the island of Hokkaido. Taken together, these islands sketch an arc across the North Pacific Ocean that is testament to the interconnected nature of the continents of Asia and North America—a link obscured even today on maps that center the Atlantic rather than the Pacific Ocean.

Another conduit connecting the two continents across the North Pacific is the Kuroshio, or Japan Current, which carries the warm waters of the western mid-Pacific north along the coast of Japan—a Pacific archipelago made up of numerous islands itself—and eastward across the North Pacific until it nears the shores of western North America, where it divides off the west coast of Haida Gwaii, which the British called Queen Charlotte's Islands.[3] Other forces that have connected the people of the Pacific Rim through history include the tsunamis produced by the enormous earthquakes that periodically rock its coasts, as was the case in 1700 when a tsunami created by a major

The North Pacific Ocean and its borderlands including key locations referred to in the text.

BEAUFORT SEA

Barrow

ALASKA

Beaver

Nome

Fairbanks

St Lawrence I.

Dawson City

BRITISH NORTH AMERICA/
CANADA

YUKON
TERRITORY

Nunivak I.

Anchorage
Cordova

Whitehorse

60°

Yukutat

Pribilof
Islands

Bristol
Bay

Kodiak I.

GULF OF
ALASKA

Juneau

BRITISH
COLUMBIA

Unalaska

Sitka

Prince Rupert

54°

Haida Gwaii
Hecate Strait

ISLANDS

Queen Charlotte Sound

Alert Bay

Vancouver Island
Georgia Strait
Strait of Juan de Fuca

Steveston

49°

Seattle

Portland

42°

UNITED
STATES

San Francisco

Los Angeles

OCEAN

Baha
California

Hawai'i

141°

earthquake along the Pacific coast of North America hit the Japanese coast without warning.[4]

It was along the northeastern coast of the Pacific Rim, where the waves of the Pacific Ocean wash ashore on the west coast of the North American continent, that the interests of Britain, Japan, and the United States converged during the late nineteenth and early twentieth centuries.[5] Both Spain and Russia had left their mark on the north Pacific coast during earlier centuries, but neither remained an active presence in the region by the end of the nineteenth century. Instead, Britain and the United States vied with each other over the boundaries of their respective territorial claims and shared with Japan a keen interest in both the marine and the land-based natural resources of the region. By the early twentieth century, the northwestern coast of North America had become a place where various territorial and ocean boundaries intersected, creating an increasingly complex and multilayered jurisdictional web. Together, Indigenous, provincial, territorial, village, municipal, national, and maritime borders created a dynamic legal landscape that Indigenous and non-Indigenous people alike negotiated in myriad ways as they moved through the spaces they delineated. People of all backgrounds, including prospectors, adventurers, and settlers from Europe, British North America and later Canada, the United States, Latin America, and Asia—including Japan, China, and the Philippines—made and remade themselves as they traveled across and between the boundaries that defined these jurisdictions according to the complex mix of obstacle and opportunity each represented.[6]

Latecomers from distant corners of the globe were not the first to create this coast as a borderlands region. Long before the imperial interests of Britain, the United States, and Japan converged along the northeastern shores of the Pacific Ocean, and even before the arrival of the Russians and the Spanish, it had functioned as a borderland between both land and sea and as an area where multiple, intersecting boundaries important to the Indigenous peoples of the region had evolved over time without reference to the imperial or national boundaries that would later be superimposed. In contrast to the way this coast was envisioned by Europeans, Alan D. McMillan and Iain McKechnie remind us, the Indigenous peoples who had lived along it for millennia regarded it as located not at the edges but at the center of the physical, cultural, and spiritual worlds in which they lived.[7] Often cloaked in fog and battered by westerly gales during fall and winter, narrow, stony beaches piled high with logs washed ashore during winter storms speak to the dense forests that cover much of the arable land. During spring and summer, streams fed by winter snow plunge down the steep cliffs that line the edges of the conti-

nental mainland, periodically interrupted by deep fjords. Protected from exposure to the waves of the open ocean by countless small islands separated by
narrow channels and waterways rich in natural resources, including cedar,
seals, sea otters, fish, shellfish, and other forms of marine life, this environment was one that had long sustained and been shaped by the Indigenous
peoples who made it their home over many centuries.[8]

This wealth of resources was one element that led to the incorporation of
this borderlands region within the framework of empire. Also a factor that
made this north Pacific borderland an object of imperial and commercial
competition was its proximity to the world's largest ocean, at once a watery
boundary in itself and a major transportation route. The northwest coast was
valuable in the eyes of both Britain and the United States not only because it
provided access to the shortest route to Asia but also because it functioned as
an outer perimeter that served at times, at least in the imagination of those at
the center, as a buffer against intrusion into the heart of the continent. The
ability of a colonial power to assert a territorial claim in the region provided
access to a wide range of both land-based and marine resources. Those that
came to be mined or harvested on an industrial scale—from the whales and
sea otters that first drew European sailors into the North Pacific, to gold, copper, lumber, and fish of various kinds—were soon integrated into far broader
economic networks that in time extended south along the Pacific coast to
Washington, Oregon, California, Mexico, Peru, and Chile and across the Pacific Ocean to Russia, Japan, China, Korea, Siberia, Australasia, and the Philippines.[9] Beginning with Russia's incorporation of the Alaskan coast into its
colonial empire and Spain's claims arising from its explorations of the waters
surrounding Vancouver Island and Haida Gwaii during the waning decades
of the eighteenth century, one empire after another laid claim to the region in
an effort to gain exclusive access to its resources, endeavors that in time not
only attracted labor migrants from around the world but also framed encounters between latecomers and the Indigenous peoples of the region in a wide
and ever-changing variety of ways.

While Britain and the United States had displaced or acquired Russian
and Spanish claims along the north Pacific coast by the end of the nineteenth
century, they were soon joined by a rapidly modernizing and ever more con-
fident Japan increasingly interested in asserting an identity as a Pacific power
and maximizing its share of the marine resources of the North Pacific, including fur seals and various fisheries. British and American commercial interests
engaged in both the harvest and the trade of marine mammal pelts had long
played a key role in linking the northwest coast of North America to Asia.

Both Britain and the United States sought to build on this foundation to establish a continuing presence in the North Pacific as the twentieth century unfolded. Even as the United States pressed westward beyond its Pacific coast to extend its influence over Alaska, Hawaii, and the Philippines, however, Japan increasingly pressed eastward both to reinforce its position as a Pacific nation that itself had a significant geopolitical role in maintaining the balance of power in the Pacific and to secure access to a share of marine resources along the north Pacific coast. By the early twentieth century, as a result, what had long been regarded by Europeans as a remote and intensely local area located at the periphery of empire had become ever more closely interconnected through travel and capital not only to centers of finance and industry in Europe and North America but to a diasporic economic network centered in Japan that extended across the Pacific.[10]

Within this broader framework, I pay particular attention to the ways that Japanese labor migrants, as subjects of an expanding non-European imperial power actively engaged in projecting itself out into the North Pacific Ocean, and Indigenous people negotiated the liminal spaces of this borderlands region. A focus on Japanese migrants permits a closer examination of ways in which they understood their presence in the North American West and their encounters with Indigenous people, as well as the reciprocal question of how Indigenous people perceived Japanese immigrants—as colonial settlers whose presence was not qualitatively different from that of Euro-Canadian or American settlers or otherwise.[11] The inclusion of Japanese migrants, active participants in that colonial endeavor and yet relegated to the margins of settler society in some of the same ways as Indigenous peoples, also helps to avoid reducing a multifaceted and complicated story of historical encounter to the simpler binaries against which historians warn.[12] As in my previous work, my approach assumes that such encounters were shaped not just by the racialized legal structures the dominant societies alone imposed but also by social and cultural considerations specific to Japanese migrants, on the one hand, and to the various Indigenous groups they encountered, on the other.[13]

Encounters between Japanese immigrants and Indigenous people along the north Pacific coast were also a product of a far larger contest between empires around the Pacific that pitted both settler nations in the Americas and Japan against Indigenous peoples and the United States and, in time, Canada against Japan. Many of the Japanese who traveled or settled in the north Pacific borderlands left no written record or, if they did, not one that has been preserved. Often all we can do is catch a glimpse of a given individual in accounts produced by others. Where prewar Japanese-language records were preserved, however, they give us an added level of access to the complex and often contradictory nature of the experiences of racialized peoples in this borderlands region. They also reveal the ambiguous and contingent nature not only of the region itself but of seemingly fixed categories of citizenship and race.[14]

Boundary drawing and law would prove to be critical tools utilized by both Canada and the United States to regulate the movement of people in both countries and to control access to local resources, each of which went hand in hand with the inscribing of racial boundaries. Both nations asserted the power not only to define the rights and privileges of their own citizens or subjects but also to limit those of Indigenous people and Asian immigrants, even as they relied on their labor to facilitate the practical integration of British Columbia and Alaska into broader, nation-based political and economic structures. Based on distinct rationales and utilizing different kinds of legal mechanisms, the separate legal constraints imposed on Japanese migrants and Indigenous people on each side of the international border often worked together to privilege Anglo-European settlers in both Canada and the United States. At times, however, both Japanese immigrants and Indigenous people themselves deployed the categories "subject" and "citizen" in an effort to position themselves more favorably in a changing world. On the one hand, the power to bestow or impose status as subject or citizen, or to withhold it, lay at the heart both of colonial practice and of processes of racialization. On the other hand, the ability to claim status as subject or citizen—or to resist such designations—could also serve as a tool that allowed Japanese immigrants and Indigenous people to position themselves more effectively in the shifting borderlands of the north Pacific coast.

National borders, abstract and largely imaginary when first drawn, acquire new meaning as they begin to shape human behavior and categories of belonging or identity.[15] Although never as simply determinative as the colonial powers that constructed them wished they were, the newly articulated national boundaries that cut across the traditional territories of Indigenous peoples—Haida, Tsimshian, Tlingit, and Tr'ondëk Hwëch'in (Hän), among others—often led, over time, to a reframing of identity as they negotiated the jurisdictional spaces that these borders produced. Identity, as various historians have noted, is mutually constructed and defined, neither entirely imposed nor wholly self-determined, but a product of multiple interactions with both the state and others.[16] Like Japanese labor migrants, Indigenous people actively negotiated the intersecting boundaries of race, class, citizenship, and identity that were a product of the evolving bodies of law on each side of the U.S.-Canada border in ways they perceived to be to their advantage, sometimes engaging in border crossings—whether of national borders or of the boundaries of race and citizenship—that themselves contributed to the infusing of such borders with new meaning.[17] Marginalized though they may have been under the law of both Canada and the United States, in short, Japanese immigrants and Indigenous people were not necessarily marginal actors in any given time and place.

Considered from a nation-based perspective, the Indigenous and settler communities of northern British Columbia, Alaska, and the Yukon appear as relatively insignificant settlements at the periphery of empire and the nation-state—distant outposts whose history would seem to tell us little of the concerns and objectives of those at the center. Considered from a regional perspective, we come to see this borderlands region as central to the development of key policies and ideas regarding matters close to the heart of each nation, including national identity, the contours of citizenship, and the nature of sovereign authority as it was understood by both Indigenous and invading peoples. Policies enforced along the national borders that cut through the region both on land and at sea shed light not only on how each nation, including Canada, the United States, and Japan, came to define itself but also, as in other borderlands areas, on how "process[es] of territorialization" unfolded within the context of each nation-state.[18] A regional lens also allows us to engage stories that are obscured by histories that center the nation-state. It brings into focus the roles of the Indigenous people who had made the north Pacific borderlands their home for millennia prior to the imposition of colonial rule both in responding to and in facilitating change. This, in turn, provides a basis for comparing the impact of the racialized legal framework imposed on both Indigenous peoples and Asian immigrants on each side of the U.S.-Canada border, including ways in which these constraints reinforced one another, as well as the strategies developed by members of both groups to counter the restrictions they faced.

Borderlands Historiographies

Although the steep mountain peaks that mark the northern stretch of the U.S.-Canada border that divides Alaska from British Columbia and the Yukon, like the tree- or ice-covered landscapes of the north Pacific coast, have captured the imagination of almost all who come into contact with them, the north Pacific borderlands have been largely ignored by borderlands historians of North America, as contrasted with the attention given to the U.S.-

Mexico border and, to a lesser extent, the border the United States shares with Canada along the forty-ninth parallel.[19] Seemingly regarded as too remote and inconsequential to be of much significance in broader national or international contexts, this region has generally been left to historians of Russian America to consider more closely, or to those who focus either on Alaska state history or on the history of British Columbia as a province.[20]

Both of the international borders that cut across the North American continent from east to west had been firmly in place for half a century or more before disagreements between Britain and the United States regarding the precise location of the B.C.-Alaska border were generally resolved in 1903. The international borders that transect the continent, as Richard White explains in his history of the American West, were historically produced, the product of a series of contingent moments that occurred over a period of eight decades, with the result that it was not geography but history that determined where they came to be drawn.[21] In North America, imperial contests and interactions with Indigenous peoples played a central role in the articulation of the national borders that were inscribed across this continent over time.[22] These boundaries, in effect, sketch time across space.[23] The same is true of the northernmost stretch of the Canada-U.S. border that separates Alaska from British Columbia and the Yukon. It differs, however, from those that transect the continent to the extent that the Pacific coastline itself played a key role in delimiting the borders of both the United States and Canada and in shaping the ways these borderlands were perceived over time. The boundary line that sets British Columbia apart from the Alaska panhandle more or less traces the height of the Coast Mountains, following what was imagined as the natural boundary that divides the watersheds on either side of those mountains. The U.S.-Canada border then bends abruptly north to follow the 141st meridian to the Arctic Ocean, slicing across the bioregion it bisects as sharply—and as illogically—as any other of North America's international borders.[24] In this and other ways, the "nature" of the borderland region along the north Pacific coast differs both literally and figuratively from that along the forty-ninth parallel or the U.S.-Mexico border, even as all three border regions also share many of the same characteristics.[25]

As along the U.S.-Mexico border, where, Juanita Sundberg argues, nonhuman actors have played as significant a role as human actors in shaping both its history and the ways it has been enforced, nonhuman actors have always played a significant role in shaping the history of the north Pacific borderlands.[26] There, as elsewhere, the terrain, including both the geographical features that contribute to boundary drawing and those that attract human endeavor, such as mineral deposits or deep natural harbors, are also factors that shape or explain human activity in the region, including enforcement-related practices on the part of government officials. The same is true of the behavior of both land and marine animal populations. State-sanctioned crossing points were far and few between along the northern stretches of the U.S.-Canada border during the nineteenth and early twentieth centuries, ensuring that enforcement was at best sporadic and uneven, even as the establishment of border crossings in itself, as along the U.S.-Mexico border and other sections of the U.S.-Canada border, gave rise to new patterns of movement across it, whether of people or of animals.[27] Early Japanese travelers, it should be noted, would not have been unfamiliar with the notion of policing or monitoring travel at border checkpoints, a practice that was actively utilized by the Tokugawa shogunate to restrict movement between domains in Japan during the Edo period in order to avoid the erosion of its own authority.[28]

Borderlands, by definition, are places where power is liminal and contested, often areas where imperial or state power has yet to be consolidated.[29] They are not, as Mary L. Dudziak and Leti Volpp explain, just geographical areas where the borders of the nation-state and the limits of its political authority are challenged or enforced. Transient and unstable, fluid and evolving, they are also areas that function as "interstitial zones of hybridization" and as contact zones between both people and ideas "that can open up new possibilities of both repression and liberation."[30]

"Borderlands, as a plural noun," Pekka Hämäläinen and Samuel Truett note, reflects a "multidirectional, multivocal vision" of the spaces surrounding any border, best understood, as Truett explains, as "a shifting mosaic of human spaces—some interwoven, others less so," that reflect both the colonial and other historical contests that unfolded across any given borderlands region over time.[31] These are places where people rooted in distinctive cultural traditions, often unfamiliar with one another's practices, encountered one another in, at times, unexpected ways.[32] The stories of such individuals, Truett reminds us, can tell us a great deal about "how ordinary people emerged from the shadows of state and corporate control to reshape the borderlands on their own terms," as well as about the worlds through which they moved.[33] A transpacific framework allows us, in turn, as David Igler and other historians of the Pacific world have shown, to situate the "more intimate realms of cultural encounters" that occurred in places like the north Pacific borderlands within the broader context of "large-scale geopolitical relations," making it possible both to identify larger historical patterns that connect different areas of the world, including new forms of labor migration, and, at the same time, to evaluate their impact on local and Indigenous populations in particular places.[34]

The formal incorporation of Alaska and British Columbia by the United States and Canada within the borders of each nation-state, together with the arrival of growing numbers of labor migrants, including Japanese set in motion by parallel processes of modernization and industrialization, brought newcomers from around the world into increasing contact with the Indigenous coastal people. Many such encounters occurred within the framework of new forms of extractive industry along the north Pacific coast, including logging, mining, and fisheries of one kind or another, all of which structured relations between Indigenous people and Japanese or other colonial settlers in different ways.[35] The maritime spaces of the Pacific Ocean, both border and borderlands region in its own right, were also places where such contacts occurred, even as they also served as a conduit both for transpacific migration and for the projection of imperial power throughout the Pacific world over many centuries.[36]

Long before European powers arrived, the north Pacific coast was already a complex borderlands region, where the maritime and land-based territories of a wide range of Indigenous peoples—Aleut, Alutiiq, Eyak, Tlingit, Haida, Tsimshian, Haisla, Heiltsuk, Nisga'a, and Kwakiutl, among others—intersected and overlapped.[37] Although the national and imperial boundaries etched across this landscape by Russian, British, and American agents during the nineteenth century were superimposed on these Indigenous territories—a practice that David A. Chang notes is itself a "hallmark of colonialism"—they were never able simply to displace Indigenous understandings of place and kinship.[38] Grounded in culturally distinct ways of conceptualizing space and delineating territories, at times overlapping and equally capable of shifting and evolving over time, the boundaries of Indigenous territories were not as rigidly mechanical as those of nation-states. More important in Indigenous contexts were the cultural landscapes that connected people to place through oral histories. Often tied to particular landforms, such oral histories infused place with both lived and spiritual dimensions that were central to their identities as distinct peoples.[39] Along the north Pacific coast as elsewhere, Julie Cruikshank explains, this produced separate yet intersecting histories of place. Mount St. Elias and Mount Fairweather, both key links in the chain of mountain peaks that mark the borders of Alaska, British Columbia, and the Yukon, Cruikshank notes by way of example, "play a significant role in both Tlingit oral traditions and European exploration narratives."[40] While the histories of Indigenous peoples along the north Pacific coast are so varied and complex

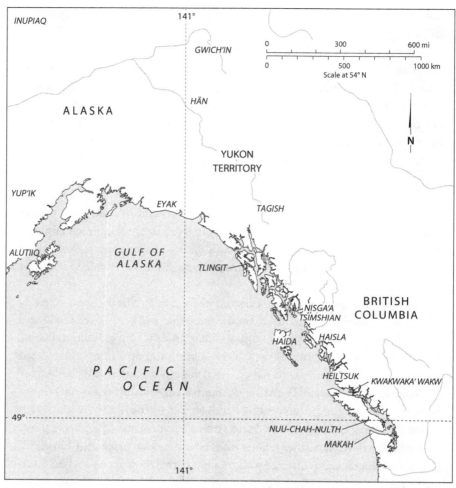

Indigenous peoples along the north Pacific coast referred to in the text and the general areas where their traditional territories are located.

that it is impossible for any book to take them fully into account, particularly a book focused on the convergence of three empires, I am acutely aware that imperial powers and colonial settlers constituted only a small subset of the significant actors in this borderlands region at any given time and that, despite the sweeping claims of European powers to overarching sovereignty, the great majority of it remained—and to a significant extent remains today—unceded Indigenous territory.[41]

Chapters

Chapter 1 traces the historical contexts that set the stage for the convergence of British, American, and Japanese interests along the Pacific coast of North America during the twentieth century. It focuses, in particular, on the legal and geopolitical contests among European imperial powers, including Russia and Spain, that help to explain the contours that the national boundaries that later cut across the northwestern reaches of the North American continent would assume, as well as the role that Indigenous resistance to colonial pressure played in the articulation of these boundaries. This chapter situates these events within the broader framework of colonial endeavor around the North Pacific Rim, particularly those that had an impact on Japan, setting in motion forces that contributed to the demise of the Tokugawa shogunate in 1867, the same year that Canada entered Confederation and the United States acquired Russia's interests in Alaska. These developments, taken together, remade the political geography of the North Pacific Rim and opened the door to Japan's own incorporation of Hokkaido, the traditional homeland of the Ainu people that is now regarded as the northernmost of Japan's four major islands. Japan's determined effort to remake itself as a modern, imperial nation, together with the demand for labor that followed from the formal incorporation of the north Pacific borderlands by Canada and the United States, in turn, created the conditions that in time led Japanese labor emigrants to cross the Pacific Ocean in search of employment.

Chapter 2 considers ways in which Indigenous people and Japanese migrants responded to the establishment of the northernmost section of the U.S.-Canada border as it was etched across the landscape in the wake of the United States' acquisition of Russian interests in Alaska. At times, members of each group seized on this newly articulated boundary to engage in complex acts of repositioning that took into account ways in which U.S. or Canadian law structured constraint and opportunity on each side of that border, only to find themselves caught in the conceptual gap between "immigrant" and "Indigene." The chapter also addresses ways in which perceptions of indigeneity rooted in Japanese history and culture shaped encounters between Japanese and Indigenous people along the north Pacific coast. While Japanese immigrants shared certain attitudes with their Euro-American neighbors, viewing the land as empty and open to settlement, they also argued that Japanese had a special connection to the Indigenous peoples of the north Pacific coast that entitled them to assert a presence there in ways Europeans could not. Though it is tempting to consider Japan's boundaries as "natural" in ways that those of Canada and the United States are not, given that Japan is an island nation, its boundaries are also a product of history and not geography alone, as demonstrated by its incorporation of Hokkaido, the Ryukyu Islands, and Taiwan within its borders during the early Meiji era.

Exclusion on various scales and in a variety of forms was central to the reimagining of the north Pacific coast as Euro-Canadian or American space, including restricting the entry of Japanese migrants at international borders, the denial of the full rights of citizenship to Japanese immigrants and Indigenous people, and barring access to certain kinds of occupations by law or in practice. On both sides of the Canada-U.S. border, exclusion also sometimes took the form of overt expulsion. Chapter 3 examines instances where Japanese and Chinese labor migrants were driven out of towns in British Columbia, Alaska, and the Yukon, arguing that the use of personal violence to enforce local and municipal boundaries was, as elsewhere, integral to the reimagining of this region as quintessentially white. Like government-sanctioned forms of exclusion, the expulsion of Japanese migrants—part of a larger pattern of racialized violence and intimidation that swept through western North America at the time—mirrored efforts to erase the Indigenous presence from the colonial landscape in both Canada and the United States. While each was positioned differently within a global context, Canada as a British dominion and the United States as an independent nation, they repeatedly worked together during the early decades of the twentieth century, up to and including World War II, to ensure that the racialized barriers they erected against both Japanese immigration and the acknowledgment of Indigenous land rights reinforced those of the other.

Chapter 4 addresses the convergence of U.S., British, and Japanese interests in the ocean waters off the northwestern coast of North America and considers the impact that the marine boundaries cutting through the waters of this environmentally sensitive region had on both Japanese immigrants and Indigenous people. On each side of the international border, the regulatory reach of the U.S. government, in particular, extended well out into coastal waters in the form of treaty agreements that pertained to the harvesting of marine mammals. Overlapping fisheries created varying spaces of encounter between Japanese immigrants and the Indigenous coastal peoples most affected by the impact of industrial-scale fisheries that often devastated the traditional fisheries on which they had relied for centuries. Both groups were the target of efforts along the B.C. coast to exclude them from some of the very fisheries that they had helped found. While Japanese often competed with Indigenous fishers, their shared local interests and mutual efforts to avoid the impact of exclusionary law and policy produced far more intricate sets of alignments and divisions among and within racialized groups than has often been recognized.[42] The many boundaries that came to structure the north Pacific coast, largely intended to divide, as such, produced not only new and unanticipated patterns of association and interconnection but also new patterns of migration across them.

As World War II approached, however, the very mobility of Japanese fishers, together with their intimate knowledge of British Columbia's coastal waters, gave rise to ever more strident allegations of smuggling and spying on both sides of the Canada-U.S. border. Along the coast of Alaska, in particular, alleged intrusions into U.S. waters by fishing vessels registered in Japan were increasingly depicted as the vanguard of a forthcoming invasion. The increasing pressure Japan brought to bear along the northwestern coast of North America during the first half of the twentieth century, reflected in ongoing disputes over both oceangoing fisheries and the hunting of sea lions and fur seals, combined with Japan's long-standing resentment of both the race-based exclusion of Japanese immigrants and the unequal treatment of Japanese settlers by the United States and Canada, heightened tensions among all three, setting the stage for policy decisions that followed the outbreak of war. Chapter 5 argues that the decisions of both nations to forcibly remove not just Japanese subjects but U.S.- and Canadian-born citizens and subjects of Japanese descent from the north Pacific coast can be understood as the culmination of prior efforts both to exclude and to expel migrants of Japanese ancestry. This chapter also considers the forced removal and detention of people of Japanese ancestry in relation both to the forced relocation of the Aleut by the U.S. government and to those taken prisoner by the Japanese Imperial Army and taken to Japan for the duration of the war.

Conclusion

During the late nineteenth and early twentieth centuries, the area surrounding the north Pacific coast emerged as a distinctive borderlands region produced, in part, by the convergence of three empires in the waters along its shores during that period. The North Pacific was an area where the interests of an expanding Japanese empire actively projecting itself out into the Pacific in a quest for a share of its marine resources encountered Euro-American powers that were themselves engaged in extending their own spheres of influence in the Pacific, in part to reinforce their ties to Asia. Despite the rocky terrain, winter storms, and rough seas that tend to isolate the north Pacific borderlands during certain parts of the year, it was an area that became increasingly connected not only to the interior of the continent but to other parts of the Pacific Rim. To see this borderland only as a remote outpost marking the northernmost edge of the United States, or the westernmost edge first of British North America and later Canada, as such, is to miss not only the central place it occupied in the lives of the Indigenous peoples who had made it their home for millennia but also the extent to which it functioned, in the eyes of Japanese settlers, as an economic hinterland for an expanding Japanese empire.

Regardless of the national boundaries etched across it, the north Pacific borderlands also functioned, in significant ways and at key times, as a region that defied the borders that divided it. Britain's determination to preserve its access to the Pacific even before Canada was organized as a separate dominion not only resulted in the formation of the colony of British Columbia but also made possible its later incorporation into the Canadian nation-state. The B.C. coast, as such, was central both to the construction of Canada as a transcontinental nation and to the reimagining of the United States as a colonial power justified in projecting its authority not just over the contiguous territories it absorbed as it expanded westward across the continent, but across the Pacific basin. The B.C. coast, however, also disrupted ties between the contiguous U.S. states and Alaska, rendering it, in effect, an island insofar as its connection to other parts of the United States was concerned—a factor that would make the B.C. coast a focus of continuing concern for the United States particularly during times of war.

The borderlands of both Alaska and British Columbia cannot be fully understood in isolation, either in a North American context, where geography and access to the Pacific Ocean help to explain the roles assigned to each within the framework of the nation-state, or within the larger context of the North Pacific Rim, where the interests of Great Britain, Canada, the United States, and Japan converged during the late nineteenth and early twentieth centuries. While the particular locus where their interests were joined and where the resulting contests were played out shifted over time depending on the issues that were of most immediate concern, for each of these imperial powers and their subjects or citizens, as well as for their Indigenous peoples, the north Pacific borderlands represented an ever-changing but always complex mix of obstacle and opportunity, vulnerability and power. Not just the Pacific coast and the northernmost stretches of the U.S.-Canada border that divide the two nation-states but the Pacific Ocean—both border and borderland itself—played a critical role in shaping both the contours of imperial power and the lives of all those who moved through and across the land- and seascapes of this borderlands region.

CHAPTER ONE

The Shifting Borderlands of the North Pacific Coast

The northwestern coast of the continent of North America, long deemed terra incognita by European explorers and mapmakers, is a creation of both land and ocean, its contours carved out by glaciers that, along some parts of the coast, still connect land and sea. Often shrouded in mist and battered by Pacific storms in winter, it is also a borderland region rich in resources that had long sustained human life. While the turbulent waves of the North Pacific obscured European knowledge of this coastline for many decades after Europeans first set foot on the eastern shores of the continent, a growing demand for whale oil increasingly lured European sailors into parts of the North Pacific they had not previously explored. In time, they developed a more complete understanding of the contours of the north Pacific coast. Where the rough waters of the Pacific had once posed a barrier to access to the northwesternmost regions of North America, the open ocean would also become in turn a ready access route for ships from around the world.[1]

By the end of the eighteenth century, Russian hunters had followed the chain of islands that stretches across the northern reaches of the Pacific Ocean from the Kuril Islands that link Hokkaido to the Kamchatka Peninsula and then the Commander and Aleutian Islands. An archipelago that itself extends a thousand miles, the Aleutian chain bisects the North Pacific and the Bering Sea, before it connects to the western tip of the long, narrow Alaskan peninsula. In contrast to the densely forested islands that lie further south along both the eastern and western coasts of the Pacific Ocean, the far more barren shores of the Aleutian Islands, like the Pribilof Islands that lie to their north, were once home to great herds of fur seals and sea lions. Further east along the southern coast of Alaska, the deep fjords and glaciers that surround the Gulf of Alaska give way to cedar-, fir-, and pine-covered archipelagos that extend another thousand miles along the Alaska panhandle and the B.C. coast to the Strait of Georgia and Puget Sound, both a part of what is also known as the Salish Sea.[2] Together, the islands that lie along the western edge of the North American continent, including Haida Gwaii and Vancouver Island, create a series of saltwater channels largely sheltered from the broad swells of the open ocean that have long facilitated travel along that coast.[3]

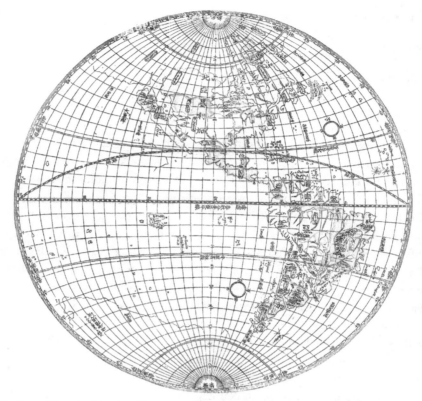

Portion of *Oranda shinyaku chikyu zenzu* (The complete map of the whole world, newly translated from Dutch sources), depicting the Western Hemisphere based on information obtained from the Dutch. Created by Hashimoto Sōkichi, 1796 (woodblock or engraved copperplate). Stanford University, Glen McLaughlin Map Collection: California as an Island.

Three major rivers flow down into the easternmost waters of the North Pacific from the coastal mountain range that now divides Alaska and British Columbia—the Skeena, the Nass, and the Stikine. The Skeena and the Nass flow into Hecate Strait just north and south of Prince Rupert, while the Stikine cuts across the Alaska panhandle just north of the town of Wrangell.[4] Together, these rivers link the north Pacific coast to the interior of the continent. Like the Fraser and Columbia Rivers to the south, the Skeena, Stikine, and Nass Rivers served as ready routes to the plateaus and mountain valleys that lie east of the coastal range, facilitating the movement of goods and people both before and after the arrival of Europeans. Railroads would follow many of the same river valleys to tie the Pacific coast to eastern Canada and the

United States, including cities like St. Louis, where many a seal or sea lion hide would be processed over the years.[5] The fact that the major rivers along the northwestern coast of North America flow directly into the Pacific Ocean distinguishes it from Siberia's eastern coast, where the major rivers of the eastern half of the Eurasian continent, with the exception of the Amur, empty into not the Pacific but the Arctic Ocean. The lack of direct access to the Pacific Ocean, the editors of *The Trans-Pacific*, an English-language journal published in Japan, observed in 1921, explained why it was not Siberia but the northwestern coast of North America that was the primary focus of resource extraction, whether of timber or of animal pelts, around the North Pacific Rim.[6]

Another feature that distinguishes the north Pacific coast of Eurasia from that of North America is the fact that far fewer harbors remain ice free in winter along Eurasia's eastern coast. Mariners understood early on that given the direction of the prevailing winds in the earth's Northern Hemisphere, the eastern coasts of its northern continents are invariably colder than their western coasts. They also recognized that this had important strategic consequences. As the Russian explorer Dmitry Zavalishin explained as early as 1824, the absence of ice-free ports in winter meant that neither the Amur River nor Sakhalin could serve as a base that would enable any power that controlled them to dominate any part of the Pacific Ocean, even its northernmost reaches. Instead, Zavalishin declared, "The key to sway over the Pacific [was] to be sought not on its Asiatic coast but on the western coast of North America. Only on this coast, even far to the north, could there be found harbors that never froze and that permitted unrestricted coming and going at all times." Harbors located as far north as latitude 57° north along the northwestern coast of North America never froze in winter, he reported, but even harbors as far south as latitude 40° north along Eurasia's eastern coast were often clogged with ice in winter.[7]

The presence of sheltered and largely ice-free inland channels along the northwest coast of North America, together with the access that the Skeena, the Nass, and the Stikine provide to the interior—all factors attractive to Europeans interested in securing access to its resources—had supported Indigenous trading networks that extended not just along the coast but deep into the interior of the continent long before the first Europeans arrived.[8] Traveling up the same river systems along the western coast of the continent, the life-sustaining salmon central to Indigenous cultures around the North Pacific Rim also linked territories as far inland as those of the Tahltan, Gitxsan, Wet'suwet'en, and Sekani peoples, among others, to the ocean,[9] as they did those of the Ainu who lived on Ainu Moshir, renamed Hokkaido by the Japanese, as

well as on the island of Sakhalin and the Kamchatka Peninsula.[10] Other resources that abound around the North Pacific Rim, and that had long sustained
the Indigenous peoples of the coastal region who had made it their home
over many centuries—Tlingit, Tsimshian, Haida, Haisla, Heiltsuk, Nisga'a,
Eyak, Alutiiq, Unangan, and others—include sea urchins, abalone, shellfish,
starfish, crab, and the kelp beds favored by sea otters.[11] These were all maritime peoples whose deep ties to coastal waters were reflected in long-standing
cultural traditions and sophisticated technologies of knowledge grounded in
many centuries of experience with the marine environment at the center of
both the spiritual and the material worlds in which they lived.[12] These knowledge systems, together with their long-honed expertise in hunting marine
mammals and the building and navigating of small boats adapted to local conditions, were among the skills Indigenous peoples had developed that non-
Indigenous invaders sought to use to their advantage. The boundaries that
these newcomers would establish over time to differentiate their own claims
to exclusive access to certain parts of northwestern North America from those
of other European powers, in short, cut across what was already a rich and
complex social and cultural landscape.

Colonial Contexts

As the eighteenth century unfolded, the same resources that had sustained
the Indigenous peoples of the North Pacific Rim for millennia attracted the
attention first of Russian and then of Spanish, British, and American colonizers. The contests that ensued among these imperial powers during the colonial period set the stage for the eventual division of these territories between
the nation-states that later replaced them. Japan's own colonization of Hokkaido and its increasing presence in the Kuril Islands was also a factor that
caused Russia to look east across the North Pacific rather than south along
the Eurasian coast for new resources. Indigenous resistance to colonial intrusion, in turn, played a key role in inhibiting the advance of Russian traders
into the heart of the North American continent and, in so doing, determining
where the boundaries of the territories claimed by European powers were
eventually drawn.

The practical incorporation of any new land area within the boundaries of
empire or a nation-state occurs in stages and may assume different forms depending on its purpose. As John R. Bockstoce notes, the rivalry among European powers in northwestern North America was initially structured around
a quest for the knowledge on which material access to commodifiable re-

sources depended.[13] "Territory had to be known before it could be controlled," Jeffers Lennox explains, "and the methods by which that knowledge was created and implemented reflected the technological, political, and ideological realities of the time."[14] Early explorations of the north Pacific coast were driven in large part by a demand for the dense pelts of sea otters highly valued in China—one of the few commodities Chinese traders were willing to accept in exchange for the tea, teak, ivory, sugar, porcelain, lacquerware, rhubarb, silk, and cotton Europeans and Americans sought to acquire.[15] The mercantile economic framework within which European nations operated made it desirable to assert exclusive control over a given area, even if there was no interest in settlement, in order to maximize the profits that could be derived from the wholesale extraction of its resources for the benefit of the mother country.[16] For that reason, contests among European powers initially centered on the "discoveries" that were key to their ability to assert territorial claims as against other European powers to areas unknown to them, based on the tenets of European international law at the time.[17]

Marine mammals, and particularly sea otters and fur seals, bore the brunt of a quest for furs that came to an end only when their populations were all but annihilated around the North Pacific Rim, much as beavers were in many parts of North America as Europeans expanded across the continent during the colonial period.[18] As Bockstoce notes, the wealth gleaned from furs and hides harvested on the North American continent and in Siberia during the seventeenth and eighteenth centuries remade the economies of Britain, France, and Russia and repositioned Europe as a power that would make itself felt around the world.[19] Mirroring the westward march of British and American colonial interests across the North American continent during the eighteenth and nineteenth centuries, the Russian empire extended its reach eastward across Siberia to Sakhalin, the Kuril Islands, and the Kamchatka Peninsula and then to the Aleutian Islands in a parallel quest for fur during the same period.[20]

The home of extensive sea otter populations of commercial interest to both Russian and Japanese traders, the Kuril Islands were also of strategic interest to the imperial governments of Russia and Japan because they linked the Kamchatka Peninsula to Hokkaido and thus controlled access to the Sea of Okhotsk. Although powerful currents, stormy winter weather, and the dense fogs that shrouded them even in summer obscured knowledge of their coasts for many centuries, both Japan and Russia were aware of their existence by the mid-seventeenth century, as were the Dutch. Both Russian and Japanese maps of the period depict the Kurils as lying just beyond the edge of empire, although historians generally agree that neither Russian nor Japanese authorities had a clear understanding of their geographical contours.[21] As John J. Stephan notes, the fact that the Kuril Islands—known as Chishima Retto (Chishima Archipelago) in Japanese—were an Ainu homeland is reflected in the names still used for the islands in Russian and Japanese today, most of which derive from those first used by the Ainu.[22] As commercial activity in the vicinity of the Kuril Islands increased during the early decades of the eighteenth century, both Russia and Japan began to acquire greater knowledge of them. An edict first issued by the Tokugawa shogunate in 1639 forbade travel outside Japan's coastal waters and imposed harsh penalties on those who violated it, making Japanese explorers more reluctant than their Russian counterparts to document their contacts with the Kuril Islands, although there were some traders who quietly defied it.[23] The shogunate's prohibition on building oceangoing vessels also meant, however, that when smaller coastal vessels were caught in storms at sea, they were often driven north and east onto the Kuril Islands and the Kamchatka Peninsula. The first Japanese to encounter Ainu people, as such, were almost certainly shipwrecked sailors, some of whom later served as translators for Russian hunters.[24] When Russians began to tighten their hold over the Kuril Islands near the Kamchatka Peninsula and to demand tribute from the Ainu inhabitants of those islands as had been their practice in other colonized regions, a substantial number of Ainu migrated south along the Kuril island chain toward Hokkaido, following long-established and familiar trade routes in an effort to retain their independence and to avoid subjugation.[25]

Tokugawa officials first began to cast their gaze north toward Ainu Moshir, an area they called Ezo that included not just Hokkaido but the Kuril Islands and areas of Sakhalin where the Ainu also lived, during the early 1600s.[26] Motivated in part by strategic concerns triggered by shifting geopolitical alignments in eastern Asia, the Tokugawa shogunate assigned the Matsumae clan responsibility for monitoring conditions in the region and managing trade ties with the Ainu in 1604.[27] Located at the northern tip of the island of Honshu, the Matsumae domain (*han*) was deemed the best positioned geographically to assume this role. Despite the shogunate's interest in establishing an outpost on Hokkaido and fostering relations with the Ainu, however, it made no attempt at this stage to incorporate Ainu territory within the borders of its realm. As Tsuyoshi Hasegawa explains, the Tokugawa shogunate was more concerned with integrating Ezo into the broader political and economic system it had established to ensure its own stability, a system that historians of Japan describe as "centralized feudalism."[28]

In limiting the right to trade with the Ainu to the Matsumae clan and prohibiting its other subjects from trading with the Ainu unless licensed to do so by the Matsumae, the Tokugawa edict resembled the charter issued by the British Crown to the Hudson's Bay Company (HBC) in 1670 giving it an exclusive right to engage in commercial activity within the region known as Rupert's Land in British North America. Both edicts constrained only the actions of that sovereign's own subjects; neither purported to constrain the actions of those who were not its subjects, including the Indigenous peoples with whom they sought to trade.[29] Even as they document the exercise of imperial power, as such, both proclamations also illustrate the limits of such power as of the time they were issued. Neither Japanese nor British imperial authorities had either the practical ability or the legal authority to impose direct constraints on those who were not their own subjects. Even as it restricted the movement of its own subjects beyond Japanese borders, the Tokugawa shogunate recognized that no such constraints applied to the Ainu, who remained free to move about as they wished, an acknowledgment similar to that in the Jay Treaty, entered into by Britain and the United States over a century later, which recognized that "Indians," as members of independent polities, were entitled "freely to pass and repass" the border they had established, as between themselves, to mark the boundaries of the areas each claimed in North America.[30] Both acknowledgments, like the earlier edicts, are testament to the fact that at the time neither Britain nor Japan assumed that legal directives pertaining to areas over which they sought to establish sole commercial access conferred any form of sovereign authority over the Indigenous peoples of those territories.

As in North America, trade between the Matsumae and the Ainu built on existing trade networks developed by the Ainu that extended to the Kuril Islands and the east coast of Asia. Japanese commercial settlements were initially confined to a small area of Ezo just across the Tsugaru Strait, but they expanded over time to the point where they began to encroach on Ainu territories further north.[31] In the 1660s, the Matsumae clan established guard posts to mark the limits of the separate areas where Japanese and Ainu lived and operated, known respectively as Wajinchi and Ezochi in Japanese, and to monitor movement across that border.[32]

Ezo also served, in effect, as a buffer zone between Russian and Japanese interests in the area. Both imperial powers were increasingly cognizant of the value inherent in establishing a presence on the Kuril Islands. Rocky and distant from the governing centers of both Russia and Japan though they were, the Kuril Islands were of interest to both in part because of the marine resources to which they provided access, including kelp, fish, and large populations of marine mammals, particularly sea otters and fur seals. Extending some seven hundred miles across the entire distance between the Kamchatka Peninsula and northeastern Hokkaido, they were also viewed by both Russia and Japan as a conduit that could potentially be used by Russia to establish a commercial presence on the island of Hokkaido.[33] In 1771 and 1772, as a result, first the Russian and then the Japanese imperial government dispatched expeditions to the Kuril Islands intended both to explore them and to establish an official presence in the area. Some Japanese sent north to assess conditions in northern Hokkaido urged the shogunate to formally incorporate the island within Japanese borders to forestall the possibility that Russia might otherwise claim substantial portions of it as its territory.[34]

As the eighteenth century unfolded, the growth of a burgeoning market for sea otter pelts in China, in particular, led to a corresponding decline in the sea otter populations of the Kuril Islands and along the coasts of Sakhalin and the Kamchatka Peninsula. Russia's exploration of the Aleutian Islands was contemporaneous with its efforts to expand its activities on the Kuril Islands, and as marine mammal populations in the western Pacific declined, Russian explorers increasingly looked east across the North Pacific for new populations to exploit. The sea otters that inhabited the icy waters around the northernmost rim of the Pacific were in demand in part because they produced the richest, densest fur most highly valued in China and Japan.[35] Also a factor directing Russian hunters and traders eastward across the Pacific Ocean was the growth of Japanese commercial activity in the southern Kuril Islands, which effectively blocked Russian expansion southward, as did Ainu resistance to Russian encroachment, which culminated in a revolt on the island that the Russians called Urup and the Japanese called Urrupu in 1770.[36]

Russian America

In 1783, four decades after Vitus Bering's first foray along the Aleutian Islands in 1741, Russia established what would become the center of its commercial operations in "Aliaska" on what Russians called Kodiak Island midway along the southern coast.[37] When sea otter numbers again began to drop because of overharvesting in the areas first colonized along the Alaskan peninsula, much as they had in the western reaches of the Pacific Ocean, the Russian American Company (RAC), chartered by the Russian imperial government in 1799 to advance its interests in North America, extended its operations further eastward along that coast.[38] The number of settlements established by the RAC remained relatively small, but it took just two decades for it to extend its commercial activities some two thousand miles along Alaska's southern coast. In 1794, the RAC established a small commercial settlement at Yakutat Bay and, in 1799, another that it called Arkhangel'sk, rebuilt nearby as Novoarkhangel'sk in 1804 after the first settlement was destroyed by the Tlingit in 1802.[39] The emergence of a Creole population that had ties both to Russian employees of the RAC and to local Indigenous groups, a consequence of the Russian imperial government's policy of supporting the cohabitation of Indigenous women and Russian men, was itself a factor in the RAC's success.[40] Much as Métis men played a key role as midlevel managers for the HBC in British North America, Creole men filled key management roles in RAC operations; as in other colonized areas of North America, Indigenous women served as interpreters and assisted their partners in building a working relationship with local Indigenous communities.[41]

Although Russia claimed the region it called Russian America by right of "discovery," as the concept was understood in European international law at the time, its geographical contours remained largely unknown. In this sense yet again, the exclusive right to engage in commercial activity granted to the RAC by the Russian imperial government paralleled that granted to the HBC a century earlier by the British Crown and that granted to the Matsumae clan by the Tokugawa shogunate.[42] Like the shogunate and the British Crown, the Russian imperial government knew almost nothing about most of the territory to which it purported to grant exclusive commercial access. With fewer than nine hundred Russian employees in all of Russian America at any given time, the RAC's efficient exploitation of fur-bearing mammals in the region relied largely on the coerced labor first of the Aleut and then of the Kodiak peoples who had hunted along the Alaskan coast for centuries.[43] It was their knowledge of land and ocean and the creatures that inhabited both, as well as their labor and finely honed technologies, that made possible Russia's success.[44] In his 1824 report, Zavalishin noted that the Kodiak "had dugout canoes whose speed was not inferior to that of the best rowboats or even whaleboats and gigs of English construction" and that they were not afraid to take either these or their small skin umiaks out on the open ocean.[45] The Aleut, he reported, "handle[d] their small skin boats as deftly as our Cossacks do horses, [pursuing] game with great speed, turning kayaks easily in all directions, so that the prey rarely manages to escape." Their skill in capturing sea otters far outweighed that of Russian hunters, whose own small boats, well adapted though they were to the more sheltered waters of the far western Pacific, could not always handle the turbulent waves of the Aleutians and in areas along the southern coast of Alaska.[46]

As in the Kuril Islands, where both Russian and Japanese commercial endeavors built on existing trade networks developed by the Ainu and other Indigenous peoples along the east coast of Asia, the RAC's commercial endeavors also took advantage of existing networks of exchange in which the Indigenous peoples with whom they came into contact along the Alaska coast already participated.[47] Early exchanges between Russians and Indigenous people were generally regarded as beneficial by both groups.[48] It was not long, however, before RAC officials began to resort to brutally coercive methods to force the participation of the Aleut and Kodiak hunters who were far more adept than they at hunting the fur-bearing mammals on which the RAC's operations depended.[49] Both overt violence and the threat of violence aided in bringing about a dramatic shift in the balance of power. Hostage taking emerged as a key strategy used to induce Aleut compliance, as was the brutal suppression of Aleut resistance, including an uprising in 1764 that was followed by harsh retribution.[50] The Aleut were vulnerable to such tactics in part because of the nature of the physical environment on the islands where they lived. As Stephen Haycox points out, the relatively barren terrain of the Aleutian Islands provided few avenues of escape and left them exposed to violent assaults in ways that the Indigenous peoples who lived in more densely forested areas were not. The Russian imperial government formally condoned the forced conscription of Indigenous men when it renewed the RAC's charter in 1821, although it also took steps at that time to constrain the practice. At any given time, it declared, the RAC could conscript only one-half of the men up to fifty years of age who lived on Kodiak Island and then only for up to three years. Intended though it may have been to limit the impact of this forced labor system on affected communities, there can be little doubt as to the degree of hardship this entailed for the families who lost their most skilled providers. Conscription was also dangerous for the hunters forced to work for the RAC. Some were sent westward across the North Pacific as far as the Kuril Islands, nearly four thousand miles from Kodiak Island, and, in the 1830s, others were sent to Fort Ross nearly two thousand miles to the south along the California coast. Still others drowned making long ocean crossings through unfamiliar waters to places such as the Pribilof Islands, where the rookeries of many thousands of sea lions were located, while others died chasing them down at sea.[51]

Although the RAC succeeded in subduing the Aleut and Kodiak communities with which they came into contact to the point where they were able to coerce several thousand of their best hunters to participate in their endeavors, they were unable to exert the same level of control over the Tlingit as

they advanced along the coast.[52] Geography and the nature of the environment was again one factor. In contrast to the rocky islands of the Aleutian
chain, where grasses and mosses constituted most of the vegetation, the forested islands of the Alexander Archipelago and nearby coastal areas provided
cover that made it easier for the Tlingit both to defend their territories and to
evade Russian incursions even if it meant temporarily abandoning coastal village sites.[53] Some villages were located on the banks of long, narrow fjords
that made them all but unassailable.[54] The Tlingit also responded to Russian
intrusion with armed resistance, impeding their advance, although it was frequently the Aleut and Kodiak hunters conscripted by the Russians who paid
the highest price.[55] Russian explorer Mikhail Vasilyev reported in 1821 that
"almost every annual hunt costs Konyagas and Aleuts their lives from Kolosh
[Tlingit] attacks," to the point where the sea otter skins collected were "steeped
in the blood of the innocent Konyagas and Aleuts." In one such attack on
Cross Sound, he added, some two hundred kayaks were lost along with the
hunters in them.[56] Much as colonial violence was displaced onto Indigenous
peoples along the U.S.-Mexico border as the historian Ned Blackhawk has
shown, in short, the same was true along the Alaska coast.[57]

Tlingit resistance also took other forms including, as the historian of Russian America Ilya Vinkovetsky explains, a reluctance to convert to Christianity for fear that this would render them little more than slaves, as they deemed
the Aleut hunters conscripted by the Russians.[58] Tlingit social structure and
cultural traditions were also a factor that allowed them to successfully resist
Russian intrusion to a greater degree than others along the southern coast of
Alaska. James R. Gibson cites a "strong clan system" as a source of Tlingit
power, arguing that it "provided solidarity against a common enemy," despite
occasional conflicts between some Tlingit groups.[59] Haycox, in turn, points
to the "strong sense of retributive justice that prevailed in Tlingit culture,"
which meant that Russians often paid a penalty for any offenses committed
against the Tlingit if they did not provide adequate compensation to the in-
jured party.[60] Demography and geography also played a role in their relative
success against Russian incursion. Not only was their population larger than
that of other Indigenous peoples along the Alaskan coast, but their territories
were positioned in such a way as to give them control of key mountain passes
into the interior and to allow them to trade directly both with coastal traders
and with Athapaskan and other peoples in the Yukon. After the Tlingit began
to trade with the Russians in the 1820s, they used their position to their advantage, favoring American and HBC traders to force the RAC to agree to
better trade terms and to obtain the permission of local Tlingit leaders before

hunting sea otters in their marine territories.[61] Tlingit resistance to RAC efforts to penetrate more deeply into the interior and to extend its operations southward along the north Pacific coast played a key role in determining where imperial and, in time, national borders would be drawn. While it also hindered British exploration and settlement of the Pacific borderlands, Tlingit interference with Russian expansion helped to preserve for Britain its foothold on the north Pacific coast.[62]

British and Spanish Exploration

Although Russia was the first European power to establish a colonial foothold in what is now Alaska, its interests along the northwestern coast of North America soon collided with those of Britain and Spain. Russia's expanding pursuits on a continent that had already been the focus of both British and Spanish colonial endeavor for some two centuries created concern among the imperial powers that had already established a presence there about the impact of its activities on their own claims. Spain's claims dated back to the treaties of Tordesillas, which had presumed, in 1494 and 1496, to divide a world almost utterly unknown to its signatories between Spain and Portugal. Occupied with the administration of its colonies in Latin America and under constant challenge by other European nations elsewhere on the continent, Spain sent the first of several expeditions to claim formal possession of areas along the Pacific coast north of New Spain only in 1741.[63] By 1774, Spanish explorers reached Nootka Sound and what they called Perez Inlet, now known as the Dixon Entrance. In 1775, they explored Vancouver Island and the southwestern coasts of what would become British Columbia and Washington State as far as the Quinault River. The same year, Juan Francisco de la Bodega y Quadra sailed north, reaching the tip of the Alexander Archipelago just north of the Dixon Entrance, and, four years later, Ignatio de Arteaga landed on what the British later named Prince of Wales Island, where he and his men became the first Europeans that the Tlingit encountered.[64] Just a year earlier, in 1778, Captain James Cook, on his third voyage around the world, had sailed north from Spanish California and along the coast of what is now British Columbia and Prince William Sound, claiming possession on behalf of the British Crown, then engaged in a battle with thirteen of its former colonies along the eastern seaboard.[65] Russian explorers had given other imperial powers their first glimpse of the Aleutian Islands and the Alaskan peninsula, long identified simply as "parts unknown" or terra incognita on European maps of the world. But the northwest coast beyond the fifty-fifth parallel remained a mystery to Europeans notwithstanding the preliminary forays of Spanish explorers. It was James Cook and, in particular, George Vancouver who sketched the contours of that coastline for European mapmakers, meticulously charting its many coves and inlets from what would become known as the Strait of Juan de Fuca to Cook's Inlet.[66]

Increasing British activity in and around Nootka Sound along the west coast of what the British called Vancouver Island, together with Russian interest in exploring the regions south of its existing operations, was of considerable concern to Spain, intent on consolidating its original claim to the region.[67] In 1776, in an effort to secure its claim to the California coast in the face of growing Russian interest in sea otter populations there, Spain established presidios at San Francisco and Monterey. Spain also established two small settlements further north, one at Nootka Sound on Vancouver Island in 1789 and the other on the Olympic Peninsula in 1792. While Britain would not establish an outpost on the Pacific coast until 1812, British merchant ships were actively engaged in efforts to develop trade ties with Indigenous peoples of the coast and regularly sheltered in the deep water harbor at Nootka Sound over the winter, both practices that Spain regarded as posing a significant threat to its own interests in the region.[68]

Although it was Russia that impinged most directly on Spain's claims under the treaties of Tordesillas, Spain was so overextended in the Americas by the end of the eighteenth century that it was in no position to defend its claims to the territories that Russia had occupied. Instead, Spain found itself more directly in conflict with Britain, which was also intent on establishing a presence along the north Pacific coast. Tensions between Britain and Spain came to a head in 1789 when several British vessels dropped anchor in Nootka Sound, refusing to recognize that Spain had an exclusive claim to the area, and Spain retaliated by seizing four of them. In 1794, Quadra and Vancouver, appointed by their respective governments to resolve the matter through negotiation, reached an agreement known as the Nootka Convention that provided for the release of the British ships. It also provided that both British and Spanish merchant vessels would be free to trade with Indigenous people along the north Pacific coast. Spain, in effect, conceded what had already long been recognized on the Atlantic coast—that not only the treaties of Tordesillas but mere "discovery" alone were no longer sufficient to sustain claims of European imperial powers to sovereignty along the north Pacific coast as against other Europeans. Instead, it was now necessary also to be able to demonstrate actual occupancy.[69]

By the 1810s, a growing British and American presence in the waters of the northeastern Pacific Ocean coincided with the decline of Russian interests in the area, complicating relations between the RAC and its Indigenous trading partners. Over and over again, the very success of Russia's commercial operations along the Alaskan coast had resulted in the collapse of the same fur-bearing mammal populations that had sustained its endeavors and, as the nineteenth century progressed, its annual harvest steadily declined.[70] Also in decline was the population of Aleut and Kodiak hunters on which the RAC's commercial operations had come to depend. Indigenous hunters were affected by disease and not provided medical care despite the brutal conditions under which they worked, and the RAC's reliance on their labor meant that the steady decrease in their numbers also undermined its ability to sustain its operations.[71] The total population of Alaska, estimated to have been about eighty thousand at the time of contact with Europeans in the 1700s, had dropped dramatically to less than half that by the 1860s owing largely to the impact of disease, although brutal working conditions, economic upheaval, and the coerced restructuring of their communities were each also a factor.[72]

The RAC's enterprises were also weakened by a need to import provisions to sustain its outposts along the Alaskan coast. The great distances between Russian America and potential sources of supply in Europe or on the east coast of Asia combined to make securing adequate supplies an ongoing problem for RAC administrators in the face of Tokugawa disinterest in opening trade talks that would have allowed Japanese merchants to fill this role.[73] In an effort both to address the problem of supply and to establish a base that would give it access to sea otter populations along the California coast, the RAC established a colony at Fort Ross, ninety miles north of San Francisco, in 1812, along with a port and a few farms.[74] Both the Russians and their Indigenous conscripts marveled at California's mild climate and abundant vegetation. In 1835, Ferdinand von Wrangel, chief manager of the RAC, wrote while on a visit to Fort Ross that "[his] wife's maid, an Unalaskan Creole, did not believe her eyes, seeing in the orchard two trees (an olive and a pear) in blossom and with fruit at the end of December at a time when on Unalaska and at Sitka it is frightful to shed a warm parka."[75] The establishment of Fort Ross, however, further exacerbated tensions not only with Britain but also with Spain, which regarded it as encroaching directly on territory long part of New Spain, to which its claim was well established.[76]

Imperial Boundaries

By the end of the eighteenth century, American traders were also an increasingly active factor along the northwest coast. While British shipowners had been the first to respond to the opportunities offered by the China trade in

the mid-eighteenth century, merchant ships from the United States had established a presence along the Pacific coast almost as soon as it was created as
a nation, in part because the vessels that sailed out of Boston under a British
flag before the Revolutionary War now sailed under a U.S. flag. The war
disrupted existing markets for cod and whale in Britain and its Caribbean
colonies, with the result that the Pacific trade offered a welcome alternative.
Shipowners sailing under the U.S. flag were also freer to operate in the Pacific
because they no longer risked forfeiture of their vessels if they violated constraints imposed on British shipping by the East India Company to protect its
monopoly among British traders in the Pacific.[77] U.S. traders soon came to
dominate the China trade, Gibson argues, because they owned their own vessels and were invested in their own success in ways that British captains employed by the East India Company were not.[78] The same kinds of Chinese
goods, including tea and porcelain, that were transported to Britain's American colonies aboard British ships before the revolution were now transported
to the newly established United States on American vessels. They, in turn,
supplied beaver pelts obtained from Indigenous people in the HBC's Columbia Department to Chinese merchants on their return trips to China.[79]

An increasing American presence in the Pacific coincided with the growing number of Americans who made their way to the Pacific coast along overland routes. Although they were still few in number during the early decades
of the nineteenth century, by the 1810s and 1820s it had become clear that
whether or not the territories along the Pacific coast would ultimately be absorbed into the United States, Americans would be a factor in shaping the
destiny of the region. The Treaty of Paris that formally brought an end to
hostilities between Britain and its former colonies in 1783 and recognized the
United States as an independent nation had extended its borders far beyond
those of the original thirteen states to the Mississippi River, doubling, with
the stroke of a pen, the size of the new nation.[80] It was only when the United
States was unexpectedly able to acquire French interests in North America in
1803, however, that it found itself in a geographical position to enter what was
an emerging contest among European imperial powers over land-based access to the Pacific Ocean, notwithstanding that the northern and western
boundaries of the territory to which the Louisiana Purchase agreement referred were poorly defined or that a majority of the Indigenous peoples who
had lived there since time immemorial neither knew of nor acceded to the
transfer of French claims to the United States.[81]

In 1818, Britain and the United States agreed to extend the boundary between Rupert's Land and the territory France had ceded along the forty-ninth

parallel to the "Stony" or Rocky Mountains. Intended to resolve several out-
standing issues related to the boundaries of territories claimed by each nation
in North America, the Convention of 1818 also addressed the rights of American fishers along the coasts of Newfoundland and Labrador, listing the bays
and creeks where they were permitted to fish until these areas were settled by
Europeans and restricting the access of foreign vessels to ocean waters within
three marine miles of shore. The agreement also addressed the area west of
the Rocky Mountains, claimed by both Britain and the United States based
on prior exploration, providing that the entire region, "together with its Harbours, Bays, and Creeks, and the Navigation of all Rivers" was to remain "free
and open . . . to the Vessels, Citizens, and Subjects" of both powers for a period of ten years.[82] The 1818 agreement did not, in fact, identify what the
boundaries of the area referred to in the agreement were, although it is often
described as if this was the case. It was subsequently interpreted, however, as
an agreement by Britain and the United States to jointly administer the region
known as the Oregon Country. Negotiators for both sides appear to have
agreed that each government had established dominion over some part of the
territory between latitude 42° and 54°40′ north, and that Russia had no valid
claim to this region south of the Dixon Entrance.[83]

Notwithstanding that Article III of the Convention of 1818 expressly declared that the purpose of the agreement was solely "to prevent disputes and
differences" between the United States and Britain and that it was not intended to undercut the claims of any other imperial power, both Spain and
Russia were immediately concerned about the implied infringement of their
own prior claims in the region. Already overextended and rapidly losing control
over its colonies in Latin America, Spain chose to negotiate its own agreement
with the United States, agreeing that latitude 42° north would mark the northern border of New Spain and ceding any prior claims it had to areas north of
that line.[84] As Gibson explains, Spain's primary interests in areas north of that
latitude were strategic and not grounded in any desire to participate in the fur
trade. Rather, it regarded the Oregon Country as a "wild and inhospitable . . .
wilderness buffer" that served to protect New Spain against intrusion on the
part of other European powers.[85]

Russia was equally concerned about the assumptions on which the 1818
convention was based. In 1790, Russian vessels had explored the Pacific coast
as far south as Haida Gwaii and the northern tip of Vancouver Island. Based
on these explorations, Russian imperial authorities had issued an ukase in
1799 declaring, based on the doctrine of discovery, that Russian America extended to the fifty-first parallel. In 1821, concerned about the growing liquor

and firearms trade that was developing between American sailors and the Indigenous people it deemed its subjects on the Alexander Archipelago, the Russian imperial government issued a further ukase granting to its subjects exclusive access to commerce along "the whole of the northwest coast of America" as far south as latitude 51° north and "from the Aleutian Islands to the eastern coast of Siberia" including the Kuril Islands as far as the island of Urup. It also declared that any foreign vessel approaching within one hundred Italian miles of any of these coasts could be confiscated, in effect asserting its exclusive jurisdiction over substantial areas of the North Pacific Ocean.[86] Both Britain and the United States issued forceful protests insisting that the attempted closure of any part of the open ocean violated fundamental principles of international maritime law. While Britain was initially willing to join the United States in negotiating a tripartite solution with Russia, however, after the Monroe Doctrine was proclaimed on December 2, 1823, Britain concluded that its interests were best served by entering into separate negotiations with Russia.[87] This also gave Britain an opportunity to clarify where the boundary between British North America and Russian America lay in the wake of the merger between the HBC and the North West Company (NWC) in 1821.[88]

The agreement reached in the Convention of 1824 between Russia and the United States, often described as establishing a clear boundary between the territories claimed by each, was far vaguer and more limited than has often been assumed. Both sides agreed that their respective subjects and citizens were free to navigate or fish "in any part of the Great Ocean," including its "interior seas, gulphs, harbours, and creeks," for a period of ten years.[89] They were also allowed to access any as yet unoccupied coasts to trade with Indigenous people. To prevent unauthorized trade in liquor and firearms, however, they were first required to obtain permission to engage in trade from the governor of any settlement established by the other power.[90] The United States agreed to establish no new settlements north of latitude 54°40′ north, while Russia agreed not to establish any new settlements south of this line, but neither formally conceded the other's right to actual possession of its claimed territories.[91] Instead, the language of the 1824 convention left open the possibility that both powers might perfect claims based on actual occupation if they did establish settlements on their side of that line. As early Vancouver Island resident Gilbert Malcolm Sproat explained, the 1824 convention was "more a modus vivendi than a mutual recognition of sovereignty."[92] While the agreement did not address British interests in the region, U.S. claims south of 54°40′ north also remained subject to the terms of its 1818 agreement with Britain, interpreted as providing for their joint occupation of the area that had come to be called the Oregon Country.[93]

The Anglo-Russian Convention of 1825 incorporated the basic provisions of the 1824 agreement between Russia and the United States, albeit not in precisely the same language, but added several clauses to address concerns arising from the geographically contiguous nature of their respective claims. In contrast to the 1824 agreement, which made general reference to 54°40′ north as a general dividing line between areas where the United States and Russia were each entitled to establish settlements but made no attempt to demarcate a formal boundary, the Anglo-Russian Convention identified, in precise terms, a "line of demarcation" between Russian and British possessions on the North American continent. Beginning at the southern tip of Prince of Wales Island near the Dixon Entrance, the 1825 agreement carved out a narrow strip of land now known as the Alaska panhandle along the west slope of the Coast Mountain Range, to the point where it intersects with longitude 141° west near Mount St. Elias, and then north along that meridian to the Arctic Ocean.[94] Russia's concession that the 141st meridian marked the eastern boundary of Russia's possessions in North America was one that Zavalishin believed his government should not have made.[95] As Julie Cruikshank has noted, however, the very vague description of the line that was to extend south of 141° west as following the "summit of the mountains situated parallel to the coast," indicates just how unimportant the precise location of the border was considered to be in 1825.[96] Although Russia wished to retain access to the trading posts that it had established along that coast, it was far more concerned with maintaining its access to trade networks that this provided than it was with maximizing its land base.[97]

In addition to demarcating the boundary between Russian and British territory, the 1825 convention also provided that British subjects would be allowed in perpetuity to freely navigate the streams and rivers that originated in British territory and flowed to the Pacific Ocean even if those waterways crossed that border. This was another concession to which Zavalishin objected, believing that it was, for all practical purposes, equivalent to relinquishing possession of these waters.[98] Other elements of the agreement included that the port of Sitka, or Novoarkhangel'sk, was to be open to British vessels and commerce for the duration of the agreement; that the ships of each power were permitted shelter in the other's ports if they were in peril; and that disputes regarding any claimed infraction of these provisions would be peacefully resolved in the courts "in a friendly manner and according to the principles of justice" and not with threats of armed conflict.[99]

For the United States and Britain, these agreements with Russia meant that both were assured of some form of access to the Pacific coast, although the question of how their asserted joint interest in the Oregon Country would be resolved was not yet clear. For Russia's part, while it had withdrawn its bar on access to the coasts of Russian America, where unauthorized traders had easily avoided detection among its many small islands and fjords, it did succeed, through the agreements, in getting both Britain and the United States to recognize its claims on the continent of North America and in the Aleutian Islands.[100] The fact that both agreements restricted Russian activity to the area north of latitude 54°40' north, however, left Fort Ross isolated. Writing in 1824, Zavalishin bitterly protested the concessions his government had made, warning that it was now inevitable that not just Fort Ross but all Alta California would "fall prey to either England or the United States, and most likely the latter." If only, he wrote, the RAC had developed Fort Ross "so as to position it between California and the boundary of the United States." This might have allowed it to serve as "an obstacle to the complete merger of California with the territory at 42° already ceded to the United States." Given reports that U.S. officials had refused to recognize existing property rights in both Louisiana and Florida, which, he declared, "had recently been unfairly taken from Spain," Zavalishin was certain that Californios and Indigenous people alike would have supported the "cession and sale of [Alta California] to the Russians."[101] Already overcommitted and primarily concerned with maintaining Russian interests north of 54°40' north, however, there was no prospect that either the RAC or the Russian imperial government would be in a position to defend Fort Ross against other imperial powers, including a rapidly expanding United States.[102] Zavalishin reassured his government, however, that Russia "had nothing to fear on the part of Mexico." Lacking its own navy, Mexico was no more able to enforce its claim to California than Spain had been.[103] Although Mexico had demanded that Russia abandon Fort Ross when it acquired Spanish interests in California in 1822 after achieving independence, it could do no more than protest when Russia did not comply with its demand.[104]

During the 1830s, tensions between local residents and Mexican officials in California grew—unrest that RAC observers believed Americans had made every effort to encourage, not least by promising aid if Californios did rebel.[105] When, in 1839, the HBC agreed to supply Sitka for ten years—the original purpose for which Fort Ross had been established—the RAC decided that it was time to sell.[106] In 1841, it sold the buildings and equipment at Fort Ross and Bodega Bay to John Sutter for $30,000—an obligation due five years later on which he chose to default, confident that neither Mexico nor any other governing authority would seek to enforce the terms of his agreement with the RAC, given that Mexico had demanded that the RAC abandon Fort Ross some two decades earlier.[107]

Dividing the Oregon Country

Even as Russian interests waned, the early decades of the nineteenth century had seen the establishment of a growing number of British and American settlements along the north Pacific coast. On the American side, these included Fort Clatsop (1805–6) and Astoria (1811–12), both near the mouth of the Columbia River. The British presence along the coast also increased when Astoria was transferred to Britain and renamed Fort George during the War of 1812. Fort Langley was erected in Stó:lō territory along the Fraser River in 1827; Fort McLoughlin was built on an island near Bella Bella in Heiltsuk territory in 1830; and, in 1831, Fort Simpson was established near the mouth of the Nass River at a place where Haida and Tsimshian people long gathered to visit and trade each summer. Britain was also concerned with consolidating its claims still further north and planned to establish a new HBC post on what was then known as Pelly's River—now the Stikine—in the hope that this would disrupt RAC access to furs originating in British North America east of the 141st meridian. Both the RAC and the Tlingit opposed this plan, and the RAC moved quickly to establish the post it called St. Dionysius Redoubt at the mouth of the Stikine in 1834, only to transfer it within a decade to the HBC, which renamed it Fort Stikine and built yet another post, called Fort Taku, still further north.[108]

Although the RAC and the HBC had faced increasing competition from American traders during the early 1830s on land as well as on sea, American traders gradually withdrew as the fur trade waned. By the 1840s, as a result, the RAC and the HBC had each come to regard the other as its chief competitor on the north Pacific coast.[109] Beginning in 1843, the HBC began to close some of the trading posts it had established just a decade or two earlier, including Fort Taku and Fort McLoughlin that year and, six years later, Fort Stikine. Instead, it moved its personnel to Vancouver Island, where Fort Victoria was slated to replace Fort Vancouver, which was located on the Columbia River, as its headquarters once the dividing line between British and U.S. interests in the Oregon Country had been settled.[110]

It was by no means certain that Oregon, which French Canadians had been the first non-Indigenous people to settle, would become part of the United States.[111] The 1844 arrival of 1,475 American emigrants in the Willamette Valley, however, had doubled the number of settlers in Oregon and raised new questions regarding its destiny. Although all these emigrants were well aware that they had traveled far beyond the existing borders of the United States and that they might not remain U.S. citizens, whether this was because the Willamette Valley became an independent republic or because it was designated British territory, their arrival created concern among some in Britain that their growing numbers might cause the United States to annex the entire Oregon Country. Although there was little public interest in the Oregon Country in either Britain or the United States, U.S. president James Polk, who had campaigned on the slogan "54-40 or fight," notified Great Britain in 1845 that the United States was no longer willing to abide by its 1818 agreement regarding the territories that lay west of the Rocky Mountains.[112] Britain and the United States had entered into that agreement, however, precisely because neither agreed just where the dividing line between their respective claims should be drawn. Nor did most regard it as a welcoming place. It was no exaggeration to say that "what Siberia is to Russia, Oregon is to the United States," declared an article published in the *North American Review* in 1846. "The road thither is equally long and wearisome," its authors wrote, and winter in Oregon, albeit not as cold as the Siberian winter, "is almost equally cheerless." It assured its readers that any effort to colonize the Oregon Country would fail, given that "vastly the greater part of Oregon is absolutely uninhabitable by civilized men." Neither side had a definitive claim, and it was not worth going to war over. Any determination of where the boundary between U.S. and British interests lay, as such, was, in their opinion, to be decided by compromise.[113]

Britain had the stronger claim north of the Columbia River based on international law as it existed at the time, a legal framework that Richard White aptly describes as "European rules for dividing up other people's countries."[114] Basing its claims on the doctrines of discovery and possession, Britain relied on James Cook's explorations of the north Pacific coast in 1778, as well as George Vancouver's careful charting of that coast between 1791 and 1795.[115] Britain also cited the land crossings of Alexander Mackenzie, who had reached the Pacific coast in 1793, and Simon Fraser, who had traveled down what became known as the Fraser River to its mouth in 1808.[116] British negotiators argued that its claim was confirmed by the Nootka Convention of 1794 which had recognized that Britain had a right equal to that of Spain to maintain a presence along the north Pacific coast. They admitted, however, that Britain's major concern was less the acquisition of title to the land at issue that it was protecting the interests of the HBC. Britain's proposal that the Columbia

River mark the boundary between the respective claims of Britain and the United States, they argued, was a simple and practical solution.[117]

The United States, in contrast, claimed the Columbia River and its entire watershed based on the voyage of the American merchant sea captain Robert Gray, who spotted and successfully navigated the river's entrance in 1792. The arrival of Meriwether Lewis and James Clark on the coast in 1806, it argued, further strengthened its claim.[118] U.S. negotiators refuted Britain's claim that the voyages of Cook and Vancouver had established title to the Columbia River, noting that both had missed the mouth of the Columbia River on their journey up the coast and that it was a Spanish explorer who had first sighted it in 1775.[119] The United States had acquired all Spain's interests north of the forty-second parallel, they argued, under the terms of the Adams-Onis Treaty in 1819.[120]

Various considerations, including the difficulties involved in defending the entire Oregon Country from halfway around the globe as well as its on-going commitments in Europe, led Great Britain to agree in 1846 that the boundary between its territories and those of the United States should run along the forty-ninth parallel to the coast. It also conceded that the Columbia River watershed should belong to the United States up to the point where it crossed the forty-ninth parallel, asking only that the international boundary turn sharply southeast in the midst of the Strait of Georgia to include all of Vancouver Island within British territory before again turning west to run through the center of the Juan de Fuca Strait to the Pacific Ocean. Subjects and citizens of both powers would be able to freely navigate these waters, and British subjects also remained free to navigate the stretch of Columbia River south of the forty-ninth parallel in the same manner that U.S. citizens did.[121] The Fraser River, which lies north of the forty-ninth parallel, however, would remain within what was now deemed British territory.[122]

Critical in the eyes of both Britain and the United States was the fact that the 1846 treaty ensured that both would have continental access to the Pacific Ocean. For the United States, in particular, extending its national borders to the Pacific gave it a far more direct stake in trade with Asia and particularly Japan, although its ports remained closed to Western nations.[123] That stake was further reinforced when, in 1848, the United States acquired Mexico's territory south of latitude 42° north to the west of Texas—which it had annexed in 1845— in exchange for $15 million under the terms of the Treaty of Guadalupe Hidalgo. In 1853, the Gadsden Purchase completed the land transfers that followed the end of the U.S. war against Mexico and produced the southwestern border of the United States as it exists today. Just half a century after the Louisiana Purchase doubled the territory of the United States, it had doubled again.[124]

From Britain's perspective, the question of where the southern boundary of its claimed territories in North America lay was settled none too soon. In 1854, less than a decade after it agreed that the forty-ninth parallel marked the boundary between British North America and the United States, the discovery of gold along the Fraser River drew some thirty thousand American miners north to pan for gold in its steep canyons.[125] In 1849, Britain had designated Vancouver Island a Crown colony based in part on fears that the United States might respond to the requests of some island residents that it annex the island. In 1858, for much the same reason, it designated the remainder of what is now British Columbia a Crown colony, merging both in 1866.[126] Britain's assumption of direct control over a region whose governance up to that time had been entrusted to the HBC, however, led to the establishment of governing structures that exerted new forms of pressure on the Indigenous peoples of what had become the B.C. coast.

The Western Pacific

As along the northwestern coast of North America, European powers brought ever more pressure to bear along the eastern coast of Eurasia as the nineteenth century progressed. While many of these efforts were directed at China, Japan also increasingly became a target. Given Japan's geographical proximity to Russia's claimed territories in the western Pacific, together with Japan's potential as a market for furs harvested in the Kuril Islands and in Russian America, Russia was the first European nation to attempt to establish trade ties with Japan. It was also motivated by the fact that the RAC had continued to struggle with the problem of supplying its outposts with needed provisions, and it viewed Japan as a potential source for such materials.[127] Russia's first formal effort to establish trade relations with Japan occurred in 1792, when a delegation sent by Catherine II was turned away at the port of Akeshi in Hokkaido. The Tokugawa shogunate continued to rebuff Russian efforts to persuade it to open Japanese ports to trade with Russian ships in need of provisions, as it would those of other European nations. When a second Russian delegation was turned away in 1804 after waiting at Nagasaki for nearly half a year, its commander retaliated by ordering two Japanese outposts, one on Sakhalin and the other in the Kuril Islands, to be destroyed. Although the Russian imperial government would disavow those attacks, the Japanese imprisoned for over a year a crew of Russian surveyors mapping the Kuril Islands to press them for information regarding Russia's intentions in the area.[128]

The discovery of new whaling grounds off the coast of Japan during the early decades of the nineteenth century led to an increase in the number of

European and American whaling ships and sealing vessels plying the waters around Japan and the Kuril Islands, increasing the pressure brought to bear on Japan to open its ports. Britain was also interested in securing harbors in the Kuril Islands where British vessels might take shelter, believing that those in the south were occupied only by Ainu and unaware that both Russia and Japan laid claim to them.[129] In 1824, Russian naval commander Otto von Kotzebue reported to Russian imperial authorities that the denial of access to Japan's ports forced European vessels in nearby waters to weather frequent storms at sea and that their crews suffered from scurvy because they could not take on fresh supplies. "Japanese do not want to have any dealings with other nations, with the exception of the Chinese and the Dutch, and treat foreigners as lepers," he explained, and "it is forbidden there on pain of death to supply foreigners with food." Japanese had no interest in the West and saw this as "a reliable means of preserving the purity of their ancient customs, with which they [were] content," although he conceded that Japanese deserved their respect for the "high level of civilization" they had attained "without any foreign influence whatever."[130] Japan's closed country policy, Inazo Nitobe would later declare, borrowing a term of art used to refer to times predating contact in North America, was grounded in "the habit of our nation from time immemorial."[131] Growing numbers of foreign ships in the western Pacific, however, also led to an increase in the number of shipwrecks along Japan's coast, including two in 1848, one near the Kuril Islands, with the result that pressure on Japan to reverse its exclusion policy did not ease.[132]

Although Russia had been the first to try to persuade Japan to establish trade relations, it was U.S. and not Russian pressure that served as the catalyst for Japan's decision to begin to open some ports to trade with the West and to establish diplomatic ties with Western nations. In 1845, even as U.S. president James Polk moved forward with plans to annex Texas and notified Great Britain that the United States planned to abrogate its 1818 agreement regarding the Oregon Country, he sent Commodore James Biddle to Japan with a formal request, presented by a Dutch interpreter, that it open its ports to American whaling vessels, only to be rebuffed ten days later. In an "explanatory edict" written in both Dutch and Chinese, Japanese officials formally notified Biddle that Japan's practice since time immemorial had been not to engage in trade with foreign parties.[133] Eight years later, in 1853, Commodore Matthew Perry, authorized by President Millard Fillmore to use more coercive measures to pressure Japan into opening its ports to U.S. vessels, was permitted to go ashore to deliver the letter he carried demanding access to Japanese ports.[134] During the eight years between Biddle's and Perry's visits, the United States had acquired California, which only heightened U.S. interest in establishing contact with Japan. When Perry returned in 1854 with additional men and warships, he was permitted to land at Kanagawa near Yokohama. At the conclusion of the negotiations that followed, Japan agreed to open the port of Shimoda at the tip of the Izu Peninsula to U.S. ships, along with the port of Hakodate in southern Hokkaido, through which much of the trade with the Ainu had passed during the previous two centuries.[135] The treaty signed at Kanagawa provided, as well, that shipwrecked American sailors could be rendered aid and a U.S. consular office opened in Shimoda.[136] Subsequent treaty negotiations conducted by Townsend Harris, the first U.S. consul in Japan, led to an agreement that provided for the opening of five additional ports in 1858. Like the treaty imposed on Qing China by Great Britain in 1842 at the end of the first Opium War, the Harris Treaty provided for foreign control of import and export duties. It also included an extraterritoriality clause, similar to one imposed on China, that allowed the United States to retain jurisdiction over its own citizens even when they committed crimes in Japan. As was noted at the time, this was a significant intrusion on the sovereign authority of another nation.[137]

During the months that followed, the Netherlands, Russia, Britain, and France all entered into treaties with Japan that closely paralleled those of the United States.[138] Russia also used its negotiations with Japan to address their respective claims in the Kuril Islands. Both had followed up on their exploratory expeditions to the Kuril Islands in the 1770s by establishing outposts and increasing hunting activities on and around the islands.[139] As late as 1854, however, both Russia and Japan remained uncertain as to just where the boundaries of the territories they claimed lay, although they shared the assumption that they were entitled to divide what they knew to be Ainu territory between them.[140] While not the subject of formal agreement, Japan and Russia exercised what was, in practice, a form of joint sovereignty over the Kuril Islands and Sakhalin not unlike that exercised by Britain and the United States in the Oregon Country before 1846.[141] Only when other European nations began to make their presence felt in the western Pacific did this dual arrangement and uncertainty as to where the boundary between their respective territories lay begin to pose a problem. Also a factor encouraging Russia and Japan to address this question was the steep drop in the size of the sea otter population in the Kuril Islands that had resulted from overhunting and yielded ever fewer profits. While the Shimoda Treaty of 1855 between Russia and Japan paralleled the 1854 Treaty of Kanagawa in key respects, it also provided that the Kuril Islands should be divided between the two at a point midway between Urup and the island known to the Japanese as Etorofu that the Russians called Iturup. Just two decades later, in the Treaty of St. Petersburg, Russia relinquished its claims to the Kuril Islands in return for Japan's relinquishment of its claims on Sakhalin.[142] At the conclusion of the Russo-Japanese War in 1905, triggered in substantial part by Japan's fears that Russian influence on the adjacent Korean peninsula might escalate to the point where Russia posed a direct danger to Japan itself, Japan would again acquire the southern half of Sakhalin.[143] Under the terms of its peace treaty with Russia, Japan also acquired "fishery rights along the coasts of Russian possessions in the Japan, Okhotsk and Bering Seas" that, in turn, encouraged the building of an oceangoing fishing fleet that would probe the far waters of the North Pacific.[144] It was the ocean itself, Nitobe wrote in 1912, that had protected Japan from the "catastrophe" that had befallen China and had allowed it to prevail in war against Russia. Japan's borders, Nitobe declared, were "guarded by waves and winds which love our land no less than do our captains and sailors."[145]

Inscribing National Borders

The year 1867 was a year of transition all around the North Pacific Rim that transformed its geopolitical landscape in ways that would have significant consequences for the Indigenous peoples on both the eastern and the western shores of the North Pacific. Not only did the United States acquire Russia's interests in Alaska and Canada enter Confederation in 1867, but it also marked the demise of the Tokugawa shogunate, which had governed Japan for over two and a half centuries. In the wake of the Meiji Restoration in 1868, the Meiji oligarchs, fiercely determined to negotiate an end to the unequal treaties that had been imposed on it by both the United States and Britain, as well as other European powers, embarked on a resolute effort to remake Japan as a modern, industrial nation that would both be recognized as civilized by the West and be powerful enough to resist Western encroachment. Meiji reforms focused on the elimination of the feudal institutions that inhibited the movement of labor needed to develop the infrastructure that Japan required to achieve its goals.[146] The Meiji government's abolition of Tokugawa-era status and caste barriers during the years immediately following the Restoration and its removal of barriers that restricted both internal and external migration during the Tokugawa period were an integral part of that process. By dissolving the historical link between status and occupation and allowing the free movement of laborers into newly industrializing urban areas, these reforms created the labor pool needed to facilitate industrialization. Industrialization, in turn, would later facilitate Japan's own quest for empire and set in motion new patterns of migration that would in time extend across the Pacific to North America.[147]

During the decades that followed the Meiji Restoration, Japan also established itself as a colonial power, incorporating first Hokkaido and then the Ryukyu Islands, which had remained a semi-independent kingdom during the Tokugawa period, within its national boundaries, much as Britain and the United States had absorbed new territories as they extended their interests across the North American continent. Once an independent people who had deflected foreign intrusions time and again, the Ainu were reframed as a colonized minority much as the Indigenous peoples of North America had been.[148] As in North America, the disruption of prior trading relationships, in this instance between the Ainu and other peoples along the eastern coast of Eurasia, had resulted in the development of a mutually dependent relationship between the Ainu and the Matsumae clan that left the Ainu economically vulnerable to further colonial intrusion in ways they were not before when Japan incorporated Ainu territories within its boundaries.[149] In time, Japan would also come to model key elements of its policy with respect to the Ainu on that of Britain and the United States.

Alaska Treaty of Cession

By the 1860s, RAC operations along the Alaska coast, comprising fewer than a dozen outposts, troubled by supply issues created by distance from sources of adequate provision, and much less profitable after the collapse of the sea otter populations on which they were founded, no longer justified, in the eyes of key figures within Russia's imperial government, the cost of maintaining a colony on the American continent.[150] Tlingit resistance had limited RAC access to new populations of fur-bearing mammals, even as its dependence on the Tlingit for food and protection while operating in their territories became a source of Tlingit power.[151] Britain's concession with regard to the HBC's forts along the Columbia River in 1846, motivated in part by the difficulties involved in defending them from halfway around the globe, in turn, had served to demonstrate how exposed Russian America also was. Russian anxiety about U.S. ambitions, particularly in the event of a gold strike that attracted miners to Alaska in the same numbers that had flooded California and the Fraser Canyon in the 1840s and 1850s, was yet another factor leading Russia to consider selling its interests on the North American continent, as were geopolitical considerations. Chief among them was a strategic decision on Russia's part to consolidate its position in the western Pacific, where it planned to make Vladivostok the center of its operations, favorably located in relation to each of Japan, the Korean peninsula, and China. While not ice free in winter, it was "a deep, safe harbor" that could be readily defended and kept clear enough of ice to function all year round.[152]

The United States, in turn, also had a variety of reasons for acquiring Russian interests in Alaska, notwithstanding the debates regarding the wisdom of that acquisition that would ensue. Although the economic opportunities that potentially flowed from access to Alaska's resources were of interest, also key were geopolitical considerations. Given its location along the Pacific Rim, the acquisition of Alaska promised to aid the United States in establishing itself as a Pacific power positioned both to dominate trade with Asia and to establish naval outposts that would facilitate its control both of the continent of North America and of key whaling and fishing grounds in the North Pacific, as well as the pelagic sealing industry.[153] Also of interest to advocates of U.S. expansion was the possibility that the transfer might encourage the annexation of British Columbia, which remained a British colony that had yet to join the Canadian confederation.[154]

Russia and the United States had certain concerns in common, including a shared desire to limit British access to the Pacific coast. It was for this reason that Russia had been willing to transfer its interests in Alaska to the United States as early as 1846, so long as the United States agreed to claim and defend the entire Oregon Country up to 54°40′. This was a proposal, however, that the United States could not accept given the 1820 Missouri Compromise and the objections Southern slave states would have raised to expansion north of 36°30′.[155] When the matter was raised again in 1859, two years after Russia's loss in the Crimean War, there was a greater degree of interest, but the U.S. Civil War intervened.[156] When the Civil War ended, Russia again proposed to sell its interests in Alaska to the United States. After a protracted period of negotiation between U.S. secretary of state William Seward and Russian diplomat Eduard de Stoeckl, Russia transferred its interests in Alaska to the United States for $7.2 million on October 18, 1867.[157] Also decided in the course of those negotiations was the ocean boundary that would now delineate American and Russian territories in the North Pacific. It was reportedly Seward himself who proposed that the international border cut down the center of the Bering Strait and divide the chain of islands that arcs across the North Pacific Rim between Russia and United States. Although the residents of Attu had closer ties to Russia than to the United States, the island of Attu and those to the east of it were denoted U.S. territory, while those to the west, known as the Komandorski or Commander Islands, were denoted Russian territory.[158]

Although it would be treated by both the United States and other European powers as a transfer of the entire region that now constitutes the state of Alaska, this interpretation contravenes the principle, well established in law, that any party can only transfer interests that it has actually acquired, and it is a matter of historical fact that Russia was able to establish a colonial presence only in a limited area along Alaska's south coast. While neither Russia nor the United States had been willing to concede in 1824 that the other had perfected its claim to full possession of its claimed territories, ironically, by 1867 it was to the United States' benefit to accept Russia's contention that the small settlements the RAC had established along the Alaskan coast had perfected Russia's claims to full possession of all Alaska.

The 1867 cession treaty, carefully written out in longhand, copied verbatim the boundary description agreed to by Britain and Russia in the Anglo-Russian Convention of 1825, including its ambiguous reference to the height of the mountains, and transferred to the United States all buildings and other infrastructure within those boundaries.[159] Uncertainty regarding just where these boundaries were located, however, remained a source of consternation for the nation-states that acquired the interests of imperial powers in the region. Whereas the imperial powers were primarily concerned with ensuring their exclusive access to trade with particular groups in a given area, with the result that the precise location of these boundaries was not of paramount concern, the nation-states that assumed their interests were far more deeply invested in precisely inscribing and enforcing clearly articulated national borders. As an example of the consternation this could cause, Bockstoce cites the provision in the 1825 convention that British subjects should build no outposts west of the 141st meridian, which separated Russian America from British North America. In 1847, unsure just where the 141st meridian was located on the ground, the HBC had built Fort Yukon at the confluence of the Yukon and the Porcupine Rivers 117 miles west of that meridian.[160] When, in 1869, the United States became aware of the error, it acted quickly to occupy the fort, relying on the terms of the Treaty of Cession, which provided for the transfer of all military posts in the ceded area to the United States, much to Britain's chagrin.[161]

The Treaty of Cession also failed to clarify the status of the Indigenous people of Alaska under U.S. law. While Article III provided that all "inhabitants of the ceded territory" who chose not to return to Russia during the three years after it was ratified would be granted the same rights as U.S. citizens, it made an exception for what it described as the "uncivilized native tribes," which were instead to be "subject to such laws and regulations as the United States may, from time to time, adopt in regard to aboriginal tribes in that country."[162] Neither side had taken any steps to consult with the Indigenous people who had lived in Alaska since time immemorial to ascertain their position regarding the sale of Russian interests in North America to the United States, nor did those negotiating the treaty, even on the Russian side, know much about a large majority of the Indigenous peoples whose homeland it was. The Tlingit repeatedly objected to the purported transfer of their territories, insisting that they had never conveyed more than a few small areas to Russia to begin with, although they decided to avoid overt resistance when they were confronted with demonstrations of U.S. military power.[163] The fact remains, however, that in the eyes of Alaska's Indigenous people, as Inupiaq scholar William L. Iggiagruk Hensley explains, the United States acquired no more than "the right to negotiate with the Indigenous populations."[164]

Canadian Confederation

Concerns that the United States might seek to annex one or more of Britain's colonies in North America after the end of the Civil War, together with fears that Britain would not be able to mount an adequate defense should that occur, were among the considerations that led three of its eastern colonies in British North America, with Britain's support, to form a confederation on July 1, 1867.[165] Questions existed, however, as to whether the Dominion of Canada had a valid claim to any of Britain's other territories in British North America, including Rupert's Land and the colony of British Columbia. It was by no means inevitable, as such, that Canada would also become a transcontinental nation. Britain had long regarded Rupert's Land and the westernmost reaches of British North America as a fur trade hinterland and not as a settlement frontier. Canadians, in turn, had often criticized the United States for its repeated absorption of new lands to the west of its original land base, the historian Doug Owram explains, and did not want to be seen as doing the same thing. Although Rupert's Land was also part of British North America, there was no clear basis in international law for its transfer to the Dominion of Canada, which included territories that France had ceded to Britain in 1763. Advocates of expansion developed a convoluted rationale to allow Canada to annex Rupert's Land on the ground that it already belonged to Canada "by right of discovery and settlement," which was approved by Britain as "just and reasonable" in 1857.[166] What had begun as a largely imaginary grant of exclusive commercial access to the vast region that drains into Hudson's Bay by Charles II to the HBC in 1670 as against other British subjects, in short, had expanded to become a claim to absolute title and overarching sovereignty in just two centuries.

Britain's transfer of Rupert's Land to the Dominion of Canada in 1870, together with British Columbia's entry into Confederation in 1871, extended Canada's borders to the Pacific. While some of Canada's leaders had initially been reluctant to extend the boundaries of the new Dominion beyond those of the three colonies that were first joined, fears that the United States might annex British Columbia following its acquisition of Russian interests in Alaska, taken together with a growing understanding of the importance of the value of a direct trade route to Asia and access to the Pacific, Patrick Lane argues, secured British Columbia's place within the Dominion of Canada.[167]

Railroads promised to do what rivers had once done and more, tying the north Pacific coast to eastern cities well beyond the reach of even the longest rivers. Completed with the aid of Chinese labor in 1886 at a time when Indigenous villages were still located near the site selected as its terminus in Vancouver, B.C., the Canadian Pacific Railway (CPR) linked the Canadian prairies and eastern Canada to Asia and the Pacific.[168] The CPR quickly positioned itself as the shortest and most direct route connecting Europe to Asia. The CPR, and not the railroads south of the Canada-U.S. border, its advertising declared, was the "great railway route across the American continent," "the highway to the Orient: across the prairies, mountains and rivers of Canada to Japan, China, Australasia and the sunny isles of the Pacific."[169] Canadian railroad boosters, like their counterparts in the United States, embraced a vision of Canada as a nation that extended from Atlantic to Pacific shores. Canada's purpose in projecting itself across the continent, however, was not just to secure a trade route to Asia or to resist encroachment by the United States, but to secure its place at the heart of the British empire.[170] As the authors of an 1897 book titled *Canada......from Ocean to Ocean* declared, the British empire extended across a quarter of the earth's land surface, and Canada constituted a third of the British empire, giving substance to the claim that it circumvented the world.[171]

Much as neither Russia nor the United States consulted Alaska's Indigenous people prior to Russia's cession of its interests there, however, neither Britain nor Canada sought the opinion of Indigenous peoples with regard to the transfer of either British Columbia or Rupert's Land to Canada, notwithstanding that the vast majority of those Indigenous residents had never agreed to relinquish title to their traditional territories to Britain to begin with.[172] Also uncertain, given the vague nature of the boundaries articulated in the 1825 agreement between Britain and Russia to which the United States was heir, was just what "the exact boundaries of this extended Canada were."[173]

The description of the boundary incorporated into the cession treaty between Russia and the United States that now delineated the northernmost stretches of the U.S.-Canada border had been taken almost verbatim from the 1825 convention between Britain and Russia, including its obscure reference to the height of the Coast Mountain Range, which did not always lie within the stipulated ten leagues from the ocean as the maps of early explorers depicted. As early as 1851, a guidebook for emigrants to British North America noted the "very vague" nature of the boundary between British North America and Russian America. The uncertain contours of that divide, its authors observed, might well give rise to "unpleasant discussions" in the future, implying that these border regions would long remain unsettled as a result.[174] By 1896, the discovery of gold in the Yukon, together with the expansion of the mining industry on the islands along the Pacific coast, made it all the more necessary to identify the precise location of the U.S.-Canada border. Determining just where it was located was key to establishing the jurisdictional authority of each nation both to grant mineral claims and to resolve any disputes that arose with regard to them. The fact that negotiations regarding coastal fisheries were underway between the United States and Britain, in turn, also made it important to determine the location of the maritime border that divided U.S. and Canadian waters.[175] The major point of contention, however, was whether the small town of Skagway, a port at the head of the Lynn Canal where prospectors traveling the most direct route to the goldfields disembarked, was located on the U.S. or the Canadian side of the international border.[176] Given that this question had yet to be resolved, the North-West Mounted Police (NWMP) stationed an officer in Skagway to maintain a Canadian presence in the recently established port town, a source of irritation for American residents who believed that Skagway was located on the U.S. side of the line.[177]

While a survey of the Alaska-Yukon boundary along the 141st meridian was successfully undertaken in 1887, confirming that the Klondike lay within Canadian borders, it was not until 1892 that a joint U.S.-Canadian survey of the boundary between northern British Columbia and the Alaska panhandle began. Continued resistance to foreign intrusion on the part of the Chilkat Tlingit, who controlled both Chilkoot Pass and White Pass well into the 1880s, had contributed to the delay.[178] Tellingly, one surveyor reported, survey posts

A Tr'ondëk Hwëch'in family near the 141st parallel in 1899. The Hän-speaking people, in the midst of whose traditional territories the Klondike is located, were among the Indigenous people displaced by the arrival of thousands of prospectors. Yukon Archives, E. A. Hegg Fonds, 82/290, #2563.

used to mark Alaska's border with British Columbia and the Yukon were re-designed "to make it more difficult to pull them out."[179] Only in 1898 did the NWMP establish posts at the summit of the two passes and begin to collect customs duties.[180]

Surveyors faced a challenging task, made all the more difficult not only by the steep and rugged terrain of the Coast Mountains but also by the problem of determining just what the contours of the borderline described in the 1825 agreement were. Notwithstanding that it was referred to in the agreement as the Portland Channel, it was generally agreed that the Portland Canal, a long, narrow fjord across from the Dixon Entrance, formed the beginning point of the borderline. The Portland Canal, American surveyor William H. Dall re-counted, "cuts into the heart of the Coast Range" for some sixty miles, "walled by mountains 3,000 to 4,000 feet high at the entrance" that increase to twice that height at its end.[181] As William Ogilvie, the Canadian astronomer who

had surveyed the 141st parallel in 1887 before turning his attention to the B.C.-
Alaska border, pointed out, the 1825 agreement stipulated that the borderline
should then follow the mountain peaks that the authors of the agreement
imagined lay in "a line parallel to the windings of the Coast," never to "exceed
the distance of ten marine leagues therefrom." But the notion that there was
any mountain range anywhere in the world that ran "along a coast-line parallel to it in the strict, or geometrical, sense of the word," Ogilvie wrote, was
simply not grounded in any real knowledge or understanding either of the
Pacific coast or of geographical formations.[182] What the 1825 agreement had
provided was less a description of an agreed-to boundary than a formula for
determining it, and even that formula was fundamentally flawed.

Equally problematic was the matter of determining what was referred to
both as "Ocean" and as "the Coast" by the original authors of the 1825 agreement. Did "Ocean" refer only to the open waters of the Pacific, or did it include the channels that surround the islands of the Alexander Archipelago
and separate it from mainland? "Coast," Sproat observed, was itself "an ambiguous term" that was used in more than one way in the agreement. Was the
coast the place "where the Mainland meets the salt water," or was it located
along the outer shores of the archipelago that face the open ocean? The latter
interpretation was decided against for purposes of determining the location
of the border described in the 1825 agreement, given that this would have
meant that Russia secured no territory at all on the mainland in a number of
areas, something for which all agreed Russia would not have negotiated.[183]
This being the case, the United States argued that the "coast" should follow
the contours of the inlets that cut deep into the mainland, sometimes for
many miles, which in turn would push the border inland to a corresponding
degree at these points. Canada contended the coastline should be defined as
cutting across the mouths of the inlets to follow a more general line. The definition proposed by the United States meant that Skagway would lie within
U.S. borders. Canada's proposal, by contrast, meant that the border would be
drawn many miles to the south, given that Skagway was located at the head of
one such inlet—the Lynn Canal—that was seventy miles in length. This would
give Canada a northern port with ready access to both the Yukon and the
Pacific—its only opportunity to secure such an ocean port given that the Alaska
panhandle blocked northern British Columbia north of Prince Rupert and
the 54th parallel from direct access to the sea.[184]

In 1903, the Alaska Boundary Tribunal ruled that Skagway lay within the
borders of the United States.[185] "Had the Canadian contention been accepted,"
Ogilvie later wrote, "Canada would have secured about seventy miles of the

length of Lynn Canal, and the ocean port at its head, Skagway." But he also observed that although its ruling was criticized in Canada, the final result "was more of a compromise than many who understood the situation expected. Canada did not secure a seaport, but on the other hand the United States did not secure the ten-marine-league limit all along the coast strip." As a result, Ogilvie noted, only the last twenty-five miles of the Stikine River lay within U.S. borders, given that the U.S.-Canada border was just twenty miles from the coast at that point and not ten marine leagues.[186] In a compromise reminiscent of that which had divided the islands of the Salish Sea between Canada and the United States in 1872, as well, a small group of islands that lie between Prince of Wales Island and the Portland Canal were divided between the two, leaving neither side entirely satisfied.[187]

Even after the precise location of the northernmost stretches of the U.S.-Canada border was largely determined, however, enforcement was neither immediate nor comprehensive. Like the U.S.-Mexico border, the border that divided Alaska from British Columbia and the Yukon "remained infrequently policed and invisibly defined, at least in the eyes of everyday borderlands residents."[188] While the NWMP set up posts along the international border, they were far and few between. Those that were built were often located close to existing Indigenous communities. Among the people hired by the NWMP to police the Alaska-Yukon border, as a result, were also Indigenous men, clearly valued enforcement officers, who may have been motivated in part by the opportunity that these positions offered to earn wages that would enable them to more easily negotiate the cash-based economies that followed from the incorporation of Indigenous territories within both U.S. and Canadian borders. The NWMP was clearly conscious, at the same time, that the power that at least some of the Indigenous men they hired had was grounded in the traditional cultural roles they filled in the context of Indigenous society. One NWMP officer, Inspector A. M. Jarvis, based at Dalton Post, not far from the mountain passes that the Tlingit had long defended, wrote in 1899, for example, that the NWMP had been "fortunate in securing the services of two of the best Indians of the Stick tribe as special constables." One of the men, he reported, was "a medicine man and the most respected and feared amongst all the Natives."[189] The special constable's willingness to navigate the shifting social and cultural borderlands along the northernmost reaches of the U.S.-Canada border, Jarvis's statement suggests, provided welcome support to the NWMP in pursuing its own mandate to preserve the peace and monitor traffic crossing the mountain passes into Canada.

Contingent Borderlands

The northern borders of both Canada and the United States were a product of several centuries of imperial maneuvering throughout the Americas that originated in Europe and spilled out across both the Atlantic and the Pacific Oceans—a series of contingent moments the consequences of which no one could have predicted at the time that they occurred.[190] Where Russia's presence on the Alaska coast had barred Britain's westward advance, the presence of New Spain constrained the ability of both Russia and Britain to extend their interests southward along the north Pacific coast. The continued involvement of both Britain and Spain in the European wars that spanned the Atlantic Ocean at key moments, including the Revolutionary War and the War of 1812, in turn, allowed Russia to establish itself along the southern coast of Alaska with relatively little initial opposition by other European powers.[191] The treaties that brought these European conflicts to an end also provided for the redrawing of imperial boundaries on the North American continent. The 1818 convention on which the joint occupation of the Oregon Country by Britain and the United States was based, for example, was itself one of a series of treaties agreed to by European powers after the end of the Napoleonic Wars, not unlike those that redrew colonial borders in North America in 1763, when France ceded many of its claimed territories in North America to Britain, and in 1783, when Britain ceded part of its claimed territory to the United States.[192]

For Britain, the edge of empire had advanced slowly westward over the course of several centuries, beginning on the shores of the Atlantic and Hudson's Bay during the 1600s, expanding first into the interior of the continent with the acquisition of French interests in North America in 1763 and then across it to the islands off its westernmost coast with the formal organization of Vancouver Island as a Crown colony in 1849. It had taken the United States, in turn, some seven decades to reach the Pacific coast and nearly a century to extend its borders to include Alaska. As heir to British North America, in contrast, Canada became a transcontinental nation just four years after 1867, having absorbed more territory within its boundaries over a far shorter period of time than either Japan or the United States; where the boundaries of the United States were repeatedly redrawn during its first hundred years, Canada's boundaries were largely determined once British Columbia entered Confederation and the transfer of Rupert's Land was complete.[193]

While Japan was not an active participant in the earliest stages of the imperial contest along the northwest coast of North America, it was not absent. Its establishment of a commercial foothold on Hokkaido in the 1700s and its ever more active presence in the Kuril Islands during the 1800s were each factors that helped to direct Russian expansion eastward across the Pacific. Japan's determined resistance to Russia's efforts to establish trade relations, in turn, aided in weakening of Russia's position on the North American continent by denying the RAC needed sources of supply and a ready market for the furs produced on the Alaskan coast, contributing to its eventual decision to sell its interests in Alaska to the United States. North America was not unknown to the Japanese. They were among those who traveled across the Pacific on Spanish vessels to Mexico in the late 1500s and early 1600s, and after Japan relaxed its restrictions on trade with the West and its prohibition on travel by Japanese subjects beyond Japanese coastal waters during the early decades of the Meiji era, Japanese migrants and fishermen also began to explore the resources of the open ocean and to travel to North America in increasing numbers.

While fears that the United States might annex British Columbia persisted for some decades, there were also Canadians who urged at one time or another that Canada incorporate parts of the United States within its boundaries. During the debates surrounding British Columbia's entry into Confederation, for example, some B.C. residents passed a resolution urging the Dominion of Canada to acquire both Maine and Alaska, so that it would comprise all lands on the continent of North America north of the forty-ninth parallel.[194] Yet, had Polk acted on his campaign promise "54-40 or fight" and won, Prince Rupert and other B.C. towns along the Skeena River, as well as Haida Gwaii, might well lie within U.S. borders today.[195] Some Americans argued as late as 1893 for what they euphemistically described as the "political reunion of the United States and Canada," one that they clearly intended the United States should dominate.[196] While no such annexation has occurred, the fact that the B.C. coast lies "athwart the United States' lines of communication with Alaska," one Canadian writer observed in 1941, ensured that it would remain a focus of U.S. interest and concern.[197]

The recasting of imperial boundaries as national borders in 1867 and 1871, following first the transfer of Russia's interests in Alaska to the United States and then the transfer of the Crown colony of British Columbia to Canada, led once again to a reframing of the northern borderlands through which Indigenous people and, later, Japanese migrants moved. At its heart would be a continuing effort to redefine the Indigenous peoples of the region as American or Canadian "Indians" and to restrict access to coastal resources based on national origin and race. The United States' ability to frame its presence in

Alaska as having stepped into Russia's shoes would allow it to obscure and overlook the presence and sovereign rights of Alaska Natives in ways it could not in the contiguous states. That Canada stepped into the shoes of Great Britain, in turn, would allow it to distance itself from the commitments Britain had made to its Indigenous allies at earlier stages. Together, the evolving bodies of law on either side of the U.S.-Canada border would produce a series of shifts in the legal, social, and cultural landscape of the north Pacific borderlands that both Indigenous people and Japanese immigrants would be forced to negotiate in ever more complex ways during the decades that followed.

CHAPTER TWO

Immigrant and Indigene

A year after word reached San Francisco that gold had been discovered on the Klondike River, Arichika Ikeda boarded a small, rundown steamer bound for Alaska along with a single companion. They had kept their plans to travel north a secret from other Japanese, not wanting, in Ikeda's words, to trigger a sudden exodus among impressionable younger men at a time when gold fever was already rampant. As the handwritten record that Ikeda kept of his journey north reveals, just one friend came to the pier to see Ikeda and his companion off as they boarded ship in February 1898. A few years later, on a return trip to Japan, Ikeda would give friends curious to learn more about his adventures on Alaska's glaciers and the Indigenous people he encountered along the way his permission to publish his diary.[1] What Ikeda did not realize was that the discovery that precipitated the Klondike gold rush, in which he also participated, had itself been made by an Indigenous man with ties to both the Athapaskan and the Tlingit peoples of the region, known to his family as Keish.[2]

The old steamer on which Ikeda sailed regularly traveled between San Francisco and the Copper River, which flows out the Chugach Mountains into the Gulf of Alaska not far from the point where the U.S.-Canada border turns sharply north.[3] Although Ikeda admired the young British captain and his "strong-hearted" and able navigator, he regarded his fellow passengers with some disdain. Where he and his travel companion occupied one of eight small first-class cabins, most of the ship's passengers slept in hammocks suspended from the ceiling of a large room that accommodated close to two hundred men.[4] An educated man who had studied English, medicine, and classical Chinese literature in Japan before traveling across the Pacific to North America, Ikeda was taken aback by the vulgar and "truly low-class" behavior of his fellow travelers, most of them *hakujin* (white people) whom he regarded as poor representatives of their society. So foul was the language they used, he wrote, that he could hardly bear to listen to them or to spend any time in their company. They were indifferent to the unsanitary conditions they created, he added, chewing tobacco and spitting on the deck and leaving their luggage lying haphazardly about the vessel.[5]

The view beyond the steamer's railings, however, provided a welcome distraction from conditions on board ship. By the time they reached Vancouver

Island on the fourth day of their journey, Ikeda wrote, the dry landscape of the California coast had given way to dense forests of cedar and pine that extended right down to the rocky shores that lined the Strait of Juan de Fuca and Puget Sound as they approached Seattle.[6] The landscape reminded a number of immigrants from coastal prefectures in Japan of home, where waterfalls not unlike those along the B.C. and Alaska coast also plunge down mountainsides and pine or fir trees cling to small, rocky islands, "exposed to the naked elements and pounding waves," that line both coasts—most famously, in Japan, those of Matsushima along its northeastern coast.[7] When his ship docked in Seattle, Ikeda disembarked and set off to find a Japanese inn where he might take a Japanese bath (*ofuro*), only to be turned away by a maid at the Yokohama Hotel—an inn he later learned was a workplace for Japanese women engaged in prostitution. Dismayed as he was to learn that there were Japanese women who worked as prostitutes in Seattle, Ikeda mused that this was inevitable as long as a majority of the eight thousand Japanese in town were men. By evening, much to his relief, he had located a Japanese restaurant and a public *ofuro*, convinced that this was the last time he would see either until he returned from his journey to the north.[8]

Seattle, Ikeda noted, was a bustling transportation hub with vessels sailing to and from Hawaii and bound for various North Pacific ports every day. A hundred additional passengers boarded the ship that he was on before it continued on its journey, steaming north past Bainbridge and Whidbey Islands into the Strait of Georgia. As they passed Vancouver, B.C., in the dark of night, Ikeda wrote, it shimmered in the distance like a faraway star. Seagulls followed in their wake and, as they made their way along the coast of Vancouver Island, they spotted pods of dolphins as well as seals and sea otters. Most intriguing to Ikeda, however, was an Indigenous village of some 450 neatly whitewashed homes located near the north end of Vancouver Island—almost certainly the Kwakwaka'wakw village of Namgis at Alert Bay—where they dropped anchor so that the steamer's passengers could watch Kwakwaka'wakw dancers perform.[9] Once they had steamed past Vancouver Island they encountered the turbulent waters of the Pacific for the first time. Even as "waves as high as mountains" crashed onto the steamer's decks, however, Ikeda found himself captivated by the beauty of the snow-covered peaks that glistened under a clear blue sky. Any who did not witness this landscape themselves, he wrote, could not begin to imagine just how breathtaking it was.[10]

On the ninth day of their journey, having crossed into Tlingit territorial waters just north of the border that cuts across the Dixon Entrance to divide Alaska from British Columbia, they came upon yet another Indigenous village. Dominated by a large Christian church, the village of New Metlakatla had been established by a group of Tsimshian people a decade or so earlier after they migrated north across the Canada-U.S. border. There were a number of shops in the village operated by *hakujin*, along with a post office to which Ikeda entrusted a letter to a friend. Curiously, he observed, the missionaries who resided there were not American but Canadian. As the steamer continued its journey, leaving the shelter of the bay alongside which the village had been built, they spotted two great carved canoes guided by Indigenous rowers through the choppy waves of the channel that led north to Ketchikan—almost certainly Haida, whose persistence in continuing to travel throughout their own island and maritime territories without regard for the international border was a source of continuing irritation to U.S. officials posted in the region.[11]

As Ikeda himself witnessed, although he may not have recognized it as such, the Haida and the Tsimshian who had settled at New Metlakatla were among the first Indigenous peoples to be caught in the shifting legal landscape produced by evolving bodies of racialized law and policy on either side of the U.S.-Canada border after British Columbia joined the Canadian confederation in 1871.[12] Although Ikeda himself encountered little interference from either U.S. or Canadian officials during the course of his voyage in 1898, in part, no doubt, because he was traveling in a first-class cabin, both he and other Japanese who arrived in this borderlands region during the years that followed would increasingly have to contend with a growing web of race-based constraints that at times extended both ways across the international border. The journey of the Tsimshian who settled at New Metlakatla was one of the first to expose the tangled and contradictory, sometimes interlocking nature of that web. Over time, as had the Tsimshian, other racialized groups and individuals living and working in this borderlands region would engage in complex acts of repositioning as they negotiated the tangled mix of constraint and opportunity that this shifting web of law and policy produced.

Metlakatla

The Tsimshian who would later embark on that journey north across the Canada-U.S. border had been converted to Christianity by William Duncan, a British missionary associated with the Church of England, who had traveled to Fort Simpson in 1858 because he imagined it as one of the most "degraded" and "savage" places in the world. Four years later a group of fifty converts moved with Duncan to a site fifteen miles south of Fort Simpson, where they built a village near the mouth of the Skeena River some twenty miles south of the Dixon Entrance.[13] Known as Metlakatla, an ancient Tsimshian word for a calm, saltwater channel, it was located on a site that had long been a meeting ground for Indigenous peoples in the region.[14] Although it had once been occupied year-round, Duncan later reported that he was told that the Tsimshian families that once lived there had resettled near the Hudson's Bay Company (HBC) trading post at Fort Simpson some twenty years earlier.[15]

By 1880, over a hundred small, sturdy homes had been built at Metlakatla, together with a church, a sawmill, and a salmon cannery.[16] It was an achievement lauded by Anglican missionary societies as far away as central Africa as an exemplar of their "civilizing mission."[17] Although Duncan was forced out of the Church Missionary Society and severed his own ties to the Anglican Church in 1881, a book written by the philanthropist and pharmaceutical company owner Henry S. Wellcome, widely distributed in Britain, Canada, and the United States after its publication in 1887, praised his efforts and portrayed Metlakatla as a model that other missionary societies should seek to emulate.[18] Among those who contacted the author to request a copy of his book was the Japanese consul based in Vancouver, B.C. Unable to locate one in any bookstore in British Columbia, the consul wrote, he wondered if Wellcome himself might send him a copy, which he gladly did.[19] At a time when Japan was actively engaged in its own "civilizing" mission in Hokkaido, inviting both British and American experts to assist in developing a body of law and policy that would determine the rights of the Ainu people whose traditional territories had been incorporated within Japan's national borders, the Japanese consul was clearly among those interested in considering Duncan's mission as a possible model.[20]

The very success of the Tsimshian who settled at Metlakatla, however, would prove to be their undoing. Faced with increasing incursions by white settlers and cannery operators intent on accessing the rich salmon fisheries of the Skeena River, the Metlakatlans asked first British colonial officials and, after 1871, B.C. provincial authorities to confirm title to their lands and resources, only to be repeatedly denied. As early as 1860, when Governor James Douglas first learned of their plans to establish a village at Metlakatla, B.C., he wrote to the British colonial secretary to recommend "withholding from [the Indians] the power to sell or otherwise alienate the title, as they are yet so ignorant and improvident that they cannot safely be trusted with the management or control of landed estate, which, if fully conveyed to them, would soon pass into other hands." Instead, he suggested, "such reserves of land

The town of Metlakatla, Alaska, under construction during the late 1800s or early 1900s after its Tsimshian residents moved north across the U.S.-Canada border to establish a new community. Alaska State Archives, Delbert E. Replogle Photograph Collection, 1897–1919, ASL-PCA-169.

should be conveyed to the Governor of the Colony for the time being in trust for the use and benefit of the Indians, leaving no power whatever in them to sell or alienate the estate."[21] While Douglas was willing to concede that the Indigenous peoples of British Columbia held some form of title to their lands, however limited he imagined it to be, B.C. officials would insist for well over a century that Aboriginal title did not exist in the province of British Columbia. It was a position that both the Metlakatlans and other Indigenous peoples all along the B.C. coast would challenge on an ongoing basis during the decades to come.[22]

In 1871, the same year that British Columbia joined Confederation, Metlakatlans openly protested the reserve boundaries that the B.C. government sought to erect around their village, challenging its authority to survey their lands and deliberately erecting a building in an area that had been set aside by B.C. officials for the Church Missionary Society.[23] While the resident bishop accused the Metlakatlans of rioting and pulling up the surveyor's stakes, Duncan insisted that they had not resorted to violence. "The only weapons ever used by the Indians were letters," he declared. The Metlakatlans had merely "asserted both verbally and in writing their claims to the land of their fathers," first by sending a committee to Ottawa to appeal to Parliament and then by traveling to London in the hope that they might have an audience with Queen Victoria, although they were not granted an opportunity to share their grievances with the Queen.[24]

Indigenous Land Rights

During the years that followed, the Tsimshian joined with the Haida and other Indigenous peoples along the north Pacific coast to argue against British Columbia's policy of denying the very existence of Aboriginal title, in stark contrast to historical practice throughout other parts of Canada and the United States, where title to Indigenous lands could only be acquired by treaty.[25] Told that title to the entire province rested in Queen Victoria and that neither Canada nor British Columbia was required to enter into treaties with Indigenous peoples in British Columbia to acquire their rights in their land, Indigenous coastal peoples questioned the basis on which title had purportedly been transferred. They, too, had a clear understanding of what areas of land were their own and had not relinquished title to places to which they had long-standing ties and where their ancestors had lived. Through what mechanism, they asked, had the Queen acquired title to their lands? As one chief wrote:

> It should not be forgotten that we occupied this land before we saw a white man. . . .
>
> We believe the land was our own, we had no cause to doubt this; and we were not a little surprised when the missionaries told us the land belonged to the Queen. Trouble would have taken place at once had they not told us that the Queen would act justly by us [and that] she would watch over us and protect our rights. . . . We never thought that in taking the Queen's flag to wave over us, and her laws to guide us, and in acknowledging her as our Queen, we were to be stripped of our land, driven from gardens we had cleared and cultivated, made to take down our houses where our fathers had lived before us, and move off the land we had always occupied.[26]

Indigenous people all along the north Pacific coast recognized such ancestral territories, often "bounded by some stream or mountain" and subdivided among families "for fishing, trapping and hunting and for berrying," to the point where trespassing on others' territories could result in conflict.[27] Native witnesses before the 1884 Metlakatla Inquiry said much the same. Asked why the Tsimshian thought the area where they lived was their own land, Tsimshian speaker Paul Legaic replied that it was because "our forefathers lived at Metlakatlah and it was their own."[28] Tsimshian women also made their voices heard. In the third of three letters to the commission, they explained that they were writing yet again "to make a most solemn protest . . . against our land being given away to any white people without our consent." Turning Queen Victoria's promise to protect them back on those who asserted it, they added, "We claim the whole of Metlakalah—the home of our forefathers, the land which was handed to us by them—to be our own property, and for our children, and we feel sure that this our land cannot be taken away from us by force while we are under the protection of the laws of our White Mother the Queen of England, which are made for the benefit of all."[29]

Duncan also advocated on behalf of the Metlakatlans with whom he lived and worked, explaining to members of the 1884 Metlakatlah Inquiry that the continued resistance on the part of British Columbia's Indigenous people was a consequence of the fact that they had never received an adequate explanation as to "how it was the Queen held all the lands."[30] He also wrote to the Department of Indian Affairs, challenging the province's refusal to recognize Aboriginal title as both unjust and hypocritical and as contrary to British principles of good governance and fair play. "Can it be right or just for the British Columbia Government to pass a law which disinherits the Indians of their lands without compensation and treats them as a conquered race—a law [that] declares the Indians have no rights to the land of their fathers, but such as are accorded them out of Charity from the Crown?" he asked. "A government that can hide its poverty and dishonesty behind the name of the Queen and then talk of her charity to those it has robbed," he declared, "is unworthy to be called British."[31]

Dominion authorities remained unmoved, as did members of the provincial government and those who sought ready access to Indigenous lands. Some B.C. officials denied out of hand that any such law existed, among them William Smithe, British Columbia's premier from 1883 to 1887, who told the Indigenous people who appealed to him to enter into treaty that there was "no such (treaty) law, either English or Dominion" and that "[those who] imagined there was . . . ha[d] been misled" on the point.[32] Miners were among those who accused the missionaries, in particular, of telling Indigenous people that in the past the British government had always compensated Indigenous people for their land but that in British Columbia it refused to do so and had effectively stolen the land. Also to blame, members of the Metlakatlah Inquiry found, were "the remarks made by Lord Dufferin when, as Governor-General, he visited British Columbia in 1876," acknowledging "the existence of Indian title and its non-extinguishment." Worse still, in their view, was the fact that his remarks had been "sedulously inculcated in the Indian mind" by those missionaries.[33] The B.C. government was willing to set aside small reserves for the Indigenous people of the province as an expression of the Queen's charity toward her subjects, they wrote. But it was fully prepared to resort to "force of arms" to see that the survey at Metlakatla was carried out. If necessary, "one of Her Majesty's vessels of war" would be sent to Metlakatla with "specific instructions to land an armed force in the event of the survey being obstructed." "The Metlakatlah Indians," they declared, "should not be allowed to defy the authority of the Indian Act, or reject the supervision of an Indian Agent."[34]

Border Crossings

Denied the ability to secure title to their traditional territories either based on Aboriginal title or by treaty, the Tsimshian living at Metlakatla began to explore other options available to them, including the possibility of securing land on the Alaskan side of the U.S.-Canada border. In January 1886, Duncan traveled to Washington, D.C., to meet with the U.S. Board of Indian Commissioners. Canadian authorities, he explained, had "declared that these Indians have no rights in the land, except such as may be accorded them in the charity of the Crown of England." At a time when the population of British Columbia was just sixty thousand, half of whom were Indigenous, Duncan told the board, the province was willing to set aside "just 2 acres a head" for them—just 60,000 of the 23,344,896 acres that constituted its land base. The rest was to be made available to white settlers. The Metlakatlans, Duncan argued, had embraced Christianity, accepted British law, and adopted white ways based on the assurance that, in doing so, they would have access to the same rights and privileges as white settlers, only to now be told that these would be denied to them. It was because they also wanted to "feel a secure tenure of the land on which they live," Duncan explained, that he had been authorized to ask whether they might settle in Alaska, "becoming freemen and citizens of that country." Other "still uncivilized" Indians, he warned, "were urging [the Tsimshian] to join in a defensive war," and they were beginning to believe that this might be the only way to address the injustice with which they were faced. Failure to assist in addressing the problem that they faced, Duncan implied, would potentially destabilize the entire region, putting not only Canadian but also American interests at risk.[35]

In February 1887, a year after his address to the Board of Indian Commissioners, Duncan and Wellcome formally applied to the U.S. Department of the Interior "on behalf of a colony of Indians residing at Metlakahtla, British Columbia" for "the privilege of removing to Alaska and there taking up lands as a colony of emigrants upon a reservation to be set aside for them by the Executive."[36] Although Congress had decided in 1871 that tribes would no longer be recognized as independent nations able to enter into treaties with the United States, the executive branch retained the authority, in its discretion, to establish reservations it deemed necessary or desirable on their behalf.[37] It was to this power that Duncan and Wellcome appealed in seeking to secure a reservation for the Tsimshian in Alaska. Their request, however, created a legal and conceptual conundrum, with which U.S. officials would continue to wrestle for decades, grounded in the contradictory and intensely racialized formulations that defined the rights of nonwhite people within the borders of the United States and linked both immigrant and "Indigene."[38]

In March 1887, Wellcome wrote urgently to Duncan from Washington, D.C., to tell him that the U.S. Department of the Interior, then responsible for governing Alaska, did not "regard Alaskans as Indians." It was "*very important,*" Wellcome advised, that Duncan "avoid *in every way* calling [the Metlakatlans] Indians" by using "the term '*natives*' or 'Aborigines' or 'Metlakahtlans' or 'Tsimsheans.'" In order to "avoid bringing them under the Indian acts," he explained, "the term *Indian* in describing your people *must be avoided.*"[39] Instead, they should simply "seek refuge as individuals in Alaska" in the hope that the U.S. government would then grant them individual homesteads, like the homesteads that "Indians" in the contiguous states were to be awarded under the 1887 Dawes Act. After all, the supporters of the Metlakatlans reasoned, the very purpose of the Dawes Act was to support Indigenous people who adopted white ways. Not only were the Tsimshian who had long lived in the area that the international border cut across indigenous to the region, but they were precisely the sort of people that the act was intended to support in their efforts to become "civilized."[40] It was a strategy that did not work.

When asked to consider the question whether "a body of about one thousand Indians, who are natives of and residents within the limits of British Columbia, about 20 miles from the line of Alaska, who have attained an advanced state of civilization, are self-supporting, and are organized into a community government by a council . . . can emigrate to Alaska . . . and then secure such rights as are accorded to the residents of that Territory who are not Indians; [or], as they wish to go as a colony, whether, under existing laws, . . . the President [has the power] to set aside a reservation for such colony," the U.S. attorney general responded that neither was an option under the existing U.S. law. "Immigration of peaceful individual Indians who have dissolved tribal relations is not prohibited by statute and is not inconsistent with the general policy of our Government," the attorney general advised, but they would have no more rights than any other foreign immigrant.[41] In fact, they had fewer rights than many other immigrants, given that, unlike those from Europe, they were not entitled to apply for naturalization, even though Canada regarded them as British subjects.[42]

The attorney general also did not believe that the U.S. president was empowered to set aside a reservation on behalf of the Metlakatlans if they migrated as a cohesive community, thereby retaining—in the eyes of the government—the very elements of their Indian identity that the Dawes Act was intended to undermine. The president's power to establish a reservation by executive order, the attorney general wrote, did "not extend to Indians not born or resident in the United States." Given that the Metlakatlans had presumably been born south of what was understood to be the borderline that divided U.S. and Canadian territory, only Congress had the power to set aside a reserve on their behalf.[43]

The Metlakatlans, in short, were regarded as "Indian" but not indigenous to Alaska and immigrant but not "white."[44] Caught in the gap between immigrant and Indigene, they were denied the benefit of both the Dawes Act and the Homestead Act, as well as access to any mechanism that they could utilize to apply for U.S. citizenship. Despite their conversion to Christianity and adoption of "white" ways, their commitment to maintaining communal ties created a problem that they could not surmount. Born though they were in Canada, where they were deemed to be British subjects, but marked as "Indian" based on both "race" and lifestyle, U.S. law also denied them a sound foundation on which to build their community.

Timing was also a factor. Had the Tsimshian moved north during the years before 1867 when the existing boundary between Russian America and British North America was recast as a national border on the U.S. side, they might well have been categorized as Alaska Natives. Even if they had done so, however, the Tsimshian would still have been denied a reservation. Like the provincial government in British Columbia, the United States also made the decision to refuse to recognize Indigenous title in Alaska. Based on the rationale that Alaska Natives were not Indians, it too adopted the position that it had no obligation to protect their traditional lands by setting aside reservations on their behalf.[45]

There was just one way for the Metlakatlans to acquire title in Alaska, former justice of the U.S. Supreme Court William Strong advised Duncan, and that was "to take possession under the law of 'squatter sovereignty.'"[46] Justice Samuel Freeman Miller agreed, explaining that this was "the only right the Settlers in Alaska then possessed" when it came to acquiring title to land.[47] Based on the assurance that it was a "moral certainty" that the Tsimshian's right to the land they settled "would be secured to them whenever the general land laws of the United States should be extended [to] the Territory of Alaska," Duncan cabled the leaders of the community at Metlakatla to let them know that he had been assured that, although there was no current law in place that would permit them to secure title to land in Alaska, their rights as squatters to the land on which they settled would be confirmed once a broader legal framework was in place.[48] In August 1887, the U.S. secretary of education went even further. Clearly unaware that his advice directly contradicted the opinion of the attorney general, he promised the Tsimshian "aid both in person and property, as soon as they became naturalized American Citizens."[49]

After receiving Duncan's message, a small group of Tsimshian traveled north across the Canada-U.S. border by canoe to find a suitable location on which to rebuild their community in Alaska. They settled on a site on one of the many forested islands of the Alexander Archipelago in Tlingit territory, alongside a bay that was largely protected from the impact of tidal currents where they had access to both halibut and various species of salmon.[50] Dominated by Mount Tamgas, the site in question was an old Tlingit winter village known as Ta'gwaan, readily identifiable as such by the carved wooden poles that surrounded it, slowly decomposing though they were.[51] Duncan reported that Annette Island was roughly twenty miles in length and eight miles wide. Although "more than three-fourths of [the island] consists of mountains and rock," he wrote, the townsite "has a beautiful pebbly beach, suitable for canoes to rest on, and a good supply of running water, and two or three small streams up which salmon ascend to spawn in summer."[52] Where the Tsimshian saw promise, however, U.S. officials saw only emptiness, dismissing the island as little more than a "lonely, rocky, and densely wooded" series of steep mountains over which Mount Tamgas towered.[53]

The first group of thirty Tsimshian moved to the site they named New Metlakatla in late July 1887. By the time Duncan returned from Washington, D.C., and arrived on August 7, thirty more Tsimshian had joined the original group. During the months that followed, more and more Tsimshian traveled north across the Dixon Entrance by canoe, some towed by a small steamship hired for that purpose, until impending winter storms made further trips too risky to undertake. By the beginning of 1888, the population of New Metlakatla

was eight hundred, twenty of whom were members of other Indigenous nations, among them Haida from both Prince of Wales Island and Haida Gwaii
and Tlingit from Cape Fox and Port Tongass.[54]

Accused by some British Columbians of manipulating the Tsimshian into
moving across the international border, both Duncan and representatives of
those who had moved north insisted that it was not true that Duncan alone
was behind the move. The decision to move to Alaska, one Tsimshian speaker
insisted, had been made at a public meeting while Duncan was away.[55] Other
observers warned that Canadian officials would try to pressure those who
had moved to return to British Columbia. Their move "to American soil [did]
not set well on the stomach of the average Canadian," one such correspondent
wrote. "Their pride is hurt by it and now their government [is] determined
not to permit it, [for] they will make you fair promises to have you remain
under the flag of Old England." "Church pride," he added, "is also touched."[56]
Among those who were most indignant was Charles Todd, the Indian agent
who had moved into Duncan's old home in Metlakatla, B.C. Todd's ire focused,
in particular, on the activities of a group of young men sent back across the
U.S.-Canada border to remove materials they had used to build the church
and homes, including doors and windows, as well as the church bell and both
sawmill and cannery machinery.[57] Five of the young men were arrested and
charged.[58] In their eyes, the materials that they had removed remained their
own, not unlike the roofing material that they had carried with them in earlier
decades when they moved from winter to summer villages.[59] The Metlakatlans' understanding of real property ownership, rooted in their own cultural
traditions, however, was directly in conflict with English common law principles, which distinguish chattel and personal property from appurtenances fixed
to the land that are deemed part of the real property and may not be removed
when that property is transferred.[60]

The Metlakatlans were also confronted with the assertion that Metlakatla,
B.C., was now a government reserve, with the result that the materials they
sought to take north were not their own but Canadian government property.[61] This was a notion that the Metlakatlans also disputed. As they explained,
"Only few of us have brought over the material of [our] dwelling houses, and
a great number of buildings are still left, including the Church, Saw-mill, Village Hall, Cannery, Guest House, etc. etc. All those buildings that were built
without cost to the British Government or the Church Missionary Society
are now seized and taken from us." They needed the materials that they themselves had purchased, they explained, so that they did not have to continue to
live in log huts in their new village in Alaska.[62] This was an argument that

Todd rejected out of hand. In March 1888, he announced that he had been instructed by the government of Canada "to prevent the further destruction of any building at Metlakatla." "The removal of any tree, shrub, timber, hay, mineral, metal, or other valuable thing from the Metlakatla Indian Reserve," Todd declared, "is contrary to law and cannot be permitted." It was his "duty as 'Indian Agent' and 'Commissioner of Police' under an act 'Respecting the Police of Canada,'" he added, "to protect the property and rights of Indians belonging to this reserve as well as the rights of Indians and others in any part of British Columbia."[63]

Most offensive in his eyes, however, was the fact that Duncan and the Tsimshian had "deserted Metlakatla and all its belongings and (as reported) forsworn [their] allegiance to [their] Queen and country." Denied access to citizenship though they were by American authorities, he did not hesitate to conclude that they were no longer British subjects. "I need not remind you," he informed Duncan, "that the destruction of the property of any Indian Reserve in Canada by citizens of the United States cannot be justified and will not be permitted."[64] Some Tsimshian who had chosen not to move to Alaska concurred, apparently hoping to use the presence of the international border to limit access by those who had moved north to fishing sites along the Nass and the Skeena Rivers. Recently opened by the B.C. government to all residents of British Columbia, the traditional fishing sites of Indigenous peoples in the province were now under ever greater pressure. The Tsimshian who had moved north "say they are Americans now," declared one Tsimshian who had remained behind, "and we don't want the American flag here."[65]

For the New Metlakatlans, neither principles of English property law nor British Columbia's claim that title to the entire province was vested in Queen Victoria was determinative. Although they may have moved north, in their eyes that move did not negate the fact that the sites on which they had built their homes in British Columbia were Tsimshian land where their ancestors had lived since time immemorial. They had never transferred title to that land to Canada, nor had they ever been compensated for their interest in it. Canada, as such, had robbed them of their place on their own land. Its position, as they saw it, was simply "Might is Right!"[66] This perception was further reinforced when Canada's superintendent general of Indian Affairs proposed in 1888 to refuse to allow them to return on even a temporary basis to participate in family or community events on the B.C. Metlakatla reserve unless they gave up all ties to New Metlakatla. His purpose, the superintendent general told the British Privy Council, was to preclude any Tsimshian who had moved across the border from "enjoying any of the privileges which they previously enjoyed in connection with lands or waters within British territory, unless they shall return to and take up their permanent residence upon the Reserve at Metlakahtla by the first of May next."[67]

Ramifications in British Columbia

Canadian concerns about the impact that the Metlakatlans' decision to relocate to Alaska would have in British Columbia were compounded by the fact that their move had spurred new resistance to the B.C. government's refusal to compensate Indigenous people for the lands they had lost.[68] In February 1888, Indigenous witnesses who appeared before a commission appointed to assess conditions along British Columbia's north coast testified that "there [would] be no peace [t]here" if the issue were not addressed. Still others were prepared to "follow [their] brethren into Alaska." Settlers might call their land a reserve, one Naas (Nisga'a) speaker explained, but there was no such word in their language. "We have the word 'land,' 'our land,' 'our property.' Your name for our land is 'reserve,' but every mountain, every stream, and all we see, we call our forefathers' land and streams." It was undisputed that the land claimed by the Nisga'a people was theirs, he added. "If you ask the Hydahs, Alaskas, Stickeens, Bella Bellas, and Fort Ruperts, they will tell you that all this country is the Naas people's land . . . [W]e don't know . . . when it was taken from us."[69]

Indigenous peoples along the B.C. coast did not reject British law out of hand, members of the commission learned. Indeed, they welcomed "a strong law" that they might use to defend the boundaries of the lands that they chose to keep for themselves not only against white settlers but against incursions by members of other Indigenous groups.[70] In the face of growing pressure on their lands by both, they were willing to accept reserves negotiated by treaty not only because this meant that they would be compensated for lands and resources to which they lost exclusive access but because reserves were bounded. Charles Russ, a subchief of the Laxgalts'ap people, testified that although he lived on the Naas River because his mother was Naas, his father, who was a chief at Metlakatla, had gone to Alaska because he did not want to live on a reserve allocated to them by the Queen and not protected by treaty. But Russ also asked, echoing the question that Indigenous people in British Columbia had posed many times before, "How did the Queen get the land from our forefathers to set it apart for us? It is ours to give to the Queen, and we don't understand how she could have it to give to us."[71]

That said, if the government continued to refuse to recognize their title in their land, Russ continued, they would also leave Canada for Alaska as the Metlakatlans had done: "We love the land; we love the places where our fathers' graves are and where our children are buried; but we will leave them and go to a new country sooner than stay where it is said 'the lands do not belong to us.'" If they did decide to move, he added, he asked that the "Government [not] persecute us or tie our hands like it did at Metlakatlah" and that it "not make trouble in our hearts but . . . let us leave in peace," in contrast to the way it had treated the Tsimshian. The commissioners were unwilling to make any such promise. As far as they were concerned, there was simply no legal ground based on which they were prepared to recognize the "alleged title of the Indians" to their lands or to compensate them for those they had lost. Moreover, one member of the commission declared, if the Naas people were "so hasty and unwise as to leave for another country, it would not be reasonable for them to expect payment for their improvements."[72]

U.S. Reverberations

In contrast to B.C. government officials and others who viewed the Metlakatlans' move across the Canada-U.S. border as a betrayal, many in the United States embraced it as a reenactment of America's founding myth and the throwing off of British tyranny. As one man who spotted a Metlakatlan canoe from the deck of a steamer characterized the moment before the Board of Indian Commissioners in 1889, he had seen "these pilgrims of this century in their boats, and saw the glint of light on their oars, as they were passing from their foreign homes to this land of freedom,—leaving the protection of the British lion to perch themselves under the wings of the American eagle."[73] In the words of another speaker before the Board of Indian Commissioners in 1894, the Tsimshian, who had given up their "splendid church and their comfortable, well-built little homes" and traveled in their canoes to an "island wilderness," were "as heroic a company as that other band who for liberty of conscience came to these shores in the Mayflower."[74]

Wellcome, among others in the United States, did not hesitate to emphasize the injustice done to the Metlakatlans, equating them with the Acadians who had been deported by the British from what is now eastern Canada in the mid-1700s, some of them to colonies that later became part of the United States. It was because they were "tired of British rule," Wellcome declared, that the Metlakatlans had sought "the protection of Uncle Sam."[75] Theirs was a story of "outrage upon, and cruelty to, a civilized Indian community" by the Dominion of Canada.[76] Their rights were "ruthlessly overridden," Wellcome wrote the editor of the *New York Herald*. "They have been coerced—imprisoned—robbed of their lands, and now force is threatened, to prevent them from taking down their own buildings, and thereby to hinder their exodus. Persecution could hardly be carried further."[77] By 1898, the same year that Ikeda visited New Metlakatla in the course of his own journey north along the Pacific coast, a visitor wrote to his congressman in Michigan to report that the Metlakatlans, who had left "the British Possession over the channel, as did our Pilgrim fathers of old, that they might have freedom to worship God, [had] changed the bleak island [in]to a comfortable village, built their homes, their church (a good one), cannery, etc."[78]

U.S. embrace of the Metlakatlans as latter-day Pilgrims akin to those who had arrived on the Mayflower, however, proved hollow when it came to surmounting race-based barriers against access to citizenship. Despite the promises U.S. officials had made regarding the protections that would be extended once they became U.S. citizens, they were instead denied even the chance to apply for naturalization.[79] As U.S. district judge John S. Bugbee advised Duncan in 1890: "I have no doubt whatever that admission to citizenship would be a great boon to them, and that they would make good, useful, and law-abiding citizens ... they have strong claims to share the rights to which, under the naturalization laws, other British subjects are entitled. But the law of the United States relating to naturalization expressly declares that its provisions 'shall apply to aliens being white persons' [which] has been construed as limiting the application of law to persons of the Caucasian race."[80] *In re Camille*, a case decided in Oregon in 1880, the judge noted, had held that the race-based bar to naturalization that had been found to apply to Asian immigrants on the ground that they were members of the "Mongolian race" in the 1878 case *In re Ah Yup* also extended to North Americans of Indigenous descent not born within U.S. borders. Frank Camille was a young man who had been born in what would later become Kamloops, B.C., in 1847, just one year after Britain and the United States agreed to the division of the Oregon Territory along the forty-ninth parallel. The son of an Indigenous mother and a British father, Camille had moved to Oregon when he was seventeen and lived there ever since. The judge conceded that if Camille were clearly a "white person" within the meaning of the law in 1880, he would be able to apply for naturalization. The judge reasoned, however, that given his parentage, Camille was "as much an Indian as a white person" and thus an alien inadmissible to citizenship just as any Asian immigrant deemed to be a member of the "Mongolian race" was.[81] The same rationale, Judge Bugbee advised Duncan, applied equally to the Metlakatlans.[82] Race, in short, trumped fitness for citizenship, regardless of the qualities of any given individual.

The anxieties of the Tsimshian of New Metlakatla engendered by the denial of any opportunity to apply for citizenship, notwithstanding the promises they had been given by U.S. government representatives, were further compounded by reports originating in British Columbia that suggested that Annette Island actually lay on the Canadian side of the border.[83] Once the precise location of the U.S.-Canada border was determined, this issue would be resolved in their favor.[84] In the interim, a bill proposing to reserve Annette Island for the exclusive use of the Metlakatlan Tsimshian was introduced in Congress.[85] Ironically, supporters of the bill included Senator Henry Dawes of Massachusetts, chair of the Senate Committee on the Territories and an original sponsor of the Dawes Act, who had visited New Metlakatla in 1889 and reported:

> [Its residents] lived in constant terror for fear their work and labor upon this island may result in the same way [as their work in building Met-lakatla in British Columbia]. The first thing they said to us when we went there was, "is it true that the Government of the United States can drive us off here at any time?" The people over on the other side, 30 miles [away], are all the time telling them that they will be driven off after they have expended their money in this way to build up this little town. Only a week before we were there a messenger from the other came over and told them that he had visited Washington, that he had seen the new President, and that the new President had told him that he was going to drive them off.[86]

The island, which lay just north of the Dixon Entrance, Dawes explained in encouraging other members of Congress to support the bill, was "good for nothing except for the wild beasts that are in the mountains and the thousand acres perhaps that run down on a level into the sea, upon which they have planted their town. . . . Nobody wants it now except there may turn up at some time somebody who desires to plunder them." The senator from Nebraska, likewise, assured his colleagues that, at the time the site was selected, "not a living soul [lived on the island] or within many miles of [it]," with the result that "no existing rights of others are affected."[87] In 1891, Congress passed the bill reserving Annette Island for the exclusive use of the Metlakatlans, only to open the land outside the immediate boundaries of their community to miners and settlers in 1896, rendering them vulnerable to outside intrusion yet again.[88]

While Congress was willing to set aside part of Annette Island for the exclusive use of the Metlakatlans, members of Congress insisted that granting them access to citizenship was impossible, given staunch public opposition to easing race-based barriers to naturalization. Also a concern was the fear that a decision to admit one group of "alien Indians" to citizenship might serve as precedent for the extension of citizenship to other groups also excluded on race-based grounds, in particular, Asian immigrants.[89] This was a concern that paralleled fears on the B.C. side of the border—where Asian immigrants could apply for naturalization but were denied the ability to vote or otherwise participate in the political process—that allowing naturalized Asian immigrants to vote would set a precedent that would in time also erode the race-based barrier against the participation of B.C. Indians in the electoral process.[90]

Similar concerns about the precedential value of any decisions made on behalf of the Tsimshian who had settled in Alaska prevented the U.S. Congress from formally designating the land set aside for their exclusive use as a reservation.[91] As the Secretary of the Interior explained in 1915, "[The 1891 act] gave the Metlakahtlans permission to live upon the land, and to use it, [but] this permission can be revoked at any time by Congress. The land is the property of the United States and the improvements thereon are also the property of the United States."[92] As for ownership of the land on which they lived in Alaska or even the homes they built upon it, in short, the position of the Tsimshian who had moved north was little different from that in British Columbia that had prompted them to leave in the first place. U.S. assumption of the authority to approve their settling in Tlingit territory, moreover, was itself grounded in a refusal to recognize the existence of Aboriginal title in Alaska that paralleled that of British Columbians. U.S. officials remained as determined as B.C. officials not to enter into treaty or set aside reservations for Alaska's Indigenous people like those that had been established elsewhere in North America. U.S. government representative James G. Swan went so far as to urge, while on a visit to Alaska, that the United States should model its policy in Alaska on that of British Columbia, given how successful the "British Columbia mission plan" and its blanket denial of Aboriginal title had proved to be. The province of British Columbia served as a geographical buffer between Alaska and the contiguous states that insulated Alaska Natives from knowledge about the treaty system, he added, which made it all the easier to avoid establishing reservations for their exclusive use.[93]

While some who opposed the extension of the treaty system to Alaska claimed to be motivated by concern for its Indigenous people, others admitted that their primary concern was ensuring unhampered access to Alaska's resources. John G. Brady, Alaska's governor from 1897 to 1906, was a particularly vocal advocate against setting aside reservations for the protection of Alaska's Indigenous people. It was understandable, he wrote, that a century earlier the United States had adopted a policy of recognizing "Indian tribes [as] domestic nations and individual members of those tribes [as] quasi-foreigners," but this policy had been driven by the need "to seek peaceful relations with organized bands of savages who might be useful as allies, but [were] dangerous as enemies." In Alaska, he insisted, there was no parallel need for concern.[94] He found deeply problematic, however, that the Alaska Natives "consider themselves the true owners of the country with all its equipments of soils, forests, streams, and water," regarding all "its game, fish, and vegetable growths [as] their personal property," while "the white man [was] an invader to be tolerated as a matter of necessity or perhaps as a matter of advantage." Refusing to set aside any part of Alaska on their behalf, Brady declared, would force them to "bow to the inevitable and [to] accept such a place in our legal structure as shall be accorded to them."[95] Reservations, Brady believed, were an "insuperable obstacle to civilization and should be abolished, the tribal organization destroyed, the lands allotted in severalty, the Indians intermingled with the whites, and the Indians treated as other men." It was for this reason that he had vehemently opposed even Congress's action in setting aside a portion of Annette Island for the exclusive use of the Tsimshian: "If we set apart a great island for them, why cannot the natives who are born Alaskans ask for island reservations; for instance, the Sitkans Branoff Island; the Hoonas, Chicagoff Islands; the Hootz-na-hoos, Admiralty Island. Where are we going to stop if we start with Annette Island? . . . There is only one manly, straightforward way for us here in Alaska—special privileges to none, equal opportunity to all, one system of laws for all, and all amenable to those laws . . . a policy that shall press Indian peculiarities to the vanishing point."[96]

Haida Gwaii

The contradiction between the United States' refusal to establish reservations to protect the traditional territories of Indigenous people native to Alaska, even as it set aside a portion of Annette Island for the Tsimshian who had moved there from Canada, tenuous though their title was, did not go unnoticed by Alaska Natives, who continued to protest the U.S. government's failure to address the question of Indigenous title in Alaska for another eight decades before Congress at last agreed to act.[97] Congress did, however, recognize that other Indigenous peoples had also been caught short by the international border. In response to lobbying by Haida people, whose traditional land and ocean territories extended from Haida Gwaii to the islands at the southern end of the Alexander Archipelago and now spanned the U.S.-Canada border, Congress included a provision in the same bill that set aside a part of Annette Island for the exclusive use of the Metlakatlans to reserve "Dahl" (Dall) and Long Islands just north of the Dixon Entrance "as a canoe and timber preserve for the Hydahs, and as such protected for their use."[98] As the report that accompanied the bill conceded, the islands had long been an important source of the timber used by the Haida to build the canoes crafted "to such a degree of perfection . . . that they have a wide reputation among the white and native people of southeastern Alaska for their superior sea-going qualities." Species of fish and game that abounded on Dall and Long Islands, it noted, had served as a critical food source for Haida people over many generations.[99]

U.S. officials also grumbled, however, about the continued mobility of the Haida people, whose big oceangoing canoes were entirely capable of traversing the rough waves of the Dixon Entrance, which marked the ocean boundary between U.S. and Canadian waters. Haida traders were long-standing trade partners of the Chilkat Tlingit, from whom they obtained furs that they carried south to trade in British Columbia, and their ongoing participation in a preexisting trade relationship that extended across the region now incorporated within the borders of the U.S. and Canadian states marked them as smugglers in the eyes of customs officials on both sides. The fact that the trade predated the establishment of the international border, one U.S. official admitted in 1876, should be regarded as an extenuating factor, noting that no customs officer had ever tried to interfere with this long-standing practice in the past.[100] Another customs inspector who "endeavored to capture the smugglers" after spotting eight Haida canoes that he assumed were transporting furs and had made no effort to pull in at the custom house, however, was determined to put an end to ongoing exchange practices now deemed "illicit trade."[101] Like the Tsimshian who had resettled in Alaska but actively maintained kinship and family ties to relatives across the B.C.-Alaska border despite efforts by Canadian officials to bar their access to their own ancestral communities, the Haida remained a mobile people, traveling throughout their traditional territories not only to trade and to maintain kinship ties but also, in time, to take advantage of new kinds of labor opportunities that developed on both sides of the border. As Haida witnesses who appeared before the Royal Commission on Indian Affairs for British Columbia (McKenna-McBride Commission) in 1916 made clear, they regarded themselves as living never in any one of Russian America, British North America, the United States, or Canada, but in Haida territory, to which they had never ceded title and which, they insisted, remained independent throughout, even as one imperial power after another laid claim to the surrounding area.[102]

Early Japanese Migrants

By the late nineteenth century, the Indigenous peoples of the north Pacific coast had been joined by other equally mobile populations from around the world who traveled throughout this borderlands region in growing numbers in search of opportunities of various kinds. Among those who traveled north along the coast and traversed many of the same ambiguous and increasingly racialized legal spaces associated with the categories of immigrant and Indigene that confronted the Tsimshian and other coastal peoples were Japanese adventurers who ventured across the Pacific after the Meiji government eased its bar on travel abroad in the mid-1880s.[103] Many of the earliest Japanese migrants to travel to the north Pacific borderlands arrived on the whaling and sealing vessels that plied the waters off the coasts of Alaska and northern British Columbia. Some jumped ship to avoid what proved to be brutal conditions aboard such whaling vessels, while others were drawn north to Alaska or the Yukon by a quest for adventure or in response to the same reports of the discovery of gold along the Klondike River that attracted men from around the Pacific Rim, including Ikeda as well as Indigenous men who lived near the Skeena River.[104]

Most of the Japanese who arrived at this time had come of age during the early decades of the Meiji era, a time when Japan endeavored to learn all it could about Western nations and was engaged in an effort to re-create itself as a modern nation that would in time take its place among the world's imperial powers. Some migrants were also students eager to develop a greater understanding of the Western technologies that many Japanese believed had played a key role in enabling the United States and Britain to persuade Japan's leaders to open its ports to the West and, later, to adopt Western modes of governance.[105] It was this heady mix of pride and curiosity, of a desire to learn and to apply that learning, that Japanese who embarked for North America during this period carried with them.[106]

At times we catch only a glimpse of individual Japanese migrants, still relatively few in number along the north Pacific coast during the 1890s. Canadian census records reveal, for example, that in 1891 a twenty-nine-year-old Japanese man named Sakamoto who worked as a mill hand was living in Metlakatla, B.C., with a family that included William Rudland, a sixty-six-year-old carpenter born in England and his wife, Mary, a fifty-five-year-old Indigenous woman born in British Columbia.[107] Although Sakamoto was the only Japanese recorded as living in Metlakatla, B.C., in 1891, the presence of a young man born in China and another born in India to an Irish father and an Indian mother, together with men from Scotland and France, speaks to the interconnected nature of the colonial world and the extent to which certain individuals moved throughout it. Sakamoto disappears from the census in subsequent years. It may be that he was among those who traveled north to Alaska or the Yukon in a search for adventure or gold, or he may have returned to Japan as others also did. Canadian census takers may also have missed his presence on a later pass through the area, as the U.S. officials may also have done who compiled population figures for Alaska in 1891 and reported just two Japanese in the entire territory.[108]

By 1898, when Ikeda arrived in Juneau on his journey north along the Pacific coast, he learned about a small Japanese community there of about fifteen people. Two Japanese residents, he was told by a local Japanese restaurant owner, were women engaged in prostitution, a fact that Ikeda again worried might tarnish Japan's reputation. Two Japanese men, he learned, had themselves left for the Klondike goldfields the previous year. One, named Matsumoto, was reportedly employed by a *hakujin*, while another had reportedly left in the company of a mining engineer. Two Japanese restaurant owners in town planned to move north to Dyea, near Skagway, at the head of the Chilkoot Trail, one of the routes gold seekers followed to reach the Yukon goldfields, crossing the international border into Canada just past the top of Chilkoot Pass.[109]

For some Japanese, their journey to the Pacific coast of North America first led through Hokkaido, formally incorporated within Japanese boundaries only in 1869. Still regarded, much as the U.S. West was, as wild and unsettled country, some Japanese had moved to Hokkaido for social or political reasons in the wake of the Meiji Restoration, while others went there to pan for gold, as did Denbei Kobayashi, who later settled in the B.C. interior.[110] Just as the United States and Canada each encouraged the settlement of its West to perfect its claims to the areas of western North America incorporated within its borders, the new Meiji government encouraged Japanese emigration to Hokkaido to reinforce its claim both against its Indigenous people, the Ainu, and against any claims that Russia might assert.[111] Like those of Alaska and the Yukon, the relatively unsettled spaces of Hokkaido appealed in part because life there was less restricted by the social and cultural constraints that ordered society elsewhere in Meiji Japan.[112] Despite the Meiji government's efforts to promote emigration to Hokkaido, however, many

Japanese looked east across the North Pacific to North America instead. One reason that its Pacific coast appealed where Hokkaido did not, one U.S. official concluded, was its more temperate climate. "There is also unoccupied land in Yezzo," he opined, but Hokkaido was "covered with snow one-half the year and abounds with mosquitoes during a very hot summer."[113]

Books penned by Japanese who traveled to Alaska and the Yukon, like that written by Ikeda, suggest that curiosity about the Indigenous people he called *dojin* was another factor that drew some adventurers north. Japanese shared certain attitudes with their Euro-American and Canadian neighbors, perceiving western lands in North America as empty—in Ikeda's words, "untrodden by men"—and its resources as available for taking.[114] Their attitudes to Indigenous people in North America, however, were also shaped in part by assumptions rooted in Japanese history and culture. Comprised of the characters *do* [土] (earth or dirt) and *jin* [人] (people), *dojin* was a term historically used to refer to Japan's own Indigenous people, the Ainu.[115] Now regarded as profoundly derogatory in nature, it was applied to Indigenous peoples around the world at the beginning of the Meiji era. Use of the term *dojin* would have invoked the negative attitudes associated with the ways in which Ainu people were historically portrayed in Japan. A British adviser hired by the Meiji government in 1871, for example, later reported that he had been told that the historical Ainu were "semi-savages" who were "savagely cruel" and "had much in common with animals."[116] Much like their European counterparts, Meiji-era Japanese tended to assume that both the Ainu and the Indigenous people of North America were doomed to extinction.[117]

Ainu, Nakayama Jinshiro, the author of a seminal prewar history of Japanese immigrants in Canada, explained in 1921, were *dojin* who lived in Hokkaido. On March 31, 1904, he wrote, a group of Hokkaido *dojin* visited Vancouver on their way to the Louisiana Purchase Exposition in St. Louis, Missouri. In Vancouver, they were invited to attend the Japanese Methodist Church by Reverend Goro Kaburagi, along with University of Chicago anthropology professor Frederick Starr, who accompanied them on their journey. The Ainu spoke about bear hunting, farming, and cattle ranching, as well as about their tattoos and their hair. Nakayama noted that the members of the group had converted to Christianity. He also emphasized, however, that while the Ainu were indigenous to Japan, the Japanese consul had reminded North Americans that they should not mistakenly be regarded as ancestors of the Japanese people as some anthropologists believed.[118]

Framed in part by ways in which the Ainu had historically been characterized, Japanese views of North America's Indigenous people were also shaped

Ainu family groups who participated in the Anthropology Exhibit at the Louisiana Purchase Exposition in St. Louis, Missouri, in 1904. Missouri History Museum, 1900–1922, #214, photograph taken by the exhibition's official photographer.

by accounts published in Japan during the early years of the Meiji period that drew heavily on English-language sources. In his *Muiken Shinshi* (A new geography of the Americas), Fukuzawa Yukichi, a major disseminator of knowledge about the West during the Meiji era, reported that North America's Native peoples were "savage by nature."[119] Hisamatsu Yoshinori agreed, describing *dojin* in North America as *yabanjin* [野蛮人] (savages, barbarians) in his 1902 history of Japanese abroad, *Shokumin Iseki* (The great achievements of our colonists). "Strong and brave, cunning, and cruel and merciless," he observed, they were not unlike Europeans insofar as these qualities were concerned. In contrast to Europeans, however, Hisamatsu told his readers, *dojin* lived a rootless life wandering from place to place and lacked houses or assets, relying on the fish they caught in rivers and streams and the big animals they hunted for food.[120] Daily newspapers were quick to capitalize on such imagery. "As is well known," the *Yomiuri Shimbun* told its readers in 1887, "*dojin* are a race that lived in America before Columbus discovered it. When Europeans began to settle and develop the land, the *dojin* gradually lost their influence and were driven into the mountains. Resilient and highly mobile, they sometimes form bands to raid travelers and to attack railroads, creating a constant problem for the U.S. government."[121]

Japanese abroad sometimes positioned themselves as less prone to negative stereotypes than Euro-Americans. "Indians [are] viewed as miserable savages by most Japanese travellers," wrote one Japanese visitor to the United States in 1877. This was understandable, in his view, because Indians lacked the "ability to change their own ways and are impoverished." But, he added, it would be "wrong to see them as wild animals as Europeans do."[122] Attitudes of this kind also persisted among Japanese immigrants in North America for a number of years after the end of the Meiji period. The *dojin* early European explorers encountered on Vancouver Island, a Japanese-language history titled *Sokuseki* (Footprint) published in 1942 recounted in a chapter on B.C. history, "lead uncivilized lives guided only by wild instincts" and had a "violent nature." They were savages, its author added, who possessed no history of their own. The dramatic drop in their numbers described in an annual report issued in 1892 by the Department of Indian Affairs, he wrote, was "entirely the inevitable result of their ignorant and unenlightened lifestyle."[123]

Still another term used by Japanese immigrants in both Canada and the United States to refer to North America's Indigenous people, also reflective of attitudes of the time, was *saibashi*, adapted from the Chinook *siwash*, both of which also acquired derogatory connotations over time.[124] As early as 1887, the *Alaskan* criticized the use of the term "siwash" to refer to Alaska Natives and, a year later in 1888, the use of the term "squaw" to refer to an "Indian woman," noting that "the one recognizes her humanity while the other classifies her as a beast." The use of such pejoratives, it noted, reflected poorly on "the refinement and character of the speaker."[125] Although some Japanese users of the terms *siwash* or *saibashi* were clearly cognizant of such negative connotations, however, this does not appear to have been true of all. Ikeda recounts in his journal, for example, that he encountered a group of Creoles near Sitka who told him that their ancestors had come to Alaska from Russia and that they called themselves "*saibashi*"—clearly an error on his part or, perhaps, on the part of his editors, who struggled to read his handwritten script.[126]

The use of such terms as *saibashi* or *dojin* to refer to Indigenous people in Canada and the United States, ironically, was also in tension with a highly idealized vision of those who lived along North America's northwestern shores. As negative as the stereotypes of Indigenous people to which they were exposed in Japan or in North America may have been, Japanese travelers also imagined that they had a special connection with Indigenous people on the Pacific coast based on kinship ties that Europeans did not share. This, some Japanese settlers suggested, entitled them to put down roots and access the resources of this borderlands region in ways that *hakujin* were not entitled to do. Reflecting on the wave-tossed objects that originated in Japan and washed up on the western shores of Haida Gwaii and other islands along the north Pacific coast, Nakayama speculated that Japanese must have ancestral connections to the Indigenous people of that coast. Japanese fishers had surely drifted eastward on the Kuroshio and been cast ashore on the eastern shores of the Pacific over the centuries. If they did not perish on some small, deserted island, he mused, they may well have been adopted into local Indigenous communities.[127] Many a Japanese traveler, after all, had remarked on what they viewed as the facial resemblance between Japanese and Indigenous people in northwestern North America.[128]

Stories of a Japanese fishing vessel that had drifted ashore on the Olympic Peninsula along the Washington coast during the winter of 1833 after encountering a big storm at sea served only to confirm this perception. The three who survived the journey across the Pacific after fourteen of their companions died, however, did not receive the welcome that Nakayama envisaged. Instead, as the historian Joshua L. Reid reports, they were enslaved by the Makah for almost a year before they were turned over to the captain of an HBC vessel in the area.[129] Kazuo Ito reports that Ranald Macdonald, the son of an HBC factor and a Chinook mother who grew up in Fort Astoria, where his father was stationed, learned some Japanese from the three survivors. His contact with the three men and interest in the pottery and fabrics recovered from the boat led him to leave for Japan in 1848 despite the Tokugawa shogunate's continuing bar against contact with the West.[130] While some HBC officials regarded the 1833 landing of the three shipwrecked Japanese as an opportunity that might allow Britain to establish a dialogue with Japan that would further the HBC's own commercial interests, however, the British government was focused at the time not on Japan but on China and did not pursue it.[131]

The 1833 landing on the Olympic Peninsula was by no means the only one along the north Pacific coast in recent memory. The Russian navigator Ivan Vasiliev is said to have named an island off the Alaska coast Japonski Island after coming upon several Japanese castaways there, and a U.S. whaling ship reportedly rescued six others near Sitka in 1843.[132] Still others cast ashore over the years, in this instance along the California coast, included a young man named Manjiro, from a small village called Naka no Hama on the west coast of Shikoku Island in Japan, who was swept out to sea by a storm while fishing in 1841, and, in 1850, Hamada Hikizo, also known as Joseph Heco.[133]

Among the Japanese men rounded up by the U.S. military in Alaska in 1941, as well, was an elderly Japanese fisherman who, after being swept out to sea and across the Pacific decades earlier, had been taken in by the Alutiiq people of the village of Seldovia in Alaska. A Japanese immigrant who encountered him at the time reported that the old man spoke a language he thought might be Russian and had all but forgotten his Japanese. Although the shipwrecked fisherman no longer remembered the year that he was lost at sea, he did recall that the railroad between Yokohama and the town of Shimbashi had just been built, which suggested to his visitor that it was 1872, just four years after the Meiji Restoration.[134]

Jujiro Wada

Among the Japanese adventurers who explored the cultural and legal border-lands of the north Pacific coast toward the end of the nineteenth century was Jujiro Wada.[135] Born in Ehime Prefecture on the island of Shikoku in 1875 eight years after the Meiji Restoration, Wada was just seventeen when he boarded a freighter bound for San Francisco in 1892 as a stowaway.[136] While Wada would later tell friends that he had traveled to the United States to study at Yale University, the fact that he was forced to hide away on board a ship to make the journey across the Pacific suggests that this was a dream that had not yet taken concrete form when he arrived in California. It was also a dream that was never realized. Within weeks of his arrival in California, Wada was abducted from a San Francisco bar one night, forced aboard a whaling ship bound for Alaskan waters, and made to sign on as a crew member for three years. It was while he worked as a cabin boy for the whaling ship's captain that he learned English and the navigational skills he would rely on when he later returned to Alaska to work as a guide and prospector. Equally important on his return to Alaska was the knowledge he acquired from Inuit people with whom he came into contact on and around Herschel Island, just east of the 141st meridian, during his time on the whaling ship. It was they who taught him how to survive in the far north and travel great distances by dog sled—a skill for which he would become well known.[137]

For Wada, the son of a former low-level samurai who had died when his son was only four, Alaska reportedly represented freedom both from the overt racial prejudice that he had encountered in California and from the social constraints that continued to order Meiji-era Japanese society.[138] Lower-level samurai families were among those most affected by the social upheavals that followed in the wake of the Meiji Restoration—which included the abolition

of samurai status in 1876—leaving many in this status category without an occupation or a role in their communities. Like members of former outcaste
groups, they were among those whom the Meiji government actively encouraged to emigrate to Hokkaido.[139] While there is no evidence that Wada himself traveled to Hokkaido before he left for North America, there is a hint that
he may have made a trip to Hokkaido at a later date. The U.S. entry card that
records Wada's arrival at Skagway in May 1923 lists as his birthplace Hakodate, the Hokkaido port that was the center of trade with the Ainu during the
Tokugawa period. Given that this is not in fact where Wada was born, it is
possible that he named it as the port from which he had embarked on his 1923
journey and that it was mistakenly recorded.[140]

Wada repeatedly traveled the length and breadth of Alaska and the Yukon
throughout the early decades of the twentieth century, moving strategically
back and forth across the U.S.-Canada border in response to the constraints
or opportunities that he encountered on one side or the other. Although
many such crossings were likely undocumented, Wada's name occasionally
appears in the records of North-West Mounted Police (NWMP) divisions
stationed along the U.S.-Canada border. The records of the NWMP division
at Dawson in the Yukon Territory for April 1908, for example, report that a
"mysterious Jap" named "Wadda" entered Canada at the Forty Mile border
crossing just north of town on April 25. He had traveled from Porcupine,
Alaska, with five dogs and a sled, and was one of ten people of various backgrounds who had entered Canada at the Forty Mile border crossing that
week.[141]

An intrepid adventurer and a capable prospector who later estimated that
he had traveled some twenty-six thousand miles by dog sled over the course
of his lifetime, Wada often prospected for gold in areas unfamiliar to non-
Indigenous travelers.[142] U.S. mining laws extended to Alaska, however, restricted the registration of mining claims to U.S. citizens or immigrants who
had declared that they intended to become a citizen.[143] In 1901, Wada applied
to become a naturalized U.S. citizen in Nome, only to have his application
refused on the same grounds as those of the Tsimshian who had settled on
Annette Island. Although they were indigenous to the region and had traveled just thirty miles across the border from their original home in British
Columbia, whereas Wada had crossed the Pacific, both were deemed aliens
born outside U.S. borders who were ineligible for citizenship because they
were not of Caucasian ancestry. Denied any chance even to apply for U.S. citizenship, Wada was also precluded from filing a claim in his own name to sites
he had identified as promising. Local mining administrators in Nome, how-

No. 834.—Return of "Wada" after a 16,000 mile Trip over the Ice, Y. T.

Jujiro Wada with his dog team on his return to Dawson City from a trip of some sixteen hundred miles to Herschel Island in the Yukon in 1908. Originally published in the *Seattle Post-Intelligencer*, July 5, 1908. Yukon Archives, Tennant Collection, 95/33 #7 PHO 448.

ever, did not hesitate to hire him to lead them to the gold mining streams to which he had hoped to register a claim on his own behalf, so that they might do so in their own names instead.[144] Although Wada would tell friends that he regarded Alaska as his home, he would be forced to make his living on the U.S. side of the border by guiding other gold seekers who met the race-based qualifications for U.S. citizenship to sites he had found. He was also forced to supplement his income by other means, running marathons, trading in furs, outfitting other prospectors, and even laying out new roads for towns such as Seward.[145] Accused at one point of fabricating news of a rich gold strike in Fairbanks by miners who "threatened to hang him for circulating false reports," Wada would continue to make a point of correcting this claim. Those who had threatened to hang him, he told a reporter some two decades later, were a group of "cold-footed miners who . . . were too lazy to work." In time, he declared, the goldfield near Fairbanks had produced millions of dollars' worth of gold, repaying the cost of acquiring Russian interests in Alaska fivefold.[146]

On the Yukon side of the international border, in contrast, Wada was permitted to stake mining claims on his own behalf and for clients. One record filed with the gold commissioner for the Yukon Territory on April 29, 1908, just four days after Wada entered Canada at Dawson, reveals that Wada recorded a claim to what he described as the "Discovery Creek on High Cache Creek 1500' in length situated about 5 miles from its mouth," a tributary of the Firth River some seventy-five miles from the Arctic coast not far from Herschel Island.[147] Wada also filed two claims for clients, each adjacent to his own. Mining law in the Yukon Territory, the *Dawson Daily News* assured its readers, permitted the registration of claims in a representative capacity and did not require those represented to have participated in the discovery itself.[148] Denied access to citizenship in the United States, Wada appears instead to have applied for naturalization as a British subject in Canada. U.S. arrival records for Ketchikan in May 1923, for example, record his "nationality" as "Canada." He was not admitted to the United States at Ketchikan at that time, probably because he was en route to Skagway, where he was admitted a few days later. From there he likely followed the trail over White Pass into Canada.[149] Later the same month, Wada filed letters patent to incorporate a company he planned to operate as Wada Placer Mines, Ltd., in Toronto, Ontario, well over three thousand miles away. He did not return to file the documents needed to formally organize the company during any one of the following three years, however, as a consequence of which the letters patent lapsed in 1926.[150]

Willing participant though Wada was in the colonial economies developing on both sides of the Canada-U.S. border and adept at negotiating the racialized legal barriers associated with each, Wada's most critical skill may well have been his ability to navigate the cultural divides between Indigenous and settler societies. Records show that he married into an Inuit community and formed close bonds with both Indigenous people and *hakujin*, engaging in business ventures with members of both groups at one time or another.[151] His interactions with the Inuit also show that he ably bridged the social and cultural divide between Meiji society, into which he was born, and his adopted community: his ties to his wife's people were clearly not circumscribed by the negative cultural assumptions about Indigenous people in North America prevalent in Japan at the time. Wada was just as skilled in navigating settler society. Although he appears most often in a fur parka in photographs taken at the time, standing by a dog sled or with the snowshoes that the Inuit taught him how to make in hand, Canadian newspapers did not fail to note that he could also look the part of a dapper and well-dressed Englishman.[152] His later years, in contrast, would be troubled by claims that first surfaced during World War I, that given his extensive knowledge of the north Pacific borderlands and the detailed maps he carried of Alaska and the Yukon, he was a Japanese spy.[153]

The ambivalent nature of Wada's place in that colonial world was also reflected in news headlines that speak to the contradictory attitudes surrounding "race" on both sides of the U.S.-Canada border at the time. Denied U.S. citizenship and suspected of spying though he was, he was also embraced in Alaska as a founder of Fairbanks and the Iditarod—a potent symbol of settler conquest of the Alaskan wilderness to this day—even as the *Dawson Daily News* on the Canadian side of the Alaska-Yukon border feted him as Dawson's own "phenomenal empire builder."[154] Like Frank Yasuda, one of his contemporaries who himself married an Inuit woman named Nevelo, Wada was hailed in both American and Canadian news accounts as a "king" or "chief" of the Inuit community he joined, even as some *hakujin* grumbled that U.S. law precluded non-Native individuals from serving as chief of a Native band.[155] As Wada would also be in later decades, Yasuda was celebrated in Japan as an individual who exemplified the Japanese spirit. Born in Miyagi Prefecture in northeastern Japan, he had reportedly left Japan for San Francisco in the mid-1880s and later traveled north to Seattle before signing on with the U.S. revenue cutter *Bear* in 1891, headed for the Bering Strait and the Arctic Ocean. In contrast to *hakujin*, who were incapable of enduring the "desolate environment" and the "endless ice and snow" of the far north for two or three months, the authors of one history of Japanese emigrants abroad wrote in 1906, Yasuda was "model fishing settler" who had persevered in a region where *hakujin* had yet to leave a footprint.[156]

Whereas Yasuda would eventually settle in what came to be known as Beaver, Alaska, Wada's status, like that of the Tsimshian, remained ambiguous. Like the Tsimshian, Wada was also caught in the legal and conceptual gap that existed between the highly racialized categories "immigrant" and "Indigene" in the colonial imagination, as well as between two distinctive ways of imagining "subject" and "citizen" on either side of the U.S.-Canada border. Although his status as an alien ineligible for U.S. citizenship reinforced his ties to Canada and shifted the focus of his activities from Alaska to the Yukon and the Northwest Territories for a period of time, he did not settle permanently in either Canada or the United States. During the final decades of his life before his death in San Diego in 1937, Wada was constantly on the move throughout North America, showing up from time to time in both New York and Seattle as well as in Toronto, and working at various times not only in Alaska and the Yukon but also in places scattered across an extended borderlands region that stretched from California to the Northwest Territories.[157]

Unlike Wada and Yasuda, who maintained their ties to the Alaska-Yukon borderlands throughout their lives, Ikeda's journey to the region ended after just six months. After exploring other opportunities in California and even northern Mexico, however, Ikeda would return to the north Pacific coast a few years later and settle in British Columbia, where he established a copper mining operation on behalf of Japanese investors on Haida Gwaii.[158] During his 1898 trip to Alaska and the Yukon, Ikeda had nearly lost his life by falling into the icy waters of Valdez Bay and, far from striking gold, had run out of supplies and money, making it necessary to run a restaurant to raise money for his return trip. He had also been forced to hunker down on glaciers battered by blizzards and shaken by seismic tremors. Had he had access to the advice and counsel of the local Tlingit and Athapaskan people based on their own deep knowledge of the landscape across which he traveled, they might well have reminded him to remain quiet and humble in the presence of the glaciers he traversed.[159] This was a lesson that Wada had clearly learned.

Conclusion

Like the travels of the Tsimshian who resettled in Alaska, Wada's journeys throughout the north Pacific borderlands reveal the complex and often contradictory mix of constraint and opportunity, promise and denial that existed on both sides of the U.S.-Canada border at the turn of the twentieth century. Skillful as Wada was in negotiating the legal and racial divides that cut across the region, they nevertheless played a significant role in shaping the contours of his life. Just two of many groups that traveled north along the B.C. coast to Alaska or the Yukon during the decades following the establishment of the U.S.-Canada border, both the Tsimshian of New Metlakatla and the Japanese adventurers who traveled through the region exposed the ironies, contradictions, and ambiguities inherent in the racialized legal categories that would be enforced with increasing rigor on each side of that boundary in the years to come. Both understood the power of borders not only to deny but also to create new kinds of opportunities and to reshape both space and aspects of identity. Both sought to reposition themselves accordingly, the Tsimshian by recasting themselves as Americans even as they continued to maintain their ties to the lands they had historically occupied in what had become British Columbia, and Japanese like Wada by assuming a Canadian identity even as his continual movement across national, state, and territorial borders and all along the Pacific coast in pursuit of his livelihood speaks to the fluid nature of his identity and his ability to adapt to the many distinct worlds this borderlands region encompassed.

The actions both of the Tsimshian and of Japanese migrants such as Wada also reveal the mutually reinforcing linkages between both the racialized legal categories that determined the status of Asian immigrants and Indigenous people and the fears of government officials on each side of the U.S.-Canada border. The nature of these ties is reflected in the legal characterization of the Metlakatlans as Indian but not Native, and yet not bona fide immigrants notwithstanding that they were deemed British subjects in Canada (a category of people that would otherwise be admissible to the United States), based on U.S. case law first directed against Chinese that also applied to bar Japanese from citizenship. The shared racial anxieties of U.S. and Canadian officials, in turn, were reflected in the reluctance of the U.S. Congress to pass legislation that would extend U.S. citizenship to the Metlakatlans for fear that this might erode the bar against admitting both Asian immigrants and Alaska Natives to the same, even as B.C. officials denied naturalized Japanese and other Asian immigrants the vote for fear that doing so might erode existing barriers against participation in the political process by B.C. Indians. Equally ironic and revealing of the shared attitudes that spanned the Canada-U.S. border is the fact that the Metlakatlans had left British Columbia in large part because they were denied title to their traditional territories under B.C. law, only to find their title to the lands on which they had settled in Alaska questioned because they did not fit squarely within either of the two racialized legal categories—immigrant and Indigene—that structured rights and entitlements in colonial society on both sides of that boundary. In that process, paradoxically, the Tsimshian themselves became settlers and colonists—ostensibly a marker of civilization but called into question in their case on grounds of race in ways that it was not for European settlers.

Notwithstanding the efforts of both nations to fix identity and impede movement at their respective borders, the continued mobility of Japanese and Indigenous people during the decades that followed itself served to infuse both the international border and the spaces it delineated with new meanings. Their very mobility, however, also provoked reaction that would lead to the further tightening of constraints faced by both groups on each side of the U.S.-Canada border. For all that their collective labor contributed to the commercial and industrial development of the north Pacific borderlands, their mobility would be used to mark them as undeserving of a central role in the evolving societies that emerged on either side of the international border and, instead, to relegate them to their margins.

CHAPTER THREE

Encounters with Law and Lawless Encounters

On a cold day in late March 1902, seventeen young Japanese men, all outfitted in similar winter coats and provided with identical rifles, were bundled into two horse-drawn sleighs bound for Atlin, B.C., on the eastern bank of a still frozen Atlin Lake. Located in Tlingit territory in the northwestern corner of British Columbia, Atlin Lake extends eighty-five miles along the eastern edge of the Coast Mountains from the Yukon Territory down into British Colum-bia.[1] Settled by miners in 1898 after gold was discovered in nearby creeks, Atlin was largely still a mining camp in 1902, more closely connected to the tiny village of Caribou Crossing some fifty miles north in the Yukon Territory and to Skagway, located roughly sixty miles to the west across the coastal moun-tain range on what had yet to be determined was the U.S. side of the border, than it was to Vancouver, over eight hundred miles to the south.[2] Unable to speak English and uncertain as they surely were about what lay ahead as they traveled across the ice of the frozen lake, the young Japanese men must never-theless have marveled at the stark and spectacular beauty of the snow-covered peaks that line the western shores of Atlin Lake.[3]

The Japanese had been hired by the Atlin Mining Company to work a hy-draulic mining operation set up on McKee Creek thirteen miles south of Atlin at the direction of the company's owners, a group of English investors based in London who referred to themselves as the Nimrod Syndicate.[4] Well aware that there was considerable hostility to the hiring of Japanese laborers by corporate interests on the part of local miners who worked their own claims on land that they had bought, R. D. Fetherstonhaugh, superintendent in charge of the op-eration, permitted the Japanese to stop in Atlin for just an hour before sending them on to McKee Creek, a strategy intended to diffuse the anger of the white miners who had gathered the day before to express their indignation at the anticipated arrival of the Japanese.[5] Their demand that the acting gold com-missioner, Edward J. Thaine, turn the Japanese miners away fell on deaf ears. Several days earlier, British Columbia's attorney general, D. M. Eberts, had no-tified Thaine and other local officials that although the B.C. government heart-ily disapproved of the hiring of Japanese labor, "as the law now [stood it was] powerless to restrain the entry of these Japanese into the district, or from carrying on any lawful calling while there."[6]

Faced with the refusal of local government officials to cooperate in driving the Japanese out of town, the miners who had participated in the indignation meeting decided to take matters into their own hands. When some miners marched to Fetherstonhaugh's home to confront him in person, he reminded them that British Columbia's Riot Act forbade rioting, to which their leaders reportedly responded, "to h—— with the Riot Act."[7] Thaine himself read the Riot Act out loud to some 150 miners as they marched past him down the narrow trail to McKee Creek, where they demanded that the Japanese leave immediately.[8] Frightened and outnumbered in a country where most did not speak the language, the Japanese men agreed to leave at the first light of day. Guy Lawrence, one of twelve special constables appointed by Thaine to maintain control of the situation, would later report that although the miners were unarmed there was "every evidence that the slightest spark might cause serious bloodshed." The Japanese men, he noted, had been provided with Winchester rifles, although he admitted that they might well have been unloaded and "just intended as a bluff."[9] The miners made clear, however, that they were willing to resort to force if the Japanese did not comply with their demand that they leave town by morning. In their own words, "We came here to get the Japs, and we are not going till we get them."[10]

When Fetherstonhaugh arrived the following morning, he attempted to negotiate with the miners, offering to dismiss the Japanese men before summer, only to be told that if they did not leave immediately, his own "position within the community" would be at risk. Fetherstonhaugh was able to extract a promise from the miners that he would be permitted to keep two Japanese cooks and that the miners would share the cost of returning the remaining fifteen to Vancouver. But the miners refused to reimburse him for the "$30 advance he had paid each of the Japanese workers." In their words, they were "all poor men and [didn't] propose to reimburse anyone for the mistakes they made."[11] Fetherstonhaugh's decision to bring Japanese miners to Atlin was, in their opinion, a miscalculation for which he alone was responsible.

"Escorted" to Atlin by ten times their number, the Japanese men again set off across the still frozen lake, retracing the journey to Skagway and along the Pacific coast that had brought them to Atlin just two days earlier.[12] Reporters who met them at the Canadian Pacific Railway (CPR) dock in Vancouver wrote that they appeared "discouraged" and "forlorn."[13] The *Atlin Claim*, in contrast, extended its hearty congratulations to "the miners, the merchants and people of Atlin" for their mutual "success achieved in dealing with the importation and deportation of Japanese labourers." A prominently displayed ad in the *Claim*, captioned "Exit Mr. Jap from Atlin Gold Fields, B.C.," offered a set of

The Atlin miners who forced recently hired Japanese laborers to leave town in March 1902 pose for a photograph, originally captioned "Parting Sendoff to Mister Jap." Yukon Archives, Atlin Historical Society Collection, 82/297, #4570.

five photographs depicting the miners who had participated in the expulsion of the Japanese from Atlin, at the price of $2 for the full set.[14] The editor of the *Claim* used the occasion to contrast the actions of Atlin's miners with those of the American miners in Skagway who, he claimed, would have resorted to force in similar circumstances. The "courteous treatment" shown the Japanese in Atlin, where its citizens had not resorted to "force or bloodshed," the editor wrote, stood in "strong contrast to what was liable to have been used on the other side of the line." For all that the "Skagway press [was] ever ready to belittle Britain or the British," he declared, residents of Skagway would surely have resorted to tactics like those that caused the death of Soapy Smith—a known gangster who died in a gunfight there in 1898—to drive the Japanese miners out of their town.[15] Within weeks, residents of Skagway, noting that the "prompt action by Atlin miners" had undercut an attempt of "English coalmine-owners to import several dozen Japanese to work in the Atlin mines," established a committee known as the Anti-Chinese Association, with branches in Atlin and Whitehorse, to ensure "that no more Asiatics are allowed to land at Skagway" and that "no more coolies" would be hired to work in any one of the three towns.[16]

As explained later in this chapter, the events in Atlin were part of a pattern of racialized violence and intimidation that extended throughout western North America during this period. They also had deeper roots in Atlin itself, where the editor of the *Atlin Claim*, a self-described "real estate and mining broker" who worked a small claim on his own property, had done all he could to encourage his readers to see Japanese laborers as a threat.[17] When he learned in October 1901, just six months before the Japanese miners who were driven out arrived in Atlin in March 1902, that another company planned to hire Japanese to work a claim on Willow Creek, the *Atlin Claim* endorsed the "hope that the ship carrying them might sink."[18] In August 1900, the editor reprinted an article first published in *The Columbian* in New Westminster, B.C., announcing that an unnamed gentleman planned to send a thousand Japanese laborers to Manitoba in the fall to harvest that year's crops at half the wages that would normally have been paid harvest workers based in Ontario. Japanese were such excellent agricultural workers, the author declared, that Manitoba farmers would "certainly prefer them to Doukhobours." He also suggested, however, that hiring Japanese would also serve the interests of those opposed to Japanese labor immigration by angering the displaced Ontario workers, who would then pressure members of Parliament from Canada's eastern provinces to reverse their position after they had voted repeatedly to strike down British Columbia's efforts to limit Japanese immigration.[19]

The March 1902 incident was just the first time that Japanese laborers were threatened with mob violence if they did not leave Atlin. In early May 1907, five years after the Japanese hired to work at McKee Creek were driven out of town, some 150 white miners surrounded the home of J. M. Ruffner, the general manager of the North Columbia Gold Mining Company, to force him to explain to those participating in yet another indignation meeting why he had hired twenty-one Japanese laborers to work the company's hydraulic mining operation. The miners warned Ruffner that if the Japanese did not "leave the camp forthwith they [would] be forcibly ejected."[20] Ruffner argued with them, insisting that he had made every effort to hire reliable white men but that there were none available, with the result that his company had operated at just 40 percent of its full capacity during the previous year. Far from undercutting the wages of non-Japanese, Ruffner argued, the "pipemen, shovel wielders, [and] common laborers" he hired received "the highest price paid

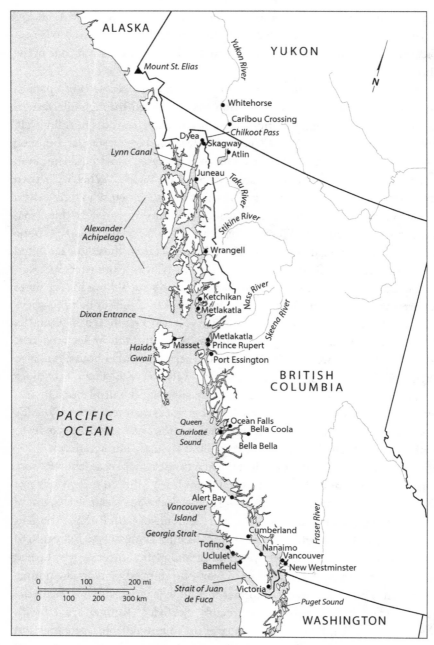

The Pacific coast of British Columbia and southeastern Alaska
including key locations referred to in the text.

for common labor on the North Pacific coast" on either side of the Alaska-B.C. border.[21] Although there were those who disputed Ruffner's claim, he was able to persuade the miners who objected to the presence of Japanese men at the camp to allow them to stay in camp through summer's end. Given that the Japanese miners had been hired in part because they were willing to "work throughout the winter," which "white miners refuse[d] to do," it was only a partial victory, but it did mean that they were not immediately driven out of town.[22]

Given the 1903 determination of the Alaska Boundary Tribunal that Skagway would be located on the U.S. side of the international border, U.S. immigration officials also kept a careful eye on the Japanese miners who traveled north to Atlin in April 1907. Only after the Japanese miners had undergone careful inspection at the U.S. immigration office in Vancouver, B.C., did U.S. officials issue permits to the Japanese that allowed them to travel through U.S. territory on their way to Atlin. As the *Vancouver Daily Province* explained, the United States had recently tightened restrictions on entry into the United States, with the result that "Uncle Sam intend[ed] to keep an especially inquisitive eye on these Japanese as they pass[ed] from Skagway to the Summit, where the Canadian boundary line [lay]."[23] Although the United States was unable to bar Japanese from transiting its territory based on the terms of its treaties with Japan, it had taken steps to make the transit privilege more difficult to exercise, by requiring persons crossing into the United States to deposit a bond of $500 at the time of entry, which amount was returned when they left U.S. territory. A policy first developed to restrict Japanese entry across the U.S.-Mexico border, the bond requirement was also applied on a discretionary basis along the Alaska border, even at Skagway, where the transit of U.S. territory was just a few miles long.[24] The fact that Ruffner was able to secure permits that allowed the Japanese miners he hired to transit U.S. territory before they headed north suggests that Ruffner, who was born in Ohio, had close ties in Seattle, and remained a U.S. citizen all his life, was able to successfully negotiate a waiver of the bond requirement.[25] The Japanese consul based in Vancouver, B.C., negotiated a similar waiver for other Japanese travelers crossing into Canada at Skagway in 1908, on the condition that they report not just their names but also those of the places where their families were registered in Japan to his office.[26] One factor U.S. officials may well have taken into account in agreeing to waive the $500 bond for Japanese traveling through Skagway was the fact that it was a critical link in the route north along the Pacific coast for all Canadians traveling from Vancouver, B.C., to northern British Columbia and the Yukon Territory given the hardships of the overland journey through the mountains of the B.C. interior. This was one reason why Canadians had hoped the Alaska Boundary Tribunal would accept the argument that Skagway lay on the Canadian side of the line when the tribunal met in 1903.[27] Also a consideration, the Toronto *Globe* declared, was the fact that "Skaguay" had been developed "with Canadian money" and was rightly a Canadian—and not an American—port.[28]

Although the Atlin miners who had demanded the expulsion of the Japanese men who arrived in May 1907 agreed that they might remain in Atlin through the end of the summer mining season, the *Atlin Claim* did not let matters rest. On August 31, 1907, the *Claim* published the remarks of William Sloan, member of Parliament for northern British Columbia. "The thin edge of the wedge of Oriental labor in the placer mines of the North," he declared, "has been driven in the Atlin camp, where the Japanese were introduced this season." The coastal areas in his constituency, "from Howe Sound northward as far as the British Columbia coast extends," he claimed, were already "flooded with Japanese labor engaging in the fisheries." For this reason, he was "unqualifiedly" opposed to "the use of the Japanese or any other Oriental labor" and intended to do all in his power to stop what he termed "the Japanese invasion."[29] When, just three weeks later in September 1907, a third group of seventy-seven Japanese arrived in Atlin to work in the mines, they were again forcibly expelled. Threatened with violence if they did not leave, some three hundred white miners banded together and "drove them aboard a river steamer" that plied the waters of Atlin Lake.[30] The "coolies," as the Japanese were referred to in both the Vancouver and the Victoria newspapers, were "almost destitute" and were to be "turned loose at Skagway," driven, as such, not just out of the village of Atlin but beyond what was now recognized as the U.S.-Canada border itself.[31]

Imperial and Transnational Contexts

Partly rooted in local concerns, the story of the forced expulsion of Japanese laborers from Atlin during the first decade of the twentieth century also unfolded within broader contexts of national, provincial, and imperial racial politics. The expulsion of the Japanese from Atlin in September 1907 was reported as far away as London, England, and Sydney, Australia, where the *Sydney Mail* told its readers that "British Columbia authorities were surprised at the expulsion, thinking the Oriental problem was acute only at Vancouver," after a large anti-Asian riot had taken place there just two weeks earlier.[32] Japanese diplomats, already deeply concerned about the Vancouver Riot and

anxious to distinguish Japanese laborers from Chinese "coolies," were morti-
fied by the characterization of Japanese subjects both as coolies and as destitute.[33] They refused, however, to be provoked by the rioters. In the words of
imperial Japanese commissioner Ishii Kikujiro, who at the time was traveling
through Vancouver on his way to Ottawa and then Washington, D.C.: "The
friendship and commercial relations between Japan and Canada are too
strong and too important to be weakened or disturbed by any 'hoodlum' element."[34] Ishii, the *Vancouver Daily Province* reported, urged his "countrymen
to preserve a dignified attitude and not to commit lawless acts" in retaliation
for the damage done during the riot. "[If a friend's] dog barked and snarled at
them [during a visit]," he reminded them, "no bitterness in consequence
should be entertained toward the friend." He was certain, he told reporters,
that Japanese living in British Columbia understood his meaning.[35] Leading
journals in Japan similarly refused to regard those "who violently advocate[d]
the expulsion of all Orientals from the American continent . . . as an index
of the great heart of the American nation," asserting instead that "such unworthy, unmanly incidents [could not] shake Japan's steadfast faith in her proved
and constant friend, America."[36]

As the expulsions of Japanese miners from Atlin reveal, the conflicts that
arose over the hiring of Japanese laborers were rooted not just in racial animus but also in the resentment local miners harbored against faraway corporate investors in large-scale industrial mining operations with which they
feared their own small operations could not compete.[37] Their ability to displace their discontent onto Japanese miners by invoking racialized divides,
even when those laborers posed no direct threat to their own jobs, made "race"
a convenient tool for Atlin's white miners in their fight against these corporate interests. Growing anxieties about their own prospects may also have
been compounded by the initial uncertainty of government officials over just
where Atlin was located in relation to the provincial border that divided British Columbia from the Yukon Territory. It was not until 1900 that this boundary,
which lay along the sixtieth parallel, was surveyed and Atlin was determined
to lie within British Columbia. This, however, meant that a number of sites in
the Atlin area were the subject of multiple and sometimes overlapping claims,
some registered in British Columbia and some in the Yukon, where different
guidelines on the permissible size of such claims applied.[38] Local miners who,
like the editor of the *Atlin Claim*, worked a small claim on their own property
would have little recourse if a dispute arose with one of the large corporations
that acted quickly to buy up and consolidate as many of these smaller claims
as possible.[39]

Equally as great a concern for Atlin residents as an influx of Japanese miners was the number of American miners who made the short trip from Skagway over the mountain passes to Atlin. Had British Columbia not recently passed an "alien bill that kept many from the United States out," one such resident wryly observed in May 1900, Americans would still outnumber Canadians in the area.[40] The presence of Americans on what was deemed British soil, however, was not the only matter that raised the ire of B.C. miners. Also a source of aggravation were the treaties into which Great Britain had entered with Japan as part of a larger effort to maintain its position as a Pacific maritime power as the United States became a more active presence there. These were the treaties that had constrained local officials in Atlin who might otherwise have supported the white miners who drove the Japanese miners out of town. Of particular concern to British Columbians was the 1894 Treaty of Commerce and Navigation, which delineated the rights of British subjects in Japan as well as those of Japanese subjects in Britain's colonies around the globe. Celebrated in Japan as the first step in securing the removal of the unequal treaties imposed on it by Western nations in the mid-1850s, the 1894 Treaty of Commerce and Navigation provided that both British and Japanese subjects "shall have full liberty to enter, travel, or reside in any part of the dominions and possession of the other . . . and enjoy full and perfect protection for their persons and property."[41] It was this principle on which the Dominion government had relied to disallow the Natal Acts passed by B.C. legislators during the years that followed in an effort to limit Japanese immigration by requiring recent immigrants to pass a language test.[42]

In January 1902, just seven weeks before the first group of Japanese laborers arrived in Atlin, Japan and Great Britain, motivated in part by a shared desire to deny Russia a port on the Pacific that was free of ice year-round, had entered into the Anglo-Japanese Alliance, cementing their ties and reaffirming the diplomatic relationship between the two imperial governments.[43] This was no doubt a key factor explaining Attorney General Eberts's restraint in responding to the Atlin Mining Company's plan to hire Japanese miners in March 1902, notwithstanding his active opposition to Japanese immigrants in other contexts. Although his advice was necessarily constrained by the terms of the alliance, however, the *Atlin Claim* did not consider itself bound by its provisions. Given that British Columbians had repeatedly "shown their loyalty and devotion to the cause of Empire," it declared, the Dominion government's repeated reliance on such treaties with Japan to disallow British Columbia's Natal Acts had given British Columbians a "legitimate grievance against His Majesty the King."[44] In April 1907, as the second group of Japanese laborers recruited to work in Atlin's gold mines embarked on their journey north, fears were high in British Columbia that its most recent Natal Act would again be struck down by the Dominion government.[45] If local residents would only unite against Japanese labor immigration, the *Claim* complained in May 1907, revealing that not everyone in town was opposed to their presence, it would cease to be just a local issue and become a problem with which Great Britain's imperial government would be forced to contend.[46]

As part of its continuing effort to foster anti-Japanese sentiment during the summer of 1907, the *Atlin Claim* republished an article titled "Japanese Invasion of B.C." reporting on a parade held in Vancouver, B.C., to welcome Prince Fushimi, a member of Japan's royal family, during his official visit to Canada. Although its author conceded that the prince had "conducted himself as became a gentleman representing a great nation," he regarded those who participated in the parade with disdain, describing them as "strutting, banzaiing, paper lantern bearers." The "presence of four or five thousand little brown men in a bunch," he wrote, was an "impressive demonstration of the fact that British Columbia is being pretty effectively invaded." The idea that Japan's success in remaking itself as "a great nation and the ally of Great Britain" meant that Canadians "should accept the Japanese as our equals," he continued, was "a piece of impudent silliness." He rejected the "hoary slop about all men having been born free and equal," declaring that "[no] Jap, Chinaman, negro nor any other colored race is the equal of any white race." Even those who belonged "to the same great and glorious Empire to which we are all proud to belong," be they "our pig-tailed brothers in empire from Hong Kong and Shanghai" or "turbaned fellow Britishers from India," the author added, were "in no sense one with us either in sentiment or physical or mental affinities." There was "no reason," he insisted, why any white Canadian "should embrace [these] fellow subjects."[47]

The expulsions of Japanese from Atlin were not only a product of racist sentiment that reverberated throughout the British empire and structured its relations with colonized peoples in its colonies around the globe, but also part of a larger wave of racially-motivated anti-Asian violence and intimidation that swept throughout the North American West, extending from the California coast deep into the interior mountain west and north across international borders into British Columbia and Alaska. Beginning in and around the California gold mines in the 1850s, periodic riots, expulsions, and rampages directed first at Chinese labor migrants escalated in the 1880s and continued well into the twentieth century despite sporadic efforts by federal officials in both Canada and the United States to maintain some semblance of control.

Among its most infamous episodes was the massacre of twenty-eight Chinese miners in Rock Springs, Wyoming, on September 2, 1885, followed a few days later by an attack on Chinese hop pickers near Squak Valley in the Washington Territory—just two of many dozen such incidents that occurred that year.[48] Violence would continue to reverberate throughout the Pacific Northwest and along the north Pacific coast during the 1880s. On November 3, 1885, residents of Tacoma, Washington, banded together to force their Chinese neighbors onto a train bound for Portland, Oregon. Three months later, in February 1886, anti-Chinese violence erupted in Seattle, triggered in part by repeated rumors that Chinese illegally crossed the U.S.-Canada border from British Columbia into the Washington Territory on a regular basis. Despite the declaration of martial law and the intervention of federal troops, the unlawful efforts to expel Chinese from Seattle were largely successful.[49] Just two weeks after the outbreak of violence in Seattle, gangs of white men drove Chinese workers in three towns along the Willamette River in Oregon—Oregon City, Beaver, and Butteville—onto river steamboats bound for Portland. In May 1887, yet another gang murdered thirty-four Chinese gold miners in what was known as Hells Canyon on the Snake River and stole their gold.[50]

Alaska was also not immune. On August 6, 1886, a mob from Juneau, Alaska, traveled to Douglas Island, separated from the mainland by just a narrow channel, where they drove Chinese laborers from their homes and places of work near the Treadwell Mine and onto a small schooner bound for Wrangell, just north of the Dixon Entrance. In response to an urgent message from the deputy U.S. marshal stationed in Juneau declaring that he was powerless to enforce the law, Governor A. P. Swineford prepared a proclamation commanding all "evil-disposed and lawless persons to at once dispense and desist from their lawless purpose" in "driving [Chinese laborers] from their homes and places of business on Douglas Island." The Chinese, he wrote, were just as "entitled to protection under laws and treaties of the United States" as any other person. His draft proclamation, however, was never published. By the time the governor arrived on August 9, the mob had disbanded and it was deemed unnecessary to publish it. The governor's efforts to secure the return of the Chinese who had been driven away and to prosecute those who had forced them to leave were also met with stalwart resistance from both the deputy U.S. marshal who originally sought his aid and the commander of the U.S. naval vessel ordered to retrieve any Chinese who wished to return.[51] As in other places where such acts of intimidation occurred, little would be done to bring the perpetrators to justice.

Expulsions such as these created new patterns of migration as Asian migrants driven out of one town moved elsewhere, sometimes across international borders. Whereas some moved on to other towns in the same or nearby states or territories, at other times race-based expulsions set in motion new migrations across international borders. Some of the Chinese miners driven out of Juneau in 1886, for example, moved south across the U.S.-Canada border to Vancouver Island or to gold-mining districts in the B.C. interior, while others left the Washington Territory for Vancouver, B.C., after a mob attacked Chinese workers in Olympia.[52] The fact that the Chinese migrants sought refuge in British Columbia in the face of an escalating pattern of violence south of the border, ironically, may have contributed to growing anxieties of anti-Chinese elements in Vancouver, where an anti-Chinese riot broke out in January 1887. Reportedly triggered by the arrival of some 250 Chinese laborers from Victoria hired to clear a 350-acre estate near Gastown, the group might well have included some who left for Vancouver Island after they were driven out of Alaska.[53] In the wake of that riot, in turn, some eighty-six Chinese laborers reportedly left Vancouver for New Westminster, B.C., while others returned to Victoria.[54]

A curious feature of this and other expulsions that used threats of violence to drive Asian migrants out of town was the pride that both observers and participants took in what they deemed to be the "peaceful" nature of their actions. Like the editor of the *Atlin Claim*, who celebrated the "nonviolent" way that Atlin's miners had "persuaded" the newly arrived Japanese to leave town, members of Vancouver's Vigilance Committee also "emphasiz[ed] the non-violent aspect of the intimidation," noting that they too had offered to pay the costs of the return of newly arrived Chinese workers to Victoria.[55] Those in Tacoma who had forced Chinese migrants onto trains bound for Portland, Oregon, in 1886, also prided themselves on the "nonviolent" nature of their action. The same was true of those who drove some thirty Japanese sawmill laborers from the town of Toledo, Oregon, in 1925. Brought in by the sawmill to stack green lumber, the hardest job at the sawmill and one that others were reluctant to do, they were forced aboard trucks and driven to a train station some fifty miles away.[56] Among them were the wives and children of several Japanese sawmill workers, as well as one Korean laborer—also a Japanese subject—and four Filipino laborers.[57]

Japanese were not initially a target of attacks on Asian labor migrants, largely because the Meiji government eased its own bar on labor emigration only in 1885.[58] As Japanese labor migrants became an increasingly visible presence along the north Pacific coast in the 1890s, however, anti-Chinese law and policy was quickly adapted, where possible, also to apply to Japanese. Japanese also increasingly became a target of mob violence, as did the South Asians who also began to arrive in greater numbers during the same period. In April 1902, just after the first group of Japanese were driven from Atlin, Skagway's Anti-Chinese Association assured all its members that it was working closely with affiliated organizations across the U.S.-Canada border in both Atlin, B.C., and Whitehorse in the Yukon Territory, to ensure that Asian labor migrants would be turned away. They had the support of both steamboat and railway workers, they announced, all along the route from Skagway, Alaska, to Dawson City, Yukon.[59] In June 1902, the *White Horse Star* reported that five Chinese men who had arrived in Whitehorse on their way to work at a placer mine near Dawson City had been forced to leave the territory and retrace their journey through Skagway back to Victoria, B.C.[60] These five, the *White Horse Star* proclaimed, were just "the forerunner[s] for a flooding of the Yukon with cheap Chinese labor." It also seized on the opportunity presented by the arrival of the five Chinese to redirect any anti-Asian hostility that its report might engender against the Japanese proprietors of local restaurants in Whitehorse that catered to working men. Japanese were able to offer meals at half the price charged by other eateries in town, the *Star* insisted, only because they reused "the refuse and leavings from higher priced restaurants," which they purportedly could be seen "carrying . . . through the back alleys" to their places of business every day. Where the *Star* claimed that Chinese had taken on most of the unskilled jobs as "cooks, waiters, laundry men, chambermaids, [and] janitors," such that Whitehorse's "white men, women and children walk the streets in a vain endeavor to secure work," the *Klondike Nugget*, based in Dawson, claimed that the presence of large numbers of Japanese threatened to leave whites in the Yukon without work.[61]

Anti-Japanese animus also extended south across the Yukon-B.C. border deep into the B.C. interior, leading to the ouster of Japanese mine workers from the Cariboo gold mine in 1904 and the threatened ejection of Japanese laborers from the Salmo sawmill near Nelson, B.C., just north of the forty-ninth parallel, in 1905, where they were told that logs floating in reservoirs would be cut loose if they did not leave of their own volition.[62] South Asian migrants, as newspapers in both Alaska and the Yukon diligently reported, were also regularly a target of mob violence on both sides of the Canada-U.S. border, notwithstanding—or perhaps because—they were already British subjects.[63] Japanese in Canada were particularly concerned about its refusal to allow the 350 passengers on the Japanese tramp steamer, the *Komagata Maru*, to land in 1914, based on what was known as the continuous passage rule, which barred the entry of anyone who did not travel directly to Canada from their home country and was directed at both Japanese and South Asian migrants. All but twenty passengers were forced to remain on board within sight of the shore in Burrard Inlet for two full months before the vessel was directed to return to India. Its passengers, Nakayama noted in 1921, included 340 Sikhs, 24 Muslims, and 12 Hindus, all of whom were British subjects.[64] While Shiozaki Yokichi, the Japanese owner of the *Komagata Maru*, later defended Canadian immigration officials on the ground that it was their duty to enforce Canadian immigration law, denying that they were "tyrannical" and "cold-blooded" as he wrote his Indian passengers claimed, others questioned Canada's action in barring them from landing.[65] The "Hindu immigrants," the *Fairbanks Daily Times* noted, were British subjects who would typically be "entitled to admission at any port under the British flag," including those in British Columbia.[66] An unnamed South Asian writer with whom Kiyoshi Karl Kawakami spoke, in turn, observed that Canadian officials had drawn "a clearly defined line between His Majesty's subjects of Canada and those of India in the face of the bold and clear proclamation of our late Queen Victoria." "It is a puzzling riddle to be solved," he said, "that in India we are British subjects, in England we are British subjects, but in Canada, to legalize our British citizenship right, we have to secure another deed to that effect."[67]

Colonial and Indigenous Contexts

As it was elsewhere throughout the North American West, anti-Asian violence along the north Pacific coast was an extension of that directed at Indigenous people by a succession of colonial powers from the time Europeans first arrived. Situated at the very core of the imperial project, violence, both actual and threatened, was regularly used to suppress Indigenous resistance to colonial intrusion, allowing imperial powers to secure the tenuous footholds in Indigenous territory that later became the basis for far-reaching claims to imperial sovereignty that extended far beyond the original outposts. Much as the Russian American Company (RAC) used violence or the threat of violence to co-opt the labor of Aleut people needed to produce the supply of furs that sustained its colonial endeavors, British and American colonizers also used both violence and the threat of violence to displace Indigenous people who stood in the way of their access to land or resources to which they laid claim.[68] At times, Britain and the United States reinforced each other in this regard. When the Tlingit reoccupied parts of Sitka after U.S. Army units were reposted to Idaho and Arizona to assist in the wars being waged against

Indigenous nations along both the U.S.-Mexico border and the forty-ninth parallel, among them Chief Joseph's band of Nez Perce, for example, white settlers appealed for aid to the British Royal Navy based on Vancouver Island, in Esquimalt, B.C. Notwithstanding that Sitka had been incorporated within the boundaries of the United States, the British Royal Navy dispatched the H.M.S. *Osprey* to Sitka to assert a military presence until a U.S. gunboat could arrive.[69]

While there were differences in the mechanics and legal technologies of exclusion as applied to Asian immigrants, on the one hand, and Indigenous peoples, on the other, on both sides of the U.S.-Canada border, efforts to forcibly exclude Japanese or other Asian migrants paralleled those of Euro-Canadian and American settlers to erase the Indigenous presence from the colonial landscape. Boundary drawing and the enforcement of the boundaries that resulted—whether by state-sanctioned or unlawful means—was itself a critical tool used to displace or to constrain the movement of Asian migrants and Indigenous people on a variety of scales. As in Atlin, national and municipal boundaries sometimes worked in tandem to restrict or to redirect the movement of members of both groups. Where Indigenous people were concerned, the establishment of bounded reservations was itself a tool used by colonial governments to open the lands between them to European settlers.[70] The establishment of Indian reserves operated in conjunction with the drawing of both municipal and private property boundaries to displace Indigenous people whom settlers wanted to see relocated outside town limits, a strategy that was also deployed in Atlin in an effort to force local Tlingit people out of town.

During the years that followed the expulsions of Japanese laborers from Atlin, its white residents turned their attention to the members of the Tlingit band whose homes were located in an area that, over time, had been incorporated within the boundaries of a part of town that white settlers hoped to develop for their own use. In 1899, one year after gold was first discovered in Atlin's creeks, the first ethnographer to travel through the Atlin area to describe its Indigenous peoples noted the presence of a village that the Tlingit called We-nah. At the time, he reported that it was located "on a point jutting out into [Atlin Lake and] separated from the town of Atlin by a small creek."[71] As Atlin grew over the course of the next two decades, it had surrounded the site. In February 1915, the Atlin Board of Trade wrote to members the Royal Commission on Indian Affairs for British Columbia (McKenna-McBride Commission), charged with adjusting reserve boundaries throughout British Columbia, that it was "the desire of the white inhabitants to have the natives removed

from the Atlin townsite."[72] The Tlingit should be removed, the board's chairman argued when the commission held hearings in Atlin that June, "because
where they are now is part of the surveyed town and . . . it is not desirable to
have the Indians right [in] what I might call the centre of the town because at
some future date the place might be required for white people when the camp
goes ahead, which we hope will be soon."[73] Their removal, the Board of Trade
urged, "should be effected at an early date, as the portion of the townsite at
present occupied by them is one of the most desirable localities in the town."
If they did not move, the board warned, it was certain to give rise to difficulties like those that had occurred elsewhere in British Columbia in places
where Indigenous people continued to oppose settler intrusion.[74]

The Board of Trade also raised the specter of disease. Some of the Tlingit
living in what they called "Indian Town" were unwell, one board member reported, and "it is a well known fact that the major part of the Indians are dying
much more rapidly than the whites and the cause of their dying off so rapidly
is attributable to tuberculosis." A site five miles from Atlin known as Five Mile
Bay was an ideal location to which to relocate the Tlingit, he suggested. From
there, they could still come to Atlin overland or by boat to pick up supplies.[75]
The board assured the members of the McKenna-McBride Commission that
the Tlingit, when approached by Indian Agent W. Scott Simpson, had indicated that they were "perfectly willing to move to some other place as long as
they get an Indian reserve."[76] Simpson himself, in contrast, testified that the
Tlingit in Atlin were "very averse to being removed from their present abode."
They had "good cause of being averse to their being removed," another witness observed, given that "they have gone to a lot of trouble putting up buildings and they have always behaved themselves remarkably well." If the Tlingit
were relocated to an isolated spot, the witness added, they might well become
a "target for a certain number of undesirable white men," who would do their
best to take advantage of them.[77]

Chief Taku Jack, leader of what B.C. officials called the Atlin Band of Indians, argued against the Board of Trade's proposal, insisting that the very endeavor in which the McKenna-McBride Commission was engaged made no
sense given that all of the land surrounding Atlin Lake was already theirs. Not
only had they all been born there and lived there long before any whites arrived, he observed, but the fact that they had named all of the places in the
area, "old names" that came from their "old forefathers" and that colonial authorities had not changed, was itself evidence that this country belonged to
them. The reason the great lake at the heart of their territory was called Atlin
was because this was the name the Tlingit had given it, Chief Taku Jack

pointed out, having first forced the commissioners to admit that they did not know that "atlin" meant "big lake." He also pointed out that white settlers had, in effect, acknowledged that the land surrounding the lake was theirs when they called his band the Atlin Indians. "You got no land to give me," he told the commissioners, "this land belongs to me." What the Tlingit wanted was not a few small reserves carved from a land base that was already theirs; it was the freedom to move throughout it and to live on it in the way they chose. "It is no good for us to have a piece of land all by ourselves," Chief Taku Jack declared. "If you give us people a piece of land we are not free."[78]

Chief Taku Jack also questioned the McKenna-McBride Commission's stated purpose in readjusting reserve boundaries throughout British Columbia. Although its members claimed that they were there to protect the Indians, their real aim appeared otherwise. "I think that you people are going to try and push us out of this country," Chief Taku Jack told them.[79] This was a process with which his people were already familiar. Although his band had been willing to maintain friendly relations with the prospectors who occasionally traveled through the area panning for gold, those who rushed to the Atlin area by the thousands after gold was discovered in its creeks in 1898 did not respond in kind. As Chief Taku Jack's daughter, Antonia Jack, later testified, the prospectors who had poured in "pushed all the natives out of their way to get to the gold, and they started to keep that place, to stay there and put up their tents." They were followed in turn by government officials, she added, who "got the policemen" after the Tlingit who did not make way for them.[80] If the government was genuinely concerned with helping them, Chief Taku Jack told the McKenna-McBride Commission in 1915, "it is better for the Government to help us . . . by giving us some work so that we can make some money to feed our children." Even a few small reserves would not allow them to do this. While he had always made a living hunting fur, younger men needed to earn wages to support their wives and children in a changing economic world. By 1915, however, the whites who ran the mining operations on Atlin's creeks hired Japanese instead. With "these Japs over here," he told the commissioners , "we cannot do anything because they are working up on the creek."[81]

Ultimately, the Atlin band received neither protection for its village site nor wage work as a result of the McKenna-McBride Commission's visit. Because its power was limited to establishing new reserves or adjusting the boundaries of existing reserves, it did not have the authority to force the Tlingit to abandon Wenah village. The commissioners warned Chief Taku Jack, however, that if the governor-general—the king's representative in Canada—were

Chilkoot Jack, who is said to have guided the first white man to the Yukon, standing in front of a wooden building in Dyea, Alaska, in 1899. He was later identified as Telegraph Jack from Atlin, B.C., a brother of Chief Taku Jack. Yukon Archives, Anton Vogee Fonds, 82/271, #58.

to tell his band that they had to move, they would have to do so.[82] When, in 1916, the McKenna-McBride Commission identified nine sites to be set aside as reserves for the Atlin band, the Wenah village site was not among them.[83] Members of the commission explained to Chief Taku Jack that it was their understanding that the land on which it was located had been bought by a Catholic priest who had transferred it to the priest who replaced him, with the result that it was now the private property either of that priest or of the Catholic Church. "That is the way the white men [treat] the Indians," Chief Jack responded dryly. "This man he put up the school in our place and now he wants the whole place."[84]

During the decades that followed, the Tlingit who lived in Atlin continued to refuse to move. In 1949, when they declined yet again to be relocated, the Department of Indian Affairs attempted to acquire title to the Wenah village site

Chief Taku Jack with "Tourist Lady." She is wearing a bracelet made from a silver dollar by Chief Taku Jack, who learned silversmithing while living in Haida Gwaii for four years. Yukon Archives, Atlin Historical Society Collection, 82/432, #27.

from British Columbia so that it could be set aside as a reserve for the Atlin band. In the face of continued opposition by the Atlin Board of Trade, however, British Columbia refused its request. Only in 1985 was a small reserve set aside on part of the Wenah village site for the band, now known as the Taku River Tlingit First Nation. In 2006, as well, the Indian Claims Commission found that Canada had breached its fiduciary duty to the Taku River Tlingit when it failed to set aside the Wenah village site as a reserve in 1916, based in part on its determination that the land in question in fact had not been purchased by the priest and was not private property at the time of the McKenna-McBride Commission's visit.[85]

Like Indigenous peoples along the forty-ninth parallel, the Tlingit were forced to choose between an identity as American or Canadian Indians and to surrender, without compensation, those parts of their original homelands that lay across the boundary that divided Canada and the United States.[86] In 1984, Canada accepted, for purposes of treaty negotiation, the provincial transboundary claim of the Taku River Tlingit First Nation to an area centered around Atlin Lake that extended south to the Stikine River and north into the Yukon where it includes Little Atlin Lake.[87] The western boundary of their claim, however, followed the rigid contours of the U.S.-Canada border, which, in effect, had severed any claims that the Taku River Tlingit previously had to areas west of the survey line. That their traditional territories did extend across the U.S.-Canada border is suggested by the fact that the B.C. government first identified the Taku River Tlingit as American Indians, a designation that would have allowed Canada to take the position that it owed them no special obligation. Indian Agent W. Scott Simpson informed B.C. officials in 1911, however, that these reports were in error. Records that described them as American Indians, he explained, were based on the fact that the Atlin Indians spent part of each year in Juneau, Alaska, where they traveled each summer to trade with the coastal Tlingit.[88] Ironically, the fact that they regularly traveled the ninety miles between Atlin and Juneau along the route that led up Taku Inlet and the north fork of the Taku River to a point where there was a short portage to Atlin Lake may explain why Atlin's Board of Trade told members of the McKenna-McBride Commission in 1916 that plans were underway to build a railway that would connect Atlin and Juneau.[89] In fact, no such railway was ever built. Far from becoming the booming town that the Board of Trade had predicted it would, Atlin today remains a small village accessible only by a narrow road some 100 miles in length that connects the northwestern corner of British Columbia to Whitehorse in the Yukon Territory. Juneau, in turn, remains accessible only by sea and, now, by air.

Scales of Exclusion

The efforts of both the U.S. and Canadian governments to open Indigenous territories to settlement went hand in hand with efforts to ensure that a majority of those who settled there were not of Asian descent. Focused in part on restricting the number of immigrants from Asia permitted to enter each country, both also denied access to the full rights of citizenship even to those who were admitted. The ability of Indigenous people in Canada to freely cross the U.S.-Canada border into the United States was protected to a degree by what was known as the Jay Treaty, into which Britain and the United States had entered in 1794.[90] Indigenous people on both sides of the border, however, also found themselves subject to closer inspection at ports of entry established by both Canada and the United States to monitor border crossings and, increasingly, to enforce exclusionary laws and policies targeting Asian migrants.[91] Although Chief Taku Jack's testimony before the McKenna-McBride Commission confirms that there were Japanese miners working on Atlin's creeks by 1915, the overall number of Japanese laborers permitted to enter the United States and Canada dropped significantly after each nation entered into Gentlemen's Agreements with Japan in 1907. Unlawful race-based efforts to exclude were directly implicated in both agreements. The U.S. Gentlemen's Agreement was the result of the diplomatic negotiations that followed the 1906 expulsion of Japanese and Korean students from San Francisco schools attended by Euro-American children and requiring them instead to attend those set aside for Chinese and African American children—developments that were closely followed in Alaska.[92] Canada's agreement, also known as the Hayashi-Lemieux Agreement, followed in the wake of the 1907 Vancouver Riot.[93] Although William Lyon Mackenzie King, appointed to investigate the causes of the riot, awarded damages to Japanese immigrants whose property was damaged, he also assured U.S. officials that Canada would limit further immigration from Japan even before his investigation was complete and told a colleague afterward that he believed that "the Japanese government was deliberately 'Japanesing' the Pacific."[94] Meiji officials feared that the anti-Japanese hostility manifested in both events might be written into law in a form targeting Japanese similar to the 1882 Chinese Exclusion Act in the United States or the Chinese head tax implemented in Canada in 1885.[95] In both Gentlemen's Agreements, the Meiji government agreed, with limited exceptions, to issue passports allowing its subjects to travel to the United States or Canada only to former residents and their immediate relatives. The United States made an exception for "settled agriculturalists," while Canada agreed to the entry of "merchants, officers, students and travelers," together with four hundred labor migrants a year.[96] Although the Anglo-Japanese Alliance had guaranteed Japanese subjects "full liberty to enter, travel and reside in any part of the Dominion of Canada," Meiji officials agreed not to insist on the "complete enjoyment of the rights and privileges" provided under the treaty.[97]

While efforts by both nations to enforce the Gentlemen's Agreements focused on barring Japanese immigrants who did not fit the permitted categories at national borders, they coincided with measures to exclude those who had lawfully entered the United States and Canada from the political process, also entangled in turn with parallel endeavors to limit Indigenous participation in the same. Although Canada and the United States had similar goals in this regard, differences in the constitutional structure of the two countries made it necessary for each to adopt different kinds of legal mechanisms to give form to shared prejudices premised on the purported inability of Asian immigrants and Indigenous people to responsibly exercise the full rights of citizenship. While the United States denied first-generation Japanese immigrants the opportunity to become naturalized citizens, it was precluded by the Fourteenth and Fifteenth Amendments from denying all children born in the United States either citizenship or the right to vote on grounds of race.[98] Canada's status as a British dominion limited its power to deny Asian immigrants the ability to be naturalized as British subjects.[99] B.C. officials, however, protested that British Columbia's "geographical contiguity to Japan" rendered it "more vulnerable to the effects of unchecked immigration" from Asia than other provinces and insisted that the province had the power to deny them the vote.[100] Given that there was no provision in the British North America Act—Canada's constitution—equivalent to the Fourteenth and Fifteenth Amendments of the U.S. Constitution, they argued, British Columbia had the power to deny the vote to naturalized British subjects born in Japan, even though it lacked the power to deny them access to naturalization.

In 1895, although there were fewer than 130 naturalized Japanese immigrants in British Columbia at the time, the B.C. legislature amended its Provincial Voters Act to provide that "no Chinaman, Japanese, or Indian shall have his name placed on the Register of Voters for any Electoral District" in British Columbia.[101] "Japanese," as used in the act, however, referred not only to "any native of the Japanese Empire or its dependencies not born to British parents" but also to "any person of the Japanese race, naturalized or not." It was a constraint, in short, based not just on national origin but on race that applied both to naturalized British subjects born in Japan and to their Canadian-born children, notwithstanding that they were British subjects by virtue of their birth in a British dominion.[102] "Indian," as used in the Provincial Voters Act, in turn, referred not to South Asians, who would be written into the act as "Hindus" when it was amended in 1907, but to "any [Indigenous] person of pure Indian blood." Not only was this a category that, on its face, was based purely on race alone, but it failed to take into account the provisions of Canada's Indian Act, which determined Indian status and provided for both the voluntary and the involuntary enfranchisement of some Indigenous people. Included among those who could be involuntarily enfranchised, regardless what their own choice may have been, were Indigenous men who earned university degrees, became members of the clergy, or were admitted to the practice of law or medicine.[103]

That B.C. officials saw the bars against participation in the political process that applied to people of Asian ancestry and Indigenous people as mutually reinforcing is apparent from the concern expressed by British Columbia's attorney general, D. M. Eberts, that rescinding voting restrictions that applied to naturalized Japanese might also lead to the erosion of legal barriers against the admission of "Indians" to the provincial franchise.[104] In 1902, even as Eberts cautioned Atlin officials that there was no lawful way to prevent the impending arrival of the Japanese miners recruited to work on its creeks, he was vigorously defending the discriminatory provisions of the Provincial Voters Act in British Columbia's courts. The case in question was an appeal from the decision of a lower court overturning these provisions in a test case brought by a naturalized British subject born in Japan and resident in British Columbia.

In October 1900, Tomekichi Homma, a naturalized British subject who had immigrated to Canada in 1883, filed suit against the registrar of voters after he rebuffed Homma's attempt to register to vote. Although the B.C. courts held, based on the law as it existed at the time, that the province did not have the power to discriminate among naturalized British subjects based on race, Eberts was determined that the British Privy Council, then the final arbiter of cases arising out of Canada, should overturn their decisions. The lower court rulings were problematic, Eberts argued, not only because they allowed Japanese immigrants to vote, but because they threatened to weaken the barrier against "Indian" participation in the political process. While the power to deny the vote to status Indians might appear clear based on the provisions of the Indian Act, he urged, an "anomalous" situation might arise where British Columbia "could legally withhold the franchise from the Indian race, born British subjects," but immigrants born in Japan who were naturalized British subjects could vote. The issue was more complicated in Canada than in the United States, he advised, because Indians in Canada were deemed British subjects, whereas in the United States they were not considered citizens.[105]

The Dominion government intervened on Homma's behalf when the appeal was heard by the British Privy Council, arguing, in part, that British Columbia's denial of the franchise was "calculated to create complications between the British and Japanese Nations." British Columbia's Provincial Voters Act, Canada pointed out, sought to impose "a perpetual exclusion from the electoral franchise" on "naturalized aliens of the Japanese race, on the score of their alien origin alone," even though they were entitled to "all the privileges of natural-born British subjects" by virtue of the fact that they had

met all of the conditions for naturalization.[106] Chief Justice Angus John Mc-
Coll, who first heard the case sitting as a county court judge on November 29,
1900, in Vancouver, had also expressed concern that, as written, the Provincial
Voters Act would establish a racialized divide that would split male British
subjects in British Columbia into two separate groups, one of which would be
deprived, from that time forward, of fundamental rights afforded to the other.
Ironically, however, he read the risk that this posed not against those who had
engineered this divide but against those who would be denied the right to participate in the political process, marking them—rather than their exclusion
from participation in the governance of the communities in which they
lived—as a potential menace to society. In the judge's words, "The existence in
the province of large numbers of persons, British subjects in name, but
doomed to perpetual exclusion from any part in the passage of legislation af-
fecting their property or civil rights, would surely not be to the advantage of
Canada, and might even become a source of national danger."[107]

The Privy Council, in contrast, treated the perpetual nature of the racial
divide created by the Provincial Voters Act as a matter of little, if any, consequence. Although it observed that the discriminatory provisions of the act
would affect not just naturalized Japanese immigrants but also their descendants who were "natural-born subjects of the King," it overturned the decisions of the B.C. courts and upheld the Provincial Voters Act as written.[108]
The Privy Council did not address the long-term consequences of its decision. Instead, it drew on language it extracted from a U.S. legal treatise that
predated the post–Civil War Fourteenth and Fifteenth Amendments and reflected the United States' own peculiar history of race and slavery, to uphold
British Columbia's power to discriminate among naturalized British subjects.[109] Eberts's warning that the failure to uphold the discriminatory provisions of the Provincial Voters Act would establish a precedent that could be
used to erode the bar against the active participation of Indigenous peoples
in the governance of their own homelands may well have factored into its
decision given the implications of such a ruling for Britain's colonies in other
parts of the world. Among them were India, Australia, New Zealand, and the
colony of Natal, to which British Columbia had already looked to craft the language tests it had passed in an effort to expel Japanese immigrants even after
they were lawfully admitted to Canada.[110]

Where Britain had long deemed the Indigenous people of territories it occupied British subjects, it had long been assumed in the United States that
Indigenous people living within its borders were not U.S. citizens given that
they remained citizens of what it acknowledged at the time of its founding

were quasi-independent tribes and nations.[111] The 1866 adoption of the same Fourteenth Amendment that ensured that the children of Japanese immigrants born in the United States could not be denied citizenship, however, had simultaneously raised the question of whether Indigenous people born within the borders of the United States were also U.S. citizens. In 1887, the Dawes Act laid out a process for the admission to U.S. citizenship of "Indians" who had severed their ties to tribal communities and otherwise met its requirements for demonstrating that they were "civilized." Like the voluntary enfranchisement provisions of Canada's 1876 Indian Act, the Dawes Act provided for a probationary period that, if successfully completed, resulted in an allotment of land to that individual.[112] On both sides of the U.S.-Canada border, however, many preferred not to avail themselves of these provisions.

Ambiguous as the status of Indigenous people living in the contiguous states was after passage of the Fourteenth Amendment, that of Alaska's Indigenous people was more uncertain still. The failure of the United States to recognize Indigenous people in Alaska as "Indians" who had clearly established rights by virtue of the fact that they were its original occupants proved to be an even more effective tool in facilitating both their marginalization and the appropriation of their homelands. The United States' 1867 treaty with Russia, carefully written out in longhand, had left open the question of what responsibilities were owed to Alaska's Indigenous peoples by the United States following its acquisition of Russian interests in Alaska. Article III of the treaty provided that "inhabitants of the ceded territory" who chose not to return to Russia were to "be admitted to the enjoyment of all the rights, advantages, and immunities of citizens of the United States, and shall be maintained and protected in the free enjoyment of their liberty, property, and religion." It made an exception, however, for those it characterized as "uncivilized native tribes," who were instead to "be subject to such laws and regulations as the United States may, from time to time, adopt in regard to aboriginal tribes in that country."[113]

The treaty's failure to adequately account for the rights of Alaska's Indigenous peoples, together with Alaska's status as a district, enabled U.S. government officials to take the position that they were not entitled to any of the special protections that applied to "Indians" elsewhere in the United States.[114] Recognized neither as U.S. citizens nor as Indians, and denied both the ability to participate in the governance of their territories and to secure title of any kind to their homelands, Alaska's Indigenous people were, if anything, even more vulnerable to colonial intrusion than those of the contiguous states.[115] It was not until 1924, when the U.S. Indian Citizenship Act was extended to Alaska, that Alaska's Indigenous people were, like others within the borders of the United States, summarily declared to be U.S. citizens. Although the Indian Citizenship Act did not require the severance of tribal relations as the Dawes Act had, however, many Indigenous people regarded the unilateral imposition of citizenship not as a welcome acknowledgment of their fundamental equality, but as the culmination of the U.S. government's long-standing effort to erase both their presence and their identity as independent peoples living within what were now the boundaries of the United States.[116]

In the same year that it unilaterally admitted all Indigenous people within its borders to citizenship, ironically, the United States also passed the Immigration Act of 1924, abrogating its Gentlemen's Agreement with Japan and barring "aliens ineligible for citizenship." This was a move that was expressly intended to target Japanese subjects given that most other Asians were already subject to exclusion based on both the Chinese Exclusion Act and the Immigration Act of 1917, which had created an Asiatic Barred Zone that included much of the rest of Asia.[117] Canada had itself amended the Hayashi-Lemieux Agreement just one year earlier in 1923 to reduce the number of Japanese labor immigrants to be admitted annually to just 150.[118] By 1924, in short, Japanese immigration to North America had been brought to a virtual standstill. These newly imposed restrictions, some Japanese believed, were deliberately timed to take advantage of the "great blow" that Japan had sustained in 1923 when large areas in Tokyo and Yokohama were devastated by the Great Kanto earthquake.[119]

Members of Congress who supported passage of the 1924 Immigration Act had argued that there was no reason to "admit those who by law cannot become naturalized," an issue that had finally been decided by the U.S. Supreme Court in 1922 in the case *Ozawa v. United States*, which had held that Japanese were precluded from applying for naturalization under U.S. law because they were not "free white persons."[120] The plaintiff, Takao Ozawa, had argued in the alternative, ironically, that Japanese immigrants should not be excluded from U.S. citizenship because they were "white" within the meaning of the 1790 Naturalization Act, given that they were descended from Japan's Indigenous people, the Ainu, categorized by anthropologists of the time as a "Caucasoid race."[121] This, he reasoned *inter alia*, meant that Japanese were not "Mongolian" and subject to exclusion on that basis as U.S. courts had held. It was an argument that the Supreme Court rejected and that some Japanese immigrants had urged him not to make, based in part on an abiding concern that Japanese not be conflated with people—the Ainu—whom they themselves continued to regard as uncivilized.[122]

Defending Japanese Immigrants

Faced with tightening restrictions on both sides of the U.S.-Canada border, Japanese diplomats endeavored to defend Japanese immigrants in part by comparing them to Indigenous peoples in both Canada and the United States, tailoring the arguments directed at each nation to its particular concerns. Like their U.S. and Canadian counterparts, Japanese writers and officials subscribed to the notion that large parts of their territories were uncultivated lands devoid of any meaningful Indigenous presence. On the Canadian side of the border, they invoked unfavorable perceptions of the United States held by Canadians. Whereas the United States was "essentially akin to a wholesale market of European peoples," wrote one Japanese advocate of emigration to Canada in 1888, there was "a heaven-sent, earthly paradise in the region of Canada with its far-extending mountains and rivers and endless prairies where the Japanese, free from competition, can work with their minds at ease."[123] In 1897, the Japanese consul in Vancouver, B.C., Nosse Tatsugoro, argued that northern Japanese were better suited than European immigrants to settle the Canadian northwest owing to racial characteristics that were a product of centuries of exposure to natural disasters in northern Japan, where the Tohoku region regularly experienced both tidal waves and extreme cold. This had made them more robust and capable of coping with Canada's harsh environment. In Nosse's words,

> [Japanese from the northern provinces of Japan] are hardy; they have strong bodies and a high stature; and they are accustomed to hardship. You have heard of the great tidal waves which sweep the coast of Japan at certain points, carrying desolation in their path? Well, this occurs in the neighborhood of these northern people. And do you know what they do? They leave the flat lands and cultivate the hillsides . . . [where] they extract crops of wheat, and millet, and apples and prunes. Now, these are the people for your Northwest. They are thrifty; they are strong; they are peaceable; and they can endure both cold and heat.[124]

Given that British Columbia was the first Canadian province that Japanese immigrants crossing the Pacific Ocean came upon, it was "natural" that they should settle the west coast of Canada, K. T. Takahashi, a self-described Japanese-Canadian, argued the same year. Japanese settlers were not responsible for the reluctance of British and other European immigrants east of the Rockies to incur the added expense of traveling to British Columbia to find work, he added. Given that British Columbia comprised a "vast area of 450,000 square miles" and had a population of just "60,000 whites and 30,000 Indians," Takahashi declared, "the presence of some eight or nine hundred Japanese scattered here and there" throughout the province could hardly disturb other settlers, nor were Japanese numerous enough to prevent European immigrants from finding jobs as some anti-Japanese agitators claimed.[125] It was Americans and not Japanese who posed the greatest danger to British Columbia and to Canada itself, Takahashi argued. "The real and most serious enemy to the bread-winners of British Columbia," he wrote, were "those predatory aliens other than Japanese who freely cross and recross the boundary line and carry all their earnings away into the American side." "As aliens," Takahashi added, noting how readily race allowed some also to cross the conceptual boundary that divided citizen from subject, "they have no right of fishing in Canadian waters, but when the season opens along the Fraser, I am told, they come and with remarkable dispatch make themselves qualified Canadians."[126] Inspector of fisheries for the Dominion government Colin B. Sword agreed with Takahashi's observation regarding the ease with which American fishers represented themselves as Canadians, conceding that it was "very difficult to tell an American citizen. If he denys [sic] his citizenship we have no means of proving otherwise."[127]

Japanese in Canada should not allow the unjust race-based constraints they faced in British Columbia to impede their progress, the editors of the *Tairiku Nippō* (Continental Daily News), a Japanese-language newspaper based in Vancouver, B.C., urged in 1909, encouraging them to consider provinces east of the Rockies that had not adopted similar discriminatory measures. "Spread before us," they wrote, "are fertile plains and dense forests stretching far and wide across thousands of miles and blessed by heaven with an abundance of natural resources, over half of which have not been cultivated or even fully explored. Beyond the Rocky Mountains along B.C.'s eastern border lie the provinces of Alberta, Saskatchewan and Manitoba, [all of] which are awaiting our advance."[128] It was to Canada's advantage to admit Japanese, Nakayama added. "Canada is a vast country, geographically speaking, her land is rich, and her weather is not . . . always inhospitable. There are a lot of trackless virgin forests as well as many unexcavated mines in the interior regions where no human being has ever set foot and which have been waiting to be explored and developed for a long time. With active efforts of our Japanese immigrants, who have a reputation for diligent and hard work, further development of Canada can be clearly anticipated."[129] Traveling across Canada three decades later, Takeo Ujo Nakano would remember how "astonished [he was] at the vastness of the land" as the train on which he was riding crossed its prairies where "a thousand miles could be taken in at a glance." "If countries with surplus land kept out the people of countries with too little land [like Japan]," he asked, should that not be regarded as a crime?[130]

On the U.S. side of the international border, Baron Rempei Kondo, president of a major steamship company that stopped in Seattle, reminded Americans in 1914 that despite the large numbers of immigrants the United States had absorbed during recent decades, land in much of the west, and particularly along the Pacific coast, was still waiting to be broken. If the United States was serious about transforming this landscape, it was imperative that it admit Japanese agriculturalists. They were especially well suited to the task, he argued, precisely because they asked for little in return and did not demand high wages. While he characterized them as "generally belong[ing] to the lower classes" and admitted that their "customs, manners, and habits [were] different from those of the Americans," he also insisted that they were "honest at heart and work[ed] earnestly," which should render any questions regarding their assimilability moot. Their hard work, Kondo argued, would "facilitat[e] the opening up of the land and increas[e] the blessings of nature to both [the United States and Japan]."[131]

Notwithstanding the arguments made by Japanese scholars and diplomats for an equal role for Japanese immigrants in colonizing the U.S. West, by 1913 California and other western states began to pass the alien land laws that denied first-generation Japanese immigrants the ability to buy, and later even to lease, the land they cultivated.[132] Arguing against the passage of alien land laws, Count Seiichiro Terashima, a highly regarded diplomat and member of Japan's House of Peers, pointed to the size of the reservations set aside for Indigenous peoples, noting that Japanese immigrants required no such accommodation. They were also far fewer in number than the "Indians" who had been settled on reserves. The fifty thousand Japanese in the Pacific states, he declared, amounted to "[just] one fifth of the Red Indians whom America is generous enough to let alone in their reservations. That she is so hard upon the Japanese as to deprive them of their land and the right to own land, is a matter that I can hardly understand." Millions of European immigrants had immigrated to the United States since the 1830s, Terashima reasoned, with the result that it "now comprise[d] quite a number of small Italies, small Syrias, [and] small Jerusalems." Surely there was room for the people of one more nation among the "many vortexes of nationality … whirling in the human sea of America." It was the "Red Indians," after all, who were originally the "masters of [the] land" that they all wished to have a hand in cultivating and not for any immigrant group to exclude any other latecomers.[133] Other Japanese intellectuals extended this argument to include all white settler nations, arguing that Japanese subjects also deserved access to regions in other parts of the world regarded as "empty" and uncultivated. Critical as they were of the displacement of Indigenous peoples by white settlers, ironically, they also imagined these areas as devoid of Indigenous inhabitants. In the words of Professor Ryutaro Nagai of Waseda University, "in Australia, South America, Canada and the United States (all white-man lands, observed) [sic] are vast tracts of unoccupied territory, yet no yellow people are permitted to enter. To seize the greater part of the earth and refuse to share it, is so manifestly unjust that it cannot continue."[134]

Japan as a Colonial Power

Disapproving as Japanese diplomats and scholars were of the ways in which the United States and other white settler nations treated Indigenous people, the Meiji government's policy toward the Ainu in Hokkaido and the Indigenous people of Taiwan paralleled that of the United States and Canada in significant respects. Among the three thousand Western advisers recruited by Meiji authorities during the 1870s in conjunction with Japan's determined effort to modernize and to secure the removal of the unequal treaties imposed on Japan during the 1850s, fifty were hired to advise the Meiji government with regard to the colonial development of Hokkaido and the legal status of the Ainu.[135] While scholars have emphasized the Meiji government's reliance on U.S. advisers, it looked not only to the United States but also to other Western nations, including Britain and France, in determining what colonial models would best serve what they regarded as Japan's own particular needs.[136] Primarily focused on developing the resource and agricultural potential of Hokkaido, the first law promulgated by the imperial government to integrate Ainu territories within a broader legal framework was the Jisho Kisoku (Land Regulation Ordinance) of 1872, which treated all of Hokkaido as *terra nullius*.[137]

In March 1899, the Meiji government passed the Hokkaido Kyūdojin Hogo Hō (Hokkaido Former Natives Protection Act). It granted the Ainu no special status, providing instead that they would thereafter be treated as commoners who might be awarded land grants of a certain size on the condition that they adopt Japanese agricultural practices.[138] The Hokkaido Kyūdojin Hogo Hō, in short, incorporated a strategy intended to facilitate their assimilation that utilized a mechanism not unlike that established by the 1887 Dawes Act. Much as the U.S. and Canadian governments did, Meiji officials justified their seizure of Ainu lands by characterizing the Ainu as a backward people in need of "protection," as the reference to "protection" in the title of the Hokkaido Kyūdojin Hogo Hō makes clear. Use of the term *kyūdojin* ("former *dojin*") reflects the negative attitudes of Meiji-era Japanese toward the Ainu.[139] At the same time, the characterization of the Ainu as "former *dojin*" erased any rights to which they might have been entitled had their status as Indigenous people continued to be recognized within a more evolved colonial framework. Only in 1912 did the Kaitakushi (Colonization Board) set aside a few small occupied village sites for the Ainu to use.[140] The Meiji government's approach in Hokkaido, as such, more closely paralleled that adopted in British Columbia and Alaska than in other parts of North America, where both Canada and the United States recognized the existence of Aboriginal title and the need to enter into treaties with Indigenous people.[141]

In contrast to its approach to the Ainu in Hokkaido, the Meiji government adopted a more overtly aggressive approach to the Indigenous people of Taiwan, modeling its approach on other aspects of U.S. and Canadian colonial policy.[142] Meiji colonial authorities essentially treated Taiwan's mountainous interior, into which its Indigenous people retreated in an effort to resist Japanese colonization, as a reservation, albeit one they were permitted to leave only when they were prepared to adopt Japanese customs and lifeways. While the pass system implemented by the Canadian government across the prairies forbade Indigenous people on reserves to leave without its permission,[143] Japanese colonial officials adopted a still harsher approach in Taiwan, using reservation boundaries in unprecedented ways to force its Indigenous people to assimilate. Writing in 1912, Inazo Nitobe, who served as a technical adviser for the Japanese Colonial Bureau of Industries in Taiwan between 1901 and 1904, explained that Meiji colonial administrators built an electrified fence around the reserve, both to prevent those within from leaving until they agreed to stop resisting colonial settlement and to deny them access to salt. Each year, he explained, the wire fence was moved several miles inland, a move that also facilitated the development of the camphor industry outside reservation boundaries.[144] When Japan first acquired the colony of Taiwan, Nitobe explained, the cost of colonial administration greatly exceeded the financial benefit derived by Japan from its newly acquired colony, but in just two decades its development of Taiwan's camphor, tea, rice, and sugar industries meant that the colony now paid for itself. Not only did this Japanese colony compare favorably to those of European powers, he declared, but it provided a model for any other colonies that Japan might acquire. In contrast to European colonial administrators, Japanese were willing to embrace the Indigenous people of Taiwan as brothers if they emerged from the hills, Nitobe wrote. Not only did Japan's colonial administration provide for their education, assimilation, and "Japanization," but it also offered them "protection of property and life." Consistent with the obligations of any colonizing power, he added, it also taught them "good government" and promulgated what it deemed to be "good laws."[145]

Given Japan's own historical experience as a target of Western imperialism just five decades earlier, its positioning of itself as a civilizing power in its own right served the dual purpose of countering any further efforts by Western imperial powers to impose colonial constraints on Japan itself or on other areas of Asia under Japan's control.[146] At the same time, Japan's very success not just in emulating but in "improving" on the expansionist and colonial practices of Britain, Canada, and the United States would, paradoxically, serve only to reinforce the suspicion with which its actions and those of its subjects who immigrated to areas along the north Pacific coast came to be viewed. During the early decades of the twentieth century, both British Columbia and the United States would continue to use the constraints each had imposed on access to the full rights of citizenship to limit Japanese access to key resources, including the rapidly expanding fisheries along the north Pacific coast. The resulting contest, in turn, would increasingly bring the United States, Canada, and Japan into direct conflict with one another.

CHAPTER FOUR

Borders at Sea

Appearing before the Royal Commission on Chinese and Japanese Immigration in 1901, William Munsie, the captain of a commercial sealing vessel based in Victoria, B.C., testified that the Japanese he had hired in recent years were "good sailor men, and trustworthy." Most sealing vessels hired twenty-four men, he reported, roughly half of whom were Indigenous and as many as four or five Japanese. Even vessels owned or captained by Indigenous men often hired one or two Japanese as sailors.[1] There was no task aboard a sealing vessel that Japanese could not do, he added, but they were never hired as hunters. Instead, those hired as hunters were Indigenous men or, on occasion, whites. Although there were Japanese hunters on Japanese vessels that operated off the coast of Japan, Munsie noted, there were none on vessels that operated along the Pacific coast of North America, "not even on Japanese schooners."[2]

Munsie's testimony reveals that valued though they were as "excellent sailors," Japanese occupied an ambiguous place aboard the commercial sealing vessels operating off the northwest coast of North America at the turn of the twentieth century. Racialized boundaries cut across the crews of the sealing vessels and ordered the spaces on board ship in ways that both reflected traditional shipboard hierarchies and shifted according to the mix of men on board. Generally, Munsie testified, Indigenous hunters lived in the forecastle and the captain and other white men lived and ate together aft. When there were three "distinct races" on board, Japanese sailors lived "aft . . . with the white men," but when there were "four distinct races" on board, the fourth being men of African descent, Indigenous hunters and boat pullers, often Japanese, ate with them at the forward end of the vessel, while the mate and sailors, who might also include Japanese, ate in the aft cabin. When white hunters were hired, however, sailors and Japanese ate together in the forecastle regardless of their role aboard the vessel, while the white hunters lived and ate aft with the captain and mate.[3]

As Munsie's comments reflect, race, class, and skill worked together to structure power relations on board ship and to apportion the tasks that enabled them to operate at sea.[4] That race was assigned the greatest weight aboard commercial sealing vessels was reflected not only in the ways that space was structured and restructured depending on the mix of men on board but also in Munsie's somewhat puzzling statement, notwithstanding his regard for the Japanese sailors he had hired over the years, that he "would be in favour of their exclusion," a comment that appears to have been prompted by a question posed by one of the commissioners before whom he was testifying.[5] Munsie's observation that Japanese never served as hunters even on the Japanese-owned vessels that operated along the north Pacific coast also suggests, however, that the social barriers that divided men on board sealing vessels were not determined by race alone. Reluctance on the part of Japanese to participate in the butchering or skinning of seals and sea lions may also have been a product of cultural taboos rooted in Japanese history that marked those who engaged in the butchering of animals or work with animal hides as "outcastes" during the Tokugawa era—taboos that persisted well into the early decades of the twentieth century among Japanese immigrants in North America.[6]

Traditional assumptions associated with historical status categories in Meiji Japan were also challenged in myriad ways, however, by the nature of the work demanded of Japanese labor migrants not just on sealing vessels but in the canneries and at whaling stations along the Pacific coast. One young woman, proud of her samurai ancestry, emigrated to Canada based on the conviction that women were treated better in North America than in Japan, married a Japanese immigrant who had settled there, and found herself living at a whaling station at Rose Harbour on Haida Gwaii, where her husband worked in the whale oil processing plant. They lived in tar shacks on the beach, she recalled, and "smelled of sweaty clothes and whale blubber." Among those they worked alongside was an older couple named Kosaka, graduates of a teachers college in Kagoshima who joked that "their education had paved the way for [them] to sweat it out in a blubber factory."[7] Work at a whaling station was not what she had imagined her life in Canada would entail, nor was work aboard a sealing vessel what other young Japanese migrants dreamed of when they ventured across the Pacific. In the words of one young man who had been hired on as a chef aboard a sealing schooner:

> Burning with high hopes
> I came to America
> Only to be cook
> On an Alaskan schooner
> Ploughing through high waves.[8]

Global Contexts

Building on the global connections first forged by the hunting of whales and sea otters, the fur seal industry came to link what Europeans had once regarded as a remote and unknown area of the Pacific to cities in Europe, Asia, and North America, among them London, Canton, and St. Louis, Missouri, where hides were processed and then redistributed at the International Fur Exchange.[9] Like the whaling industry, the pelagic sealing industry had drawn European mariners into the far reaches of the North Pacific Ocean, where a ruthless and unrelenting hunt for seals and sea lions unfolded across its entire rim from the mid-eighteenth century on.[10] The quest for fur seal and sea otter pelts triggered Russia's incorporation of Alaska within its imperial boundaries in 1799, half a century after Vitus Bering sailed into the fifty-three-mile wide strait that separates Eurasia from North America and bears his name.[11] U.S. interest in dominating the pelagic sealing industry, in turn, was a key motivation for its acquisition of Russian interests in Alaska in 1867. Britain's interest in the North Pacific sealing industry, likewise, helps to explain its determination to preserve its continental access to the Pacific Ocean by retaining British Columbia among its imperial possessions at the time.[12]

The relentless quest for seals and sea lions exacerbated tensions between Britain and the United States during the decades that followed. In the mid-1880s, even though British sealing vessels based in Victoria, B.C., had operated in the Bering Sea without objection for nearly two decades, the United States "laid claim to exclusive jurisdiction in the Bering Sea," arguing that it was a *mare clausum*, or "closed sea," to which British vessels did not have access. Britain insisted that "the Bering Sea was a part of the high seas." The United States brought the issue to a head by seizing several Victoria-based sealing vessels operating in the Bering Sea in 1886 and 1887. The arbitration tribunal asked to resolve the dispute in 1893 sided with Britain, ruling that the Bering Sea was not a closed sea. But it also limited sealing operations in the Bering Sea to six weeks or so a year and established a protected zone that extended sixty miles out to sea in the area around the Pribilof Islands. It also extended far beyond them, including the "whole waters of the North Pacific Ocean washing the shores of North America" and reaching "from those shores across the ocean to the 180th meridian, an area which covered practically 5,000,000 square miles of open ocean," where seals could be found. While only Britain and the United States were bound by the ruling, it would soon become the foundation for claims that a rapidly industrializing Japan, which shared with Britain and the United States a keen interest in both the ocean- and

land-based resources of the North Pacific Rim, acted illegally in not comply-
ing with its provisions.[13]

The growing pressure Japan would bring to bear on the rookeries of the
central Pacific during the first half of the twentieth century mirrored the
pressure brought to bear on its own northern coasts during previous decades. Beginning in the mid-1800s, British and American ships had aggres-
sively pursued both whales and sea otters along the coasts of the Kuril Islands
and in the waters around Hokkaido. One master of the hunt, Henry James Snow,
would later write that this was what triggered Japan's own interest in developing deep sea fisheries. By the 1900s, Japanese vessels had begun to venture far
out into the eastern Pacific, probing the waters off the coasts of Alaska and
British Columbia in search not only of whales and fur seals but also of salmon
and other fish that could sustain deep sea fisheries.[14] The fact that the seal
and sea otter rookeries along Japan's northern coasts had been all but destroyed by British and American hunters during earlier decades may well
have justified, for at least some Japanese, the extension of their own hunting
activities into the waters of the eastern Pacific.[15]

Although the pelagic sealing industry began to wane toward the end of the
nineteenth century, with the result that Victoria, B.C., no longer served as its
center to the degree it once had, the sealing industry would remain a focal
point in the contest over the marine resources of the North Pacific between
the United States, Britain, and Japan throughout the early decades of the
twentieth century. The same was true of a range of new industrial-scale
fisheries that evolved in response to the demands of an ever more closely
interconnected global market, among them the salmon, herring, and halibut
fisheries—all resources on which the Indigenous peoples of the north Pacific
coast had relied for millennia.[16] The development of these new fisheries, in
turn, attracted growing numbers of labor migrants from around the world.
Both travel and capital, as a result, would increasingly connect British Columbia and Alaska to Mexico, Central America, Peru, and Chile, as well as,
across the Pacific Ocean, to Japan, China, the Philippines, and Australia.

Transpacific Shipping Routes

The emergence of industrial-scale fisheries along the B.C. and Alaska coasts,
together with a growing demand for labor in the canneries and other emerging industries, encouraged the rapid development of transpacific shipping. By
1891, the Canadian Pacific Railway (CPR) coordinated its operations with
those of the Royal Mail Steamship Lines in Vancouver, B.C., establishing the
CPR, in the eyes of its promoters, as "the great highway across the continent

to and from Europe, Japan, China, Australasia and around the world."[17] Regular steamer service from Yokohama to Seattle was established in 1896, allowing passengers on Japan's Nihon Yusen Kaisha, or NYK Line, to connect with the Great Northern Railway in Seattle and to ports further south along the coast.[18] Direct steamship service soon linked both Vancouver and Seattle with "Hawaii, Fiji, New Zealand and Australia; with China and Japan; with San Francisco [and] with Alaska and Northern gold fields."[19] By 1901, the Toronto *Globe* informed its readers that the "intermittent coastal steamboat" of earlier days had been "displaced by the scores of liners carrying on the immense coastwise traffic of the North Pacific Ocean."[20] The increase in ocean-going ships worried some B.C. newspapermen. While the new shipping lines facilitated travel between North America and Asia, Vancouver's *Daily Province* warned in 1907, it also meant that Japanese would now be "coming as fast as passage can be obtained for them."[21]

North of Seattle and Vancouver, Juneau and Prince Rupert, located on either side of the Alaska-B.C. border, became critical ports of call for the oceangoing steamers that plied the coastal waters of the North Pacific, including whalers, fishing fleets, and naval vessels patrolling the area. As members of Congress observed in 1890, Juneau was a critical link in the ocean route from "Puget Sound to all the principal canneries, settlements and mining camps of southeastern Alaska."[22] On the B.C. side of the border, Prince Rupert emerged as Canada's northernmost port along the route up the coast and across the Pacific to Japan. Given the curvature of the earth, *The Globe* reported in 1901, Prince Rupert was four hundred miles closer to Asia than Vancouver was. "With the world-wide development of Chinese and Japanese trade, and the opening of Russian ports of commerce on the Pacific," *The Globe* predicted, the transpacific trade would certainly, "before many years rival, if not indeed eventually exceed, the gigantic traffic of the Atlantic."[23] Both Canadian and Japanese promoters were convinced that when the Grand Trunk Pacific was completed, Prince Rupert, its terminus, would outstrip Vancouver as the major port on the north Pacific coast and develop close trading ties with Japan. In 1921, Nakayama Jinshiro reported that Mitsui, one of the leading *zaibatsu* (conglomerates) in Japan, was just one of several Japanese enterprises that had planned to establish direct shipping routes between Japan and Prince Rupert as soon as this occurred.[24] Prince Rupert was located just twenty miles south of the Alaska-B.C. border on the same latitude as London, he noted, and boasted a harbor that did not freeze over in winter.[25]

The Meiji government's own keen interest in the port of Prince Rupert was reflected in the award it gave Charles Melville Hays, president of the

Grand Trunk Pacific Railway, in 1904 to express its appreciation for his efforts to build closer ties with Japan.[26] Not only would Prince Rupert provide Japan with a more direct connection to the markets of eastern North America, but it was located midway between the Skeena and the Nass Rivers, the heart of British Columbia's commercial salmon fishery along its north-central coast, and served as the working hub of the coastal lumber industry.[27] As Nakayama observed, dense forests of spruce, hemlock, balsam, and cedar extended deep into the B.C. interior. Prince Rupert was the center of the industry, however, both because it was far easier to move the timber by water than on land and because it could be loaded aboard ships bound for Nagasaki, Yokohama, Kobe, and Osaka to be shipped on to buyers in Australia, China, Germany, and France.[28] Together with Japan, itself already a major market for B.C. timber, one enthusiastic booster declared, the B.C. timber industry had "the world for a market."[29]

Labor Migrants

Indigenous people had been the first to take on the new jobs created by industrial-scale fisheries along the north Pacific coast. Just as work aboard commercial sealing vessels offered Indigenous men a chance to participate in the colonial economy, notwithstanding that the pelagic sealing industry had long depended on the appropriation of both their skills and their resources, so did work as fishermen or in the canneries and whaling stations. For many Indigenous people along the B.C. and Alaska coasts, however, wage work in the canneries was balanced by their participation in the seasonal rounds that had long played a key role in sustaining their people.[30] As a spokesperson for the Nisga'a people who live along the Nass River explained, each year began with the arrival of ooligan, followed by the arrival of herring and halibut. When spring came they planted gardens and gathered wild berries, and when the salmon runs began in late June they caught and prepared salmon in quantities that would last through winter, as they had for many centuries. Summer tasks included drying the berries they had gathered and stripping bark from trees both for food and to make mats.[31] Although the length of each season varied along the coast, the sockeye salmon run along the northern B.C. coast was at its peak in July, declining in mid-August as the coho run began, lasting through the end of September when dog salmon, valued by Japanese fishers but not by whites, began their two-month run.[32] When the sockeye and coho runs ended in late September, however, Ryuichi Yoshida, a Japanese fisher who settled in Prince Rupert, later recalled, most of those who worked in the canneries left by steamship, with Indigenous fishers and cannery workers returning to their villages and Japanese to Vancouver or Seattle.[33]

Much like the Indigenous people of the coast, Japanese migrants also comprised a fluid, mobile population that often remained connected through village or prefectural ties to kinship networks that, in their case, extended across the Pacific Ocean to Japan.[34] Given the seasonal nature of the coastal fisheries, many Japanese labor migrants moved from one industry to another on a seasonal basis throughout the year. The same men who worked aboard fishing vessels or in canneries along the north Pacific coast during the spring, summer, and fall, for example, might turn to work in the sawmills during the winter, given the demand for lumber needed in the mines and to build the railroads.[35] Takeshe Uyeyama, a Nanaimo, B.C., fisherman, later reported, for example, that for many years he and other fishermen had regularly traveled south each winter when they could not fish to work on the railways or in sawmills on the U.S. side of the border. Only when U.S. immigration officials began to enforce the border more rigorously did he settle north of the border, becoming a Japanese Canadian, even as his cousin remained in the United States and became a Japanese American.[36] At one point, some sixty people from the whaling village of Taiji worked at a sawmill in Mukilteo, located south of the border on Puget Sound in Washington State, while other Japanese immigrants commuted by ferry from their homes in Prince Rupert to work at sawmills on Haida Gwaii during the off-season.[37] There were also instances when young Japanese men hired to go to Alaska to work on the railroad opted to take cannery jobs instead, as did one man who left his job on the railroad to work in the salmon canneries at New Metlakatla, established by the Tsimshian who had emigrated to Alaska from British Columbia in the 1880s.[38]

The burgeoning number of canneries created a wide range of spaces where Indigenous people encountered Japanese immigrants on both the fishing grounds and the cannery floor all along the north Pacific coast. In some instances, the canneries displaced Indigenous villages, as did the cannery located at Klinkon, halfway between Juneau and Ketchikan.[39] At times, Japanese fishermen and cannery workers were brought in to provide additional labor when the number of Indigenous workers was not great enough to keep production lines operating, as was the case in Metlakatla, B.C., after the Tsimshian fishermen who had supplied local salmon canneries with fish moved north to Alaska.[40] In some places, Japanese migrants worked alongside Indigenous men and women in salmon canneries both in British Columbia and in southeastern Alaska.[41] In others, Indigenous people resisted the importation of Asian labor, as did the Tlingit in Sitka and Chilkat and the Alutiiq on Kodiak Island, along the south-central coast of Alaska.[42] The hiring of Japanese labor migrants also sometimes discouraged the Indigenous workers who had previously held the same positions. Indigenous men had once worked at the whaling stations along the coast, one northern chief testified in 1915, but they no longer sought work there because the whaling stations were now "full of Japs and [the operators] have cut down the wages on account of the Japanese."[43]

Most of the canneries were operated by distant corporations that delegated the task of securing an adequate labor supply to labor contractors with close ties to immigrant communities in major cities all along the Pacific coast, including Seattle, San Francisco, and Vancouver, B.C. While workers bound for canneries in Alaska were often recruited in Washington or California, many of those who worked in one or another of the many canneries clustered around the mouth of the Skeena River and, to a lesser extent, that of the Nass River in northern British Columbia were based in Victoria or Vancouver.[44] Ishitaro Sugitani, a Hokkaido native who settled in San Francisco after a gold mining venture on which he had embarked in Alaska with a white partner failed to prosper, was reportedly the first to contract with an Alaska cannery operator to supply Japanese laborers in 1903.[45] Also prominent among the San Francisco labor contractors who recruited Japanese to work in Alaska's salmon canneries was Kosuke Sakamaki, who emigrated to North America from Mie Prefecture in the late 1800s after converting to Catholicism in Japan; he became known as the "Alaska Boss" based on his work as a recruiter for the Alaska Packers Company.[46] In 1901, approximately nine thousand cannery workers made the trip north to Alaska, roughly half of them Chinese and the other half Italian and Norwegian laborers.[47] When the number of Chinese labor migrants began to drop following the renewal of the Chinese Exclusion Act in 1892 and again in 1902, Japanese laborers increasingly made up the shortfall.[48] The Japanese cannery workers who were part of the first group to go to Alaska appear to have been hired by a Chinese contractor to work at a cannery at Bristol Bay in 1900 after cannery operators asked for Japanese because they hoped to save money on labor.[49] Although Japanese would outnumber Chinese in Bristol Bay for a time, Mack Mori later reported that Japanese quickly came to identify the Bristol Bay canneries as ones to avoid, preferring those in southeastern Alaska, which were not as large and dirty and where one did not have to wait to be paid until after one returned home.[50]

When the fish came in by the thousands, Mori recalled, work in the canneries was hard and relentless. The first task was sorting the various kinds of salmon—king, silver, chum, pink, and coho—into separate bins. One man ran a butchering machine, cutting the heads off the fish, while others, including women, scraped and cleaned them to prepare the salmon for cooking.

Experienced fillers then stuffed the cans, which were labeled and boxed once they had cooled.[51] Some cannery workers were as young as fourteen, George Yanagimachi reported, as he himself was when he first hired on, and accidents occurred at times when workers went without sleep for days at a time.[52] Although the canneries located far from population centers were largely staffed by men, those located near towns like Cordova or Ketchikan hired local Indigenous women, as well as Euro-American and Japanese women, who sometimes worked with babies on their backs and passed on their positions to other women in their family when they had to relinquish them.[53] When her mother became unable to do her job at Ketchikan's oldest cannery, Irene Takizawa later told an interviewer, she took her mother's place as her oldest daughter even though she herself was still just sixteen. They "worked for peanuts," she recalled, "twenty-five cents an hour, piling cans, back-breaking work."[54] Hard as the work in the Alaska canneries could be, however, the wages were still higher than those for agricultural work or laboring jobs in cities such as Seattle.[55] The cannery where Yanagimachi worked, moreover, he reported, did not subtract wages when there was no work to do.[56] For young men like the *nisei* university students who gradually replaced many *issei*, it was a temporary job that offered the chance of adventure in the north. For others like Isamu Taguchi, who traveled to southeastern Alaska to work in the canneries in Ketchikan, in Cordova, or on Prince of Wales Island each summer from 1893 to 1939, it was a critical source of income throughout his lifetime.[57]

Cannery workers comprised an ethnically diverse society, the demographic distribution of which varied both from one region to another along the north Pacific coast and over time. As on sealing vessels, living arrangements in the canneries, often a jumble of small wooden buildings surrounding a larger barnlike structure where the fish were processed, reflected the racialized divides of the time, albeit not always in the same way at every cannery or in every region. Allan Okabe, the son of a Japanese father and a Tsimshian mother, explained, for example, that when he worked for the Pacific Cannery on the Skeena River, "the Chinese bunkhouse was always on the 'other' side of the rail tracks and was not painted at all and had outhouses," while Indigenous families lived in small houses in "Indian villages" alongside the Skeena River with "community rows of outhouses perched over the river." The Indigenous villages, he added, were "further segregated into Nisga'a, Tsimshian, Gitksan, Haida, and Haisla with clusters of housing for each different nation." The Japanese village, in turn, included a "bathhouse and bunkhouse" along with small homes with "white-washed walls and [maroon or] green paint on doors and front window frames."[58]

A Japanese woman on a cannery dock at the Sunnyside Cannery on the Skeena River. The small house in front of which she is standing was typical of the housing provided to Japanese cannery workers with families. A second photo taken at the same time depicts a man with a baby standing in front of the same house. City of Richmond Archives, British Columbia Packers Limited Fonds, 2001 84 9 601.

While both Japanese and Chinese labor contractors tried to recruit laborers of their own background, they also hired others when cannery operators requested that they do so.[59] When tensions between Chinese and Japanese began to grow as a result of Japan's invasion of north China, some contractors deliberately sent Japanese and Chinese men to different canneries to eliminate any conflict between them. Like Japanese consular officials, Japanese labor migrants also tended to regard Chinese workers with disdain, viewing them as less sophisticated than they themselves were as representatives of a modern imperial power.[60] Asked many years later whether there was prejudice among Japanese cannery workers against Koreans, Mori candidly admitted that there was, even though the Koreans worked side by side with them and also spoke Japanese and ate miso soup every morning, given that Japan had annexed Korea in 1910 and consequently regarded Koreans as Japanese subjects.[61]

Although Chinese and Japanese laborers came to predominate in canneries on both sides of the U.S.-Canada border as compared to those workers from other parts of Asia, they were also joined by migrants from countries along the entire Pacific coast, including Chile, Peru, and Mexico, as well as from other places around the world, including Hawaii, Puerto Rico, and Portugal.[62] In both Canada and the United States, racialized immigration laws and restrictions that limited the access of Asian migrants to the full rights of citizenship played a significant role in shaping the demographic contours of both the fishing and the canning industries. Following U.S. annexation of the Philippines after the end of the Spanish-American War in 1898, the peculiar status assigned to Filipinos by the U.S. government, which categorized them as "nationals" but not "citizens," meant that Filipinos would play a greater role in the Alaska canneries than they did in British Columbia. Much as Japanese cannery workers had helped to make up for the loss of Chinese laborers in the wake of the Chinese Exclusion Acts, Filipino workers helped to make up the labor shortfall in the Alaska canneries when the number of Japanese migrants dropped in the wake of the 1907 Gentlemen's Agreement and again after passage of the 1924 Immigration Act. As U.S. "nationals," Filipinos occupied an ambiguous position. While they were not regarded as aliens and subject to the kinds of immigration restrictions that applied to other Asian migrants, they were also not afforded the full rights of citizenship and faced race-based discrimination in the Pacific states.[63] Japanese cannery workers reported that they sympathized with Filipinos, whose homeland, they felt, had been unjustly seized by the United States, as they believed Hawaii had also been in 1897.[64] Japan had issued a protest at the time in which Britain refused to join, and the United States failed to honor its promise to Japan that the status of Japanese nationals in Hawaii would remain unchanged.[65] It was because they felt aggrieved in much the same way as the people of the Philippines, Yanagimachi later recalled, that there was "no friction at all" among them even as the number of Filipino workers in the Alaska canneries grew during the decades that followed.[66]

Much as status as citizen or subject, resident or national, taken together with bodies of exclusionary law and policy targeting Asian migrants, was a key factor shaping the demographic contours of the cannery workforce on each side of the U.S.-Canada border, status as a citizen or subject was also critical in determining who was able to participate as a fisher in the commercial fishing industry in both Canada and Alaska. Whereas Japanese fishermen in Canada, who were able to be naturalized as British subjects, came to predominate in British Columbia's northern waters, this was not the case in Alaska, where the fact that they were barred from applying for naturalization ensured that first-generation Japanese remained alien workers. While Japanese cannery workers became an important part of the workforce in both British Columbia and Alaska, far more Japanese turned to fishing in British Columbia, where they could apply to become naturalized British subjects, than on the U.S. side of the border. In 1909, for example, it was estimated that there were 8,000 Japanese in British Columbia, one-third of whom were fishermen, but just 913 Japanese in Alaska one year later, in 1910.[67] By 1922, the Japanese consulate in Seattle counted just 320 Japanese settlers in Alaska, fewer than 30 of whom identified as fishery workers.[68] In contrast to British Columbia, where Japanese fishers would play a prominent part in the coastal fisheries, in southeastern Alaska Tlingit fishers outnumbered others by a factor of four to one in 1897 and would continue to do so through the 1920s. Rather than Japanese fishers, Scandinavian, Danish, German, and Italian fishermen were recruited in San Francisco and other Pacific ports each year to travel north to work alongside them.[69]

In the Pacific Northwest, Washington and Oregon also limited Japanese access to coastal fisheries including those of the Puget Sound. Although anti-Japanese agitators in California tried to do the same, however, their efforts were frustrated by the cannery companies that the Japanese fishers helped to supply. Although Japanese fishers worked out of ports all along the California coast, including Monterey, San Diego, and Long Beach, the largest group of Japanese fishing families lived in a small village on Terminal Island, near Los Angeles.[70] Established in 1899, East San Pedro was described by one former resident as "a Japanese village on American soil."[71] Many of the Japanese fishers who settled there hailed from Wakayama Prefecture, a majority of them from the whaling village of Taiji.[72] Bob Kumamoto later described East San Pedro as a "shanty town" where its residents "lived in tiny wooden shacks . . . cramped together in a jungle-like maze of dwellings, their jerry-built frame cottages . . . surrounded with fishing nets, chicken coops, rabbit pens, and wild bamboo."[73] Although some had fished the waters of San Pedro Harbor for two decades or more, in the wake of the Gentlemen's Agreement of 1907, barred as they were from becoming U.S. citizens, even residents who had lived there or elsewhere in the United States for decades but had no passport or documentary record to demonstrate this were forced for the first time to find ways to prove that they were prior residents.[74]

In British Columbia, in contrast, Japanese fishers had established themselves early in the commercial fishing industry centered around the small town of Steveston at the mouth of Fraser River. Built on Lulu Island near a point where two Coast Salish villages—Kwayo7xw ("bubbling water") and Kwlhayam ("place where there are driftwood logs on the beach") were located—Steveston has also been described as "a Japanese village," in this instance on Canadian soil.[75] Like the residents of Terminal Island, many of the Japanese fishers based in Steveston hailed from Wakayama Prefecture. The largest group emigrated to Canada from Mio-mura following the collapse of the sardine fishery in Osaka Bay in the 1890s. Japanese had always lived along the ocean and fished the waters of the Pacific, one Wakayama fisherman explained. When they first arrived on its easternmost shores, he argued, they had played a key role in establishing the commercial fishery both on the Fraser River and elsewhere along the B.C. coast. It was for that reason that he and others were convinced that they were entitled to participate both in the Fraser River fishery and in other fisheries along the B.C. coast.[76] These were men who had grown up on the shores of the western Pacific, Nakayama later explained. Accustomed to navigating the wild waves off the coast of Japan, he wrote, they had a natural talent for fishing.[77] Also key was the fact that they were already familiar with the kinds of knowledge that fishermen needed to acquire regarding the prevailing currents and the timing of tides, as well as the life cycles of the fish and where particular fish were likely to be found at given times of the year.[78]

While the authors of a Japanese-language book on Japanese abroad complained in 1906 that Japanese immigrants preferred to settle in British Columbia than in Alaska, despite the fact that Alaska was closer to Japan and replete with resources that would also benefit Japan, they failed to take into account the distances that fishermen would have to travel along the Pacific coast.[79] The distance between northern British Columbia and Vancouver was considerably shorter than that between Alaska and California, and fish caught off Vancouver Island were preferred even in Seattle because they were far fresher than those that made the journey from Alaska.[80] The milder weather along the B.C. coast may also have been a factor that influenced the decision of at least some Japanese immigrants regarding where to settle, as was the fact that the landscape of the B.C. coast reminded many of that along Japan's Pacific coast. Kazuichi Tasaka, for example, would later report that his grandfather first settled in Portland, Oregon, in the late 1880s, but after traveling north to fish sev-

The Atagi Boatworks in Steveston, B.C., circa 1915. Both Japanese flags and a Canadian flag, with the Union Jack in the upper left corner, wave in the breeze above two recently completed fishing vessels. City of Richmond Archives, City of Richmond Collection, 2009 16 111.

eral times during the summer he decided to make Salt Spring Island, B.C., his home because the forested islands in the Gulf of Georgia reminded him of those along the coast of Ehime Prefecture on Shikoku, where he was raised.[81]

Japanese Pioneers

The Japanese who first ventured north along British Columbia's west coast were proudly embraced by the Japanese community as *kusawake*, pioneers who had "parted the grass" or blazed a trail for other Japanese in an unfamiliar land.[82] Fishermen, wrote the authors of one Meiji-era account of Japanese emigrants abroad, often served as pioneers for farming communities that followed in their wake.[83] A founding story that recounts the dangers surmounted by those who "discovered" the northern salmon fishery, first recorded by Jinshiro Nakayama in the 1920s, is often cited as evidence of the role Japanese fishermen played in establishing the commercial fishing industry along British Columbia's north coast. In 1890, Nakayama wrote, Yasukichi Yoshizawa and Shiga Aikawa began to worry that the sawmill at Hastings Mill in Vancouver, where Japanese labor migrants first found work when they arrived in the 1880s, could not continue to absorb more workers.[84] The sawmill was located in Gastown, on the south shore of Burrard Inlet near the Indigenous village that still occupied the site where the Japanese Language School would later be built.[85] Determined to find a solution that would open up new possibilities for Japanese, Yoshizawa and Aikawa recruited three others to travel north with them along the B.C. coast as far as the Skeena River to see what other employment opportunities might exist. While Yoshizawa had served as an officer in the Japanese navy and been trained in navigation, they had just one unfinished chart of the B.C. coast to guide them. They launched the rowboat they had acquired from the beach near Hastings Mill on April 8, 1890, cheered on by friends who had come to see them off. Realizing that what they estimated to be a 500-mile journey might take as long as three months, Nakayama wrote, they carried on regardless, facing with tenacity and grit the dangers and hardships that confronted them. They also benefited from the aid of those they encountered along the way. When they reached Seymour Narrows, well known for its raging tidal currents, for example, they came upon a boat skippered by *hakujin*, who advised them to wait until low tide the following morning when it was safe to cross. When their food supplies ran low, they shot wild ducks near shore, dug for clams, or dangled a line to catch fish and, in one instance, an octopus. When they neared Alert Bay at the northern end of Vancouver Island, they heard several gun shots and pulled into shore by the Kwakwaka'wakw village of Namgis. There they bartered tobacco and soap for the halibut they saw drying on racks, as they would again at other Indigenous villages along the way. That night they decided to sleep in their boat, only to discover when they awoke that their anchor had come loose and that they had drifted onto the beach during the night. Noticing that their boat was surrounded by numerous wolf tracks, they realized that it was only the lantern that they had left burning through the night that had saved them from harm.[86]

After forty-two days, having endured many hardships along the way, they reached the mouth of the Skeena River. There, Nakayama's story continues, they found over a hundred white and Indigenous men working to build a cannery. None of them had ever seen anyone from Japan before, and they were reportedly greatly impressed by the "pioneering spirit" of the five men. All five were hired as firewood cutters, but only Aikawa and Yoshizawa decided to stay on.[87] Their fellow travelers left for Seattle after learning that construction workers were in demand there as it began to rebuild following a fire that had destroyed its central business district the year before. When the sockeye season began two months later, both hired on as boat pullers, Aikawa for an

Indigenous fisherman and Yoshizawa for a white fisherman. Both men rowed out to the fishing grounds in a small Columbia boat—so called because they had first been used on the Columbia River in Oregon and Washington State—where they cast their 200-fathom-long drift nets and caught both "giant spring and graceful sockeye salmon."[88] In the spring of 1895, Yoshizawa traveled further north to Nisga'a territory along the Nass River to participate in the ooligan fishery. A mainstay of Indigenous peoples along the north Pacific coast for centuries, ooligan were prized on both sides of the B.C.-Alaska border as both a valuable trade item and a source of nutrition. The first fish to return to its spawning stream each spring, it was called the preserver fish by the Tsimshian and *ha'liimootkw*, or "savior," by the Nisga'a.[89]

Both Aikawa and Yoshizawa reportedly developed close ties with the Indigenous people with whom they came into contact. Aikawa was born in 1868, the first year of the Meiji period, and left for San Francisco in 1887, where he worked as a laborer for three years before deciding to go to Seattle, where, Shimada and Ariiso tell us, he thought he would find more adventurous men than in California given that Seattle served as the home port for a number of deep-sea fishing vessels, including those of poachers who fished the waters surrounding the Kuril Islands.[90] In Seattle, he recruited a group of five men to hunt sea otters on Kodiak Island in Alaska, only to decide as he traveled north along the B.C. coast to focus instead on salmon fishing. In 1905, after fishing for some fifteen years in the Lax-Kw'alaams area, where Metlakatla and other Tsimshian villages were located and where he and Yoshizawa had ended their journey north in 1890, he moved to Bella Bella in Heiltsuk territory, where he established the Bella Bella Marine Products Company, Ltd., intending to salt chum salmon and can abalone for export to Japan. As unsophisticated and rough as Aikawa may have looked, Shimada and Ariiso wrote the following year, his role in establishing a commercial salmon fishery that extended across the B.C.-Alaska border made him "a hero among Japanese in Canada."[91]

Yoshizawa, in turn, learned both Chinook jargon and English during his years fishing on the Skeena River and often served as an interpreter for Indigenous people in Namu, Bella Bella, and Kimsquit, by all accounts gaining both the affection of his Indigenous neighbors and the trust of the *hakujin* who negotiated with them, to the point where he came to be called "Saibashi Yasu" (Indian Yasu) by other Japanese.[92] Yoshizawa and the other earliest Japanese pioneers, Nakayama would later write, were all "[men] of ability and full of vitality." Rather than "engage in wordy warfare," they "preferred to win success with sheer talent" and, in so doing, laid the foundation on which subsequent generations of Japanese were able to build. "To develop virgin lands," Nakayama declared, "a man of action is needed rather than a man of words."[93]

The successful recruitment of other Japanese by both Aikawa and Yoshizawa, including some who had only recently arrived in Victoria, B.C., on a ship from Japan in 1891, would in time have a dramatic impact on Indigenous people along the coast.[94] Within a year of their arrival at the mouth of the Skeena River, Japanese fishers had started to explore the waters of the open ocean on the western side of Haida Gwaii, where five signed on with a Swedish fishboat captain named Charlie Namba, who had reportedly lived in Japan long enough to learn some Japanese.[95] By 1893, Nakayama reports, Japanese fishers were active in Rivers Inlet and along British Columbia's central coast, and by 1900 they were fishing on the Nass River just south of the Alaska border. Among the "virgin fisheries" that Japanese "discovered" during the first years of the twentieth century were those in China Hat (1900), Bella Bella (1907), and Smith Inlet (1908). They also developed existing fisheries at Kimsquit, Kingcome Inlet, Alert Bay, and Klemtu, among others, he reports. Where salmon had once been regarded only as food for Indigenous people, by the early twentieth century, Nakayama wrote, due in part to the efforts of Japanese fishers, it had become one of British Columbia's most lucrative commercial fisheries.[96]

Coastal Fisheries

In 1899, concerned about the growing number of Japanese immigrants participating in British Columbia's fisheries along the Fraser River, Canada's Department of Marine and Fisheries restricted independent fishing licenses to British subjects.[97] That status as a British subject was required to obtain a commercial fishing license reinforced the place of the Canadian state, already responsible for regulating coastal fisheries, at the center of contests over access to fishery resources along the B.C. coast.[98] It also ensured that proposed restrictions on access to naturalization, should they be implemented, would serve the dual purpose of limiting access to British Columbia's fishery resources, even as it exposed Japanese immigrants to claims that they applied for naturalization only because it was a prerequisite to obtaining a fishing license.[99] The fact that Japanese immigrants who were awarded fishing licenses were no longer Japanese subjects but British subjects of Japanese origin hampered Japan's ability to protest British Columbia's efforts to restrict the number of licenses issued to *nikkei* fishermen based on the Anglo-Japanese Alliance, which provided that Japanese subjects "shall in all that relates to the pursuit of their industries, callings, professions and educational studies be placed in all respects on the same footing as the subjects or citizens of the most favoured nation."[100] The requirement that one be a British subject to obtain a commercial fishing license was also not met with disapproval by all Japanese. In limiting fishing licenses to naturalized British subjects, Kiyoshi Karl Kawakami told his readers in 1914, for example, the Dominion government's motivation was just "to secure desired labour for the promotion of the salmon industry without at the same time admitting ignorant fishermen into citizenship."[101] Not noted by Kawakami was that one factor that encouraged Japanese immigrants to turn to fishing may have been the fact that they were not listed on British Columbia's provincial voter lists, which meant they were barred from a range of alternative occupations, including law, hand logging, pharmacy, public works projects, and mining.[102]

Salmon

Despite the constraints imposed, by 1913 *nikkei* fishermen were awarded more than half of the licenses issued for the salmon fisheries on British Columbia's northern coast that year. Many of these were not independent but "attached licenses" issued in the first instance to cannery owners who then distributed them to the fishermen they hired.[103] Nakayama attributed the success of *nikkei* fishermen to what he described as distinctive cultural traits, as reflected in their diligence, cooperation, and productivity. They were dependable and had worked hard both to identify new fishing grounds and to develop their relationships with the cannery companies. Another factor, Nakayama declared, was the courage that Japanese fishers displayed in venturing out into the rough waters of the open ocean, where the waves, pushed along by strong westerly winds, were sometimes high enough to swamp most fishing boats. White and Indigenous fishers had been afraid to venture out onto the open ocean, he claimed, until they saw how successful Japanese fishers were when they braved these waters.[104] This was why they were sought after by white cannery owners, Nakayama wrote, adding that the only reason that white politicians opposed Japanese was because they wanted to attract and protect white fishermen.[105]

Indigenous fishers, in contrast, testified before the McKenna-McBride Commission that the reason cannery owners preferred to hire *nikkei* fishers was that they were willing to "operate on Sundays and during prescribed closed days of the fishing season" and also resorted to other means they regarded as questionable to maximize their catch.[106] According to Nakayama, when commission members visited Indigenous communities—in his words, *dojin buraku*, a phrase that invokes derogatory associations both with indigeneity and with outcaste status—Indigenous fishers complained that Japanese fishers had encroached on their traditional fishing territories and engaged in fishing operations that were in competition with their own.[107] He also claimed that Indigenous witnesses had told the commissioners that the Japanese government secretly funded Japanese fishermen who were willing to spy on Canada and that this was why they had top-notch gear. Based on these claims, he wrote, Indigenous fishermen asked that they be provided with boats and gear that would allow them to compete with Japanese.[108] The English-language record of the McKenna-McBride Commission's report reflects that Indigenous fishers did feel displaced by their Japanese counterparts. When "too many Japs [get all of] the licenses and the [cannery] boats," a Nisga'a spokesman testified, "us Indians have to go even up to Ketchikan," north of the B.C.-Alaska border, "to get work." Cannery operators, he added, had "intimated to us that if they had enough Japs they would push the Indians out altogether."[109] In some areas, canneries would hire an Indigenous fisherman only if he also had a wife who could work in the cannery. As one Indigenous man at Rivers Inlet testified, "This is our own country, but in spite of that, because I have no right to work in the Cannery, I cannot get a boat to fish with, and therefore I can get no money. The Japanese and the white man came here and they have no wives, but they are given work whenever they want it." But in the case of an Indigenous man, even if work was available, "wherever he goes an Indian is called a Siwash and [if] he is a Siwash he is not given work."[110]

Although B.C. officials publicly defended Indigenous fishers as against Japanese, the low number of independent licenses issued to Indigenous fishers was itself the result of a deliberate, racialized policy intended to privilege any fishers who could be categorized as "white." In 1913, for example, Tsimshian fishers living on British Columbia's north coast reported that they had been told that they would not be permitted to purchase independent fishing licenses because they were intended "only for white men who owned their boat and Net [sic]." In arguing for access to independent fishing licenses, they pointed not only to their deep historical ties to the region but also to their status as British subjects. "We are natives of this Country," wrote one group of Indigenous men, "and as Fishing is one of our means of livelihood, and we are loyal British subjects, we think it only right and fair that if we have the money to purchase a Licence, and other qualifications necessary, we be allowed to have these independent Licences."[111] Others invoked Canada's obligations to them, declaring, "As wards of the government and non-treaty Indians, we want the same privileges as white men, the Chinese, Japanese and other foreigners. We are sufficiently advanced in the manner and customs of the white man to warrant full considerations and justice in this matter."[112] When a Nisga'a delegation traveled to Ottawa to bring this matter to the attention of fisheries officials there, however, they were assured that "Japs" would also be denied independent licenses, which would be reserved for white men alone.[113] Indigenous fishers were not issued independent licenses at the Nass Agency, Indian Agent C. C. Perry admitted, because cannery operators worried that "if independent licenses were granted to the Indians, the Japs would want them," and they, "being naturalized British subjects, are entitled to them." Although he conceded that "Indians are well able to provide their own boats and gear" and that they would "get a better price for their catch" as independent fishermen, it was his opinion that Indigenous fishers were already "provided with plenty of work at the canneries."[114]

In 1916, the McKenna-McBride Commission agreed with Indigenous fishermen that the Fisheries Department's policy of denying fishing licenses to Indigenous fishers amounted to "racial discrimination" and that it was unjust. "Applications of North British Columbia Indians," it declared, should be "considered and dealt with upon their individual merits and not refused because of the applicant being an Indian, the Indians of British Columbia being British subjects and as such entitled to equal consideration with their fellow British subjects."[115] Notwithstanding its findings, however, policies restricting the participation of Indigenous fishermen in British Columbia's coastal fisheries—and particularly their access to independent licenses for British Columbia's northern coastal fisheries—did not change until 1919.[116] When a policy shift did occur, it coincided with the first of a series of graduated annual reductions in the number of licenses to be issued *nikkei* fishermen in an effort to restrict their access to British Columbia's coastal fisheries, beginning by limiting the number of licenses issued in 1920 to that issued in 1919.[117] Only then did the Fisheries Department begin to support Indigenous participation in British Columbia's commercial fisheries. It did so not because it recognized this as an inherent Aboriginal right, notwithstanding Canada's failure to enter into treaties with most of British Columbia's Indigenous peoples, however, but based on the Crown's presumed acquisition of these rights and the obligations it assumed when it established reserves. British Columbia's defense of Indigenous fishermen also allowed it to emphasize the "foreignness" of the "Japanese" fishermen it feared might limit opportunities for the Euro-Canadians it sought to recruit as settlers, notwithstanding that these "Japanese" fishers were, by law, required to be British subjects, whether by birth or by naturalization.

In 1922, the B.C. Fisheries Commission again reduced the number of licenses issued to "Oriental" fishermen by up to 50 percent along its southern coast. In response to the concerns of canners that "men unaccustomed to fishing the conditions on the Skeena" would not be able to navigate its rough waters and unpredictable currents, however, it reduced the number of licenses issued to *nikkei* fishermen along the Skeena and the Nass Rivers by only 10 percent. The need for highly skilled fishermen familiar with coastal waters, however, was one that it anticipated would soon be rendered moot by changing technologies. "In 1924," it observed, "when gasoline boats come into use, there will be much less trouble in replacing Orientals."[118] Just one year later, the federal Department of Marine and Fisheries declared that its "policy of eliminating the Oriental from the fisheries of the province with a view to placing the entire industry in the hands of white British subjects and Canadian Indians . . . appear[ed] to be working out well."[119]

Matters surrounding gasoline engine boats came to a head in 1928, however, when the ban against their use, which had continued to apply in the Skeena River district even after it was lifted elsewhere, was lifted with respect to Indigenous and white fishermen but was maintained against *nikkei* fishermen. As Mitsuo Yesaki explains, British Columbia's coastal salmon fishery was divided into three districts. By 1924, all fishers in Fishing Districts 1 and 3, which covered the waters off the coasts of southern British Columbia and Vancouver Island, were permitted to use gas engine boats. This was not true, however, of Fishing District 2, where *nikkei* fishers predominated in a region that "extended from Cape Caution to the Alaska border" and included the Nass and Skeena River areas, the Rivers and Smith's Inlet areas, Haida Gwaii, and the central coast.[120] Rintaro Hayashi, a fisherman who was active in the Steveston-based Japanese Fishermen's Association, later explained that the ostensible reasons for the original ban included the reported sensitivity of salmon to the noisy putter of gasoline engines and concerns that the use of motorized vessels would result in overfishing. But the real concern, Hayashi explained, was the desire of cannery owners to maintain control over all commercial fishing in the area by requiring that fishermen, who might otherwise set themselves up as independent operators if they had access to gas engine boats, rent Columbia boats from them.[121] Although one translation of Hayashi's account suggests that he attributed the ban to a "covert agreement" between "white fishing companies" and government authorities and that "Japanese fishermen were denied this new advantage without any reason" when the ban was lifted, his original text offers a more complex reason for the failure to include *nikkei* fishermen when this occurred. Hayashi reports that a rumor circulating at the time suggested that some *nikkei* bosses, joined by certain *nikkei* fishermen whom he describes as having dubious backgrounds, told fisheries officials that *nikkei* fishers in Fishing District 2 did not mind being denied the use of gas engine boats as long as they were not subjected to any further reductions in the number of licenses issued to *nikkei* fishermen in Fishing Districts 1 and 3.[122]

In the spring of 1929, Jun Kizawa, a fisherman born in Wakayama Prefecture who had studied law at Waseda University in Tokyo before immigrating to Canada and being naturalized as a British subject, decided to challenge the ongoing ban against the use of gas engine boats by *nikkei* fishers by engaging in a protest fishery that he hoped would provide a foundation for a test case that would bring the matter before the courts.[123] According to Hayashi, Kizawa encountered some resistance from *nikkei* fishermen in the Skeena district who wanted to avoid trouble as long as their own licenses were secure, but the Steveston-based Japanese Fishermen's Association, of which he was a member, extended its support.[124] When reports that the Department of Fisheries might lift the ban on its own accord came to nought, Kizawa cabled his supporters in Steveston to let them know that he was determined to "proceed the course firmly."[125] On June 12, 1929, the Amalgamated Fishermen's Association informed him that his request for funds to purchase a gas engine boat for this purpose had been approved.[126] When he headed out to fish in the old boat he had acquired expecting that it would be seized, he was detained and charged with violating the ban against the use of gas engine boats by *nikkei* fishermen as he had anticipated he would be. Just one week later, on June 19, however, the justice of the peace who heard the charge against Kizawa dismissed it on the ground that, as a naturalized British subject, he was entitled to the same "rights accorded any other British subject."[127]

Kizawa's case was not appealed. Instead, it was effectively rendered moot by a decision of the British Privy Council in October 1929 that affirmed a ruling by Canada's Supreme Court in 1928 in a case filed by the Amalgamated Fishermen's Association, on behalf of all Japanese fishermen in British Columbia, to challenge the provisions of the Fisheries Act on which the Department of Fisheries relied to discriminate against *nikkei* fishermen on race-based grounds, and particularly its "policy of reducing the number of licenses granted to . . . Japanese fishermen year by year so that they will be eliminated in the course of five years from all part[s] in the fishing industry in British Columbia."[128] The Privy Council agreed with the Supreme Court that nothing in the act gave the Department of Fisheries the discretion to deny a fishing license to any British subject who properly applied and paid for that license, regardless of background or country of origin.[129] Canada responded almost immediately by revising the Fisheries Act to give the minister of fisheries "absolute discretion" to withhold a license, a power that he presumably could have exercised on race-based grounds as on any other, but it also lifted the ban on the use of gas engine boats by *nikkei* fishers at the same time.[130]

In 1931, Kizawa, now secretary of the Skeena Fishermen's Association, joined with the Prince Rupert Japanese Association and the Northern B.C. Salmon Fishermen's Association, a predominantly white organization, in an effort to bring an end to what had come to be known as the attachment system, which bound *nikkei* fishermen in the Skeena River district to particular canneries as a condition of receiving a license. In a letter written with the approval of the Skeena Fishermen's Association, the Northern B.C. Salmon Fishermen's Association explained that the system "gave the Japanese Contractor a strangle hold on [the *nikkei*] fisherman. In fact the contractor owned him, as far as his means of earning a living was concerned."[131] Kizawa, in turn, explained in a message written in Japanese to all the fishermen of the district that their purpose in working together to abolish what he characterized as "Slave licenses" was to place Japanese fishers on the same footing as any other fishermen so that they could also sell their catches wherever they wanted.[132] Ironically, even though Euro-Canadians frequently criticized the attachment system as an example of "Oriental slavery," the Department of Fisheries' own regulations required Japanese fishermen to sell their catch to the cannery to which they were attached.[133] At one meeting with government officials and other salmon fishermen, Kizawa was joined by Ushizo Suga, the first Japanese immigrant to establish a family in Prince Rupert and a representative of the Prince Rupert Japanese Association, who reminded all present that fishers of Japanese ancestry born in Canada were British subjects and equally entitled to fishing licenses as any other British subject. Suga urged that "bona fide residents of the district" be given priority over seasonal participants in the salmon fishery regardless of race or national origin. White representatives of the Northern B.C. Salmon Fishermen's Association agreed. While Japanese had once "been regarded as a danger to the interests of white fishermen," a Mr. Anderson admitted, "since then, the times had changed in the industry."[134]

Their collective efforts were successful. On December 22, 1931, the Vancouver *Province* announced that "attachment of Japanese to canneries" would end with the start of the new fishing season. "Japanese fishermen," it declared, were now "free" and able to decide for themselves to whom they wished to sell their catches.[135] There were some difficulties with its implementation that were a result of resistance on the part of both white cannery owners and "Japanese bosses," however. Because many Japanese fishermen did not read

English, they simply failed to inform them of the change, Kizawa explained, with the result that "Japanese fishermen still allow[ed] the contractors to sell them like sheep to the canneries at so much per head."[136]

Another matter also remained to be addressed. The restriction of fishing licenses to those who were British subjects had long given rise to claims that Japanese Canadian fishers obtained their naturalization papers by fraud.[137] In 1932, the Department of Fisheries notified Kizawa, in his role as secretary of the Skeena Fishermen's Association, that it would withhold licenses from any fishers whose naturalization papers were "found to be fraudulent" or where there was "good reason to suspect [their] qualifications" pending further investigation. But it assured Kizawa that any licenses that were withheld would be issued to local applicants whose papers were in order, including Japanese Canadians, as Suga had urged.[138] An internal memorandum from a member of the Skeena Fishermen's Association noted that the Royal Canadian Mounted Police (RCMP) had kept a close eye on those applying for fishing licenses and had "already picked up a few illegals" who had presented naturalization papers that were determined to be false.[139] Unclear, however, was whether all of these belonged to individuals who had not been born in Canada. Particularly when they lived in places distant from centers of government, Japanese parents did not always register their children's births, with the result that even second-generation Japanese Canadians sometimes found themselves in a position where borrowing another's naturalization certificate was the most efficient way to obtain a fishing license.[140] Evidence does exist that naturalization certificates were sometimes shared among Japanese immigrants.[141] Others, in turn, candidly admitted that they applied to become naturalized British subjects precisely because this was a prerequisite to obtaining a fishing license. In 1923, the Kanada Nihonjinkai (Japanese Association of Canada) reported that a survey it had conducted two years earlier had revealed that about one-fifth of the Japanese fishermen who had obtained fishing licenses had done so by utilizing naturalization certificates borrowed from others and that they were not in fact British subjects. This practice, the association reported, was most prevalent in Fishing District 2 along British Columbia's northern coast. As such, it reminded its members, Japanese were in no position to insist that all fishers were naturalized.[142]

In 1933, the Fisheries Department informed the Skeena Fishermen's Association that eighty-three licenses issued to its members would not be renewed because their naturalization papers were "irregular."[143] What government officials overlooked when they targeted *nikkei* fishers and criticized them for borrowing naturalization papers or exaggerating the number of years that they had lived in Canada when they applied to be naturalized was that fishermen of European ancestry had long done the same.[144] As recently as 1927, the Fisheries Department's own annual report admitted that despite the fact that fishing licenses were issued only to British subjects, "1460 unnaturalized white immigrants in Canada [were] granted licenses in order to fill the vacancies left by Orientals" who had been forced out of the fishing industry.[145] When it came to enforcement, as well, the department applied a different standard against Japanese fishers as contrasted with whites. While fisheries officers were permitted to assume that white fishers met the requisite standard based on their word alone, enforcement officers were instructed "in the case of Japanese [to] insist upon the production of naturalization papers showing licensee to be a British subject."[146]

Although Japanese Canadians had prevailed in the courts, the demographic profile of the coastal salmon fishery nevertheless changed dramatically by 1930. Between 1922 and 1930, the number of *nikkei* fishermen along British Columbia's northern coast had dropped by 1,253 men.[147] Fishery officials, however, were at a loss to explain why the catch of *nikkei* fishers, who held just one-eighth of the number of the licenses issued throughout the 1930s, continued to "exceed that of other fishermen." Perhaps it was that they tended to stay out on the fishing grounds longer than other fishermen, one official suggested. Another speculated that the dramatic reduction in the number of *nikkei* fishermen during the 1920s meant that "the poorer fishermen were let go and the very cream of the fishermen were kept on," whereas "the average [skill] of Indians and whites [was] spread over all classes—efficient or inefficient."[148]

Although the B.C. government's primary concern was always the interests of the Euro-Canadian fishers it hoped to induce to settle along the B.C. coast, the numbers of licenses issued suggest that Indigenous fishers were able to establish a somewhat stronger foothold in the coastal fishing industry during the 1920s as a result of the restrictions imposed on *nikkei* fishermen. By the 1930s, the numbers of Indigenous fishermen living in areas such as Alert Bay, Fort Simpson, and Haida Gwaii had greatly increased and many had also acquired gasoline engine boats.[149] The adoption of new technologies, however, did not mean the abandonment of tradition either in British Columbia or in Alaska. As Tlingit scholar Nora Marks Dauenhauer recalled, for example, although her father, a Tlingit, "eagerly embraced new technology, his values and those of the extended family were very conservative. He was the first to get a gas or diesel engine, but we were among the last families who still followed a traditional subsistence lifestyle, and who still spoke only Tlingit at home."[150]

Herring

Although debates as to whether it was permissible to distinguish among British subjects on race-based grounds in granting access to fishing licenses came to a head in the context of the salmon industry, it remained an issue in this and other fisheries up to the outbreak of the Second World War as salmon stocks were increasingly depleted by the overfishing not just of salmon but also of species such as herring on which salmon depended for food at critical times of the year. Given that Japanese fishers had a particular interest in harvesting herring, the herring fishery also became a site of contest over access to marine resources that directly engaged the question of what it meant to be a British subject in Canada. All along the north Pacific coast, herring, like salmon, had long served as an essential spiritual, cultural, and economic resource, to the point where anthropologists have described it as a "cultural keystone species."[151] Deeply embedded in the history and culture of Indigenous peoples around the North Pacific Rim, for many the arrival of herring in coastal waters each year marked the beginning of spring. Known as *heroki*, or "the fish that brings spring," to the Ainu on the western shores of the Pacific, where it had been one factor that drove Japanese expansion into Hokkaido, for example, it also signaled the start of the Heiltsuk new year on its eastern shores.[152] And like salmon, herring was also a focus both of trade and of early regulatory constraints both in Japan and in North America.[153]

The commercial harvest of herring along the eastern shores of the North Pacific began in 1876 when Canada's Dominion government authorized the taking of herring as a bait fish in an effort to bolster the salmon and halibut fisheries, expanding dramatically around the turn of the century in response to the demand for imported salt herring in China and Japan.[154] Japanese entrepreneurs based in Nanaimo, B.C., on the east coast of Vancouver Island, had been among the first to see the potential inherent in salting both herring and chum salmon for Asian markets, where both products came to be regarded as a welcome and relatively inexpensive food source for poorer populations, and in using herring to produce fish oil and fertilizer for export to Asia.[155] The herring fishery was most active between October, when the salmon runs had largely ended, through March. Because herring congregated in schools, spotting them required special skill on the part of those who fished for them: in the fall, they scanned the ocean for bubbles rising from the depths; in the spring, they fished at night, locating the herring by listening for the splashes made by those that jumped out of the water.[156]

Among the first to acquire a herring saltery and a fish oil and fertilizer reduction plant in the Nanaimo area was Arichika Ikeda, who had turned to
fishing the waters along the B.C. coast a few years after he returned from his
1898 trip to Alaska. Although Ikeda was forced to close the fertilizer reduction plant after the use of herring for nonfood purposes was banned in 1905,
he continued to manage the herring saltery he had bought in 1903 from the
three Japanese men who had established it four years earlier on behalf of
Awaya, Ikeda and Company, Ltd., an enterprise he established with a partner
based in Japan.[157] By 1907, his was one of ten salteries managed by Japanese in
the Nanaimo area, and within the decade there would be as many as twenty
operating along the B.C. coast and exporting salt herring to Japan, Korea,
Manchuria, and China.[158] At times, Japanese saltery operators competed
with one another, turning in others that they believed might not have com-
plied with licensing requirements.[159] In 1910, for example, "one Korenaga"
notified fishery officers that "T. Ode of Desert Bay" and "H. Tsuchiya of Sech-
elt have not paid their licenses" and suggested that there was some irregular-
ity involving R. Tabata of Nanaimo, although this proved not to be the case.[160]
The fact remains that Japanese saltery operators had effectively remade the
economy of Nanaimo. It was as a result of their success in developing the
herring saltery business, Kawakami wrote in 1914, that Nanaimo, which had
once been known as the Coal City, had instead come to be known as the
Herring City.[161]

The very success of Ikeda and others who exported salt herring to Asia,
however, also made them a target of white residents in Nanaimo who believed that they were impinging on their own access to these resources. Local
merchants reportedly boycotted Japanese Canadian fishers as early as 1903,
and Nanaimo's municipal government did what it could to restrict their participation in local fisheries, passing a resolution in February 1910 advocating
their expulsion from the city.[162] In July 1910, fires fed by "an accumulation of
grease and other combustible[s]," which were believed to have been deliberately set, destroyed three Japanese-run salteries along the waterfront in
Nanaimo.[163] In July 1912, four more Japanese-run herring salteries on nearby
Newcastle Island were destroyed by a fire that reportedly started on the
grounds of the saltery run by Korenaga. According to newspapers of the time,
locals believed that the fires were arson intended to drive Japanese fishers and
entrepreneurs out of town.[164]

Ikeda, however, was not to be deterred, and continued to explore other
options, including fisheries on both sides of the Alaska-B.C. border. In 1904,
he had purchased a steamship named the *Azuma Maru* to export fish prod-

Kaoru Ikeda with baby Arimoto and, from left to right, T. Shimoisaka, Arichika Ikeda, and Captain Shibuya, circa 1917. Haida Gwaii Museum at Ḵay Llangaay, Skidegate, B.C., Phillips Dalzell Fonds, Chisato Tokunaga Collection, 1907–1915, Ph. 02400.

ucts produced by a saltery he planned to establish in Dutch Harbor on Amak-nak Island in the middle of the Aleutian chain. Alaska, after all, as Nakayama explained to his readers, was just three thousand miles from Japan and, as such, closer to Japan than it was to the United States, which meant that transportation to Japan cost far less than it did to the U.S. states. Ikeda was the right man to embark on such a venture, Nakayama declared, given that he had conducted surveys in Alaska for the Japanese government in the past and had the backing of Japan's Ministry of Agriculture and Trade, which was interested in developing deep sea fisheries in the North Pacific Ocean.[165] Ikeda also actively explored new opportunities south of the Alaska-B.C. border, including in the waters around Haida Gwaii. Other Japanese entrepreneurs had also identified Haida Gwaii as a promising base for export industries with ties to Japan given that it was a hundred miles closer to Japan than Prince Rupert. Among them was Masatoro Mukai, who established a saltery on Moresby Island to salt chum salmon he bought from *nikkei* and Haida fishers for export to Japan in the early 1900s and later grew potatoes at Sandspit that he sold in Prince Rupert.[166] Yasuyuki Sawada, in turn, established a fish processing plant on Haida Gwaii with an eye to exporting dried fish and fish oil to Japan. He also purchased land on an island that "*hakujin* had already abandoned," where he hoped a Japanese village would develop unhindered by racial animus.[167]

Jinsaburo Oikawa, who settled in southern British Columbia on two small islands in the Fraser River, had also dreamed of establishing a Japanese village on Haida Gwaii. The industries that he developed focused on salting dog salmon and salmon roe, which he had been told in Japan "hairy barbarians," or *ketō*—as *hakujin* were also called—did not eat even though it was reportedly as good as that in Hokkaido.[168] Oikawa was motivated not only by his desire to live free of racial discrimination but also by the wish to avoid the prefectural biases that structured Japanese immigrant society and resonated more strongly than their shared identity as Japanese subjects in some places.[169] When he first arrived in Canada, he later wrote, he worked among fishermen from Wakayama Prefecture who spoke a regional dialect different from his own and made him feel as if he was a "complete outsider."[170] Oikawa hoped that salting salmon roe would give migrants from the Tohoku region in northeastern Japan their own distinct area of endeavor, much as those from Wakayama Prefecture predominated in the coastal fisheries and those from Shiga Prefecture in the forest industry.[171]

In 1906, Oikawa smuggled a group of eighty-three migrants from Miyagi Prefecture who had been unable to obtain passports in Japan out of a lesser known port on its northeastern coast in a sailboat he chartered called the *Suian Maru*, bound for the small island in the Fraser River that whites called Lion — Island and Japanese Oikawa-jima, where they planned to settle.[172] As they approached the Canadian coast, Oikawa insisted that they instead sail north to Haida Gwaii to establish the village he dreamed of there. Not only were the Queen Charlotte Islands as large as Shikoku in Japan, his friend Goro Kaburagi had reportedly told him, but there were "only a few Indians and even fewer Whites living there." Immediately adjacent to some of the richest fishing grounds in British Columbia, Kuichi Airan, as Japanese immigrants called Haida Gwaii, was a place that had yet to be "touched by the White man's hands." There, Kaburagi suggested, they could "build a church and create a little Japan in Canada."[173] Oikawa hoped that he could get permission from Canadian government authorities to bring three or four hundred settlers over from Japan but also reportedly recognized that his only option might be to smuggle them in.[174] Reminded that the Queen Charlotte Islands were located within the borders of the Canadian nation-state, however, he is said to have responded, "In this Canada, there are French who have built a French-only land, there are Germans who have built farm colonies for Germans, and the English have built English towns. What is so strange about one island in Canada for Japanese?"[175]

Unable to find a place to put ashore along the rocky coast of Haida Gwaii and faced with growing discord among his passengers, who had already spent forty-eight days aboard the small vessel on which they had crossed the Pacific, Oikawa turned back toward the Strait of Juan de Fuca, where his passengers went ashore on Vancouver Island. Oikawa would abandon his dream of establishing a "Japanese utopia the size of Shikoku" on Kuichi Airan, however, only when the Japanese consul intervened and told him in no uncertain terms not to proceed with his plan. Not only did the consul "have it on good authority that the Canadian authorities ha[d] authorized the Coast Guard to open fire on any such vessels that approach[ed] the Queen Charlotte Islands," but it could "result in a serious diplomatic incident between Japan and Canada." "The honour of Japan is at stake," the consul reportedly told Oikawa, and "the days of phantom immigrant ships are over." "Japanese who are here already," the consul said, "must concentrate on co-operating with their neighbors, studying hard, and assimilating into the local population."[176]

The collective efforts of Japanese entrepreneurs to develop new export businesses based on previously untapped resources also led to the establishment of other promising industries. It was while Ikeda was searching for new fishing grounds near Haida Gwaii to supply the salt herring market he had opened in China in 1906, his son-in-law later recalled, that he learned that there was copper ore along the shores of Guuna GawGa (Bare Bay), where two Haida villages had once been located.[177] Within a year, Ikeda staked a series of overlapping mining claims on behalf of Awaya, Ikeda and Company around what settlers would come to call Ikeda Bay, assigning the claims such whimsical names as Peach, Lily, Sweet Pea, Pansy, Violet, Wisteria, Lotus, Persimmon, Cherry, Apricot, Bamboo, and Rose.[178] Ikeda Mine would prove to be the only commercially viable copper mine in the area at the time.[179] By 1908, it employed 150 miners, most of them Japanese and many brought directly from Japan for that purpose, to the point where the area surrounding the mine came to known as "little Japan."[180] Its facilities included a 275-foot dock, a deep and accessible harbor, ore bunkers, and a tram line from the mine down to Ikeda Bay.[181] Residents celebrated Dominion Day, which marks Canada's confederation, on July 1, as well as the Meiji emperor's birthday on November 3.[182]

In contrast to the herring salteries in Nanaimo, the success of Ikeda Mine attracted not the ire but the admiration of his white neighbors. These included both the provincial constable and the stipendiary magistrate based in Jedway, some four miles away, who visited Ikeda Mine on a regular basis, often joining Ikeda and Joseph Marco, the German American mining engineer he hired, for dinner.[183] In August 1908, Ikeda welcomed British Columbia's attorney general and other officials with a large arch built on the pier from which flew Canada's flag, with the Union Jack still in one corner, crossed with that of Japan, the *hi no maru*.[184] Even the Prince Rupert *Empire*, which had stridently opposed Japanese immigration and the hiring of Japanese laborers by the Grand Trunk Pacific Railway, expressed its grudging admiration for Ikeda's mining operation, holding it up as an example that "might be followed to advantage by companies managed and doctored by white men."[185] Haida leaders also visited on occasion, although there is no evidence that any Haida were employed at the mine, and Ikeda shared with white settlers the assumption that the Haida had long abandoned Moresby Island, notwithstanding their own insistence that they had never surrendered their own claims to any part of their territories.[186]

Copper prices surged with the outbreak of war in Europe in 1914, as did the demand for lumber and canned fish. While B.C. industrialists rallied to meet the demand, Canada was in no position to defend its own west coast. More concerned with defending Canada's Atlantic coast, Great Britain responded to the presence of German vessels near the mouth of the Strait of Juan de Fuca, where they posed a potential danger to the ports of Victoria and Vancouver, by asking Japan, which had entered the war as its ally in accordance with the Anglo-Japanese Alliance, to take on the task of protecting the B.C. coast. The arrival of Japanese warships in Burrard Inlet in August 1914 was warmly welcomed by many in British Columbia.[187] Nakayama would proudly declare a few years later that the participation of "our motherland, the Empire of the Rising Sun," on Great Britain's side in the war had forced B.C. officials to reconsider their hostility toward Japanese immigrants.[188] Anti-Japanese sentiment rebounded, however, when soldiers returned from the front.[189] Copper prices dropped precipitously following the end of the war, leading to the suspension of mining operations at Ikeda Mine.[190] Demand for salt salmon and herring also dropped in Japan during a postwar economic downturn, even as herring runs along the B.C. and Alaska coasts that had once seemed inexhaustible disappeared entirely or were so depleted that they seemed on the verge of doing so.[191]

Indigenous peoples all along the north Pacific coast had long complained of the impact of industrial scale fishing on both the herring and the salmon runs on which they had long depended to sustain them through the winter.[192] Herring had once been "so thick you could walk on them," Tsimshian speaker Moses Johnson told the McKenna-McBride Commission in 1915, but over time their numbers had been reduced to a point where there were almost none left to be caught. The demise of one species also had an impact on the other. "The spring salmon follow the herring," he explained, "and if the herring are driven from here there are no spring salmon."[193] Although the many canneries operating along the coast were primarily responsible for the decline in numbers, however, *nikkei* fishermen were also a focus of Tsimshian complaints.[194] Local canners allowed Japanese fishers to use seine nets even on spawning grounds immediately adjacent to their reserves, Tsimshian witnesses testified, while the Tsimshian residents of those reserves were denied licenses of any kind to fish for herring. Also troubling was the fact that Japanese fishermen, in their view, caught more herring than they needed, so that many went to waste.[195] Even when fisheries officers sent Japanese fishermen away from the shore, Tsimshian witnesses reported, they moved just a short way down the coast and carried on. When one fisheries officer insisted that Japanese did not fish close to the reserve during the spawning season, Moses Johnson wryly responded, "[The officer] was at Prince Rupert and could not see, whereas I was on the ground and could see."[196] Indian Agent C. C. Perry also confirmed the Tsimshian accounts, noting that white British subjects had done the same. When he spoke to the cannery manager about this, the manager "replied that if the Indians didn't shut up," he would contact the Dominion government to demand that it forbid their practice of gathering herring spawn for food. "Far more harm was done to the fisheries by Indians robbing the spawning grounds," the manager declared, than by all the fish caught for the canneries. Neither Perry nor the members of the McKenna-McBride Commission were swayed by his claim. As both dryly observed, the Tsimshian had gathered herring spawn every spring as long as could be remembered and it had not yet had a negative impact on the number of herring that returned each year.[197]

Bolstered by the strong demand for salt herring in Shanghai and Hong Kong, as well as in Korea, Taiwan, and Manchuria, fish salteries in Nanaimo and elsewhere along the Pacific coast survived the postwar downturn, searching out new fishing grounds to replace those that had been depleted.[198] While B.C. residents would take great pride in the herring industry as it rebounded, many criticized the fact that it remained "largely in the hands of Japanese fishermen." In 1924, B.C. fishery officials predicted that Japanese could "be as easily eliminated from that fishery as they are being eliminated from the salmon fisheries of the north, by yearly reducing the number of licenses issued to Japanese."[199] Complaints nevertheless persisted. For a number of months, a Miss Caldwell of Ganges, B.C., wrote in 1928, Japanese fishing boats filled with herring bound for Japan had passed many times an hour. Even "local Indians tell us they cannot get a fresh herring except [when] they buy them from the Japs, who are disinclined to sell them in small quantities." "We wouldn't mind the Japs getting some fish if they need them," she added, "if we might have some also for ourselves and our domestic animals, cats and dogs, etc."[200] "Surely," declared a Prince Rupert resident north along the coast, "it is as important to feed the Canadian hen as it is to feed the Oriental humans."[201] Others, however, objected to such racist diatribe, including a Mr. McInnes, who, in contrast, "demanded fair treatment for Japanese, who established the saltery herring industry," and characterized the effort to force Japanese fishers out of the fishing industry both "un-British" and as "camouflaged confiscation."[202]

Also a growing source of irritation during the interwar period was the belief that the dry salt herring business gave "the bulk of its freight money to Japanese Maru boats."[203] Japanese shipping lines, V. J. Creeden complained, were "subsidized by the Japanese government," which purportedly gave "secret rebates" that were "payable in Japan to consignees," who were "closely affiliated with those engaged in packing and shipping from British Columbia." He did concede that Canadian steamships declined to carry salt herring because passengers objected to its odor. But he also claimed that saltery owners sent all of their profits to Japan, where they also resided, each year, returning only when "the season opens for packing Dry Salt Salmon" in the early fall. Japanese saltery managers, he alleged, also did not comply with a newly adopted regulation that required that half of those hired to work in B.C. salteries be "White and/or Native Indian labour." Instead, he claimed, "Japanese packers contend in a very subtle manner that White labour is not dependable and will not stay with the employment." Still another strategy employed by Japanese saltery owners, according to Creeden, involved agreements with non-Japanese in whose names the saltery licenses were issued, a strategy not unlike that utilized by Japanese farmers south of the border to avoid the impact of alien land laws. Creeden cited as an example what he described as the "camouflaged identity of Messrs. Bush-Mack & Co.," which, he alleged, existed solely "to supply T. Matsuyama & Co. with Dry Salt Herrings for sale and shipment to Messrs. Eiwa Yoko of Shanghai." The only way to address the problem, he believed, was to replace the transpacific trade with Japan with trade ties to other corners of the British empire, obtaining salt from the West Indies and purchasing nets elsewhere than from Japan.[204]

Harry E. Hoffman of Kyuquot Sound on Vancouver Island's northwest coast offered a still more complex series of allegations. The salmon saltery near his home on Kyuquot Sound that was "supposed to be owned by a white man, G. L. Davis," he reported, was instead "run by Japs and [had] all Japs working there." He also alleged that "at least 70 per cent of the fish taken . . .

last season were caught illegally, either by towing sets or inside the limit" and reported that he had seen "one Indian in the mouth of the creek near [his] home catch over 200" for the saltery. They had developed a strategy to avoid enforcement, he claimed: "This man Davis had small gas boats towing the skiff while the seine boat towed the other end of the net. They also used these boats to signal when the fishery officer was coming [and that] does not give the officer a chance to enforce the law."[205]

Ultimately, however, it was not complaints by white settlers but events across the Pacific that would have the greatest impact on the salt herring industry in British Columbia. By the early 1930s, the outbreak of hostilities in Manchuria had swept across the Pacific Ocean in the form of a boycott of all Japanese-made products organized by China in the wake of Japan's invasion of its northern territories. Because some B.C. salteries were widely reported to be financed by companies with close ties to Japan, salt fish originating in Canada was also included in the boycott even though, as B.C. officials admitted, British Columbia's salteries were "largely operated" not by Japanese subjects but "by naturalized and Canadian-born Japanese."[206] By August 1933, as a result of the boycott, they were "virtually out of business and the salteries closed." Even this news did not mollify those who were determined to complain. "The Japanese fishing of herring must be eliminated absolutely to re-establish this industry," one B.C. resident declared. Given that "the great majority of Japanese in B.C. are naturalized and are entitled to obtain a license," fishery officials responded, there was not much that they could do to achieve this end. But there was no reason for concern, they added: the "Japanese" were "practically down and out," and there was nothing to stop "white operators from stepping in to take their place."[207]

Halibut

Despite the strident rhetoric surrounding Japanese Canadian participation in the salmon and herring fisheries, facilitated by the ready conflation of Japanese nationals with naturalized Japanese immigrants and Canadian-born British subjects—a persistent practice intended to imply that their claim to a share of British Columbia's natural resources was somehow illegitimate—the halibut fishery was one from which they were not excluded. Given its great promise, Nakayama later wrote, it was unfortunate that Japanese did not establish themselves in the halibut fishery to the same degree as in other fisheries. He recognized, however, that their relative lack of interest in the halibut fishery was also the reason that fisheries officials had not taken steps to limit the number of halibut licenses issued to Japanese Canadian fishers.[208] North of the international border in Alaska, where Japanese immigrants were denied any opportunity to apply for U.S. citizenship, they remained foreign nationals excluded from all commercial fisheries on that basis regardless of how deep the roots they had put down in Alaska may have been. By 1912, commercial fishing licenses in Alaska were restricted to Native Alaskans and U.S. citizens or those who had declared that they intended to become a citizen, with the result that Japanese immigrants who settled in Alaska did not have the same opportunity to establish themselves as fishermen as those in British Columbia.[209] "The Jap is barred from citizenship," the *Ketchikan Miner* assured its readers in 1912, and in no position "to interfere with our fishing industry." Had "the Jap" been able "to secure a monopoly of the herring business," it warned, it would have been "only a step from that to the salmon and halibut industries." Alaska should not allow its fisheries to "be stolen by a crowd of foreigners who do not contribute a cent to our district."[210] The *Fairbanks Daily Times* equated Alaska's legislation barring Japanese from its fisheries with California's alien land laws. Both bills, it explained, were motivated by a shared desire to repel the "Japanese invasion," but Alaska's approach was the wiser. Whereas, it claimed, Alaska's law barring aliens ineligible for citizenship from participation in its fisheries was "directed against all foreigners alike," Californians had tried "to single out the Japs in their efforts to thwart the[ir] colonization plans," making it more likely that their bill would be overturned. There was great danger, the *Fairbanks Daily Times* declared, in "permitting the Japs to secure too strong a foothold at any point along the Pacific coast."[211]

The halibut fishery was particularly vulnerable to claims of poaching, given that the best halibut grounds along the north Pacific coat were located along the banks of the Juan de Fuca Strait and the Dixon Entrance, both of them channels through which separate sections of the U.S.-Canada border ran. The Makah were among those who had traditionally fished for halibut along the banks of what the Spanish had called the Juan de Fuca Strait.[212] The Haida, in turn, had long gathered every year to fish the halibut banks off the northern end of Graham Island, which were among the richest in the region. It was for this reason that Ikeda had explored the waters around Haida Gwaii in a search for new fishing grounds, before being diverted by other opportunities.[213] There were also rich halibut banks along the Alaska coast, where nearly all the early European explorers had observed that halibut were second only to salmon as a food source for Indigenous coastal peoples. It was only after the Northern Pacific Railway reached its terminus in Seattle in 1888, however, that commercial halibut fishing in the north Pacific borderlands began in

Arichika Ikeda, standing by a boat on a beach across from Ikeda Mine together with several young Japanese men. Ikeda's partner Shinazo Awaya stands on the boat with his hand on a large halibut with the wharf and ore bunkers visible behind him, circa 1909. Three more halibut are visible on the ground. Haida Gwaii Museum at Kay Llangaay, Skidegate, B.C., Phillips Dalzell Fonds, Chisato Tokunaga Collection, 1907–1915, Ph. 02398.

earnest. A railroad link to eastern markets was key because halibut were preserved on ice, unlike herring and salmon, which could also be salted or canned. Also a factor that facilitated the development of the halibut industry, a B.C. Fisheries Commission report noted, was "the coming to the north [Pacific] coast of men and boats from the halibut fishery of the North Atlantic."[214]

The impact of the commercial fishery was apparent in just two decades. As late as 1907, halibut were still so numerous on both the Masset and the Ketchikan banks of the Hecate Strait that men recalled seeing "halibut swimming up to the door."[215] By 1910, however, the banks around the Dixon Entrance and the Strait of Juan de Fuca were so depleted that the halibut fishery had become a deep-sea fishery. So dramatic were the years of "overproduction and expansion" that followed that, by 1914, the B.C. government had become concerned about the need to take steps to "preserve the species from the almost total depletion" that was sure to occur if nothing were done. While the outbreak of the First World War gave halibut a respite, completion of the Grand Trunk Pacific Railway, which had its terminus in Prince Rupert and provided a still more direct link between the most productive North Pacific halibut grounds and eastern markets than Seattle, ensured both the resurgence of the halibut fishery after the war ended and Prince Rupert's place as its regional center.[216]

In the halibut as well as other fisheries, the fact that Japanese settlers in Alaska remained foreign nationals facilitated not only their conflation with Japanese subjects resident in Japan but also the characterization of any Japanese resident of Alaska caught fishing without a license not as a citizen who had failed to comply with regulatory licensing requirements, generally regarded as a minor infraction, but as a poacher engaged in an act of piracy.[217] Fears that Japan might encroach on Alaskan waters dated back to the early 1900s. In 1905, for example, Seward's *Daily Gateway* had blared the headline "Run Out Jap Fishermen" after "U.S. military vessels confiscated dried salmon from Japanese fishing schooners deemed as poachers." A similar incident, it stated, had occurred a year before during which the Japanese crew were reportedly "very fresh with American fishmen." It was "to discourage Japanese encroachment on American preserves" that the U.S. revenue cutter *Commodore Perry* had been sent to Alaskan waters at the time.[218] Japanese Canadian fishers who drifted into Alaskan waters in search of halibut were also sometimes targeted and charged with poaching, as was one young fisherman who was caught and fined after he crossed the nautical boundary that divides the coastal waters of British Columbia from those of Alaska in search of good halibut.[219] In 1913, determined to stop what U.S. government officials regarded as an "invasion of Alaska waters by foreign halibut fishermen," the secretary of commerce, then responsible for governing what was now the territory of Alaska, requested police boats that could be used to intercept the Japanese, Russian, and Canadian fishermen believed to be encroaching into Alaskan waters.[220] When "Japanese-manned vessels with Canadian registry" were spotted fishing for halibut along the Alaska coast in 1939, however, Japanese living in Alaska defended them, telling reporters that if the boats were close to shore, it was only because they were forced to take refuge there by "weather or mechanical trouble."[221]

Sealers and "Poachers"

Claims alleging that Japanese poachers were active along Alaska's western coasts had also long been raised in connection with the sealing industry. Among the oldest of the maritime industries to attract Euro-American sailors to the north Pacific coast but eclipsed for a time by the rhetoric surrounding other industrial-scale fisheries, sealing once again emerged as a key focus of dispute among imperial powers in the North Pacific during the 1930s.

Although British and Canadian sealers dominated the pelagic sealing industry through 1902, the Meiji government offered Japanese sealers a ten-dollar
bonus to support the development of its sealing industry in 1906, in the wake
of the destruction of many of the rookeries along its northern coasts by British
and American seal hunters during the second half of the nineteenth century.
In July 1906, Japanese hunters went ashore on St. Paul Island to slaughter
seals there. Discovered by Indigenous men assigned to guard the seal islands,
some surrendered but others refused to comply. After firing a warning round,
the guards were ordered to fire on them, killing five Japanese and leading to
the arrest of a dozen more even as others made their escape, returning to their
sealing schooners on the small boats they had used to reach shore. Some two
hundred dead seals were left behind.[222] Reports that Japanese seal poachers
were active in Alaskan waters would continue to circulate, including claims
that they posed a danger to Indigenous people along the Alaskan coast, who
were sometimes forced to provide them with food.[223] "If this Japanese poaching business continues," the *Douglas Island News* declared in May 1909, "all
the jails in Alaska will be full of Japs."[224] The pursuit of both seals and halibut
also drew vessels registered in Japan deep into Hecate Strait, which divides
Haida Gwaii from the continental mainland and is nearly a hundred miles
wide, exacerbating fears that Japan was encroaching in both Canadian and
American waters. "The sealing question," the *Fairbanks Daily Times* predicted
in 1911, "is the rock upon which Japan and American friendship will split."[225]

In July 1911, the United States, Britain, Japan, and Russia entered into the
North Pacific Fur Seal Convention, agreeing to outlaw the pelagic hunting of
fur seals on the waters of the open ocean north of the thirtieth parallel in the
Bering Sea, the Sea of Okhotsk, the waters of Kamchatka, and the Sea of
Japan. In 1867, when the United States acquired Russian interests in Alaska,
the seal population of the Pribilof Islands had been estimated to be over 2
million. By 1911, just 123,600 seals remained. In exchange for payments based
on the value of the skins taken each year, all of the parties to the agreement
acknowledged that the United States had the jurisdictional authority to manage the onshore hunting of seals in these islands for commercial purposes.[226]
The U.S. Congress acted almost immediately to impose a moratorium of five
years on the hunting of seals in the rookeries that served as their breeding
grounds on the Pribilof Islands to give the herds a chance to recover; similar
protections were extended to the Japanese and Russian rookeries.[227] Only
Indigenous peoples around the North Pacific Rim, including both the Aleut
and the Ainu, were exempted from the constraints imposed under the treaty,
although they were required to use traditional technologies, including canoes

and handmade spears, to hunt for seals.[228] During the months before the North Pacific Fur Seal Convention was ratified in November 1911, however, British and Russian cutters captured several Japanese sealing vessels operating in Canadian waters and in the waters near the Komandorski Islands.[229]

On December 1, 1926, two weeks before the initial fifteen-year term of the North Pacific Fur Seal Convention expired, Arichika Ikeda, now special commissioner for Canada on behalf of the Japanese imperial government's Department of Agriculture and Commerce, forwarded a translated copy of a letter outlining Japan's position to John P. Babcock at the Bureau of Fisheries in Victoria, B.C., and assuring Babcock that his government "now thoroughly understood [his] admirable opinion." It was willing to find a way to settle the matter, he wrote, but the Japanese people were so strongly opposed to the treaty that it was hard put to find a way to "soothe them."[230] Amendments proposed by Japan included both a greater percentage of the seal skins taken in the Pribilof Islands and a request that its share of seal skins be sent directly to Japan for processing and dyeing, rather than to St. Louis. Japan also requested that it be permitted to hunt fur seals on islands along the coast of Japan and Sakhalin during the fall migration in "the manner permitted to Indians off the coast of B.C. and Alaska, where some thousands of skins are annually taken," seeking to position itself, in effect, as simultaneously both an Indigenous and a modern nation.[231] Captain Charles Spring, like William Munsie, the master of a sealing schooner that was once part of the Canadian fleet, argued in response that "in order to be fair, Japan should show that she has a class among her people" equivalent to the Indigenous people of the B.C. coast "accustomed to hunt the Seals for its meat for food for themselves."[232] Ironically, however, even as the United States insisted that it was important that Russia remain a party to any agreement, it was unwilling to call the parties together to renegotiate the treaty because it refused to recognize the new Russian government.[233]

By 1930, Japan's request to renegotiate the North Pacific Fur Seal Convention had still not been acted on. Its ever more urgent request for such a renegotiation, however, had expanded to include the additional claim that the seal herds of the North Pacific had grown so large that they were decimating the supply of fish needed to feed the Japanese population.[234] While Japan was by no means alone in seeking to justify the continued slaughter of seals and sea lions on the ground that they purportedly posed a danger to salmon, this was an argument roundly refuted by scientists whose studies showed that "seals subsisted largely on octopus and squid," which were also "known to be of injury to salmon," while "sea lions [were] primarily mollusk and crustacea eaters."[235] As the 1930s progressed, an increasing number of Japanese floating canneries and mother ships were spotted off Alaska's west coast.[236] In response, Miller Freemen, chairman of the Joint Committee for Protection of Pacific Fisheries, urged the United States to assert sole jurisdiction over the entire length of the continental shelf, warning that "unless fishing within sight of the Pacific Coast by aliens is checked, our salmon resources may be destroyed at any time."[237] Responding to repeated criticism in 1939, one Japanese fisheries official declared that "the Japanese people regard it as their inevitable fate or even sacred mission to develop riches hidden in the sea" and to "exploit [both] resources in the northern seas and southern waters." This was why Japanese fishermen were operating floating canneries and fish meal factories "in the Okhotsk and Behring Sea and off Alaska." "Japanese fishermen," he insisted, were "neither reckless [catchers] nor lawless trespassers." Invoking the same rationale that European imperial powers used to justify their own seizure of Indigenous lands and resources in North America, he added that Japanese also "firmly believe that all the marine resources of high seas are endowed to those who exploit and utilize them for useful purposes."[238]

THE DETERMINED CONFLATION of Japanese nationals with naturalized and Canadian-born British subjects of Japanese ancestry, together with the fact that Japanese in Alaska had no option but to remain Japanese subjects, also continued to cause problems in inland waters along the coast. In 1938, Vancouver's *Daily Province* reported, a group of white fishers drove seven "Japanese" fishing vessels away from Bull Harbor, located off the northern tip of Vancouver Island and named after the seals that had long abandoned it. As the *Daily Province* reported:

> Advancing in solid formation, almost hull to hull, sixty trolling boats, manned by white fishermen, bore down on a group of seven Japanese fishing boats . . . as they lay at anchor in Bull Harbor early this morning, and with a force that was irresistible, pushed them slowly outside the harbor, anchors and all. Despite the shouts of the astonished Japanese, the white boats kept steadily, relentlessly on, without heat or violence. [Once] the Japanese boats were clear of the anchoring ground, they were allowed to get under way, and the entire white fleet escorted them eastward past Shushartie Bay . . . , where they were left with warnings not to return to this fishing area again.

Reminiscent of the expulsion efforts of earlier decades, both in its aggression and in its assertion that it was a "peaceful" response, the decision to drive the fishing boats out of the harbor followed an indignation meeting at which the "Japanese" fishers were warned to "get out." In response to an appeal for support from the seven fishers, fisheries officials sent a government boat to meet with the white fishers to explain that the seven vessels were legally entitled to fish in the Bull Harbor area. It was only then that the white fishers had decided to take matters into their own hands.[239]

Growing tensions along the B.C. and Alaska coasts reflected the steady rise in hostility among the imperial powers over access to both fishery and marine mammal resources and in response to such events as Japan's invasion of China. These tensions coincided with growing conflict between Japan and Russia over the coastal waters of the western Pacific, which led Japan to warn Russia in 1939 that it might act to defend its "bitterly contested fishing rights off the coast of eastern Siberia."[240] Japanese fishing operations in the eastern Pacific, the *Fairbanks Daily News-Miner* reported, had increased in the wake of its dispute with Russia in the western Pacific, posing a danger not only to Alaska but also to British Columbia and to all three U.S. Pacific states. "If the Japanese should be successful in their attack upon the Bristol Bay fishery," the *News-Miner* predicted, "they will undoubtedly follow on down the American Coast operating against the fisheries of the region wherever they find it profitable."[241]

In 1940, Japan declared its intention to abrogate the Fur Seal Convention, which had still not been renegotiated despite its repeated requests that this occur. In abrogating the convention, the *Alaska Miner* declared, Japan was also "throwing overboard indefinitely the more important 'gentlemen's agreement'" pertaining to the taking of salmon along the B.C. and Alaska coasts. The active presence of Japanese sealing vessels in the Pribilof Islands, it predicted, would also increase the pressure on Alaska's salmon runs and trigger new rounds of salmon disputes. In the past, vessels registered in Japan had operated "further west around Dutch Harbor and Unalaska [and] around the Aleutians or along the northern side of the Alaska peninsula to Bristol Bay," the *Alaska Miner* reported, but in August 1940 "four Jap 'fish' boats were sighted at Katalla, on the southern extremity of the Alaska peninsula and just over one hundred miles from the Kodiak Navy Base now under construction." Equating these fish boats with "[thieves] sneaking in one's back door," it raised the question whether they were genuine fish boats or actually "Jap naval vessels." "Every Jap has always been looked upon as a spy," it declared, promising that "at the first sign of Jap poachers and their so-called 'fishboats,' Alaska fishermen will go after them with three-fold vigor," not only because they were encroaching on marine resources Alaskans regarded as their own but also based on a "natural hatred" for "all participants of the Nazi Axis." Perhaps, the editors of the *Alaska Miner* mused, "an Alaska fish war will precipitate putting the 'sunrise kingdom' back where Commodore Perry found them in 1853."[242]

Noting the growing tensions surrounding these disputes as he prepared his final draft of his history of Canada and the Japanese in 1940, Nakayama himself observed, "Ominous clouds have recently begun to gather over the Ocean." "While the Japanese-Canadians sincerely hope that these dark clouds will be cleared up in the near future," he mused, "they are in a difficult situation sandwiched between their fatherland and their adopted motherland on both sides of the Pacific Ocean."[243]

CHAPTER FIVE

The Pacific Borderlands in Wartime

The same Pacific ocean boundary that had long served as a gateway to its wealth of marine resources was also increasingly seen as a point of vulnerability as tensions among the imperial powers that had a stake in controlling or accessing those resources escalated. Rumblings of war and rumors that Japanese spies had infiltrated the north Pacific coast ahead of a planned invasion of British Columbia and Alaska, and indeed the entire Pacific coast, date back to the earliest years of the twentieth century. They grew louder with the onset of the First World War despite Japan's role as an ally of both Britain and the United States in that war. In Alaska, Jujiro Wada, who had resigned himself to making a living by guiding other prospectors to promising gold mining sites given that he, as a Japanese subject, was denied the opportunity to become a U.S. citizen as was required to stake a claim, was accused of spying on behalf of Japan's imperial government based on the carefully drawn maps that depicted promising claims, as well as the best routes to use to reach them, that were found among his possessions.[1] In 1923, the *Cordova Daily Times* revived these accusations, warning its readers that Japan, which had retained control of German colonial interests in China and the western Pacific at the end of the war, was now "casting covetous eyes on Alaska's defenseless territory" and planned to include it within its "grip." Wada's extensive knowledge of the north and his ability to travel easily across its wide expanses was the primary "evidence" on which his accuser's claims rested. For what other reason, his accuser asked, would anyone develop the degree of familiarity with Alaska and the Yukon needed to travel throughout the region in all seasons of the year as Wada had?[2]

In British Columbia, as well, the very mobility of Japanese Canadian fishermen, together with their deep familiarity with British Columbia's coastal waters, would repeatedly be turned against them, cited as evidence to suggest that there must be Japanese spies among them.[3] As J. A. Motherwell, chief inspector of fisheries, would remind the International Fisheries Commission in 1939, the Japanese Canadian fishermen who lived near the Fraser River regularly "wander up as far as the Naas River during the fishing season and return to the areas around their homes after the sockeye fishing is through up North." "The salmon trollers," in particular, were "pretty well scattered all over the coast, . . . [from] Dixon's Entrance which is just south of the International

Boundary; and in the north, and around the Queen Charlotte Islands . . . and down Hecate Straits and around the north end of Vancouver Island, and around to [the] Alert Bay area, and all down the west coast of Vancouver Island and in the Gulf of Georgia in certain seasons of the year."[4]

As early as 1914, the same year, ironically, that the Japanese Imperial Navy acceded to Great Britain's request that it send vessels to defend the B.C. coast against the potential threat posed by German submarines spotted near the Juan de Fuca Strait, rumors that Japanese naval officers disguised as fishers based both in Steveston and in Prince Rupert were preparing charts of British Columbia's coastal waters on its behalf were also rampant.[5] By 1933, B.C. member of Parliament Thomas Reid did not hesitate to declare as established fact the oft-repeated allegation that many Japanese Canadian fishermen were actually "Japanese naval officers spying on the B.C. coast." A year later the Royal Canadian Mounted Police (RCMP) reported that a Japanese informant not only had confirmed this but had also alleged that "many Jap fishermen belong[ed] to the samurai group" and that they knew "every inch of the area in which they fish[ed]."[6]

Claims that there were former naval officers among the Japanese immigrants who settled in British Columbia were not entirely unfounded. As Richard White and other Western historians have noted, popular myths often resonate in part because they contain elements of truth, even as they sustain false narratives by failing to tell more complete stories.[7] Yasukichi Yoshizawa, who journeyed north along the B.C. coast in 1890 in search of opportunities for Japanese migrants, was himself a former naval officer trained in navigation, one reason he felt able to undertake such a trip with the aid of just a single roughly drawn nautical chart.[8] The same was true of the secretary of the Japanese Fishermen's Association, Jujiro Takenouchi, also known as James Tenning.[9] Among those who emigrated to North America after the Russo-Japanese War ended in 1905, as well, were soldiers and sailors unable to find work in Japan when they returned from the front.[10] But allegations that these sailors remained in the employ of Japan's Imperial Navy were at best unproved, and the notion that a majority of the Japanese Canadian fishers along the B.C. coast were former samurai was neither a statistical probability nor true of most, particularly those from fishing communities in Japan, where they occupied a very different place within the rigidly stratified social structure of the Tokugawa period than samurai did.[11] Although there were also former samurai among those who emigrated to North America after the Meiji Restoration, among them Tomekichi Homma, who worked as a fisher for a time after he first arrived in British Columbia in 1883, samurai constituted less than 7 percent of Japan's population during the Tokugawa period, making it highly unlikely that they ever constituted a majority of any group of emigrants in North America, including those involved in the fishing industry. While visiting naval officers were welcomed by Japanese settlers in both Canada and the United States, especially during the First World War, this was in large part because they exemplified the transformation Japan had undergone in becoming a modern imperial power, as well as its role as an ally of both Britain and the United States during that war, rather than for nefarious reasons.

Rumors that Japanese naval officers were active along the eastern shores of the Pacific Ocean, however, resonated along the entire length of the Pacific coast, including south of the U.S.-Mexico border in Baja California. In 1934, these rumors were seemingly confirmed by the report of a U.S. intelligence officer, later proved unfounded, alleging that a fishing fleet under the command of "Japanese naval officers," including some fishing boats from California, had assembled in Magdalena Bay to prepare an advance base for the Imperial Navy on its shores.[12] Japanese fishers operating out of California ports "*know every* foot of the North and South American coast, including where cables are located and where mines could be laid," the Los Angeles district attorney charged, a claim duly repeated by Alaska's *Fairbanks Daily News-Miner*.[13] U.S. counterintelligence agents reportedly admitted the same year that there was no stretch of the Pacific coast of North America, from Alaska to the Panama Canal, that was not vulnerable to Japanese espionage, given that the enormous distances involved.[14] When an ongoing investigation of the "vague reports of Japanese naval officers posing as fishermen" along the Pacific coast that had circulated for years led to the seizure of nineteen unregistered fishing vessels crewed by Japanese off the coast of Hawaii in July 1941, the *Victoria Daily Times* told its readers that "expensive radio and photographic [equipment], together with navigational charts of a type unconnected with fishermen's work" had been found on board. The customs officers who had seized the vessels, in contrast, reported finding nothing of concern.[15]

During the 1930s, exaggerated claims of this kind also circulated throughout Canada, together with warnings that the alleged activities of Japanese naval officers along the Pacific coast posed a danger to all Canadians. In 1937, Nova Scotia's *Halifax Herald* published a cartoon framed by cherry blossoms and depicting a bespectacled Japanese soldier armed with both sword and pistol looming over a Canada lying in the shadow of the Japanese flag. The Anglican archdeacon of Quebec, it declared, had been "'informed on good authority' that Japanese naval officers in disguise" were "living in so-called 'fishing villages' in British Columbia."[16] Japanese naval officers, the *Toronto*

Star warned its readers in 1938, together with the "40,000 Japanese" allegedly residing in Vancouver alone, "represented a serious threat to Canadian security."[17] In July of that year, more than two years before Japan entered into the Tripartite Pact with Germany and Italy, yet another article claimed that the Japanese spies long rumored to be active in British Columbia were working with German counterparts in the province. One Japanese naval officer, the article alleged, had already established five advance naval bases in small, remote inlets located along the west coast of Vancouver Island, most of them inaccessible by land, where fuel and various other supplies had been stored in anticipation of a possible naval attack against Vancouver and other cities all along the Pacific coast.[18]

Claims that Japanese spies and saboteurs traveled freely among the many small channels and islands that line the B.C. and Alaska coasts resonated in turn with claims that Japanese boats had landed individuals surreptitiously on the west coasts of Vancouver Island or Haida Gwaii.[19] Where suspicions related to smuggling and illicit border crossings had once been directed mainly against Indigenous peoples like the Haida, who had continued to travel throughout their maritime territories without reference to the international border that divided British Columbia and Alaska during the nineteenth century, such suspicions were over time redirected against Japanese. As early as 1901, B.C. newspapers alleged that Japanese migrants were smuggling into Canada from the United States through the Gulf Islands just south of the forty-ninth parallel and that Japanese vessels had put migrants ashore at places that were not ports of entry.[20] In 1910, the *Nicola Valley News* reported that George H. Cowan, member of Parliament for Vancouver, B.C., had claimed that Japanese migrants were being smuggled into British Columbia through Haida Gwaii as a way of avoiding the constraints of the Gentlemen's Agreement that Japan had acceded to in 1907 at Canada's request in the wake of the Vancouver Riot. This charge, it asserted, had been "substantiated by fishermen and others in close touch with [the] Queen Charlotte islands." If verified, it would prove once and for all that the persistent rumors regarding such activity were accurate and that the "Mikado's government" could not be counted on to honor the commitments it made in such agreements.[21] In August 1913, reports circulated that Canada's Dominion government had ordered that a search be undertaken for a "Japanese junk which landed eleven Japanese at Bella Coola," located across Hecate Strait, southeast of Haida Gwaii, on the B.C. mainland. Just nine of those who had been landed were apprehended, and one later escaped. The vessel that put them ashore, however, had last been seen "becalmed well within the three-mile limit," and, if intercepted,

B.C. newspapers assured their readers, its captain would be subject to a penalty of $600 per person set ashore.[22]

As in the case of claims that some Japanese immigrants had previously served in Japan's Imperial Navy, suspicions that Japanese were occasionally put ashore in out-of-the-way places were not entirely without foundation. An elderly *issei* man whom Kazuo Ito interviewed in the 1960s conceded that "in 1893 ten young people from [Mio-mura] landed secretly at Steveston, at the mouth of the Frazer [*sic*] River." Early Japanese pioneers in Canada included some, such as Yasukichi Yoshizawa, Ito adds, who had stowed away on an oceangoing steamer or crossed the border into Canada from the United States.[23] The 1906 arrival of the group of immigrants from Miyagi Prefecture who had left Japan surreptitiously in a small vessel they chartered themselves to avoid the Meiji government's own constraints on labor emigration and settled on Oikawa-jima likewise seemed to confirm that this was a persistent pattern given their decision to cast ashore on Vancouver Island. As earlier migrants may also have been, they were clearly unaware that failure to comply with Japan's emigration restrictions would not have barred them from entering Canada under the existing law at the time as long as they reported to an immigration officer on arrival and passed a medical inspection.[24] Rumors circulating at the time suggest that at least some of the Japanese miners brought from Japan to work at the Ikeda Mine on Moresby Island in Haida Gwaii during the early decades of the twentieth century also disembarked without first traveling to Victoria or another port of entry. An RCMP investigation assigned to follow up on claims that Haida Gwaii served as a base for Japanese spies who entered Canada surreptitiously, however, concluded in 1921 that there was nothing to fear in this regard. "The Japanese mine and nearby wireless station had been closed," its report noted, and "shoals made the coast there of little use as a base for submarines or large war vessels."[25] Despite its findings, reports that "a smuggling ring . . . operated in the dark of night using the far side of the Queen Charlotte Islands as a landing site" persisted even among Japanese settlers well into the 1930s.[26]

Fueled in part by Japan's efforts to secure a greater share of the maritime resources of the Pacific Ocean, reports that Japanese migrants were illegally put ashore along the B.C. coast also reinforced claims made north of the B.C.-Alaska border that men on board Japanese schooners had deserted or that Japanese seal poachers operating in Alaskan waters had landed Japanese migrants on remote islands off the Alaska coast. In May 1908, for example, the *Douglas Island News* reported that "a Japanese sailing vessel landed four Japs on an island near Sitka," where they were found by Alaska Natives "in a half

starved condition," with the result, the *Alaska Prospector* added, that "the Indians on the Island were forced to provide the Japanese with food until the
latter could make their way to Sitka."[27] In 1914, in turn, several students who
wanted to study at American universities but were not granted passports in
Japan to travel to the United States signed on as seamen aboard a steamer
bound for Nome, Alaska, where they jumped ship in the hope that, once they
were on U.S. soil, they would then be able to make their way south to the
contiguous states.[28]

In response to such persistent reports of illicit entry, Japanese diplomats
endeavored to turn cases where Japanese had entered the United States or
Canada illegally to their advantage, arguing that North Americans should not
blame the Japanese government for the behavior of a few bad actors. In 1914,
Kahei Otani, a former member of the House of Peers, cited instances of illegal entry as proof of the effectiveness of the restrictions on emigration to
North America that the Japanese government had put in place in accordance
with the Gentlemen's Agreements. He cited as an example the report that
"last fall 15 reckless Japanese attempted, to the astonishment of some Americans, to cross the Pacific Ocean in a boat of ten tons." If Japan was not actively
enforcing its obligations under these agreements, he asked, why would any
emigrant risk their lives to reach the United States?[29] While a few dozen Japanese might enter the United States surreptitiously across the U.S.-Mexico
border every year, the authors of a book titled *Japan and the California Problem* wrote in 1921, "it is absurd to imagine that any wholesale smuggling is being practiced through the connivance of Japanese officials and under the
noses of competent [U.S.] officers who patrol the borders and coasts." The
Gentlemen's Agreement into which Japan had entered with Canada, they reminded their readers, had greatly reduced the number of Japanese permitted
to enter that country each year. This, they argued, had largely eliminated the
danger that Japanese might smuggle into the United States across the Canada-
U.S. border or, for that matter, anywhere along its Pacific coast, with the exception of occasional deserters who did not return to their ships. The absence
of a parallel gentlemen's agreement with Mexico, they declared, made the
U.S.-Mexico border the only real "danger zone," but even there the number of
illegal migrants was far lower than U.S. immigration officials alleged.[30]

Diplomatic Tensions

Diplomatic tensions among the imperial powers, a product of geopolitical
maneuvering related to the balance of power in the Pacific as well as the

continuing contest over the marine resources of the North Pacific, had also risen steadily during the years following the First World War, building on what was already a growing sense of frustration in Japan with anti-Japanese sentiment in the United States, which Japan would increasingly come to believe motivated U.S. criticism of Japan's own efforts to build an empire as Britain and the United States had already done.[31] A survey of leading Japanese-language journals by a London *Times* correspondent in Tokyo in October 1906 observed that while Japanese were increasingly disillusioned by reports that Japanese immigrants in the Pacific coast states were the target of racially motivated acts of hostility, they were not yet willing to believe that the racist attitudes that motivated the attacks permeated all levels of government or defined American policy toward Japan in any broader sense. Instead, he explained, most of Japan's leading journals

> note the strong contrast between America's attitude towards Japan in the days of Perry, who, with the cannon's voice, proclaimed the doctrines of universal brotherhood and the common right of all nations to nature's gifts, and the attitude of a section of Americans today, who violently advocate the expulsion of all Orientals from the American continent, but the leading journals decline to regard the action of the Pacific slope as an index of the great heart of the American nation, and declare that such unworthy, unmanly incidents cannot shake Japan's steadfast faith in her proved and constant friend, America.[32]

Much as the United States and Britain had invoked the role of civilizing power to justify both their own acquisition of new territories in North America and the pressure brought to bear on Japan to open its ports to trade with the West and to adopt Western ways in the 1850s, Japan characterized its own mission in Asia as an exercise in bestowing the benefits of civilization on the people of China, Korea, and Taiwan.[33] Whereas "Western nations have long believed that on their shoulders alone rested the responsibility of colonizing the yet unopened portions of the globe, and extending to the inhabitants the benefits of civilization," Japanese Diet member Yosaburo Takekoshi wrote in 1907, "now we Japanese, rising from the ocean in the extreme Orient, wish as a nation to take part in this great and glorious work."[34] Japan's own acquisition of new colonies in Asia, he added, also offered a solution to the persistent problem of Japanese emigration modeled after that of England itself: "[Japan] has many would-be colonists, but so far has had no colonies to which they could be sent. Germany has many colonists but has few colonies. France has colonies but has few colonists. England has both colonies and colonists. Such is the opinion of the world. Japan formerly had colonists but had no colonies. Now Korea has room for 10,000,000 immigrants, and Formosa for 2,000,000. So we have today both colonies and colonists, like England."[35]

While Japan's allies during the First World War agreed that it be allowed to retain the islands it had seized in the western North Pacific that were formerly part of Germany's colonial empire, Woodrow Wilson's failure in 1919 to support the inclusion of a racial equality clause in the League of Nations Covenant, which provided that "the principle of equality of nations and the just treatment of their nationals," including those residing in foreign countries, would from then on serve as the foundation for international relations, was deeply felt as a betrayal in Japan. Equally dismaying was Great Britain's unilateral abrogation of the Anglo-Japanese Alliance in 1921, replaced a year later by the Washington Naval Treaty, which limited key naval vessels in the Pacific to a five-five-three ratio as between the United States, Britain, and Japan.[36] Purportedly based on the fact that the United States and Britain had more wide-ranging interests in and around the Pacific Ocean, Nakayama Jinshiro wrote, Britain and the United States were really motivated by fear of Japan's growing naval power in the North Pacific.[37] As early as 1914, U.S. Navy rear admiral Charles E. Vreeland reportedly declared, Japan already had a naval fleet large enough to threaten the Pacific coast of North America—a capacity that Britain was entirely willing to take advantage of to protect Canada's Pacific coast during the war, but that quickly became a source of concern for both Britain and the United States at war's end.[38]

Growing opposition on the part of the U.S. government to Japan's dealings with China, beginning in 1915 when it opposed Japan's Twenty-One Demands and, later, its opposition to Japan's efforts to expand its base in Manchuria, was also regarded by many in Japan as deeply hypocritical.[39] In their view, Japan's absorption of contiguous territories and its efforts to secure access to the raw materials needed to support its growing industries were directly modeled on colonial practices developed and later honed first by Britain and then the United States.[40] As Konoe Fumimaro, a Japanese delegate at the Paris Peace Conference in 1919 and Japan's prime minister prior to the outbreak of the Second World War in 1945, wrote in 1918, what the United States and Great Britain meant by peace was "a status quo that is to their advantage which they dignify with the name of humanism" intended to deny late-developing nations the same opportunity to acquire new lands and build an empire as they had.[41] Particularly ironic was the fact that the United States had been complicit in Japan's expansionist plans from the start. Like other

European powers, it had not objected to Japan's absorption of either Hokkaido or the Ryukyu Islands during the early decades of the Meiji era, nor did it object to Japan's acquisition of Taiwan as a colony at the conclusion of the first Sino-Japanese War in 1896. The United States had also assured Japan in 1905 that it would not object either to its incorporation of Korea within the borders of an expanding empire or to its assumption of control over Korean foreign relations.[42] Japanese leaders were convinced that criticism of its role in China stemmed from the fact that not just the United States but also Great Britain, France, Germany, and Russia were all equally interested in asserting their own position and influence there. Only when Japan's interests began to challenge those of the United States, they observed, did it begin to criticize Japan for its efforts to do the same. Each nation, ironically, justified what it deemed its own special interest in China based in part on its "territorial propinquity" to China, a rationale that clearly provided stronger support for Japan's position than that of the United States.[43]

Passage of the 1924 Immigration Act, which all but barred further Japanese immigration to the United States, in turn, was regarded as so deeply humiliating in light of the many efforts Japan had made to address race-based concerns related to immigration, whether by restricting emigration from Japan or by identifying alternate destinations in Asia or Latin America, that it triggered public demonstrations in Japan.[44] Based on their own observations in Japan at the time, the sociologists Hugh H. Smythe and Mabel M. Smythe would later write that the 1924 Immigration Act and the U.S. Supreme Court's 1922 decision in *Ozawa v. United States* upholding the denial of citizenship to first-generation Japanese immigrants "were nationally resented as racial insults and helped to bring on Pearl Harbor and rallied the people against the United States in the Pacific phase of the Second World War."[45] Although Izumi Hirobe would disagree that the Immigration Act was a direct cause of the war, in that its repeal would not have averted war, he points out that both Emperor Hirohito and Fujita Kikuichi, the squadron leader who led the attack on Pearl Harbor in December 1941, identified "Japan's aggrieved response" to the 1924 Immigration Act "as one of the principal causes of the deadly clash" between the two nations during the Second World War.[46] The Japanese-language *Taihoku Nippo*, based in Seattle, may have put it best. Passage of the 1924 Immigration Act, it wrote, had planted "the seeds of a racial war," not in the sense that "any intelligent Japanese thinks for a moment of waging war upon America over a matter that is fundamentally domestic in character," but in the sense that it engendered a level of resentment on the part of some Japanese as of that date that would make it more difficult for

人格の人

二重

"TWO-FACED UNCLE SAM"
The Tokyo *Miyako* shows the American nation as a two-faced being,
one face being that of a gentleman and the other that of a fiend.

A political cartoon originally published in the *Miyako Shimbun* in response to U.S. passage of the 1924 Immigration Act depicted Uncle Sam as a man with a two-faced personality, republished by *The Trans-Pacific* in spring 1924.

"those who seek ways of international peace and progressive democracy in Japan . . . for decades to come."[47]

Japan's ambassador to the United States, Hanihara Masanao, had tried to warn members of Congress that the 1924 Immigration Act would have this effect only to find that his use of the phrase "grave consequences"—wording that he insisted was first suggested by U.S. secretary of state Charles E. Hughes—was deliberately misread by anti-Japanese agitators as a threat to go to war.[48] As Hanihara explained at a welcome dinner held for the new U.S. ambassador to Japan in 1930, "The resentment Japan feels toward the United States for passing the immigration law of 1924 excluding Japanese 'will never die so long as the wound inflicted remains unhealed.'"[49] Hughes himself agreed, writing that in passing the Immigration Act, Congress had "undone the work of the Washington Conference and implanted the seeds of an antagonism which are sure to bear fruit in the future." By the mid-1930s, in the wake of the League of Nations' condemnation of Japan's aggressive move into Manchuria, Japan would indeed withdraw both from the League of Nations and from the Washington Treaty system.[50]

Rumors that Japan might declare war on the United States or Great Britain or invade the Pacific coast of both Canada and the United States had begun to circulate even before Japan's victory in the Russo-Japanese War in 1905, the first time that an Asian nation defeated a Western power and a moment celebrated throughout Asia.[51] Admiral Togo Heihachiro, who led Japan to victory in its final battle against the Russian fleet, gave a series of speeches on the west coast of the United States after the war in which he sought to reassure Americans that Japan had no such intentions and expressed his appreciation to the United States for its fair handling of the treaty negotiations. "Whatever Europe might do in its selfish schemes," he had reportedly told his audiences, "America could be depended upon to be both fair and kind." By 1914, Kiyoshi Karl Kawakami would write that the United States' attitude to Japan had changed so dramatically during the decade that followed the signing of the Treaty of Portsmouth that it now appeared to regard Japan as a menace and war as unavoidable.[52] Inazo Nitobe sought to respond to fears that Japan posed a danger to the United States by refuting the notion that Japan had any interest in going to war, and particularly not with the United States. If war with the United States were ever to break out, he declared, it would not be Japan that initiated it. No other nation, he pointed out, had avoided war for over two and a half centuries as Japan had during the Tokugawa era. Japan was actively building a stronger navy only because it was needed to defend its greatly extended coastline, given Japan's incorporation of Korea and Sakhalin within the borders of its expanding empire in the wake of the Russo-Japanese War, awarded to it by the Treaty of Portsmouth. Even racially motivated attacks on Japanese, he insisted, would not cause Japan to go to war. While Japanese would not forget that they had been poorly treated by Americans, they would bear these insults "like gentlemen."[53] As such, Nitobe wrote, it remained his "sincere hope" that the "rumours of war will prove but a transient dream, a horrible nightmare that passes with the coming of the dawn," and that, instead, "lasting peace shall reign over the Pacific."[54] Baron Rempei Kondo agreed. Although an increasing number of Americans predicted that Japan might go to war with the United States, he noted in 1914, "there is no Japanese who advocates a war with America, although we are often called by the foreigners a bellicose race." Given the huge losses that such a war would entail for both countries, he urged, both nations should do all they could to ensure that it remained "an impossibility."[55]

Not all Japanese leaders were as certain that a race war with the United States and Britain could be avoided. In a letter to Premier Ōkuma Shigenobu, Yamagata Aritomo, another of the Meiji oligarchs who had governed Japan since 1868, expressed his concern that the racial animus directed at Japanese by Americans in California and by the British toward South Asians in South Africa would lead to a "bitter clash in the future between white and colored peoples."[56] In 1918, future prime minister Konoe Fumimaro wrote that it was incumbent on Japan to insist that Great Britain and the United States "change their arrogant and insulting attitude," "revise all laws that call for discriminatory treatment of Orientals," and "rescind immigration restrictions against Orientals."[57] Even Takao Ozawa had warned when he argued his case for access to citizenship before the U.S. District Court in Hawaii, years before it reached the U.S. Supreme Court, that "if the United States persisted in discriminating against Japan . . . the final result will be the greatest war between the European and Asiatic people."[58] In 1916, the *Alaska Daily Empire* had noted the publication of a book in Japan that urged Japanese to go to war against the United States in retaliation for its "'inhuman treatment of the Japanese immigrants'" and, in so doing, take possession of "California, Hawaii, and the Philippine Islands." "'The hearts of 60,000,000 of Japanese are inflamed with courage,'" its author reportedly declared, and they "'[would storm] like the strong winds of the heavens'" in order to "prove to the bluffing Americans that the Japanese people do not know defeat and that her soldiers cannot be beaten."[59] If Japan and the United States went to war, the *Fairbanks Daily News-Miner* predicted some years later, Japan would time its invasion of Alaska to coincide with the return of the salmon to their freshwater spawning streams along the Pacific coast to ensure an adequate food supply.[60] Only the Great Kanto earthquake in 1923, the *Alaska Miner* later opined, had prevented Japan from going to war at that time.[61]

IRONICALLY, Japanese immigrant acceptance of Western attitudes to settlement, together with their active participation in the colonization of western regions of both the United States and Canada, as well as their embrace of a pioneering role, itself served to reinforce perceptions that Japanese immigrants posed a threat to Euro-American settlers along the Pacific coast. As Eiichiro Azuma explains, "Many educated Issei considered themselves to be modern settler colonists intent on conquering a wilderness, just like their Anglo-Saxon predecessors, for the sake of advancing civilization," a stance that, ironically, "compounded the public notion of a Japanese threat and conspiracy."[62] Much as the persistent conflation of Japanese who had settled decades

earlier along the coasts of Alaska and British Columbia with Japanese subjects in Japan reinforced perceptions that *nikkei* fishermen posed a threat, the
parallel conflation of the efforts of Japanese farmers who had settled in the
B.C. interior or the Pacific coast states to acquire land with what the *New York
Times* described in 1923 as Japan's "growing appetite for new territory" in Asia
was also invoked to suggest that they represented the vanguard of a coming
invasion on both sides of the Canada-U.S. border.[63] Still others characterized
the commercial enterprises established by Japanese immigrants along the
Pacific coast of North America as further evidence of such an invasion.
Although the Japanese consul in Vancouver, B.C., would vigorously reject as
"sheer rumor" claims made in the 1930s that ownership of a majority of these
businesses had been transferred to the large conglomerates, or *zaibatsu*, that
played a key role in urging on Japan's pursuit of raw materials, for example,
reports that Mitsui had assumed control of iron mines on Haida Gwaii or that
a Japanese pulp company had acquired extensive timber interests there would
continue to make the rounds.[64]

The Japanese empire, reasoned the authors of an article published in *Maclean's* magazine in 1933, already extended from Sakhalin and the Kuril Islands
almost as far as the equator in the western Pacific. "Asiatic expansion," which
in their minds included Japanese immigrant communities in North America,
extended "thousands of miles . . . from California to the Yukon," as well as
into Latin America, along the eastern shores of the Pacific. The presence of
Japanese immigrants in these areas, they suggested, was "evidence" of Japan's
intention to extend its empire across the Pacific at some point in the future.[65]
But for the strength of "the white man's navies," another writer warned, Euro-
Americans might well find themselves displaced by Asian immigrants in much
the same way that white settlers had displaced Indigenous peoples.[66] The fact
that some Japanese settlers in Canada or the United States had ties to Manchuria
or that Japanese officials previously posted to Mukden had been transferred to
Japanese consulates in the United States or Canada, as was the case in Vancouver, B.C., in 1911, also bolstered the perception that Japanese immigrant
settlements in North America served much the same purpose as those in Manchuria. The "national genius that governed the Manchurian adventure," one article declared, was the same as that "directing the peaceful penetration into
Canada, only the weapons are different." Where Japan resorted to military
force to gain control in Manchuria, it claimed, Japan was using commercial
activity to achieve the same end in British Columbia.[67]

Among those with ties both to British Columbia and to Manchuria was
Yamazaki Yasushi, the author of a Japanese-language history of Japanese im-

Shoki Kayamori in Yakutat, Alaska, with a rifle, two dogs, and an otter. Alaska State Library, Kayamori Photograph Collection, 1913–1939, ASL-P55-714.

migrants in Canada titled *Sokuseki* (Footprint), who visited Manchuria four times during the interwar period to spend time with a sister whose husband was reportedly the chief of a band of mounted bandits, before returning permanently to Japan in 1934.[68] North of the B.C.-Alaska border, Shoki Kayamori, a cannery worker who had worked for a time at a dye works in Seattle, settled in Yakutat, a Tlingit village located in Eyak territory, in 1912, and regularly sent letters and gifts to his nephew's family in Manchukuo after his widowed mother moved there following Kayamori's father's death.[69] Japanese settlers based in North America who visited Manchuria noted that it embodied the same qualities that had made the American West appealing to Japanese migrants. A Japanese settler in Oregon who visited Manchuria with his wife in 1938, for example, described it as "a magnificent place!" Its vast expanses were such that it was capable of absorbing millions of settlers, he exclaimed; like the

United States, Manchuria had room for many, as contrasted with Japan, which was far more densely settled.[70]

As the 1930s drew to a close, an increasing number of reports regarding opportunities available to Japanese immigrants in Manchukuo appeared in Japanese American newspapers. In the spring of 1939, for example, the Seattle-based *Japanese American Courier* published a front page article informing its readers that Manchukuo was recruiting new immigrants. A Japanese government official based in Hsinking, the capital of Manchukuo, it reported, had visited Tokyo to confer with representatives of the Colonization Bureau of the Overseas Affairs Ministry there. Manchukuo, he had said, "require[d] all kinds of persons for the development of the country," and people of all classes were therefore encouraged to emigrate to Manchukuo.[71] Two articles published in 1941 made clear that emigration to newly colonized areas also provided a way to contribute to Japan's larger imperial project. In January 1941, the *Japanese American Courier* reported, "3400 young colonizers including 156 girls . . . who had completed their studies at the Colonial Development Labor Training Institute" were about to leave Japan to go to Manchukuo to farm.[72] In February 1941, it published the story of a young Ainu woman from the Ainu village of Ochiho on Karafuto (Sakhalin), who after she graduated from sewing school had left for Hsinking to contribute what she could to the development of Japan's colonies in Manchuria. "We, too," the Ainu villagers who gave her "a grand send-off" were reported to have said, "are adjusting our lives to the new structure."[73]

By the 1930s—partly as a result of reports like these—Japanese emigration to the United States and Canada had all but ceased, and the overall direction of Japanese migration across the North Pacific had essentially been reversed.[74] Claims that Japanese migrants continued to enter British Columbia or the Pacific coast states illegally in substantial numbers persisted, however, among those who believed that they derived some benefit from allegations of this kind. In fact, during the decades that followed passage of the 1924 Immigration Act and Canada's revisions to its Gentlemen's Agreement with Japan in 1923 and 1928, the flow of Japanese migration to the Americas, such as it was, had largely been rerouted to South America, particularly Peru and Brazil.[75]

Despite Japan's efforts to address the concerns that had been raised over time regarding Japanese immigration to the United States, and the fact that emigration to both Canada and the United States had all but ceased, the authors of *Zaibeinihonjinshi* (History of Japanese in America), published by the Japanese Association of America, observed in 1940, U.S. hostility to Japan and its people had continued unabated. This hostility was the result not of any failure on Japan's part to control emigration, they wrote, but of a deep and persistent form of racism that was deeply rooted in U.S. history. The presence of both "Indians" and enslaved Africans at the time of its very founding had produced a form of racism that had been directed one after the other at Irish, Jewish, Italian, German, Scandinavian, Chinese, Filipino, and now Japanese migrants, despite U.S. claims that it was a nation founded on the principles of "Liberty, Justice, Equality, and Brotherhood." Anglo-Saxons, they declared, "bound their sense of superiority together with their racism." Not only had Native people been the targets of it, but it had also been directed at those of Spanish and Mexican ancestry who had lived in California at the time it was acquired by the United States. It was because of this deeply rooted form of racism that, rather than supporting Japan, a nation that had long regarded the United States as both friend and mentor, the authors of *Zaibeinihonjinshi* declared, the United States had instead "encouraged China's policy of discrimination, resistance, and contempt toward Japan and, jointly with England, France, Holland, and China, blocked Japan's expansion of its foreign trade."[76]

Outbreak of War

News of Japan's attack on Pearl Harbor from a base in the Kuril Islands on December 7, 1941, together with its invasion of Hong Kong and the Philippines, tore into any sense that the Pacific Ocean served as a buffer that protected the Pacific coast of North America from events unfolding elsewhere in the world and seemed to confirm the oft-repeated rumors of years past that Japan might one day invade Alaska or British Columbia. Where the broad expanses of the Pacific Ocean may once have appeared to protect isolated communities along its shores from the immediate impact of distant conflicts, their accessibility to the open ocean now seemed to render them particularly vulnerable. Distance was, in effect, reimagined, as were both scale and terrain. The many small interconnected channels, islands, and fjords that made these watery borderlands such a complex space and shielded much of the continental mainland from direct exposure to the Pacific Ocean also had the power to obscure the presence of intruders, as did the vast expanses of the Pacific itself. The six aircraft carriers from which the attack on Pearl Harbor was launched, after all, had made the journey from the island of Etorofu (Iturup), where the convoy had assembled, to a point within striking distance of Hawaii unobserved.[77] How much easier it would be for smaller boats to slip unnoticed between the many islands that lined the coast of British Columbia and Alaska or to drop anchor in one of its many inlets.

On the one hand, exaggerated fears of this kind speak to the sense of vulnerability and uncertainty that those living along a coast exposed to the Pacific Ocean and far from the centers of power in both Canada and the United States felt in the wake of Japan's attack on Pearl Harbor. In fact, as Muriel Kitagawa wrote in 1945, the intricate geography of the B.C. coast—much like that of the Alaska panhandle—was such that British Columbia "was never in real danger of either invasion or sabotage." Marked by "thousands of coves and bays, canyons and impassable mountains," she pointed out, it was "hardly developed enough to be of any worth to an enemy needing roads and supplies." If that were not the case, Kitagawa astutely observed, Canada would not have left that coast as "thinly defended" as it did during the war.[78] While some Japanese immigrants found it hard to break their ties to Japan and hoped, at the very least, that Japan would not lose the war, others felt betrayed by Japan's leaders, who had, in effect, abandoned them to the strident claims made by anti-Japanese agitators over the years regarding the danger Japan purportedly posed.[79] The "sneak attack on Pearl Harbor," James Sakamoto wrote in 1942, had placed Japanese in North America in an impossibly difficult position, with the result that "by nightfall on December 7, the bitterest foe that Tokio had in this country was the Japanese people as a class."[80] Not only did Japanese Americans and Japanese Canadians share in the anxieties of their neighbors, but some also feared that if Japan did invade, they would be regarded as traitors by members of its imperial forces.[81]

During the weeks that followed the outbreak of the Pacific War, claims that Japanese settlers in British Columbia and Alaska were spies or collaborators who posed a danger to the United States and Canada only increased in intensity, drowning out the more moderate voices that had always argued against such extreme allegations.[82] Within months, no matter what the nature of their ties was to the communities in which they lived, Japanese immigrants and their children would be forcibly removed from coastal areas on both sides of the Canada-U.S. border. Relying on questionable rationalizations grounded in substantial part on decades of unfounded rumors, the forced removal of people of Japanese ancestry from the coasts of North America and subsequent confinement by both governments ripped through the lives of those who lived in the small, scattered communities that dotted the coastline of both Alaska and British Columbia, as well as those of Japanese settlers in the Pacific coast states. Although some warned that Japan might drop down through British Columbia to invade the United States across the forth-ninth parallel from bases in Alaska, much as Germany had used Belgium in the European war, others argued that the difficulties Japan would encounter in supplying any outposts it established in Alaska—the same problem that Russia had faced and that contributed to its decision to sell its interests in Alaska to the United States in 1867—together with difficulties involved in traveling through the mountains of the B.C. interior and the absence of any land-based route connecting the territory to the states made it utterly impractical. Less hard to imagine, however, was the possibility that Japan might establish airstrips on one or more of the small islands along the coast and use the shelter of its many fjords and inlets to mount raids against coastal communities.[83]

Both Canada and the United States acted quickly to round up individuals with ties to organizations seen as having connections with Japan, including prominent *issei* and community leaders, living in cities all along the Pacific coast. In Juneau, where there were fewer than three dozen residents of Japanese ancestry in December 1941, all *issei* men were rounded up and housed in a jail that overlooked the city. Among them was Hikohachi Fukuyama, who arrived in British Columbia in 1903, where he worked for an English tea company before moving north across the B.C.-Alaska border to settle in Juneau in 1906. There he worked for a few years as a cook for a federal district court judge before marrying a woman chosen for him by his family in Japan and opening a laundry.[84] A few nights after the arrest of the *issei* men in town, Mack Mori, who had worked in the canneries before taking a job at the laundry in Juneau, recalls, the Federal Bureau of Investigation (FBI) took Fukuyama's wife, already frightened by her husband's arrest, and the wife of another man into custody, leaving the care of their children in Mori's hands until the women were released twelve hours later.[85] Although many of the *issei* men arrested during the days immediately after the attack on Pearl Harbor remained in custody, still unclear in both Canada and the United States was what would be the fate of their families, including their *nisei* children, who were native-born citizens or subjects in both countries. Left without the support of the men who were often the primary breadwinners in the family, and with no way to know what lay ahead, the uncertainty their mothers faced as to what awaited them and their children would take a tremendous toll during the months that followed.

The more immediate concern all along the Pacific coast for both the U.S. and Canadian governments was the Japanese American or Canadian–owned fishing boats that had repeatedly been characterized over the years as instruments of war. These included the tuna boats operating out of California ports that, it was alleged, could be "transformed into torpedo boats in less than four hours," a claim that was also widely circulated in British Columbia and Alaska in relation to other kinds of vessels.[86] Japanese fishing boats along the B.C.

coast, the Anglican archdeacon of Quebec had asserted in 1937, "concealed sixteen-inch guns ready to spring into action the day the Japanese should declare war," another allegation that received wide traction notwithstanding that munitions experts pointed out that "the concussion from a sixteen-inch gun would blow any fishing boat clear across the Rocky Mountains."[87] Harder to counter were claims that Japanese-owned fishing boats could potentially be used to mine or sabotage isolated ports along the north Pacific coast. A single fishing boat with three men aboard, a highway engineer in Alaska opined in 1940, could destroy Alaska's defense capability by attacking Seward, the only port in Alaska accessible all year round, and dynamiting the oil tanks where much of Alaska's oil supply was stored. If they also destroyed the channel markers that guided ships into port, he added, it would "render the harbor as dangerous as a mine field owing to hidden reefs."[88] In British Columbia, Vancouver alderman H. D. Wilson took matters a step further, warning British Columbians that "marine mines may have been secreted along the British Columbia coastline in readiness for mining local waters at an instant's notice."[89] If Britain were to find itself at war with Japan, the *Financial News* warned after Japan entered into the Tripartite Alliance with Germany and Italy in the fall of 1940, it was critical that the Japanese Canadian fishing fleet be immobilized right away.[90] The immediacy with which the Canadian government acted to do just that on December 7, 1941, suggests that it had taken such advice to heart.

Within a matter of hours of Japan's attack on Hawaii, the Royal Canadian Navy ordered all fishing boats owned by Japanese Canadian fishermen on the B.C. coast to remain in or return to port. On December 8, the navy set in motion its plan for impounding their vessels, beginning with a search for any weapons on board.[91] Some did have rifles on board, the daughter of one fisherman who had fished the west coast of Vancouver Island later said, but they were used to shoot the sea lions that came after their catch—a right for which white fishers had also lobbied—and not any other purpose. On December 15, all Japanese Canadian fishermen who moored their boats in Tofino, on the west coast of Vancouver Island, were ordered to take them south around Vancouver Island and across the Strait of Georgia to a slough near New Westminster just upriver from Lion Island—once Oikawa-jima—on the Fraser River. Each vessel, she explained, was assigned a sailor tasked with making sure that they "wouldn't turn the boat around and go to Japan."[92] Those based at Ucluelet and Bamfield were next to leave, escorted by the H.M.C.S. *Givenchy* and joined by other fishing boats along the way until they formed a convoy of some sixty vessels. Several fishers reportedly mistook a light near Neah Bay

Confiscated boats of Japanese Canadian fishers from the west coast of
Vancouver Island being held in Bamfield Harbour, B.C., where they were
forced to take shelter for two days because of harsh wintry weather as they
made their way under escort by the Canadian Navy to the Fraser River a few
days after December 7, 1941. Nikkei National Museum, Margaret Wright
Collection, 2001.20.3.6.

on the U.S. side of the international border for the lighthouse at Carmanah
Point by the entrance to the Strait of Juan de Fuca, which had darkened its
lights to obscure its location, and found themselves in American waters,
quickly turning back toward Victoria when they were met by warning shots.[93]
One fisher, who became separated from the rest and drifted into U.S. waters
when their vessels split to avoid a tugboat towing a wide load as they neared
Active Pass, was intercepted on the U.S. side of the line and would later die of
injuries reportedly inflicted before he was handed back over to Canadian
authorities.[94]

Japanese Canadian fishermen in the Skeena River area on British Columbia's northern coast, in turn, were ordered to take their fishing boats to Seal
Cove near Prince Rupert on December 15. From there, they were towed south
in two long lines, stopping at the Heiltsuk village of Bella Bella along the way

to repair two boats that had overturned under tow and filled with water. From there they continued into Queen Charlotte Sound, where high tides and driftwood tossed about by the large waves of the open ocean sank one fishing boat and cut others adrift, forcing them to go after them. These delays, taken together with the wintry weather, meant that the trip along the coast, which normally took just a few days, lasted two weeks.[95] While most of the fishermen who delivered their boats to the mooring on the Fraser River where they were ordered to leave them were initially allowed to return to their homes in Port Essington and elsewhere along the coast, they and their families remained as uncertain of what the future held as did Japanese American families in Alaska.

Barely three weeks later, on January 16, 1942, the Custodian of Enemy Property ordered that the 1,337 fishing boats it had impounded be sold to fishers of "other than Japanese origin." The removal of so many vessels from the coastal fishing fleet, government officials had realized, threatened to undermine key components of the fishing industry at a time when wartime demand for fish was growing rapidly. The sale began with the auction of some 1,100 boats, many at prices well below the value their owners assigned to them.[96] Canneries purchased 660 of the 887 boats initially sold, while 227 were bought by smaller companies or individuals, including both white and Indigenous fishers. Government agencies acquired another 150 vessels, among them the British admiralty (20), the Canadian armed services (43), and the B.C. Custodian of Enemy Property (187).[97] A further 181 were too badly damaged from the journey to the Fraser River or the crowded moorings to be sold.[98] In still other cases, Japanese Canadian fishermen had arranged to sell their boats themselves before they could be confiscated by the Canadian government, among them Thomas Tsutomu Kimoto, whose daughter later reported that he had sold his fishing boat to an Indigenous fisher to avoid this outcome.[99]

Forced Removal: British Columbia

Uncertain as to what the fate of the Japanese American *nisei*, born citizens of the United States, was to be, the *Japanese American Courier*, which had regularly reported the departure of cannery workers based in the Seattle area for the Alaska canneries and their return at the end of the season each year, kept a careful eye on the impact of unfolding events on Japanese Canadians north of the forty-ninth parallel. On January 16, 1942, it informed its readers that "in Canada Japanese face[d] evacuation." Not only had the Canadian government determined that 23,428 "Japanese people and other enemy aliens" in British

Columbia were to be removed from the coast, it noted, but it had mandated the sale of the Japanese Canadian fishing vessels it had impounded.[100] Even the *Japanese American Courier*, ironically, failed to note that a majority of the 23,428 individuals it described as "Japanese" were actually Canadian-born British subjects who happened to be of Japanese ancestry.

Even as it issued the removal order, the Canadian government was already aware that Japanese Canadians posed no danger. Prime Minister William Lyon Mackenzie King himself had declared rumors that they posed a danger "unfounded and irresponsible," and, as the *Tairiku Nippō* reported, a special committee assigned to evaluate claims that they were a threat had concluded there was no evidence to support such allegations.[101] As Ken Adachi explained in *The Enemy That Never Was*, an RCMP representative informed federal and provincial officials at that meeting in Ottawa on January 8 and 9, 1942, that "the few potentially subversive Japanese had already been interned and that no further internment was necessary." The navy concurred, believing it had neutralized any danger when it immobilized Japanese Canadian fishermen on the day that Pearl Harbor was bombed, as did the army, which agreed that Japanese Canadians not already in custody did not pose the "slightest menace to national security." Although they were vigorously opposed by provincial officials, representatives of some federal government agencies who attended the meeting went so far as to argue that Canada would be best served by allowing all experienced fishermen already familiar with the B.C. coast to contribute to Canada's wartime food production industries.[102]

Regardless, nearly all Japanese and Japanese Canadian men in British Columbia who were not already under arrest, including both Japanese subjects and naturalized and Canadian-born British subjects, were sent to road camps, where they were put to work building roads in the B.C. interior east of the Coast Mountains that marked the eastern edge of what had been denoted the protected area.[103] Among them was Ryuichi Yoshida, who had long fished the Skeena River but was working aboard a packer in December 1941 because the fish runs were low that year. Ordered to return to shore within hours of the attack on Pearl Harbor on December 7, he was interrogated and released after explaining that he had immigrated to Canada in 1910 and had not returned to Japan in three decades. The mood in Vancouver was so hostile at the time, he later recalled, that he feared a race riot far worse than that of 1907 might break out at any moment.[104] Sent to a road camp near Revelstoke, B.C., not far from the site where thirty Japanese railroad workers had died along with twenty-eight other men in an avalanche in March 1910, he was put to work building a road through a series of deep mountain passes. Hard as the work was, he remembered, it was not as hard as the work he had regularly done as a fisherman.[105]

The forced removal of all Japanese Canadians who lived along the B.C. coast, regardless of age, nationality, or place of birth, began on March 14 based on orders-in-council issued by Canada on February 23 and March 4 that empowered the British Columbia Security Commission to effect their removal and made clear that the directive applied not only to Japanese nationals or persons born in Japan but also to British subjects born in Canada.[106] A day earlier, the Union Steamship Company, the Canadian Pacific Railway (CPR), and the Canadian National Railway (CNR) had submitted a joint plan to the B.C. Security Commission for the removal of all remaining Japanese Canadians from the B.C. coast.[107] The first Japanese Canadians directed to leave their homes were those who lived on the west coast of Vancouver Island, followed by those living in Alert Bay and on northern Vancouver Island, on March 15. On March 16, those living in the Nass River area just south of the Dixon Entrance, which marked the Alaska-B.C. border, were ordered to leave, followed by those who lived in and around Bella Coola on March 18.[108] On March 20, Japanese Canadians in the Prince Rupert area, ranging from 206 living in Prince Rupert itself to 3 living in what was identified only as "Jap Inlet," were directed to board a special CNR train bound for Vancouver, B.C., where Hastings Park, a racetrack and livestock exhibition hall, had hastily been repurposed to serve as what was euphemistically described as an assembly center. The steamships assigned to pick up those who remained stopped at a further three dozen ports and inlets, taking aboard a total of 1,839 individuals, from 409 at Ocean Falls to a couple of dozen or sometimes just 2 or 3 individuals in other locations.[109] Japanese Canadians living on Haida Gwaii were among the last of those living in more remote communities along British Columbia's north coast to leave their homes, boarding the steamships bound for Vancouver on March 26 and 27.[110]

Forced removals from inland towns on Vancouver Island that were not predominantly fishing communities followed. On April 17, the *Japanese American Courier* reported that many were ready to go given that the prior removal of their husbands and fathers had left them with no means of support and, in some cases, virtually destitute. More than five hundred were reportedly packed and ready to go in Cumberland, a coal mining community that was one of the first where Japanese immigrants had settled in the late 1800s, and in Victoria some two hundred Japanese Canadians reportedly waited for the steamship that would take them to Vancouver.[111] Not all, however, were prepared to leave without protest. Ray Iwasaki would later recall, for example, that when the ferry that picked his family up on Salt Spring Island stopped to take others aboard at Mayne Island, his father disembarked and refused to reboard, insisting he had committed no crime and did not deserve to be imprisoned, until friends and family persuaded him to reembark.[112] On April 24, 1942, the *Japanese American Courier* reported that its sister publication, the *New Canadian*, had confirmed that the removal of people of Japanese descent from the entire British Columbia coast other than Howe Sound and Vancouver was complete.[113] By June 1942, no Japanese Canadians remained in Steveston. The "once-thriving Jap village was now deserted," one newspaper reported, and white families had begun to move into the buildings that now stood empty. A number of Indigenous families based at Campbell River on Vancouver Island were also on their way. Where whites planned to settle permanently in the homes that had been left empty in Steveston, however, one Indigenous fisher told a reporter, they planned to return to Campbell River at the end of the fishing season.[114]

Although *nikkeijin* who lived in Vancouver were permitted to remain in their homes while the removal of coastal residents was underway, those brought in from the coast and British Columbia's island communities were housed at Hastings Park, some in stables and others in large buildings lined with rows of beds that offered little privacy and, despite efforts to clean them, reeked of animal manure.[115] For weeks after they arrived at Hastings Park, Henry Shimizu, whose parents owned the Dominion Café in Prince Rupert, later recounted, his father remained convinced that Canadian government officials would realize that "all of this was a mistake" and that they would be allowed to return to Prince Rupert. After some months, however, it became apparent that this was not to be. Rather than being allowed to return to Prince Rupert, they were put aboard a train for Slocan City, one of the ghost towns in the B.C. interior where Japanese Canadians would be confined for the duration of the war, and then taken by truck to New Denver.[116] The dwellings that awaited them, said Ryuichi Yoshida, whose work crew was sent to New Denver to build them, were constructed by amateurs who knew little about what they were doing.[117] The small shacks consisted of a common kitchen and living area located between two other rooms, each assigned to an entire family. During the particularly cold and bitter winter of 1942–43, snow drifted through the cracks that formed in the walls of many as the green wood with which they had been built slowly dried.[118]

Fishermen who had worked on the Skeena River or lived in Port Essington were among those assigned to Sandon, an abandoned mining town located in a dark and narrow valley about eight miles from New Denver.[119] An order

that forbade fishing along the B.C. coast for the duration of the war was reportedly enforced, at least during the first years of the war, even in the lakes
beside which some of the detention camps were located.[120] While the mountainous landscape of the B.C. interior reminded some *issei* of the narrow
mountain valleys in Japan where they had been born, their dramatic beauty
was no substitute for the open waters of the Pacific for those who had lived
along its shores. Although the camps erected in British Columbia's interior
valleys were not surrounded by barbed wire and watchtowers did not loom
over them as in the United States, an RCMP detachment assigned to each
camp restricted travel in or out.[121] A pass system not unlike that imposed on
Indigenous people on the Canadian prairies during the late nineteenth century,
which required them to obtain a pass to leave their reserves, was now implemented to monitor and control the movement of Japanese Canadians and, at
least initially, tightly enforced.[122]

Forced Removal: Alaska

In the United States as in Canada, fisher families were also among the first to
be targeted after the outbreak of war with Japan, among them the thirty-five
hundred *nikkei* residents of East San Pedro on Terminal Island, most of whom
worked either as fishers or in canneries located on the island.[123] Separated
from Los Angeles by a small drawbridge, the island was cut off from the mainland a day after the attack on Pearl Harbor.[124] Although hundreds of *issei* and
nisei men regarded as potentially dangerous, including all *issei* in possession
of a valid fishing license, were arrested within a matter of hours or days following the attack, local officials demanded that the federal government remove those who remained on the island, most of them women and U.S.-born
children, even though federal officials had not yet determined whether it
would require people of Japanese ancestry born in the United States to be
removed from the coast.[125] Writing in 1979, Bob Kumamoto noted how ironic
the persistent belief was that a majority of the fishermen who lived and
worked on Terminal Island had links to Japan's military. "Instead of a poor and
outcast group of fishermen" living in what he described as a "shanty town," he
recalled, "they were regarded as an armed enemy fleet ready to wage maritime
war."[126]

On February 10, "all Japanese aliens"—first-generation Japanese immigrants who had been denied the opportunity even to apply for citizenship—
were notified that they had to leave their homes on Terminal Island within
the week. The U.S.-born Japanese Americans who still remained on the

island were informed on February 25 that they had to do the same within forty-eight hours.[127] Late in March, former residents of Terminal Island who had already moved once to the mainland were among the first to leave Los Angeles for what was euphemistically called the Manzanar Relocation Center in the Owens Valley, a once fertile valley sacrificed to ensure a steady water supply for the city of Los Angeles.[128] Japanese Americans who lived on Whidbey Island and in the San Juan Islands, part of the same archipelago as the Gulf Islands north of the Canada-U.S. border, had themselves been largely cut off from contact with other parts of the Puget Sound area at the end of January, forbidden to travel aboard the ferries linking the islands to the mainland unless they first obtained a travel permit.[129] On March 30, those living on Bainbridge Island, near Seattle, regarded as the most strategically vulnerable of the islands in Puget Sound, were the first to be directed to leave their homes, followed within days by the Japanese American residents on other islands in the sound, a good number of whom, ironically, were not fishers but farmers.[130]

On February 20, after weeks of uncertainty about what the fate of U.S.-born citizens of Japanese ancestry was to be, President Franklin D. Roosevelt issued an order that made clear that "any and all aliens and citizens" were subject to removal from any region deemed "important to National Defense."[131] Despite later claims that this was done to protect Japanese Americans from growing anti-Japanese sentiment, its preamble makes clear that it was grounded in the pattern of rumor and innuendo already well established even before the outbreak of war. Japanese Americans were to be removed from designated military areas, it declared, because "the successful prosecution of the war require[d] every possible protection against espionage and against sabotage to national defense material, . . . premises, . . . and utilities."[132] It was not until March 6 that the *Japanese American Courier* was able to report to its readers that the designated military areas from which "Japanese Americans [were] to be excluded" included "the western two-thirds of Washington, the western half of Oregon and California, and the southern portion of Arizona," where "Mexican Japanese" were required to leave their homes on both sides of the U.S.-Mexico border.[133] Just three weeks later, all of Alaska was also identified as a designated military area.[134] "It is difficult to see why an American of Japanese ancestry is more dangerous to the national safety than one of German or Italian parentage," the editors of the *Japanese American Courier* mused on April 3, 1942, urging all Japanese Americans at the same time to cooperate with the removal order as a way of demonstrating that they in fact posed no threat to the country of their birth.[135]

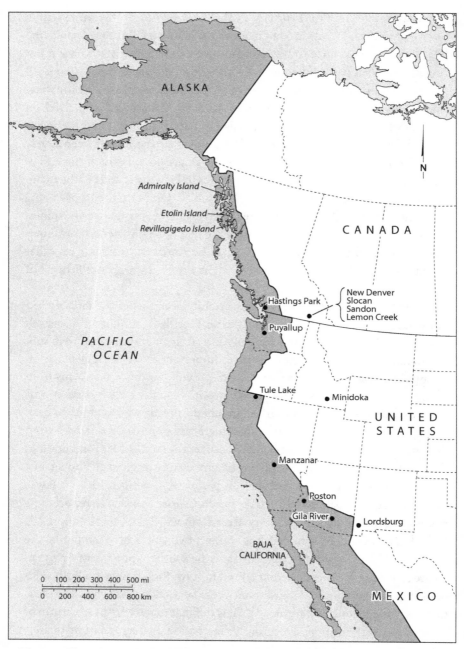

The areas along the Pacific coast of North America from which people of
Japanese ancestry were forcibly removed during World War II, including
those in British Columbia, Mexico, and Alaska, together with the detention
camps referred to in the text.

In contrast to the states of Washington, Oregon, and California, just parts of which were designated military areas, all of the territory of Alaska was designated a military zone. As early as February 19, the date on which President Roosevelt signed Executive Order 9066, Alaska's governor, Ernest Gruening, began to raise concerns about U.S. military policy in Alaska. The U.S. Navy, he pointed out in a letter to the secretary of the Interior in Washington, D.C., had "little, if any, experience with conditions in Alaska," and he was "at a loss to understand" its decision to designate all of Alaska as a military defense zone. Given that the navy's three bases were all located on islands off the Alaska coast, Navy personnel had little knowledge of its interior. Even if a policy made sense in places like Sitka, Anchorage, and Kodiak, where these bases were located, it made no sense, he wrote, "to apply it to the whole Territory with an area of 586,000 square miles in which the preponderance of communities are not in defense areas and, from the standpoint of defense, are probably as safe as the communities in the States . . . along the Pacific coast [to which] evacuated families are freely permitted to go." The situation in Alaska, he noted, was "not analogous to [that] in the Hawaiian Islands or in Puerto Rico." Was it possible that U.S. military officials had "perhaps unknowingly merely applied to Alaska what may be a reasonable policy in the other offshore territories?"[136]

Gruening's query had no apparent effect on U.S. military policy in Alaska. On April 7, "all persons being of Japanese race of greater than half blood," as well as all men and boys of Japanese ancestry seventeen or older of "half blood" in Alaska were directed to report to the nearest army post by April 20 in preparation for their removal to the "continental limits of the United States." In the interim, all persons of Japanese ancestry were forbidden to travel outside their home community without first obtaining a travel permit, as were German and Italian aliens in Alaska who had not elected to become U.S. citizens.[137] The removal order created immediate confusion. Although persons living in places far from an army outpost were initially allowed to report by letter or telegram pending a direct order to report in person, those living in small towns in the vicinity of a military base such as Wrangell and Petersburg were uncertain just what they were required to do.[138] While many Japanese immigrants in Alaska lived in Juneau, Anchorage, and Ketchikan, others were scattered across the length and breadth of Alaska, including the towns of Fairbanks, Seward, and Yakutat, as well as a range of smaller communities. On April 14, Earl N. Ohmer, president and general manager of the Alaskan Glacier Sea Food Company in Petersburg, wrote to acting governor E. L. Bartlett asking him to clarify what was required so that he might allay the fears of his employees, including the "old Jap women [who] have been working for me for years, [and] are of course all scared."[139]

Elderly *issei*, including old timers who had spent many years in Alaska without returning to Japan or having any significant contact with other Japanese, were among those brought into military bases. Harry Sotaro Kawabe, who had settled in Seward after emigrating to the United States in 1906 and was arrested there on December 7, 1942, would later tell Kazuo Ito that he was taken to the U.S. Army base in Anchorage along with a dozen other Japanese men who had lived in Alaska for decades, some of them, including a man named Nakamura, in Indigenous communities. Given that the war began in the middle of winter, he recalled, some were out in the wilderness working their traplines deep in the mountains, far from any place that might conceivably be a target of sabotage, when they were ordered to report. "As if by mutual agreement," he told Ito, "none of them admitted to knowing that the war had begun." His own biases were also apparent. "You could not tell them from Indians," he said. "They didn't bathe or shave, wore filthy fur coats and had a vacant expression." Some had all but forgotten their Japanese, and it would be months before they began to speak a few words again. Among them was a Japanese fisher whose fishing boat had washed ashore in the Aleutian Islands in the 1870s and who had reportedly become a chief in Seldovia, a village accessible only by boat, located by Kachemak Bay on the Kenai Peninsula. Still another member of the group held at the U.S. Army base was a Korean—then regarded by both Japan and the United States as a Japanese subject—who had married an Alaska Native girl.[140]

U.S. government policy would tear mixed-race families apart, forcing women to choose whether to accompany their husbands and children to choose between accompanying a father subject to deportation or remaining with their mother in Alaska. This raised questions in turn about just which federal agency was responsible for the welfare of mixed-race children who, on the one hand, were marked by their Japanese ancestry but, on the other hand, were the responsibility of the Alaska Indian Service.[141] "Japanese women legally married to white men" were exempt from the removal order, as, in time, those "married to Indians or Eskimos" were later declared to be.[142] As even General S. B. Buckner acknowledged, however, this did not address the question whether an Indigenous woman married to a Japanese or "half Japanese half Alaska Indian man" was permitted to accompany him voluntarily if she so chose to preserve the family unit. Nor did it resolve the problem that the deportation of Japanese men married to Indigenous women posed in terms of leaving their families without any means of support. Among those that would require support once their primary breadwinners were removed, Buckner admitted, were families like those of John Eyon and Chotaro Miyasato in Wrangell, who had a total of eleven dependents; Tom Foode in Cordova, who supported seven dependents; and Sam (Saburo) Kito, whose wife, Amelia, and three children lived in Petersburg; as well as other mixed-race families in Ekuk, Ugashik, Seward, and other outlying communities.[143] While some of the women qualified for public assistance in the form of a mother's grant and additional aid from general relief funds as was needed to sustain their family, this was emergency funding set to expire at the end of June. Caught in the jurisdictional gap between two branches of government, their families, who were deemed "native peoples living in the native manner," territorial officials argued, should be the responsibility of the Office of Indian Affairs once their part-Japanese husbands and fathers were forcibly removed and "placed in technical custody because of war defense developments."[144]

The dilemma that the strict racial categories applied to Indigenous and Japanese people created for some families is evident in the position in which a seventeen-year-old named Henry Hope found himself in the wake of the removal order. As Alice Stuart explained in a letter to Governor Gruening in an effort to prevent his being forced to go to California one week later, Henry, she wrote, was the biological son of an "Eskimo mother" and a Japanese father, whom he had never met. Instead, he had been adopted when he was a baby by the couple who had given him their name and were both Indigenous, his adoptive mother an Athapaskan Indian and his adoptive father an "Eskimo." Henry had "never been below the Arctic circle until the other day when he was sent into Fairbanks to register because he is of Japanese descent," Stuart explained, adding that "he has never even seen a Jap, nor does he wish to." Rather, he had "spent all of his life in the hills, or around Wiseman where he went to school and completed the seventh grade." Henry was a responsible young man who worked as a freighter and Caterpillar operator for a mining operation and was his family's primary source of support. "He loves the rivers and mountains of his native home and has no desire to leave it," Stuart wrote. "Would it not perhaps be possible to find some way that he might return to the Arctic instead of being shipped out to California?"[145] Acting governor Bartlett, clearly moved by Stuart's letter and aware that the removal order created a predicament for people in Hope's position, wrote to Governor Gruening, then in San Francisco, noting that Hope posed no danger to Alaska and asking him to inquire whether the Western Defense Command had the discretion to consider the particular circumstances of his case, as Alaskan officials did not.[146] Its response, as Bartlett explained to Stuart, was that the Western Defense Command was unwilling to make any exceptions for anyone with the requisite degree of Japanese blood, regardless of the cultural context in which they were raised. Bartlett also expressed his own regret that it was regarded as necessary to "take Henry away from his homeland." It was "one of the cruel things about war which really hurt," he admitted, precisely because Henry Hope posed no danger whatsoever to the United States.[147]

Others would also question the need to forcibly remove Japanese men whose lives were deeply rooted in the Indigenous communities that they had long since come to call home. Mamie Attunga Moto Karmun recalled that her father, George Moto (shortened from Yamamoto), had enjoyed his life in Deering, an Inupiaq village located on the southern shore of Kotzebue Sound along Alaska's northwest coast. He had never gone back to Japan, and she did not remember him ever receiving a letter from Japan. He had always been so kind to everyone over the years, she added, that even after the attack on Pearl Harbor almost no one's attitude toward him changed.[148] He and his three sons, all of whom had children of their own, were nevertheless taken away by plane with barely a day's notice. Those left behind did not learn where they had been taken until her father was able to send them some money he had earned working as a watchman at a dam in Idaho. Her Inupiaq mother, however, who had worked as a midwife for many years and worried that her grandchildren had lost their fathers, would never know that her husband and sons were safe. "She really went old that year after they were gone," Karmun recalled, and died around a year after they were taken away.[149]

Frank Yasuda, likewise, his daughter Hana Elavgak Yasuda Kangas recalled, regularly assisted people of all backgrounds in Beaver, Alaska, who did not know how to read or write, helping them fill out government forms or place their Sears orders at his store. He cheerfully allowed her mother, Nevelo, "an Inupiat Eskimo from Barrow," to do what Kangas described as "her Eskimo cultural thing," allowing friends to select from among new bolts of fabric when they came in, invariably choosing the brightest and leaving the darker, plainer colors to be sold. Before taking Yasuda into custody, ironically, army officers first met with him to ask his advice about what type of clothing he recommended that soldiers wear to ensure that they survived the cold winters in Alaska. An officer at Ladd Air Force Base had reportedly suggested using caribou hides, Kangas recalled, but Yasuda had advised against this, explaining that when they got wet, caribou hides no longer protected the wearer from the cold. "Woolens and down," he said, were a far more practical option. Only later did the army officers who had sought his advice return and inform him that he was required to accompany them.[150] Like George Moto and the

George Moto (short for Yamamoto) and family members including, from right to left, Sally P. Moto and grandchildren Bessie Moto (age 4), Harry Karmun (age 4), and Gilbert S. Karmun (age 6) in Deering, Alaska, in 1942. University of Alaska, Fairbanks, Alaska and Polar Regions Collections and Archives, Alaska's Japanese Pioneers Research Project, UAF-1991-45-3.

other *issei* men taken into custody in Alaska, Yasuda was first held at an army facility near Metlakatla on Annette Island just north of the U.S.-Canada border, the same island on which the Tsimshian who left Canada for the United States during the 1880s had settled, before being transferred to detention facilities in the continental interior of the United States.[151]

All along the Pacific coast, the anguish generated by accusations of disloyalty also had tragic consequences. In Alaska, Shoki Kayamori, the former cannery worker who had settled in Yakutat in 1912, was among those regarded with particular suspicion by the FBI, likely because he was an avid photographer who documented both the lives of his Tlingit and Eyak neighbors and the dramatic landscape in the area, including Mount St. Elias, visible from Yakutat. Born in 1877, just a decade after the start of the Meiji era, Kayamori had left Japan for Seattle in 1903, a decision that allowed him to avoid conscription at a time when Japan was actively preparing for war with Russia. Reportedly fearing arrest by U.S. soldiers—and, if he did leave Japan to avoid conscription, possibly also the arrival of Japanese troops at a time when rumors were rampant that a Japanese invasion was imminent—he committed suicide on December 9, two days after Japan's attack on Pearl Harbor.[152] He was not the only Japanese immigrant to do so. In March 1942, Hideo Murata, a World War I veteran, committed suicide after being directed to leave his home in San Luis Obispo, having first tucked a certificate that declared him to be "an honorary citizen of Monterey County" into his pocket.[153] And in early April, Tae Okumura, a young mother in Seattle anxious about having been separated from her husband, who was arrested immediately after the attack on Pearl Harbor, and uncertain about her ability to care for her six-year-old son in the face of her own pending removal from her home, also took her life. That she was separated from most of her relatives, members of a family that extended across the Pacific Ocean, may also have been a factor; while one sister lived in Seattle, another sister was in Shanghai and her mother and brother were in Japan. "Please God and America," she wrote in her final note, "forgive us if we did any wrong."[154]

ALTHOUGH *ISSEI* MEN all along the Pacific coast, including those in Alaska, were quickly rounded up after the war began, many of their children, U.S.-born citizens who had gone to school in Alaska, were not initially concerned for themselves. Some young *nisei* men, including Patrick Hagiwara, from Ketchikan, had joined the National Guard more than a year before the outbreak of war, while others, such as Mack Mori, were ordered to report to the army base in Haines, Alaska, to comply with the draft. Only after the war began, Hagiwara recalled, did his "motives and allegiance" come to be questioned, including, in one instance, allegations that he had been spotted up on "a mountain using flashlights trying to signal the Japanese."[155] Before he and other Japanese American National Guard members were transferred to stateside military bases as required by the removal order, ironically, he was assigned to guard *issei* elders and friends who were to be sent to Annette Island. When the troop vessel aboard which he was traveling a few weeks later stopped at Annette Island on the way south, in turn, he was allowed to say a quick farewell to his father and the other *issei* men.[156] Mori, who knew a number of the thirty or forty Japanese detainees being held at the army base in Haines, was also permitted to go shake hands with them once he explained that they were friends. He would not, however, be allowed to join the army. Instead, he was sent back to Juneau until transportation to a detention camp in the continental interior of the United States could be arranged.[157]

In all, a total of 218 persons of Japanese ancestry made the journey south in April 1942 on a large navy troop transport through the archipelagos that line the coasts of Alaska and British Columbia to the Puget Sound. Ninety-two were first-generation Japanese residents of Alaska, who remained Japanese subjects because they were denied the chance to apply for naturalization, and 126 were U.S.-born citizens of Japanese ancestry. Over the course of a two-day period, the vessel stopped first at Petersburg and Wrangell and then at Ketchikan, where the 34 who left Juneau were joined by 59 others, the single-largest group living in any town in Alaska. Ninety-four of those who came aboard were from seventeen other towns and villages in Alaska, including Beaver, Nome, Seward, Deering, Bristol Bay, Kodiak, Bethel, Chichagof Island, and Valdez, located in Prince William Sound.[158] The commanding officer looked tough, Komatsu Ohashi remembered, but his demeanor was friendly and they were well fed while on board the troop transport, although they would be treated more poorly when they reached Washington State.[159] While some of the women on board the ship were fearful, not knowing what lay ahead for their children, Hope Ohashi found the journey "interesting." Her grandfather had arrived in 1909 and settled in Ketchikan, where he ran a boardinghouse and a grocery store on Stedman Street at the heart of what was both the Japanese and the Indigenous community there. Born in Ketchikan in 1927, Hope Ohashi had lived in Ketchikan all her life and was eager to learn what the world beyond it was like. When they arrived in Seattle on April 27, 1942, her father was taken first to Tacoma, Washington, and then sent to the Lordsburg detention facility in New Mexico, as were many of the other *issei* men from Alaska. Their families, in turn, were taken to Puyallup, south of Seattle, to a fairground that had been commandeered to serve as the major assembly center for Washington State, where they remained until early fall.[160]

At the Puyallup Assembly Center, former Alaska residents were housed together at one end of the camp in what was known as Alaska Row.[161] Amelia Kito, who had been allowed to accompany her husband on the journey south, Hope Ohashi recalled, was one of her neighbors. Kito's father-in-law, Tom Kito, had come to Alaska in 1914 at the age of fifteen to work on a seasonal basis at the canneries in Cordova and Ketchikan; he settled in Petersburg in 1920, where he ran a cold storage business and married a woman who had one Indigenous parent and one Swedish parent.[162] Amelia Kito herself was Alaska Native as well. Pregnant and with no source of income, Kito, who had three children and was expecting a fourth in May, struggled to make ends meet. She gave birth to her son Harry, who would later be killed in Vietnam, at the Puyallup Assembly Center, where, Hope recalled, she reassured the anxious and inexperienced hospital staff that they need not worry because she herself was an experienced midwife.[163]

When Japanese Americans from Seattle arrived, Hope Ohashi and her mother, Komatsu, recalled, they initially regarded those who had lived in

Alaska with some disdain, insisting that the mess hall was reserved for Seattle Japanese, until a *"hakujin* officer" intervened and made clear that all had equal access. "They thought we were Indians or something," Hope Ohashi explained.[164] Similar divisions existed in other detention camps.[165] Ed Suguro, who was among those sent to Tule Lake, where seven Alaskans were also sent, later reported, for example, "We didn't get along too well, because, you know how Japanese people can be very chauvinistic. Californians thought they were better than we were." Japanese Americans who had lived in the Pacific Northwest, on the other hand, thought "they were a little bit better because they were a little more assimilated and they came from smaller Japanese communities," as compared with the Californians, who, they assumed, "lived in ghetto-like, self-contained communities." Those from the Pacific Northwest called them "California colored people," Suguro recalled, in part because they were more tanned by the sun, whereas the Californians called those from Washington and Oregon "chibi lily" because they were less tanned—both terms also arguably intended to invoke broader racial divides.[166]

Social divides existed not just between Alaska residents and those from Seattle and the Pacific states, however, but also among Alaskans, including between those who were solely of Japanese ancestry and those of both Japanese and Alaska Native ancestry. Their forced removal to the Puyallup Assembly Center had brought into contact for the first time those who had lived in more urban communities in Alaska and those who had lived in outlying areas, including its far northern communities. "We met people there who didn't even know they were Japanese," Helen Nakashima recalled, among them the Foode boys, one of whom was blond, who had no idea that they had a Japanese grandfather.[167] Isamu Taguchi recalled several men from Barrow, Alaska, with whom other Japanese Americans from Alaska rarely mingled, who also learned only after the war broke out that they were half Japanese and, before being deported from Alaska, had had no contact with other Japanese.[168] Unable to speak Japanese and unfamiliar with Japanese culture, George Yanagimachi remembered, those like "the Indian fella" who had just "a little bit of Japanese blood in him" had the hardest time adjusting to their new circumstances. "They were different," he said, regarded as "other" by those who viewed themselves as Japanese Americans.[169]

Even in Ketchikan, where a number of Japanese business owners had rented land from their Indigenous neighbors on Stedman Street, their parents had chided them for playing with Indigenous children, Patrick Hagiwara recalled. He was reluctant to call it a "stigma," he said, but it was clear that they were deemed "considerably low class."[170] Cherry Tsuruko Tatsuda Fujioka explained that even though her father's grocery store was located near Stedman Street and most of his customers were their Indigenous neighbors, "the protectiveness of our mothers did not allow us to mix too much." While they "lived among Natives and kind of grew up with them, to a certain degree," she added, the fact that the Tlingit children were sent to a different school also limited their interaction with them.[171] That some who lived in the small urban Japanese immigrant communities in Alaska also remained conscious of historical status differences rooted in Japanese history and culture, in turn, was reflected in the refusal of some mothers to allow their children to attend the Japanese-language school in Ketchikan because the Japanese teacher there reportedly spoke a low-class dialect, in contrast to the more polite "true Japanese language" of the Meiji era, and they did not want the teacher "to contaminate the kids with this kind of crude Japanese."[172]

After more than four months at the Puyallup Assembly Center, the Alaska families who had been housed there were sent to the Minidoka War Relocation Center, a detention camp in Hunt, Idaho, along with others from Washington and Oregon.[173] The windows of the train that carried them eastward across the Rockies were blacked out so that they would not know where they were, but the soot still worked its way in and combined with the sweat on their faces to make them look like "kuronbo-san" (people of African descent), Abe Hagiwara recalled. Like his brother Patrick, Abe would also join the 442nd Infantry Regiment, made up entirely of Japanese American soldiers, to fight in Europe.[174] The Minidoka site was a "God-forsaken place, way out in the desert," Irene Takizawa later told an interviewer.[175] When they arrived, construction was not yet completed, Mack Mori recalled, and "then, the wind started blowing, *neh*. Sandstorm. *Hidoi yo* [It was awful]." The Portland people arrived just as the wind came up, he remembered, and one woman was crying, overwhelmed by the barren landscape and fearing that they would never leave. The wind might be blowing that day, but the next day it would not, he told her in an effort to give her something to be happy about.[176] Isamu Taguchi was also dismayed both by the facility and by the barren expanses that surrounded it. Minidoka was all "sage, and flat and hot. Hot country back there," he later told an interviewer. "It was just a bunch of farms and it was kind of discouraging. And then there were barracks and we didn't appreciate that. . . . Just one small room for [five] of us . . . about 16 × 20."[177]

Some found ways to make the best they could of the challenging environment in which they found themselves. Winters were much colder than in Ketchikan, Hope Ohashi remembered, explaining in a mix of English and Japanese that "Ketchikan *no ho nanka* never *anna-ni samuku natta koto nai*

[Ketchikan never got as cold as it was there]." But Minidoka was "all right" and "good enough," in her view. Boys played baseball, no one was called "Jap," and they did not have to worry about having enough food. In this sense, she said, "*Amerika ni otta hito wa* [those who spent the war in America were] lucky," as compared both with those who spent the duration of the war in Japan and those who went to Europe with the 442nd. Those interned at other camps including Tule Lake, she acknowledged, had a harder time, but some, she thought, were "looking for trouble, too, some of those pro-Japan ones, huh?" During wartime, she explained, you had to be willing to just "get along."[178] Much as he missed his home in Beaver, Alaska, Frank Yasuda's daughter Hana Elavgak Yasuda Kangas later reported, he adapted as best he could to the constraints and arid environment of the detention facilities where he was incarcerated. While Yasuda could no longer speak much Japanese, she said, he could still understand it and took advantage of the chance to visit with others from Japan for the first time in many years so he could hear it spoken.[179] Generally, Isamu Taguchi recalled, they were free to do what they wanted at Minidoka, visiting friends or working during the week and, in his case, going to church on Sundays. After a time, they were allowed to leave the camp to go to Twin Falls to dig potatoes or "top sugar beets," he added, and he did this whenever he could. It was "pretty good," he said, explaining that if the families for whom "[we worked] didn't feed us in their homes they made arrangements for us to eat in restaurants in town."[180]

Concerns arose within a month of the arrival of Japanese Americans from Alaska and the Pacific Northwest in Hunt, Idaho, regarding the impact of the upheaval on those of both Japanese and Native decent. In a memorandum addressed to Dillon S. Myer, director of the War Relocation Authority, Carl V. Sandoz, a counselor assigned to the Minidoka detention camp, noted that many of those in this group had been forced to leave their homes in remote areas of Alaska and to board planes that connected directly with ocean transport with little, if any, meaningful notice. There were forty-two individuals of mixed descent. Ten were children under the age of ten; nine were children between ten and twenty; sixteen were young adults between twenty and thirty; and seven were adults between thirty and forty years of age.[181] One family, Sandoz wrote, was "part Eskimo" and the others were "part Indian." Despite the War Relocation Authority's determination that they were part Japanese, none "consider[ed] themselves persons of Japanese ancestry," and they were also "not accepted [as such] in the community [t]here."[182]

On December 31, 1942, James H. Condit, who had taught at the Sheldon Jackson School for Indians in Sitka, Alaska, for a period of ten years, appealed to Anthony J. Dimond on behalf of two boys, Joseph and Henry Ozawa, the sons of an Indigenous mother and a Japanese father, who, together with their older brother, had been placed at the school by their mother, who had raised all three. Their father had taken no interest in them and was a "virtual stranger to his own sons," Condit wrote. The boys were "decidedly Indian, taking after their mother" and very much rooted in the Native community in which they had grown up, with no ties to anyone of Japanese descent. Joseph Ozawa, he explained, had written to the school superintendent to ask why the children of Japanese fathers and Caucasian mothers were permitted to stay in Alaska whereas the children of Japanese fathers and Indigenous mothers were forcibly removed and whether this practice improperly discriminated between the children of Caucasian and Indigenous mothers. The Ozawas worked as fishermen during the summers, Condit noted, and if they were permitted to return to Alaska, they would surely "render a greater service in helping with the salmon intake than in raising vegetables in whatever agricultural area they may be placed." Also deserving of note when it came to questions regarding their status as American citizens, he added, was that "these boys, born in the United States, have mothers who are more truly 'American' than the rest of us since their mothers were here when we white folks arrived." Might they not be allowed to return to Alaska, where they had been born and had deep ancestral ties, "so that they may engage in the fishing industry, their natural occupation, and thus aid in the food production so essential to the winning of the war?"[183]

On January 21, 1943, uncertain just where the Ozawa boys had been incarcerated, Myer directed the project directors of the Gila River and Poston detention camps "to identify and accept applications for [indefinite] leave from Joseph Ozawa and Henry Ozawa" so they could be forwarded to military authorities at Fort Richardson in Alaska for consideration.[184] In April, however, Condit was notified that military authorities in Alaska intended categorically to deny all such requests given that it was regarded as a war zone and because it was General Buckner's policy "not to permit entrance back to Alaska of any persons of full blooded or half blooded Japanese parentage." This, he conceded, meant that he was unable to do anything more on behalf of the Ozawa brothers. Condit also, however, reminded Myer that it was important to distinguish between culture and ancestry and warned that incarcerating individuals who had no actual ties to Japan might itself undermine the loyalty of those in question. As a consequence of the deportation order, Joseph and Henry, as well as an older brother who was married to an Alaska Native woman, were separated not just from family and friends but also "from their natural habitat and occupations." "Would it not be logical," he asked, "that under such conditions they may become embittered and transformed from loyal American citizens, as they have been, to pro-Japanese aliens?"[185] Problematic as his characterization of the Ozawa boys as "natural" extensions of their environment was, Condit understood, as others did not, that the injustice visited on them might itself have the effect of persuading them or others in their position to identify more strongly with Japan than they had ever had reason to do before.

While Myer agreed that there was indeed "danger of losing the fealty" of young men such as the Ozawas as a consequence of their removal from Alaska and incarceration stateside, the War Relocation Authority did not have the power to override "the determination of military authorities that all persons of Japanese ancestry should be removed from Alaska" regardless of their circumstances. Myer indicated, however, that it was his hope that they might be released from the detention centers where they were being held and given the chance to "be placed in productive work" in areas outside designated military zones, as some five thousand Japanese Americans had already been.[186] For most, however, this meant relocating to the East Coast or the Midwest. Charles Foode, who did receive an indefinite leave permit to work on farms outside Minidoka, wrote in the fall of 1943 that moving to these parts of the country was no substitute for being allowed to return to Alaska. He asked in a letter to Governor Gruening when he and his three brothers, who had been taken from their jobs and "put in one of those Jap camps," would be able to rejoin their family in Alaska. "We are half Japanese and half Alaska Indian," he explained, and "our sisters and brothers are still in Cordova with our mother." Although they had all been issued indefinite leave permits to help with the harvest, they wanted to return to Alaska by the spring of 1944, he said, "so we can go back to fishing, and our folks."[187] Like Myer, however, territorial officials in Alaska were powerless to intervene on behalf of those in Foode's position. While he understood their situation, the acting governor of Alaska explained to Foode, much as Myer had to Condit, "control of the evacuation of persons of Japanese ancestry from the Territory was and is entirely within the jurisdiction of the War Department."[188]

The Aleut Relocations

Unfamiliar with Alaska, its landscape, or its people, Captain Ralph C. Parker, the U.S. Navy commander responsible for Alaska, wrote Governor Gruening in August 1941, five full months before Japan's attack on Pearl Harbor, to ask for information that would allow the navy to plan for the evacuation of Alaska's white residents if war broke out. "The Bering Sea Coast and the Aleutian

Chain are strategically in exposed positions, and in the event of war in the Pacific, their liability to possible enemy raids, and the more certain curtailment of their supplies, and medical care from outside, might dictate the evacuation of white inhabitants, wholly or in part," he explained. As such, he asked that the governor of Alaska send him a "list of ports and places in geographic order along the coast from east to west, and from south to north, starting with points west of Kodiak," together with a list of the white residents in each location. He also asked the governor to indicate whether it was more practical to evacuate each group by sea or by air should the need arise. Names were helpful but not required, Parker said, as was the "data on natives (round numbers only)," given that they were clearly not his primary concern.[189] In the wake of Japan's attack on Pearl Harbor on December 7, the commander of the Naval Air Station at Dutch Harbor cabled the Bureau of Indian Affairs in Juneau, to ask what plans were for the evacuation of the 160 Aleut women and children who lived on Unalaska, the Aleutian island deemed most vulnerable to attack, only to learn that no plans had been made.[190] As U.S. citizens, the superintendent of the Alaska Indian Service told him, the Aleut were free to go where they wished, ideally "to other villages on the Alaskan Peninsula or nearby islands" rather than to Seattle. The Alaska Indian Service did not have funds to assist them with that move, but it had told the non-Native teachers it employed that they were expected to continue to assist their Native students and to travel with them if they were evacuated, unless the U.S. military forbade them to do so.[191] At a meeting of interested agencies on March 18 in acting governor Bartlett's office in Juneau, participants agreed that if Japan were to invade Alaska, some effort should be made to assist the Aleut in moving to other locations, with certain caveats:

1. ... [N]o general attempt should be made even in case of actual enemy attack, to evacuate Eskimos or other primitive natives of Alaska. It is felt these people could never adjust themselves to life outside of their present environment, whereas they could "take to the hills" in case of danger and be practically self-sufficient for a considerable period.
2. It is felt, however, that six months' supply of staple food should be widely distributed in Alaska, for natives as well as whites.
3. It is felt also that the approximately 150 Aleut women and children at Unalaska should be moved to other villages less exposed (to both military and social dangers). The Office of Indian Affairs has canvassed

their groups and learned their preferences as to the places they would like to be moved. These places are King Cove, Akutan, Sand Point, Squaw Harbor, Belkofsky, Kanatak, Karluk, Chignik, Perryville and False Pass. At Karluk, False Pass and Chignik there are living quarters available at canneries not to be operated this year. Three teachers from the Unalaska Government school could be assigned to Alaska Peninsula or Aleutian Island villages which would gain most markedly in population.

4. Other exposed positions from which some natives should probably be moved include Seward (Jesse Lee Home) and Yakutat, where (school enrollment [was already] down from 90 to 30).[192]

Three months later, on the morning of June 3, 1942, General Buckner wired the governor of Alaska to report that Dutch Harbor had been bombed by a small group of Japanese planes that morning.[193] Like the attack on Pearl Harbor, Japan's attack on the Aleutian Islands had also been launched from a base in the Kuril Islands.[194] On June 5, Canada's minister of labor informed the House of Commons that "the Japanese hit-and-run raid on Dutch Harbour signalled the need for increased precautionary measures in the British Columbia coastal area." He planned to begin by ordering the immediate removal from the B.C. coast of some six thousand persons he considered a danger to "Indian schools" in Manitoba, Alberta, and the B.C. interior.[195] On June 6, Japanese forces landed on the island of Kiska (Qisxa), and, on June 7, they landed on the island of Attu, about fifteen hundred miles west of the city of Anchorage and over two thousand miles west of Juneau.[196] Although U.S. military officials tried to keep the attack from becoming general knowledge to avoid alarming civilians who lived along the Alaska coast, fears that a Japanese invasion was imminent and concerns about just how far it would penetrate along that coast were already high.[197] On June 13, Susan Marks, a resident of Hoonah, a Tlingit village on Chichagof Island thirty miles west of Juneau, wrote to Governor Gruening to ask whether civilians would be evacuated if it proved "impossible to hold Alaska from being taken by the Japs." She begged him to act before the "Jap submarines" she assumed were operating in Alaskan waters cut off any chance of escape and even one Alaska resident was taken prisoner by "the Japs." Alaskans were "depending upon our government to see that we are never taken prisoners by the Japs," she reminded him, adding, "We love Alaska and would like to keep it. But if our government knows it can't be held we should all be evacuated and . . . not wait until the last minute like what was done in Singapore."[198]

The more immediate concern in the minds of army officials, however, was evacuating the Aleut and other Native people on Atka and in the Pribilof Islands near Kiska and Attu to ensure their safety.[199] On June 4, prior to the landings of Japanese forces on Kiska and Attu, Gruening had written to Secretary of the Interior Harold L. Ickes expressing his concern that the very act of evacuating the 450 individuals, most of them Indigenous, from these islands would itself expose them to danger, given that Japanese naval vessels were active in the area, although there were also fears that if Japanese forces did invade, they "might conceivably exterminate all the natives." Gruening noted, moreover, that General Buckner believed that "it would be a great mistake to evacuate these natives," given that "evacuating them [would itself come] pretty close to destroying them," since they would then "be subject to the deterioration of contact with the white man, would likely fall prey to drink and disease, and probably would never get back to their historic habitat." Gruening also reminded Ickes that many residents of the Aleutian Islands had yet to be consulted, arguing that "the pros and cons of so momentous a decision, the possible risks and alternatives [must] be presented to them understandingly, sympathetically and clearly." This could no longer be done by radio, however, given that radio communications might well be intercepted by Japanese naval vessels. Instead, it would require someone to travel to the islands to discuss the matter with them.[200]

In the end, there would be no meaningful opportunity to consult with the Aleut residents of Atka and other nearby islands before a decision was made. On June 17, 1942, ten days after Japanese forces landed on Attu, Captain Parker informed officials in Anchorage that they now appeared to be in control of that island. Unknown was the fate of its non-Native residents, who had presumably been taken prisoner, but whether they were still on the island or on the way to a prisoner of war camp in Japan he could not say.[201] The landing of Japanese troops on Attu also rendered moot the debate regarding the evacuation of its Indigenous residents. As Gruening conceded in a letter to Ickes on June 20, U.S. officials also did not know what had happened to them. He could only hope, he wrote, "that they are prisoners of war and will be treated decently." The army had acted immediately to evacuate those living on Atka and in the Pribilofs, however, and their arrival in southeastern Alaska was imminent.[202]

The question of where the Aleut hastily evacuated from the islands of the Aleutian chain would be housed was caught up in the tangled web of jurisdictional boundaries that delineated the authority of the various agencies involved in the evacuation. As Gruening explained to Ickes, these included

the Office of Indian Affairs (which has jurisdiction over the natives of
Atka and over possible future evacuees from such places as Nunivak,
St. Lawrence Island, Umnak Island and Unalaska); the Fish and Wildlife
Service (which has jurisdiction over the Pribilof natives); the Army
(which is handling the evacuation); the Navy (because the Army did not
know whether the evacuees would come on Army or Navy vessels); the
Social Security Board (which includes the Federal Employment Service);
United States Marshal's Office (because the establishment of these new
colonies may involve certain aspects of law enforcement, particularly in
regard to liquor); the Territorial Health Department and the Public
Health Service (both because health problems particularly with a view to
avoiding epidemics will be involved in the selection of these new sites);
and the U.S. Forest Service (since the localities planned for resettlement
are within the Tongass National Forest).[203]

After his meeting with representatives of each agency, Gruening reported
that the participants had reached a consensus regarding the jurisdictional authority of two of the agencies: the Office of Indian Affairs was responsible for
the Aleut who lived on the other Aleutian Islands, whereas the Fish and Wildlife Service was responsible for the four hundred Alaska Natives who lived on
the Pribilof Islands given their role in the fur seal industry. It would make far
more sense, he told Ickes, if the Office of Indian Affairs were also to be assigned responsibility for the Pribilof Islanders while they were in southeastern Alaska so that there was just one agency involved in providing for all
evacuees and the Fish and Wildlife Service could concentrate on matters related to the fur seal industry.[204] Abandoned canneries had already been identified as sites that might be used to accommodate the Aleut, who would
eventually be housed in four separate locations—at Funter Bay and Killisnoo
on Admiralty Island not far from Juneau, at Burnette Inlet on Etolin Island
near Wrangell, and at Ward Lake on Revillagigedo Island some thirty miles
north of the Dixon Entrance.[205]

ON JUNE 18, even as the Atka Natives were in the process of being removed to
southeast Alaska, word came that the Japanese were continuing their advance,
raising new fears about whether other islands in the Aleutian chain would be
attacked, in particular Umnak and Nikolski Islands, as well as Unalaska.[206]
U.S. officials would not know for some time what had happened to those who
lived on Attu. Only later would they learn that Charles Foster Jones, who was
employed by the Alaska Indian Service, had been shot after he refused to fix

the radio he destroyed or that his wife, Etta Jones, who served as school-teacher and nurse on the island, had been taken prisoner and put aboard a ship bound for Japan on June 15. In response to concerns expressed by friends who worried about how close Attu was to Japan when they first arrived on Attu in August 1941, Etta had reportedly replied, "What would Japan want with Attu?" "Attu looks good to us," she wrote at the time, explaining that there were nine or ten houses in the village, "all well painted, large and fur-nished," as well as a "beautiful Russian Orthodox Church." Its forty-five resi-dents already spoke some English, which surprised her given how isolated their village was. "They rarely see other people," she explained, "except men on the occasional Coast Guard cutters that put in here."[207] A report prepared by Charles Jones for the Office of Indian Affairs described the Aleut on Attu—or Unangan, as they preferred to be called—as "a proud people; proud of the fact that they differ somewhat from the people of Atka and Unalaska." They do not "intermingle with the Japanese [and], in fact, dislike and distrust the Japs," he explained. In fact, "they accuse them of stealing their foxes, and even of killing some of their trappers years ago."[208] Nick Golodoff, who was not yet seven when the Japanese landed on Attu, also remembered times when people assumed to be Japanese were spotted from afar or left tracks on the beach.[209]

Although some two thousand Japanese troops who landed on the far side of the island poured down the mountain above the village, shooting while the Unangan were in church, on June 7, the Japanese did not "exterminate" all of them as U.S. military authorities had imagined they might. They did, how-ever, confine them to their homes and prevent them from moving freely about, making it difficult for them to gather food and to hunt or fish.[210] The officers of the Japanese Imperial Army who landed on Attu—some of whom had previously fought in China—carried English-Japanese dictionaries and were accompanied by a Japanese American interpreter named Kaoru (Karl) Kasukabe, who had lived in Pocatello, Idaho, as a child but had returned to Japan with his mother while still a youngster, while his father remained in Pocatello. Kasukabe distributed copies of a proclamation that declared, in English, that the Imperial Army "had come to rescue [the Unangan] from the tyranny and exploitation of the Americans" and that they had nothing to fear as long as they obeyed its orders.[211] Fukuzawa Mikizo, one of the Imperial Army officers who had landed on Attu, informed his superiors that the school where Etta Jones taught was in fact a U.S. Navy communications post and that the United States was preparing to remove all of the Aleut, both on Attu and on the other Aleutian Islands, in order to establish military bases on

Japanese shrine on Kiska Island in the western Aleutian Islands, August 1943. Alaska State Library, U.S. Navy Bureau of Aeronautics Photograph Collection, ASL-P430-82.

them. When the soldiers of the Japanese Imperial Army arrived, Fukuzawa wrote, the Aleut were relieved to learn that they were Japanese and not German, as he claimed the U.S. military had led them to believe would invade, and that the Aleut "felt a kind of kinship [to Japanese] because of the similarity of facial features."[212]

In mid-September, when the Japanese Imperial Army decided to withdraw from Attu, it put the forty Unangan still on Attu aboard a freighter last used to carry coal, before transferring them to another ship bound for Japan at Kiska. On September 27, they arrived in Otaru, a city on the west coast of Hokkaido in what was historically Ainu territory, some sixteen hundred miles west of Attu. As civilian detainees rather than prisoners of war, the Unangan were able to stay together, housed in a five-room building but carefully guarded for two years, before being moved to another part of the city.[213] Described in a book published in Japan in 1906 as "docile and diligent like our Ainu natives," they were put to work digging clay.[214] Although the Unangan would later say that they were treated less harshly than Chinese or Korean prisoners, Japanese sources acknowledge that the Unangan were also beaten and verbally abused.[215] Poorly fed, particularly as food supplies throughout Japan grew scarcer as the war ground on, twenty-one Unangan, including four children born in Otaru, died of diseases including tuberculosis and beriberi, among them Nick Golodoff's father, an older sister, and two brothers. Just twenty-four would survive their forced confinement in Japan, among them Golodoff's younger sister, the only baby born in Japan to do so.[216] Etta Jones, who had arrived in Japan on or about June 22, 1942, also survived, although she would not return to Attu after the war. Held first at the Bund Hotel in Yokohama, she was moved to the Yokohama Yacht Club in July, along with eighteen Australian nurses who had been captured in New Guinea in January 1942. Two years later, in July 1944, they were moved again, this time to Totsuka, a village near Yokohama. There they were put to work digging trenches meant to serve as air raid shelters as U.S. bombing raids intensified and, in the spring of 1945, found themselves watching growing numbers of Japanese civilians who, having lost their homes to the fires that swept through Tokyo and Yokohama in their wake, trudged by the building where they were held.[217]

Returning Home

Attu would be retaken after a bitter and hard-fought battle that began on May 11, 1943. Unfamiliar with the topography of the island and unprepared for the steep and rough terrain, beset by fog and gale-force winds, and mired in tundra that the cold rain turned to mud, U.S. troops and the Canadian observers who accompanied them fought the entrenched Japanese soldiers for almost three weeks until the battle ended on May 30.[218] As when Japanese Imperial Army troops had landed one year earlier, those who went ashore included *nisei* interpreters, some of them *kibei* or *kika nisei* born in the United States or Canada but educated in Japan who had later returned to the country of their birth.[219] While both sides sustained devastating losses on Attu, the taking of Kiska, which had been heavily bombed by U.S. and Canadian aircraft as part of a joint mission, would prove anticlimactic. When they went ashore on August 18, U.S. and Canadian soldiers realized that Japan had already abandoned Kiska and evacuated all of its military personnel three weeks earlier.[220]

Only at the end of 1944, a year and a half after Attu and Kiska had been retaken, did the army officials in Alaska agree that three Japanese *issei*, Frank Yasuda, Sam (Saburo) Kito, and Harry Okegawa, who had asked that they be allowed to return to what army officials called their "former homes," now be permitted to do so, together with four of their family members.[221] By the middle of January 1945, fourteen more Alaskans assigned to the Minidoka Relocation Center had asked to do the same.[222] While layers of administrative red tape repeatedly delayed their return, forcing the War Relocation Authority to cancel reservations already made for Yasuda's return to Beaver, Alaska, at one stage, by May 1945, with some exceptions, the necessary clearances were in place.[223] In a number of instances, military authorities in Alaska themselves provided transportation to those returning to their homes, given that regular plane service to a number of the communities where they had lived did not exist.[224] Other Alaskans, however, would be denied the ability to return until the fall of 1945. Although the exclusion order for the Pacific states was revoked in full on September 4, that for Alaska would not be revoked in full until November 1945.[225]

Just over half of the Unangan who had been forcibly removed and imprisoned in Japan returned to Alaska in November after a circuitous journey around the Pacific Rim, first aboard a U.S. Army plane, which flew south from Otaru over the ruins of Nagasaki to Okinawa, and then a ship that stopped at Manila, San Francisco, and Seattle, before heading north again to the Aleutian Islands. When they arrived, however, they were told that their homes on Attu had been destroyed and their numbers were now too few to make it possible for them to resettle there.[226] While the Pribilof Islanders who were evacuated to southeastern Alaska after Japan's attacks on Kiska and Attu were permitted to return in 1944, the Aleut from Atka and other Aleutian Islands were able to begin returning home only in 1945. They, too, had suffered during the war, housed in crowded and unsanitary conditions in canneries never intended for wintertime occupation and exposed to disease, to which some of their family members also succumbed.[227]

Some first-generation Japanese who had been removed from Alaska in 1942 also did not return, among them George Oshima, the only *issei* immigrant other than Frank Yasuda who had lived in Beaver.[228] Still others were permanently separated by the war. While George Moto did return to Deering, the Inupiaq village that had become his home, he would never again see his Inupiaq wife, who had died a year after her husband and sons were taken away by plane.[229] In British Columbia, Tomekichi Hashimoto was separated from his wife, who was in Japan when the war began and for its duration, and died in May 1944 in the B.C. interior without seeing her again.[230] Others who spent the war years in Japan included Mack Mori's sister, Mary, who was also in Japan when war broke out and was forced to remain there until it ended, as well as Mary Kiyooka's daughter Mariko, who spent the war years with family in Kyoto and Hokkaido, where they struggled to make ends meet.[231] Shig (Shigeru) Kuwabara, whose father had emigrated to Canada after the end of the Russo-Japanese War and settled on the Skeena River, was held in a prisoner-of-war camp in Petawawa, Ontario, for the duration of the war, but would return to salmon fishing at Port Edward in 1949. Roy Uyeda, born at the Celtic Cannery in Vancouver, on the other hand, was among the Canadian-born British subjects expatriated to Japan by the Canadian government in 1946, together with his father and two sisters. Although they had hoped to reunite with his brother Tom, who was also stranded in Japan when the war began, they would learn that, deemed a Japanese subject by Japan's imperial government, he had been drafted into the Japanese army and sent to Burma with his unit, where he died.[232]

Many *issei* men were also separated from their families for all or part of the war. On the U.S. side of the border, they remained Japanese subjects because they had never had the option of applying to become U.S. citizens; in Canada, they included both men who remained Japanese subjects and those who were naturalized British subjects.[233] Many of the *issei* men who settled in Alaska were confined at the Lordsburg detention facility in New Mexico for close to two years before being allowed to rejoin their families at Minidoka in November 1943. Some had been moved from one detention center to another in the course of their journey. Chokichi Hagiwara, who had arrived in Alaska in 1909 and settled in Ketchikan, for example, was first sent to Missoula, Montana, then to Lordsburg, and from there to a detention camp in Santa Fe, New Mexico, before being allowed to rejoin his family at Minidoka.[234] The family of Harvey Shirai, the son of a Japanese father and a Tsimshian mother, who was married to a Tlingit woman and also lived in Ketchikan, appears to have been the most widely scattered.[235] Whereas Harvey Shirai was among those confined at Minidoka in Hunt, Idaho, his twenty-four-year-old wife, Minnie, an Alaska Native woman who had chosen to accompany her husband in an effort to keep her family together, spent much of the war at a facility near Seattle, Washington, where she was treated for tuberculosis, while their three children were sent to what was called the "children's village" at Manzanar in California.[236] When she was released in March 1944, a U.S. government lawyer explained that because Minnie had "no Japanese blood, there was nothing in the exclusion orders or regulations of the Western Defense Command to prevent her from continuing to live in Seattle," although she could also choose to live in Manzanar if War Relocation Authority officials allowed. Military officials in Alaska, in turn, indicated that they did not object to her return to Alaska as long as she did not "become a public charge," the lawyer added, noting that there was actually no legal ground on which they could bar her from Alaska even if she did become a public charge. While her children would be permitted to join her in Alaska if she did return there, given that they were just "one-quarter Japanese blood," however, they would not be allowed to join her if she remained in Washington. Military authorities in Alaska, he explained, excluded only people who were at least one-half Japanese, but the Western Defense Command in Washington State did "not permit the return to the evacuated area of children of a mixed marriage when the husband [was] of Japanese blood," regardless of degree.[237]

While restrictions on the return of people of Japanese ancestry to the coasts of Oregon, Washington, and California were lifted in their entirety on September 4, 1945, and restrictions on the return of Japanese Americans to Alaska that November, in British Columbia such restraints were not lifted until 1949.[238] Among those who would never return to the coast was Tome-kichi Homma, who had fought for the franchise in the early 1900s and passed away on October 28, 1945, near Slocan, deep in the B.C. interior, without be-ing allowed to return to the coast even though the war had come to an end two months earlier.[239] His room in the camp where he was confined, his son Keay Homma later recalled, was almost bare: just a single portrait of the king and queen hung on one of the walls—ongoing, if mute, testimony both to his loyalty and to his belief that he was entitled to all of the rights normally af-forded a naturalized British subject.[240] Jun Kizawa, who had successfully challenged the ban on the use of gasoline engine boats by fishers in the Skeena River area in the 1920s, was sent to Greenwood, the first detention camp to be built in the B.C. interior, just eight miles north of the forty-ninth parallel; he passed away in nearby Grand Forks in February 1950.[241] While Arichika Ikeda had passed away in 1939, having established a copper mine in Haida Gwaii in the 1910s as well as a number of other businesses, his wife, Kaoru, who was relocated first to Slocan and then to New Denver, passed away in the spring of 1946, without ever returning to the coast. Three years earlier, in late 1943, she had written a tanka that reflected on her forced removal and con-finement far from the coast:

> I thought
> It would only be temporary
> In this Mountain country
> Accumulate another year
> As snow deepens.[242]

Just a few families and individuals were able to avoid expulsion altogether, including, in Canada, Japanese immigrant families in the Yukon, which had not been included in the protected area. Alaska, in effect, was deemed a sufficient buffer against attack from the Pacific.[243] Some assumed non-Japanese identities when the war began. Among them was Isamu Taguchi's mother, who sold vegetables at Seattle's Pike Street Market after his father died and was given a button to wear at work declaring her to be Chinese.[244] An Oregon woman who reportedly did not "look Japanese" was also able to avoid being forcibly relocated during the war by hiding this part of her identity.[245] In Alaska, Japanese women married to white or Indigenous men were permitted to remain in the territory, while in Canada this rule was also applied to *issei* and *nisei* men married to women not of Japanese descent. Ninety-four Japanese Canadian men and women were allowed to remain in or return to the protected zone on this basis. Among them was Yoshizo Takeuchi, a World War I veteran who had married an English woman he met in Europe while overseas and settled in Prince Rupert after he returned from the war. Although his family was initially sent to Hastings Park, his wife and children were released one month later and he was permitted to rejoin them in the protected zone in November 1943, after spending a year at the detention camp in Lemon Creek, B.C., and allowed to start fishing on the Fraser River and in Rivers Inlet again in 1944.[246] There also appear to have been a few individuals who were already so deeply embedded in Indigenous communities that they were also not removed or, possibly, not even recognized as being of Japanese descent. Among them were the descendants of Imakichi Kawashima, born in Japan around 1870, who had settled in Bella Bella, where he was known by his adopted name, Joe Vickers, and worked in the fish saltery. Records reflect that he married a Kwakiutl woman in 1907, and in 1921 a man by the name of Joe Vickers, a fisherman born around 1867, was listed in the census as the head of a Kwakiutl family living in Bella Bella. While he himself died before the war began, there is no indication that his descendants were among those forcibly removed from the coast.[247]

Despite such occasional examples, however, relations between Japanese Canadian and Indigenous fishers along the B.C. coast would take time to mend. The contest between Japanese and Indigenous fishers along that coast during the interwar period had itself served, at times, to reinforce allegations that Japanese Canadian fishermen were spying for Japan,[248] and fears that Japan might launch a seaborne invasion during the Second World War appear to have worked their way into the songs and dances of at least some Indigenous peoples along the B.C. coast.[249] Relations between the two groups were also complicated by the fact that cannery managers, particularly along British Columbia's north coast, hired Indigenous fishers to take the place of the Japanese Canadian fishermen who were forbidden to fish for the duration of the war, making the vessels that they had purchased at auction from the Custodian of Enemy Property available to them at little more than cost, a practice that provided new opportunities to Indigenous people along the coast but did not sit well with the former owners of the boats that had been seized.[250] Although Indigenous leaders had long argued for an equal place in the B.C. fishing industry, however, some also recognized the injustice visited upon their Japanese Canadian neighbors. Kwakiutl elder Ga'axsta'las, for example, had long complained that "the Japs" held most of the gillnet licenses on the Nimpkish River at the north end of Vancouver Island, whereas "the Indian, who was the original there, and to whom the reserve belongs, and who has had his food there from that river," did not, arguing that Kwakiutl fishers "should be protected from the Japs." But she and her children also clearly felt for the Japanese families they had come to know and who were forced to leave, including that of the Cook family barber, who, they said, was Japanese, as well as the "Suki-yama" and "Fugiyama" families, who managed the dog salmon saltery and fish plant at Cook Wharf.[251] While the Cook family left the processing equipment untouched, there were other Indigenous fishers, Ryuichi Yoshida recalled, who "didn't like it all" when *nikkei* fishers returned in the early 1950s, and "caused a lot of trouble," "interfer[ing] with us putting our nets in the sea."[252]

Some Indigenous leaders had supported Canada's policies not only of barring the return of Japanese Canadians to the B.C. coast until 1949 but also of requiring Canadians of Japanese ancestry to choose between dispersal (resettlement in eastern Canada, still further from the B.C. coast than the detention camps in the B.C. interior) and "repatriation"—or, in the case of those born in Canada, expatriation—to Japan.[253] Both were policies crafted in part to ensure that the small *nikkei* fishing communities that had existed along the coast before the war would not be reestablished.[254] Japanese Canadians, the Co-operative Committee on Japanese Canadians wrote in July 1945 after the "repatriation" policy was announced, had "hoped that [British] justice and fair play would eventually prevail, and that when the war was over attitudes would change."[255] It was undisputed that despite the losses they had sustained and the trying conditions in which they had lived in hastily erected camps and reclaimed ghost towns, Japanese Canadians had remained loyal throughout the war, and they would continue to cooperate. "What kind of Canadians would we be if we [lost faith] now?" asked the author of one letter included with the brief.[256]

Forced to choose between moving east of the Rockies or being exiled to Japan regardless of whether they were familiar with it, some Canadian-born children felt they had no choice but to accompany their *issei* parents, who had lost everything they had worked for. Still others chose to go to Japan in the "desperate hope" that they would be able to reconnect with children or elderly parents whom they had not heard from in several years, some who had been living in Hiroshima when the war began. Among them was Uno Kimura, whose fruit farm in Mission, B.C., was seized and sold by the Custodian of Enemy Property in 1943 and whose parents had returned to Japan in 1938 after working for thirty-six years in British Columbia's coastal fishing industry.[257] Although some would rescind their decision to go to Japan when given the chance, nearly four thousand individuals—roughly one-fifth of those who lived in British Columbia before the war began—were deported or exiled. Of this number, just over half were Canadian-born, one-third were Japanese subjects, and one-seventh were naturalized British subjects.[258] While the repatriation program was ended in 1947, Canada's forced dispersal policy, which effectively extended its wartime "evacuation policy" into the postwar period, was not rescinded until 1949.[259] The same year, Canada guaranteed all Canadians, including those of Japanese ancestry, the right to vote in federal elections. Just three weeks before the federal franchise took effect, the B.C. legislature amended British Columbia's Provincial Voters Act to do the same, granting both Japanese Canadians and Indigenous people living on reserves the right to vote in provincial elections.[260]

Defending the Pacific Borderlands

Despite the persistent rumors that had plagued Japanese immigrants in Alaska and British Columbia during the first half of the twentieth century that Japan was intent on extending its empire across the North Pacific, the northern stretch of the U.S.-Canada border that divides Alaska from British Columbia was never strongly defended by either nation during the war. While those living in the few small villages along the Dixon Entrance were instructed to dim their lights at night, the general lack of concern on the part of military authorities was reflected in the absence of any meaningful effort to shore up defenses along that section of the U.S.-Canada border. On the west coast of Moresby and Graham Islands, which overlooked the shipping lanes that connected Alaska with the U.S. states, the Royal Canadian Air Force set up two small airfields and a series of eight small coast-watching outposts, each staffed by a maximum of just four men, who were instructed to radio

Prince Rupert or the air station at Alliford Bay if they saw anything unusual. Other than the arrival of a Canadian naval vessel that they initially feared might be Japanese and the shots that rang out when a whale was taken nearby, one coast watcher later recalled, there was little besides the "pounding, ever-changing moods of the whole Pacific," the "sounds of gulls and wind and rain and surf," and the smell of "moss on conifer," however, to occupy them.[261]

Attu and Kiska, at the westernmost end of the Aleutian Islands that extended out toward the Kamchatka Peninsula and, just beyond it, the Kuril Islands, were for a time a focal point for the United States and Japan. Both powers imagined the islands at the end of the Aleutian chain as a place where an advance base might be built that would allow the other to proceed east or west along the North Pacific Rim to mount an attack. Both nations, each unaware that the other never seriously considered using the Kuril and Aleutian island chains to launch an invasion against territories they claimed as their own, however, were focused less on using the islands to mount an attack than on defending existing perimeters.[262] The very distances that seemed to render the north Pacific coast vulnerable, paradoxically, made utilizing the island chain to invade either the continent of North America or the Japanese empire eminently impractical.[263] While Japan's seizure of two rocky and relatively barren islands at the end of the Aleutian chain may have appeared insignificant to others, however, its long frustrated efforts to secure what it regarded as its fair share of the marine resources of the North Pacific, given that Western nations had freely availed themselves of the same in its waters during earlier decades, also helps to explain its interest in occupying and establishing a claim to those islands. Its occupation of them, as such, was also partly responsive to the United States' persistent unwillingness to cooperate with Japan's efforts to secure a negotiated resolution regarding what it deemed the inequitable distribution of the proceeds generated by the lucrative hunt for seals in the waters surrounding them.

Not only did the Japanese Imperial Navy not advance to any significant degree beyond the Aleutian outposts from which it withdrew in 1943, but it also never attempted to establish a foothold in Hawaii, despite indications that Japanese imperial authorities envisioned the Hawaiian Islands as part of an extended Pacific maritime empire. As Keiichi Takeuchi, later a professor at Hitotsubashi University, recalls, the officially sanctioned geography textbook he was assigned in elementary school during the war described the Hawaiian Islands as part of what was imagined, in effect, as a Japanese "sea of islands," even if it was never formally designated a part of the Japanese empire.[264] Forty percent of Hawaii's population was of Japanese ancestry, its authors explained, and so extensive was their contribution to the Hawaiian economy, they wrote, that "we can consider Hawaii as Japanese Islands."[265] This was a vision of Hawaii that was already apparent decades earlier after the United States annexed Hawaii, leading a prominent Japanese-language newspaper in Hawaii to predict as early as 1906 that "if ever trouble arises between the United States and Japan, Hawaii will be the 'fuse' that will cause the explosion."[266] In British Columbia, likewise, observers predicted in 1908 that if the United States and Japan were ever to go to war over the immigration issue, the Hawaiian Islands would be "easy prey" for Japan.[267]

The irony inherent in these competing visions of Hawaii as Japanese or American space, as well as the claim that the forced removal of U.S.- and Canadian-born citizens and subjects of Japanese ancestry from Alaska and the B.C. coast was warranted, is demonstrated by the fact that Japanese Americans in Hawaii were never subjected to parallel measures, precisely because, as the authors of Takeuchi's geography textbook noted, they played such a central role in Hawaii's economy.[268] For Japan's part, just as ironic was the fact that a campaign intended to challenge a history of racism, restriction, and exclusion and to secure what Japan regarded as its fair share of the world's resources, including the marine resources of the North Pacific, provided instead for the escalation of the very stereotypes it sought to confront and, for a time, appeared to prove those who persisted in spreading rumors that characterized Japanese migrants as a threat to both American and Canadian settlers along the north Pacific coast right.

Afterword

The onset of war brought to a head the contradictions inherent in the racialized legal structures that had been erected over time on both sides of the U.S.-Canada border, only to be further complicated by wartime policy measures motivated by many of the same considerations that had shaped the bodies of law and policy applied both to Asian immigrants and to Indigenous people by each nation. The forced removal of those of Japanese ancestry from the coast in both Canada and the United States, regardless of their status as citizens or subjects, accomplished, at least for a time, what prior efforts to expel and exclude had not. It can, as such, be understood as the culmination both of prior efforts to exclude and of an ongoing contest among the expanding imperial powers with a stake in the North Pacific—the United States, Britain, Japan, and Russia—over its marine resources and for strategic advantage.

The Pacific Ocean was as important to the north Pacific borderlands, and how they were imagined at any given time, as the land-based territories that it comprised, at once a gateway to Asia and the resources of the North Pacific or a conduit for the dangers that it behooved some to suggest that the open ocean might hold. Even before the land-based 100-mile-wide coastal exclusion zone was established after the outbreak of World War II, as a result, B.C.'s coastal waters had, in effect, already been declared a prohibited zone as those in key areas along the Alaska coast would also be. While the perceived—or asserted—vulnerability of the north Pacific coast was based in part on its complexity, including the thousands of small islands, channels, fjords, and inlets that define its contours, however, these qualities, together with the enormous distances over which it stretches and its often steep and rocky terrain, were also the very factors that protected it from a seaborne invasion.

Persistent fears of spying and espionage on both sides of the U.S.-Canada border were part of a larger pattern of rumor and innuendo that extended across the Pacific Ocean as far as India and Australia. Rooted in a mix of racial animus and concern on the part of Britain and the United States about Japan's emergence as a competitor in Asia, these rumors failed to take into account the actual limits of Japan's ability to mount such operations. Such fears also conflated Japan's quest for the many kinds of knowledge that would aid it in remaking itself as a modern nation that followed the imposition of unequal treaties on Japan by Western nations and defined the Meiji era, with what was imagined to be a far more nefarious form of information gathering.[1] Such insinuations, in turn, served the dual purpose of appearing to justify constraints imposed by both Canada and the United States on access to naturalization and the rights normally extended to citizen or subject.

While the power to bestow or impose status as citizen or subject—or to withhold it—was at the heart of both colonial practice and processes of racialization, the corresponding ability to claim status as subject or citizen, or to resist such designations, was also a tool deployed from time to time by both Japanese immigrants and Indigenous people to position themselves more effectively within a colonial framework. The same was true of the crossing of national borders. Powerful ways of organizing difference as they were, however, neither race nor the categories "citizen" and "subject" were ever solely determinative of interrelationships between or within differing racial groups. Neither national nor territorial borders succeeded in severing the kinship networks that connected Indigenous people across them, and borderlands people often saw themselves as having ties to, or even as independent of, both Canada and the United States. Racism and the continued denial of access to the full rights of citizenship also served, in some cases, to reinforce ties to Japan that might otherwise have weakened over time.[2]

Both Japanese diplomats and Japanese immigrants responded to white racism by turning race itself back on white North Americans in ways that included, at varying times and places, not just challenging race but mobilizing and reproducing it in a bid for inclusion. In arguing against race-based exclusion in both the United States and Canada, Japanese officials argued not against the colonial project but for the right of Japanese immigrants and Japan as a nation to participate in it. This was an endeavor to which Japan committed itself during the first half of the twentieth century, actively working to incorporate new territories much as Britain and the United States had done during an earlier era, and as the United States continued to do elsewhere in the Pacific during the same era. Other imperial powers perceived Japan and Japanese immigrants as a threat, at least in part, precisely because they too had come to view colonization and empire as a marker of civilization. Born into a world that was itself a product of imperial expansion and eager to participate in the development of extractive industries along the north Pacific coast, Japanese entrepreneurs carried with them visions of empire similar to those that motivated their Euro-Canadian and American counterparts, notwithstanding that they were also the object of racial discrimination.

Boundary drawing, law, and the racialization of space were essential tools in the arsenal of each imperial power. Despite their respective claims that Canada was heir to British justice and fair play and that the United States was founded on the rule of law, both nations ignored or avoided key principles of international and domestic law where it served their purposes, even as they invoked the law to cloak questionable practices in an aura of legitimacy. Imperial boundaries originally intended to delineate the vaguely defined and largely unknown areas over which European powers sought to assert their authority as against one another—establishing, in effect, zones of influence that made no claim to outright ownership or the formal acquisition of title— "morphed" over time into claims of overarching sovereign authority that purported to erase or greatly diminish, by their very assertion, the interests of Indigenous peoples in that land. The same disregard for legal principle was evident in the lack of due process afforded both U.S. citizens and British subjects of Japanese ancestry resident in Canada prior to their forced removal from the coast and their incarceration during World War II.[3]

Law and national borders were deployed together not just to facilitate the absorption of Indigenous territories, but to secure Asian and Indigenous labor even as they worked to exclude those laborers from a role in governance. The desire to limit access to the same resources they helped to develop, in short, was always in tension with the desire to mobilize the labor needed for the development of fledgling industries along the Pacific coast. Even as borders worked to constrain movement, the removal or displacement of particular populations at particular times—whether these were Indigenous people forced aside by extractive industry of one kind or another or those of Aleut or Japanese ancestry forced to leave their homes during World War II—itself proved to be an essential tool in the consolidation of empire.

Mechanisms first developed to limit the rights of Indigenous people were also utilized to restrict those of Japanese Americans and Japanese Canadians, reflected in the repurposing of spaces set aside as "Indian schools" or reservations to house people of Japanese ancestry during World War II.[4] In the United States, the rigid emphasis on Japanese blood degree applied to Japanese Americans in Alaska, regardless of the cultural context in which they were raised, and even when it was acknowledged that they posed no danger, mirrored its reliance on blood quantum to limit its obligations to Indigenous people, much as the forced removal of people of Japanese ancestry from the coast mirrored the removal of Indigenous people from areas opened for settlement.[5] The same impulse was reflected in Canada's exile and deportation of its own citizens and refusal to allow Japanese Canadians to return to the coast for four years after Japan surrendered. Both wartime and postwar policy, these parallels make clear, were shaped less by security concerns than by racial animus.

Both border and borderland, the North Pacific Ocean, as all places do, signified different things to different people over time. For Britain and the United States, it represented, at critical moments, ready access both to Asian markets and to its wealth of marine resources. Once an ultimate "frontier" in the eyes of some Americans, the Pacific Ocean also came to serve in time as a fluid waterway that linked Alaska and the contiguous states.[6] For some Japanese and B.C. officials, in turn, it was a reminder of British Columbia's "geographical contiguity to Japan," a factor that made the two immediate neighbors and allowed some Japanese to view the north Pacific coast as an economic hinterland replete with resources of benefit to Japan, even as it enabled some Canadians to characterize it as a point of vulnerability and the arrival of Japanese immigrants as a threat.[7] While the Meiji- and Taisho-era Japanese immigrants who returned to Japan, both before and after World War II, found it profoundly changed, for those living along the eastern shores of the North Pacific Ocean during the early decades of the twentieth century, the ocean also served as a connecting thread to the older Japan they remembered. As one prewar immigrant wrote at the time:

Warm to the sad heart,
The thought of Pacific Sea
Touching Japan shores,
I found some solace
Listening to the sound of waves.[8]

Notes

Acknowledgments

1. "Aboriginal law" is a term of art used in Canada to describe the body of law developed by the colonial, provincial, and federal governments pertaining to Indigenous people. Aboriginal law is known as federal Indian law in the United States.

2. Ronald K. Inouye, Carol Hoshiko, and Kazumi Heshiki, *Alaska's Japanese Pioneers: Faces, Voices, Stories* (Fairbanks: Alaska's Japanese Pioneers Research Project, 1994), 58–59, interview with Alice Mikami Snodgrass.

Note on Terminology

1. Amanda Murphy and Kelly Black, "Unsettling Settler Belonging: (Re)naming and Territory Making in the Pacific Northwest," *American Review of Canadian Studies* 45, no. 3 (2015): 315–31; Julie Cruikshank, *Do Glaciers Listen? Local Knowledge, Colonial Encounters, and Social Imagination* (Vancouver: UBC Press, 2005), 19, citing Felix Driver, *Geography Militant: Cultures of Exploration and Empire* (Oxford, UK: Blackwell, 2001).

2. Named Queen Charlotte's Islands by Captain George Dixon in 1787, the islands of Haida Gwaii were referred to by Japanese Canadians as "Kuichi Airan," a shortened, phonetic form. C. Nogero, *Queen Charlotte Islands (Illustrated)* (Jedway: Jedway, B.C. Commercial Association, 1909), 8; Masako Fukawa, ed., *Nikkei Fishermen on the BC Coast: Their Biographies and Photographs* (Madeira Park, B.C.: Harbour Publishing, 2007), 204. In 2009, the Canadian government agreed that the islands be renamed Haida Gwaii (X̱aayda Gwayy'). Haida Gwaii Reconciliation Act, SBC Chap. 17, 59 Eliz. 2 (2010).

3. For the same reason, I avoid the use of macrons in Japanese place-names, for example, Ryukyu instead of Ryūkyū, Hokkaido instead of Hokkaidō.

4. Alaska was reorganized as a state only in 1959.

5. Benjamin Hoy describes the complex nature of Indigenous identity today, which can include the use of both exonyms (names used by outsiders to describe the group) and autonyms (a group's own name for itself), as well as a range of subdivisions important to members of any given group. Benjamin Hoy, *A Line of Blood and Dirt: Creating the Canada–United States Border across Indigenous Lands* (New York: Oxford University Press, 2021), ix, xiii–xiv.

6. See Society of Writers, Editors and Translators, Tokyo, *Japan Style Sheet: The SWET Guide for Writers, Editors and Translators* (Berkeley, CA: Stone Bridge Press, 1998), 33–36. Where a given author or individual uses the macrons that signal a long vowel sound in Japanese when his or her name is transliterated into English, I provide it in endnotes, but I generally do not use macrons in the text to avoid confusion in cases where a name is rendered in more than one way in different sources and to facilitate readability. For the arguments for and against the use of macrons, see Society of Writers, Editors and Translators, *Japan Style Sheet*, 17–18.

7. As I discuss in chapter 4, the easy conflation of Japanese subjects both with naturalized British subjects born in Japan and with those of Japanese ancestry who were American or Canadian citizens by birth was a strategy often utilized by anti-Japanese elements to suggest that the latter were suspect in some way. For different reasons, prewar Japanese-language sources also often did not distinguish the two, using such terms as *nihonjin* (Japanese) or *waga dōhō* (our compatriots) to refer not just to Japanese nationals but also to persons of Japanese ancestry who were U.S. or Canadian nationals. The use of *nikkei* and *nikkeijin* in prewar Japanese-language sources was relatively rare.

8. While some people of Japanese ancestry have embraced the term "Nikkei," which refers to any person of Japanese ancestry living abroad regardless of their status as citizen or subject of any given nation, there are others who resist it. Among them is Grace Eiko Thomson, a Japanese Canadian elder, who was forcibly removed from the coast as a child along with her family. Thomson argues that "Nikkei" erases the century-long struggle by Japanese Canadians to achieve full recognition as Canadian citizens and redress for their wartime incarceration. Grace Eiko Thomson, *Chiru Sakura—Falling Cherry Blossoms: A Mother & Daughter's Journey through Racism, Internment and Oppression* (Halfmoon Bay, B.C.: Caitlin Press, 2021), 169. See also Greater Vancouver Japanese Canadian Citizens Association Museum Name-Change Committee, "Re: Re-naming of Nikkei National Museum," *The Bulletin* (*Geppō*), April 4, 2021, 12.

9. Terms utilized for the forced relocation of persons of Japanese ancestry inland during World War II also include "internment," "confinement," and "incarceration." Terms used to describe the sites where they were forcibly detained include "internment camp," "concentration camp," and "incarceration camp." For the evolving discussion of the various alternatives and their implications in both the United States and Canada, see Roger Daniels, "Words Do Matter: A Note on Inappropriate Terminology and the Incarceration of the Japanese Americans," in *Nikkei in the Pacific Northwest: Japanese Americans and Japanese Canadians in the Twentieth Century*, ed. Louis Fiset and Gail M. Nomura (Seattle: University of Washington Press, 2006), 183–207; Roy Miki, *Redress: Inside the Japanese Canadian Call for Justice* (Vancouver, B.C.: Raincoast Books, 2004), 2n1; Greg Robinson, *A Tragedy of Democracy: Japanese Confinement in North America* (New York: Columbia University Press, 2010), vii–viii; Connie Y. Chiang, *Nature behind Barbed Wire: An Environmental History of the Japanese American Incarceration* (New York: Oxford University Press, 2018), xiii–xv; and Denshō: The Japanese American Legacy Project, "Terminology," accessed November 1, 2021, https://www.densho .org/terminology, noting that "detention camp" can be used interchangeably to refer to the various types of camps established to house persons of Japanese ancestry in the United States during World War II.

Introduction

1. See, e.g., Guillaume Delisle, *Circumpolar Map*, 1714, in William W. Fitzhugh and Aron Crowell, *Crossroads of Continents: Cultures of Siberia and Alaska* (Washington, D.C.: Smithsonian Institution Press, 1988), 8.

2. Alan D. McMillan and Iain McKechnie, "Investigating Indigenous Adaptations to British Columbia's Exposed Outer Coast: Introduction to *These Outer Shores*," in "These Outer Shores: Archaeological Insights into Indigenous Lifeways along the Ex-

posed Coasts of British Columbia," special issue, *BC Studies*, no. 187 (Autumn 2015): 11–12.

3. Hideo Kawai, "Hydrography of the Kuroshio Extension," in *Kuroshio: Physical Aspects of the Japan Current*, ed. Henry Stommel and Kozo Yoshida (Seattle: University of Washington Press, 1972), 235–36. *Kuroshio* means "black current." Rintaro Hayashi, *Kuroshio no hate ni* (At the end of the black current) (Tokyo: Nichibo Shuppansha, 1971).

4. Archaeological evidence and oral histories reflect the impact of major earthquakes and tsunamis on Indigenous peoples around the Pacific Rim. Alan D. McMillan and Ian Hutchinson, "When the Mountain Dwarfs Danced: Aboriginal Traditions of Paleoseismic Events along the Cascadia Subduction Zone of Western North America," *Ethnohistory* 49, no. 1 (Winter 2002): 44, 46, 60, citing K. Satake, K. Shimazaki, Y. Tsuji, and K. Uyeda, "Time and Size of a Giant Earthquake in Cascadia Inferred from Japanese Tsunami Records of January 1700," *Nature* 379 (1996): 246–49. For Japanese records of the tsunami engendered by the Cascadia earthquake in 1700, see Brian F. Atwater, Satoko Musumi-Rokkaku, Kenji Satake, Yoshinobu Tsuji, Kazue Ueda, and David K. Yamaguchi, *The Orphan Tsunami of 1700: Japanese Clues to a Parent Earthquake in North America* [Minashigo Genroku tsunami: Oya-jishin wa Hokubei nishi kaigan ni ita] (Reston, Va.: U.S. Geological Survey in association with University of Washington Press, 2005).

5. As such, this study complicates the "two empire paradigm" developed by Eiichiro Azuma in his well-regarded *Between Two Empires: Race, History, and Transnationalism in Japanese America* (New York: Oxford University Press, 2005). See also Eiichiro Azuma, "Remapping a Pre–World War Two Japanese Diaspora: Transpacific Migration as an Articulation of Japan's Colonial Expansionism," in *Connecting Seas and Connected Ocean Rims: Indian, Atlantic, and Pacific Oceans and China Seas Migrations from the 1830s to the 1930s*, ed. Donna R. Gabaccia and Dirk Hoerder, Studies in Global Social History 8 (Leiden: Brill, 2011), 418–19. While Canada is also important to this story, it remained, even after its confederation in 1867, a dominion of Great Britain, which retained control over its foreign relations. See chapter 1.

6. For the importance of engaging multiple scales, including global, transnational, national, regional, and local, to understand the history of any given place, see Richard White, "The Naturalization of Nature," *Journal of American History* 86 (December 1999): 976–86.

7. McMillan and McKechnie argue that even the outer shores that face directly onto the Pacific were never peripheral in the eyes of the Indigenous people who lived along the coast. McMillan and McKechnie, "Investigating Indigenous Adaptations," 6.

8. See McMillan and McKechnie, "Investigating Indigenous Adaptations," 14, emphasizing the role that Indigenous people played in shaping the coastal environment. See also Fitzhugh and Crowell, *Crossroads of Continents*, 236–37, noting the complex mix of Indigenous cultures that existed prior to contact and how early European explorers described the people they encountered as contented with their ways of life.

9. For a comprehensive examination of the incorporation of various locations around the Pacific Rim into larger economic networks during the eighteenth and nineteenth centuries, see David Igler, *The Great Ocean: Pacific Worlds from Captain Cook to the Gold Rush* (New York: Oxford University Press, 2013).

10. Andrea Geiger, "Haida Gwaii as North Pacific Borderland, Ikeda Mine as Alternative West: 1906–1910," *Pacific Northwest Quarterly* 108, no. 4 (Fall 2017): 122. For a contemporary

account of such ties, see Archer Wall Douglas, "Inland America and the Orient: Mississippi Valley Has Products Which Far East Needs and Vice Versa," *The Trans-Pacific* 1, no. 1 (September 1919): 45.

11. Paige Raibmon notes the importance of decentering our analysis of colonial processes by also examining the role of non-Europeans in colonial contexts, including Chinese immigrants. Paige Raibmon, "Unmaking Native Space: A Genealogy of Indian Policy, Settler Practice, and the Microtechniques of Dispossession," in *The Power of Promises: Rethinking Indian Treaties in the Pacific Northwest*, ed. Alexandra Harmon (Seattle: University of Washington Press, 2008), 69–70. Although the literature on contact relations between Indigenous people and Anglo settlers is instructive, the same imbalance of power did not always exist between Japanese immigrants and Indigenous people. See, e.g., John Sutton Lutz, *Makúk: A New History of Aboriginal-White Relations* (Vancouver: UBC Press, 2008).

12. For one compelling argument against reducing stories of historical encounter to simple binaries, see Alex Calder, Jonathan Lamb, and Bridget Orr, "Introduction: Postcoloniality and the Pacific," in *Voyages and Beaches: Pacific Encounters, 1769–1840*, ed. Alex Calder, Jonathan Lamb, and Bridget Orr (Honolulu: University of Hawai'i Press, 1999), 1. See also Pekka Hämäläinen and Samuel Truett, "On Borderlands," *Journal of American History* 98, no. 2 (September 2011): 352.

13. See, e.g., Andrea Geiger, *Subverting Exclusion: Transpacific Encounters with Race, Caste, and Borders, 1885–1928* (New Haven, Conn.: Yale University Press, 2011).

14. Race, as a socially and legally constructed category, any number of scholars have shown, is inherently unstable. See, e.g., Matthew Frye Jacobson, *Whiteness of a Different Color: European Immigrants and the Alchemy of Race* (Cambridge: Harvard University Press, 1999), 139; Neil Foley, *The White Scourge: Mexicans, Blacks, and Poor Whites in Texas Cotton Culture* (Berkeley: University of California Press, 1999).

15. In Robert Karrow's words, "Maps . . . tell us not only where things are but also who we are." Robert Karrow, introduction to *Maps: Finding Our Place in the World*, ed. James Akerman and Robert Karrow (Chicago: University of Chicago Press, 2007), 17.

16. See, e.g., Gloria Anzaldúa, preface to *Borderlands / La Frontera: The New Mestiza* (San Francisco: Aunt Lute Books, 1999); and Eric V. Meeks, *Border Citizens: The Making of Indians, Mexicans, and Anglos in Arizona* (Austin: University of Texas Press, 2007), 1–2. Once national borders are established, Bethel Saler and Carolyn Podruchny observe, those on either side tend to assume the inevitability of the identities they impose, a tendency to which even historians are prone. Bethel Saler and Carolyn Podruchny, "Glass Curtains and Storied Landscapes: The Fur Trade, National Boundaries, and Historians," in *Bridging National Borders in North America: Transnational and Comparative Histories*, ed. Benjamin H. Johnson and Andrew R. Graybill (Durham, N.C.: Duke University Press, 2010), 275. Writing across national borders, as a result, "requires historians to defy the trail left by the documentary record." Theodore Binnema, "The Case for Cross-National and Comparative History: The Northwestern Plains as Bioregion," in *The Borderlands of the American and Canadian Wests: Essays on the Regional History of the Forty-Ninth Parallel*, ed. Sterling Evans (Lincoln: University of Nebraska Press, 2006), 18.

17. See, e.g., Michel Hogue, "Between Race and Nation: The Creation of a Métis Borderland on the Northern Plains," in *Bridging National Borders in North America: Transnational*

and Comparative Histories, ed. Benjamin H. Johnson and Andrew R. Graybill (Durham, N.C.: Duke University Press, 2010), 60–61.

18. Samuel Truett and Elliott Young, "Introduction: Making Transnational History: Nations, Regions, and Borderlands," in *Continental Crossroads: Remapping U.S.-Mexico Borderlands History*, ed. Samuel Truett and Elliott Young (Durham, N.C.: Duke University Press, 2004), 2, quoted in Benjamin H. Johnson and Andrew J. Graybill, "Introduction: Borders and Their Historians in North America," in *Bridging National Borders in North America: Transnational and Comparative Histories*, ed. Benjamin H. Johnson and Andrew R. Graybill (Durham, N.C.: Duke University Press, 2010), 8–9, also noting that borders are "site[s] where national notions of race and citizenship [are] forged."

19. An exception is Julie Cruikshank, who, although she does not identify herself as a borderlands scholar, offers a compelling and deeply thoughtful analysis of the borderlands region surrounding the St. Elias Mountains during the colonial period and draws heavily on Indigenous sources. Julie Cruikshank, *Do Glaciers Listen? Local Knowledge, Colonial Encounters, and Social Imagination* (Vancouver: UBC Press, 2005).

20. This approach parallels the tendency of historians to focus on one side or another of other sections of the U.S.-Canada border. See Andrew R. Graybill, *Policing the Great Plains: Rangers, Mounties, and the North American Frontier, 1875–1910* (Lincoln: University of Nebraska Press, 2007), 2, noting that "writers and scholars have long confined their studies to either one side of the 49th parallel or the other, imposing intellectual parameters seemingly no less arbitrary than the international border itself." For citations to histories of Russian America and to provincial and state histories of British Columbia and Alaska, see chapter 1.

21. Richard White, *"It's Your Misfortune and None of My Own": A New History of the American West* (Norman: University of Oklahoma Press, 1991), 3–4, 61–84.

22. See, e.g., Jeremy Adelman and Stephen Aron, "From Borderlands to Borders: Empires, Nation-States, and the Peoples in between in North American History," *American Historical Review* 104, no. 3 (June 1999): 814–41.

23. See Michiel Baud and Willem Van Schendel, "Toward a Comparative History of Borderlands," *Journal of World History* 8, no. 2 (1997): 212.

24. Cruikshank, *Do Glaciers Listen?*, 213, noting the "curious angles" of the U.S.-Canada border as it turns west and north.

25. The dual sense in which I refer to the "nature" of the north Pacific borderlands invokes the way it is used by Lissa K. Wadewitz in her study of the section of the U.S.-Canada border that divides the waters of Puget Sound and the Gulf of Georgia, known collectively as the Salish Sea, between British Columbia and Washington State. See Lissa K. Wadewitz, *The Nature of Borders: Salmon, Boundaries, and Bandits on the Salish Sea* (Seattle: University of Washington Press, 2012).

26. Juanita Sundberg, "Diabolic *Caminos* in the Desert and Cat Fights on the Río: A Posthumanist Political Ecology of Boundary Enforcement in the United States–Mexico Borderlands," *Annals of the Association of American Geographers* 101, no. 2 (2011): 318. See also Cruikshank, *Do Glaciers Listen?*, 4, identifying nature as a category of analysis that is as important as race, class, and gender.

27. See Rachel St. John, *Line in the Sand: A History of the Western U.S.-Mexico Border* (Princeton, N.J.: Princeton University Press, 2011); and Michel Hogue, *Metis and the*

Medicine Line: Creating a Border and Dividing a People (Chapel Hill: University of North Carolina Press, 2015), noting that the establishment of both the U.S.-Mexico border and the forty-ninth parallel produced new patterns of movement across each. Although national boundaries concentrate the power of a nation-state along a given borderline, their purpose is as much to monitor as to bar crossings of it. Enforcement practices, as such, are never intended solely to exclude. In Richard White's words, national borders in North America are best described as "a series of doors pretending to be walls." White, *"It's Your Misfortune,"* 3.

28. See, e.g., Takahiro Yamamoto, "Japan's Passport System and the Opening of [Japan's] Borders, 1866–1878," *The Historical Journal* 60, no. 4 (2017): 997–1021; "Sekisho," *The Japan Magazine* (December 1914): 449–50.

29. See, e.g., Adelman and Aron, "From Borderlands to Borders."

30. Mary L. Dudziak and Leti Volpp, "Introduction: Legal Borderlands: Law and the Construction of American Borders," *American Quarterly* 57, no. 3 (September 2005): 595–96, 599, 602. See also Mary Louise Pratt, describing contact zones as "social spaces where cultures meet, clash, and grapple with each other, often in contexts of highly asymmetrical relations of power." Mary Louise Pratt, "Arts of the Contact Zone," *Profession*, 1991, 34.

31. Hämäläinen and Truett, "On Borderlands," 343; Samuel Truett, *Fugitive Landscapes: The Forgotten History of the U.S.-Mexico Borderlands* (New Haven, Conn.: Yale University Press, 2006), 2.

32. See, e.g., Hämäläinen and Truett, "On Borderlands," 348. As Gloria Anzaldúa writes, borderlands can be "site[s] where many different cultures 'touch' each other, and the permeable, flexible, and ambiguous shifting grounds lend themselves to hybrid images. The border is the locus of resistance, of rupture, implosion and explosion, and of putting together the fragments and creating a new assemblage." Gloria Anzaldúa, "Border Arte: Nepantla, el Lugar de la Frontera," in *The Gloria Anzaldúa Reader*, ed. AnaLouise Keating (Durham, N.C.: Duke University Press, 2009), 177.

33. Samuel Truett, *Fugitive Landscapes: The Forgotten History of the U.S.-Mexico Borderlands* (New Haven, Conn.: Yale University Press, 2006), 9, noting the importance of "track[ing] historical border crossers along their own, local pathways."

34. David Igler, "Exploring the Concept of Empire in Pacific History: Individuals, Nations, and Ocean Space prior to 1850," *History Compass* 12, no. 11 (2014): 879. See also Igler, *Great Ocean*, 4, noting the role of both the imperial and the personal in shaping encounters in the Pacific world. See also David A. Chang, "Borderlands in a World at Sea: Concow Indians, Native Hawaiians, and South Chinese in Indigenous, Global, and National Spaces," *Journal of American History* 98, no. 2 (September 2011): 384, noting the need to be attentive to the many "spaces where global history became local." Despite the role played by imperial actors, Julie Cruikshank argues, "the aftermaths of colonialism are always local." Cruikshank, *Do Glaciers Listen?*, 9.

35. Along many areas of the north Pacific coast, colonial endeavor focused less on settlement than on resource extraction. For this reason, forms of colonialism other than "settler colonialism" can be helpful in understanding the impact of colonial development in this region over time. See Patricia Nelson Limerick, "Comments on Settler Colonialism and the American West," *Journal of the West* 56, no. 4 (Fall 2017): 90–96, describing settler colonialism as a concept that is over-determinative and often applied in ways that lack historical specificity and do not account for change over time. For a discussion of some of the many

forms that colonialism could assume, see Nancy Shoemaker, "A Typology of Colonialism," *Perspectives on History*, October 2015, http://historians.org/publications-and-directories /perspectives on history/october-2015/a-typology-of-colonialism. See also Dean Itsuji Saranillio, "Why Asian Settler Colonialism Matters: A Thought Piece on Critiques, Debates, and Indigenous Difference," *Settler Colonial Studies* 3, no. 3–4 (2013): 280–94.

36. Historical studies that explore the movement of laborers and others around the Pacific Rim include Igler, *Great Ocean*; Matt Matsuda, *Pacific Worlds: A History of Seas, Peoples, and Cultures* (Cambridge: Cambridge University Press, 2012); David A. Chang, *The World and All the Things upon It: Native Hawaiian Geographies of Exploration* (Minneapolis: University of Minnesota Press, 2016); and Gregory Rosenthal, *Beyond Hawai'i: Native Labor in the Pacific World* (Berkeley: University of California Press, 2018).

37. As Joshua L. Reid shows in his study of the maritime world of the Makah, coastal waters functioned as maritime borderlands for Indigenous peoples along the coast, to the point where they included the ocean itself as part of the country they inhabited. Joshua L. Reid, *The Sea Is My Country: The Maritime World of the Makahs* (New Haven, Conn.: Yale University Press, 2015).

38. Chang, "Borderlands in a World at Sea," 388, noting that the "refusal of non-Indians to recognize bounded native territories has been a hallmark of colonialism." See also Paige Raibmon, "How to Talk about Relations between Indigenous Peoples and Europeans," *The Tyee*, September 28, 2018, https://thetyee.ca/Opinion/2018/09/28/Relations-Indigenous -Peoples-Europeans/. Raibmon notes that terms such as "'natural resources' [are] limited concept[s] that cannot accurately represent Indigenous ontologies in which animacy, kin and utility are differently configured."

39. See, e.g., Jeffers Lennox, *Homelands and Empires: Indigenous Spaces, Imperial Fictions, and the Competition for Territory in Northeastern North America, 1690–1763* (Toronto: University of Toronto Press, 2017), 3; and Saler and Podruchny, "Glass Curtains and Storied Landscapes," 292, quoting Colin Calloway, *One Vast Winter Count: The Native American West before Lewis and Clark* (Lincoln: University of Nebraska Press, 2003), 11, noting that Indigenous borders relied not on identifying "fixed points within a bounded space but on patterns of intersecting lines."

40. Cruikshank, *Do Glaciers Listen?*, 25.

41. See Cruikshank, *Do Glaciers Listen?*, 9, warning against "an intellectual imperialism that once again presents Europe as the key historical agent, as though no other actors existed."

42. Andrea Geiger, "Disentangling Law and History: Nikkei Challenges to Race-Based Exclusion from British Columbia's Coastal Fisheries, 1920–2007," *Southern California Quarterly* 100, no. 3 (Fall 2018): 264.

Chapter One

1. Donald D. Johnson, *The United States in the Pacific: Private Interests and Public Policies, 1784–1899*, with Gary Dean Best (Westport, Conn.: Praeger, 1995), xv.

2. Together with the Strait of Juan de Fuca, the Strait of Georgia and Puget Sound were designated the Salish Sea by the Geographic Names Board of Canada and the Washington State Board of Geographical Names in 2009, a name intended to supplement, rather than

replace, the existing names of the various bodies of water that constitute the Salish Sea. See Brian Justin Tucker, "Inventing the Salish Sea: Exploring the Performative Act of Place Naming off the Pacific Coast of North America" (master's thesis, University of Victoria, 2013), 8, 111, 139.

3. Stephen Haycox, *Alaska: An American Colony* (Seattle: University of Washington Press, 2002), 9.

4. The Stikine, Skeena, and Nass Rivers have their origins high on the Spatsizi Plateau, an area long recognized by the Indigenous peoples of the area as the Sacred Headwaters. Wade Davis, *The Sacred Headwaters: The Fight to Save the Stikine, Skeena, and Nass* (Vancouver, B.C.: Greystone Books, 2012), 7. "Stikine" means "great river." Eliza Ruhamah Scidmore, *Appleton's Guide-Book to Alaska and the Northwest Coast* (New York: D. Appleton, 1899), 69. The town of Wrangell is located near the mouth of the Stikine River on the site of a Russian outpost called Fort St. Dionysius and later renamed Fort Stikine by the British. Anton Money, "A Voyage Up the Stikine," pt. 1, *Alaska Sportsman*, August 1964, 46.

5. Eric Jay Dolin, *Fur, Fortune, and Empire: The Epic History of the Fur Trade in America* (New York: W. W. Norton, 2010), 312–14.

6. *The Trans-Pacific*, vol. 2, no. 3 (September 1921), referring to these three Siberian rivers as "the Ob, the Irtish, and the Yenisei."

7. Dmitry Zavalishin, "[Alta] California in 1824," in *California through Russian Eyes, 1806–1848*, comp., trans., and ed. James R. Gibson, with the assistance of Alexie A. Istomin (Norman: University of Oklahoma Press, 2013), 274.

8. See, e.g., Julie Cruikshank in collaboration with Angela Sidney, Kitty Smith, and Annie Ned, *Life Lived like a Story: Life Stories of Three Yukon Native Elders* (Lincoln: University of Nebraska Press, 1990), 5, 8. Similar trade networks existed across the North Pacific between the Ainu and other coastal peoples on the Eurasian continent and along the Kuril Islands. Kaoru Tezuka, "Long-Distance Trade Networks and Shipping in the Ezo Region," *Arctic Anthropology* 35, no. 1 (1998): 352, 355.

9. Davis, *Sacred Headwaters*, vii. The same was true further south where the Fraser and the Columbia Rivers linked areas as far as the high desert of what is now eastern Washington State and the B.C. interior to the ocean. See, e.g., Gloria Bird, "Kettle Falls on the Columbia, circa 1937," in *First Fish, First People: Salmon Tales of the North Pacific Rim*, ed. Judith Roche and Meg McHutchison (Seattle: University of Washington Press, 1998), 52.

10. "Ainu Moshir" means "the peaceful land of the people." Shigeru Kayano, "Traditional Ainu Life: Living off the Interest," trans. Jan Corddry Langill with Rie Taki, in *First Fish, First People: Salmon Tales of the North Pacific Rim*, ed. Judith Roche and Meg McHutchison (Seattle: University of Washington Press, 1998), 23. For the importance of salmon to the Indigenous peoples around the Pacific Rim including those of the Kamchatka Peninsula, Sakhalin, and Alaska, see Benedict J. Colombi and James F. Brooks, eds., *Keystone Nations: Indigenous Peoples and Salmon across the North Pacific* (Santa Fe, N. Mex.: School for Advanced Research Press, 2012).

11. James R. Gibson, *Otter Skins, Boston Ships and China Goods: The Maritime Fur Trade of the Northwest Coast, 1785–1841* (Montreal: McGill-Queen's University Press, 1992), 7. See also John J. Stephan, *The Kuril Islands: Russo-Japanese Frontier in the Pacific* (Oxford, U.K.: Clarendon Press, 1974), 18–19, describing the marine resources of the Kuril Islands; and Brett L. Walker, *The Conquest of Ainu Lands: Ecology and Culture in Japanese Expansion,*

1590–1800 (Berkeley: University of California Press, 2001), 45, describing the marine resources harvested by Japanese in Ezochi.

12. See, e.g., Alan D. McMillan and Iain McKechnie, "Investigating Indigenous Adaptations to British Columbia's Exposed Outer Coast: Introduction to *These Outer Shores*," in "These Outer Shores: Archaeological Insights into Indigenous Lifeways along the Exposed Coasts of British Columbia," special issue, *BC Studies*, no. 187 (Autumn 2015): 11–12. Also see Walker, *Conquest of Ainu Lands*, 6, noting that Ainu Moshir remains the spiritual center of the Ainu world, and 15, describing the Ainu as a maritime people.

13. John R. Bockstoce, *Furs and Frontiers in the Far North: The Contest among Native and Foreign Nations for the Bering Strait Fur Trade* (New Haven, Conn.: Yale University Press, 2009), 115.

14. Jeffers Lennox, *Homelands and Empires: Indigenous Spaces, Imperial Fictions, and the Competition for Territory in Northeastern North America, 1690–1763* (Toronto: University of Toronto Press, 2017), 256.

15. For a detailed list of the various products traded, see Gibson, *Otter Skins*, 12, 37–38.

16. Haycox, *Alaska*, 93.

17. Francis Paul Prucha, *The Great Father: The United States Government and the American Indians*, abridged ed. (Lincoln: University of Nebraska Press, 1984), 6.

18. Sites of sea otter extirpation ranged from Baja California to the coast of Chile and across the North Pacific Ocean to that of Siberia. David Igler, *The Great Ocean: Pacific Worlds from Captain Cook to the Gold Rush* (New York: Oxford University Press, 2013), 103, 105, 114. See also Ryan Tucker Jones, "A 'Havoc Made among Them': Animals, Empire, and Extinction in the Russian North Pacific, 1741–1810," *Environmental History* 16 (September 2011): 585–609.

19. Gibson, *Otter Skins*, 12; Bockstoce, *Furs and Frontiers*, xi, 41–51, providing a comprehensive list of furs taken along the eastern coast of the North Pacific.

20. Gibson refers to the quest for fur as a "fur rush" equal in its intensity to the gold rushes that would follow later in the nineteenth century. Gibson, *Otter Skins*, 12–13; James R. Gibson, introduction to *California through Russian Eyes, 1806–1848*, comp., trans., and ed. James R. Gibson, with the assistance of Alexie A. Istomin (Norman: University of Oklahoma Press, 2013), 16. For a detailed description of Russia's eastward expansion across Siberia, see Haycox, *Alaska*, 40–52.

21. Stephan, *Kuril Islands*, vii, 12, 16. See also Hiroshi Kimura, *The Kurillian Knot: A History of Japanese-Russian Border Negotiations*, trans. Mark Ealey (Stanford, Calif.: Stanford University Press, 2008), 1, 3, 6, explaining that the Russians first learned of the Kuril Islands from Dutch maps dating from the 1600s. What the Japanese called the Chishima rettō (archipelago) was called Kuril'skie Ostrova by the Russians. It has thirty-six islands that extend some 750 miles at the same latitudes as those between the northern tip of Vancouver Island and southern Oregon. Kimura, *Kurillian Knot*, 11. Those that continue to be the subject of dispute between Russia and Japan, referred to as the Northern Territories in Japan, include the three islands known, in Japanese, as Kunashiri (Kunashir in Russian), Etorofu (Iturup), Shikotan, and a small group known as the Habomai Islands. All but one of these lie fewer than sixteen kilometers off the coast of Hokkaido. Northern Territories Issue Association, "'A Border Yet Unresolved': Japan's Northern Territories" (Tokyo, 1981), 3.

22. Stephan, *Kuril Islands*, 25–27 (early contacts with the Ainu); appendix B ("Russian and Japanese Place-Names in the Kuril Islands"), 248.

23. Stephan, *Kuril Islands*, 41–47, 54–55; Tsuyoshi Hasegawa, *The Northern Territories Dispute and Russo-Japanese Relations* (Berkeley: University of California, International and Area Studies, 1998), vol. 1:15. See also "Gohei: The Castaway," *Japan Magazine* 3 (April 1910): 225–27, for an example of one individual who defied the shogun's edict forbidding trade with foreign vessels.

24. Kimura, *Kurillian Knot*, 6–7.

25. Stephan, *Kuril Islands*, 48–50.

26. Hasegawa, *Northern Territories Dispute*, vol. 1:19, noting the vague nature of the boundaries.

27. Walker, *Conquest of Ainu Lands*, 6, 36, noting that the Tokugawa were interested in gold mines in Ezo.

28. Hasegawa, *Northern Territories Dispute*, vol. 1:19; Walker, *Conquest of Ainu Lands*, 39, noting that a popular 1713 encyclopedia described Ezochi as "a foreign land," except for Fukuyama castle at the southern tip of Wajinchi, which was regarded as "a portal to 'barbarian land.'" For a detailed discussion of centralized feudalism, see Kenneth B. Pyle, *The Making of Modern Japan*, 2nd ed. (Lexington, Mass.: D. C. Heath, 1996), 25–27, noting that the Tokugawa were particularly concerned with preventing alignments between defeated *han* and foreign powers.

29. Charles II, Royal Charter Incorporating the Hudson's Bay Company, 1670. For a translation of the Tokugawa edict, see Walker, *Conquest of Ainu Lands*, 37. And see Walker, 39, noting parallels between the charters issued to the Massachusetts Bay Company and those issued by the Matsumae domain to merchants authorized to develop commercial endeavors in Hokkaido.

30. Treaty of Amity, Commerce, and Navigation, between His Britannic Majesty and the United States of America, November 19, 1794, entered into force October 28, 1795 (known as the Jay Treaty); Walker, *Conquest of Ainu Lands*, 37.

31. The pelts of sea otters hunted by Ainu hunters were among the goods traded to merchants licensed by the Matsumae domain together with kelp and other marine products. Archaeological evidence of sea otter hunting on Hokkaido dates back some ten thousand years; it is also recounted in Ainu oral histories. Richard Ravalli, *Sea Otters: A History* (Lincoln: University of Nebraska Press, 2018), xxiv, xx, xxii.

32. Walker, *Conquest of Ainu Lands*, 44, explaining that although guard posts were established along its length, the boundary between the separate areas where Japanese and Ainu lived and operated was a "permeable, porous line" that extended from Kumaishi to Shinori by 1669. Kimura, *Kurillian Knot*, 4.

33. See Stephan, *Kuril Islands*, 1, 6, for Japanese perspective; Kimura, *Kurillian Knot*, 7, for Russian perspective.

34. Kimura, *Kurillian Knot*, 6.

35. Ravalli, *Sea Otters*, xiii.

36. Walker, *Conquest of Ainu Lands*, 162–63. "Urup," like the names of a number of the other Kuril Islands, is derived from an Ainu word. Stephan, *Kuril Islands*, 248.

37. Ilya Vinkovetsky, *Russian America: An Overseas Colony of a Continental Empire, 1804–1867* (New York: Oxford University Press, 2011), ix, noting that "Alaska" is derived from Aliaska,

a name the Russians adapted from the Aleut. Sonja Luehrmann, *Alutiiq Villages under Russian and U.S. Rule* (Fairbanks: University of Alaska Press, 2008), 22, referring to Kodiak Island as the "center of a periphery."

38. Gibson notes that the RAC was "modelled upon the British East India Company and the Hudson's Bay Company." Gibson, *Otter Skins*, 13.

39. Gibson, *Otter Skins*, 13–14; Haycox, *Alaska*, 97–98. Novo-Arkhangel'sk was renamed Sitka under U.S. rule.

40. Vinkovetsky, *Russian America*, 140–41, explaining that Russian men were encouraged to cohabit with Native women and encouraged to remain monogamous to enhance "social stability and [the] appearance of moral order," and arguing that Native women also benefited from their relationships with Russian men in that they were generally able to provide a more stable economic foundation and because such partnerships served to elevate the women's status within the local community.

41. Haycox notes that Russia could control the area it colonized in Alaska only "with the labor of the approximately fifteen hundred Creoles in the colony and the several thousand Aleuts [it] subjugated." Haycox, *Alaska*, 90. See also Luehrmann, *Alutiiq Villages*, 117, noting that the term "creole" (*kreoly*) derives from Spanish, Portuguese, and French practice and was first used in Alaska around 1816; she argues that this "seems to indicate that Russians thought of the offspring of Alaskan marriages as distinguished by extraterritorial birth rather than racial descent."

42. Haycox, *Alaska*, 88–89.

43. Haycox, *Alaska*, 58, noting that the number of Russians in Russian America averaged just 600 at any one time and never exceeded 823.

44. Igler, *Great Ocean*, 103.

45. Zavalishin, "[Alta] California in 1824," 253.

46. Otto von Kotzebue, "Alta California and the Russian Colony of Ross [1824]," in *California through Russian Eyes, 1806–1848*, comp., trans., and ed. James R. Gibson, with the assistance of Alexie A. Istomin (Norman: University of Oklahoma Press, 2013), 309.

47. Russian merchants built on existing and wide-ranging interactive trade routes along the Pacific coast as far as what is now southern British Columbia. William W. Fitzhugh and Aron Crowell, *Crossroads of Continents: Cultures of Siberia and Alaska* (Washington, D.C.: Smithsonian Institution Press, 1988), 10–11, 228 (maps).

48. Bockstoce, *Furs and Frontiers*, xi, noting that early trade was "almost always regarded as advantageous by both parties." See also Gibson *Otter Skins*, 269, arguing that "for Northwest coast Indians, the trade was neither just destructive ('looting') nor just constructive ('enriching') but both," and noting that "Euroamerican goods supplemented rather than supplanted Indian products and served to further, not initiate, change."

49. Gibson, *Otter Skins*, 14, noting that "the RAC benefited from the enserfment of Aleuts and Kodiaks, the world's best hunters of sea otters."

50. Vinkovetsky, *Russian America*, 12; Luehrmann, *Alutiiq Villages*, 6. See also Haycox, *Alaska*, 59, noting that Aleut attacks on Russian vessels in 1757 and 1762 were among those brutally suppressed and followed by harsh retribution.

51. Haycox, *Alaska*, 94, noting that the RAC relocated Aleut at will, sending them to places as distant as the Kuril Islands and California; Stephan, *Kuril Islands*, 85, noting the establishment of Aleut colonies on Urup in 1828 and on Simushir in 1830. See also David

Igler, "Exploring the Concept of Empire in Pacific History: Individuals, Nations, and Ocean Space prior to 1850," *History Compass* 12, no. 11 (2014): 882; and Igler, *Great Ocean*, 108, citing Lydia T. Black, "The Nature of Evil: Of Whales and Sea Otters," in *Indians, Animals, and the Fur Trade: A Critique of "Keepers of the Game,"* ed. Shepard Krech III (Athens: University of Georgia Press, 1981), 120; and Jones, "'Havoc Made among Them.'"

52. Haycox, *Alaska*, 123. See also Ted C. Hinckley, *The Canoe Rocks: Alaska's Tlingit and the Euroamerican Frontier, 1800–1912* (Lanham, Md.: University Press of America, 1996).

53. Haycox, *Alaska*, 57–58, 131. See also Scidmore, *Appleton's Guide-Book*, 141, describing the landscape of the Aleutian Islands and noting that it was replete with wildflowers in summer.

54. Gibson, *Otter Skins*, 17.

55. See, e.g., Vinkovetsky, *Russian America*, 123, citing an instance where "incursion into Tlingit waters in 1809–1810 led to violence." Gibson, *Otter Skins*, 17.

56. Mikhail Vasilyev, "Remarks on [Alta] California [1821]," in *California through Russian Eyes, 1806–1848*, comp., trans., and ed. James R. Gibson, with the assistance of Alexie A. Istomin (Norman: University of Oklahoma Press, 2013), 190–91. Vasilyev uses "Konyagas" to refer to the Kodiak hunters who were also conscripted.

57. Blackhawk describes in detail the "intertwined violent and hybrid effects of colonial encounters in the Spanish borderlands" and explains that "like their many neighbors, the Ute and Comanche adapted to colonial violence in kind, redirecting it against New Mexico while also displacing it onto more distant native groups." Ned Blackhawk, "The Displacement of Violence: Ute Diplomacy and the Making of New Mexico's Eighteenth-Century Northern Borderlands," *Ethnohistory* 54, no. 4 (Fall 2007): 740–42.

58. Vinkovetsky, *Russian America*, 132.

59. Gibson, *Otter Skins*, 17.

60. Haycox, *Alaska*, 131. Igler notes that Indigenous people in the Pacific Northwest also "exerted a great deal of power . . . by manipulating competition, hard bargaining, and at times, committing violence against outsiders." It was they who "did the actual hunting and preparation of furs and pelts, and their power derived in part from this role as suppliers," as well as "from tight-knit kinship groups and well-established regional trading networks." Igler, *Great Ocean*, 34–35, citing Robin Fisher, *Contact and Conflict: Indian-European Relations in British Columbia, 1774–1890* (Vancouver: UBC Press, 1977), 1–48, and Daniel W. Clayton, *Islands of Truth: The Imperial Fashioning of Vancouver Island* (Vancouver: UBC Press, 2000), 78.

61. Vinkovetsky, *Russian America*, 104, 115–16, explaining that Tlingit power was rooted in "their continuing independence, their large numbers, the strategic location of their territory, and various social factors." See also Julie Cruikshank, *Do Glaciers Listen? Local Knowledge, Colonial Encounters, and Social Imagination* (Vancouver: UBC Press, 2005), 213, explaining that "coastal Tlingit traders on the Lynn Canal appropriated the role of middlemen in the nineteenth century, blockaded the few accessible passes to the interior, and compelled both their Athapaskan trading partners and Euro-Americans to deal through them."

62. Andrei Val'terovich Grinev, *The Tlingit Indians in Russian America, 1741–1867*, trans. Richard L. Bland and Katerina G. Solovjova (Lincoln: University of Nebraska Press, 2005), 275–77.

63. Haycox, *Alaska*, 59.

64. Haycox, *Alaska*, 63–64; James R. Gibson, "Russian Dependence upon the Natives of Russian America," Kennan Institute Occasional Paper 70 (Washington, D.C.: Kennan Institute for Advanced Russian Studies, Woodrow Wilson Center, 1979), republished as "Russian Dependence on the Natives of Alaska," in *An Alaska Anthology: Interpreting the Past*, ed. Stephen Haycox and Mary Childers Mangusso (Seattle: University of Washington Press, 1996), 21–42.

65. There is an extensive literature on Captain Cook's voyages including his own journals. Recent studies include Igler, *Great Ocean*, 5, 82–85; and Anne Salmond, *The Trial of the Cannibal Dog: The Remarkable Story of Captain Cook's Encounters in the South Seas* (New Haven, Conn.: Yale University Press, 2003).

66. Haycox, *Alaska*, 45, 66, 80, explaining that while Cook's "journals revealed the geography of the [north Pacific coast of North America] and solved the geographic puzzle," George Vancouver conducted an "extensive survey of the coast from Juan de Fuca Strait to Cook Inlet." See also Gibson, *Otter Skins*, 25, noting that Vancouver's "detailed charting of the coast was to assist trading vessels as late as the 1820s."

67. Gibson, *Otter Skins*, 13, noting that Russian exploration extended as far south as Haida Gwaii.

68. Haycox, *Alaska*, 63–65. See also Jean Barman, *The West beyond the West: A History of British Columbia* (Toronto: University of Toronto Press, 1991), 25–27; and John Gibson, *A Small and Charming World* (Toronto: Collins, 1972), 161, noting that Nootka Sound "provided shelter from westerly gales and there were safe anchorages in twenty fathoms of water."

69. Haycox, *Alaska*, 76–77.

70. Vinkovetsky, *Russian America*, 123.

71. Igler, *Great Ocean*, 37; Vasilyev, "Remarks on [Alta] California," 191, stating, "The native inhabitants are decreasing annually, and venereal disease—brought by the Russians—also plays a part in the toll. The company [leaves the sick] without any care."

72. The 80,000 population figure includes about 15,000 Tlingit who lived on what is now the Alaska panhandle; 1,800 Haida on what is now known as Prince of Wales Island off the southern tip of the panhandle; 3,500 Sugpiaq or Alutiiq on Kodiak Island and the Kenai Peninsula on the south-central coast of Alaska; 15,000–18,000 Unangan or—as the Russians called them—Aleut, in the Aleutian Islands; 19,500 Yupiit or Yupik along Alaska's western coast; 10,000 Inupiat along its northernmost coast; and about 11,000 Athapaskans who lived along its interior waterways, including roughly 2,200 in the vicinity of what would become the Alaska-Yukon border. Eric Sandberg et al., *A History of Alaska Population Settlement* ([Juneau]: Alaska Department of Labor and Workforce Development, April 2013), 4, citing Steve J. Langdon, *The Native People of Alaska* (Anchorage: Greatland Graphics, 2002) (noting that these are the figures adopted by Alaska Native Heritage Center). It is estimated that the Indigenous population in the Aleutians and on Kodiak Island was reduced by as much as 80 percent and in south-central Alaska and along the Alaska panhandle by as much as 50 percent. Sandberg et al., *History of Alaska Population Settlement*, 6. The first U.S. census of Alaska conducted in 1880 counted 33,426 residents; of these, 430 were identified as white and 1,756 as "Creole" or persons of both Russian and Indigenous descent. Sandberg et al., *History of Alaska Population Settlement*, 8. On the western shores of the

Pacific, disease similarly facilitated Japanese colonial expansion in Hokkaido. Walker, *Conquest of Ainu Lands*, 177–78.

73. Gibson, introduction to *California through Russian Eyes*, 16–18, 20, noting that "the trip from European Russia was long, arduous, and dangerous [and] could take as long as a year" by sea and as long as two years overland.

74. William L. Iggiagruk Hensley, "There Are Two Versions of the Story of How the U.S. Purchased Alaska from Russia: The Tale of 'Seward's Folly' Must Also Be Seen through the Eyes of Alaska's Native Population," *Smithsonian Magazine*, March 29, 2017, https://www.smithsonianmag.com/history/why-russia-gave-alaska-americas-gateway-arctic-180962714/; originally published by *The Conversation*. Hensley identifies himself as Inupiaq.

75. "Ferdinand von Wrangell's Diary of a Journey from New Archangel to St. Petersburg, 1835–1836," *California through Russian Eyes, 1806–1848*, comp., trans., and ed. James R. Gibson, with the assistance of Alexie A. Istomin (Norman: University of Oklahoma Press, 2013), 368. See also Alexander Rotchev, "A New Eldorado in California [1849]," in *California through Russian Eyes, 1806–1848*, comp., trans., and ed. James R. Gibson, with the assistance of Alexie A. Istomin (Norman: University of Oklahoma Press, 2013), 459–60, exclaiming, "What an enchanting land is California!"

76. Gibson, introduction to *California through Russian Eyes*, 18.

77. Gibson, *Otter Skins*, 18, 23, 36.

78. Gibson, *Otter Skins*, 34–35.

79. Gibson, *Otter Skins*, 37, 62; Kariann Akemi Yokota, "Transatlantic and Transpacific Connections in Early American History," *Pacific Historical Review* 83, no. 2 (2014): 209. The HBC's Columbia Department stretched along the Pacific coast from California to Russian America. Richard Somerset Mackie, *Trading beyond the Mountains: The British Fur Trade on the Pacific, 1793–1843* (Vancouver: UBC Press, 1997), xvi (map).

80. The 1783 Treaty of Paris defined the northern boundary of the United States, as it existed at the time, as between it and Britain as far as Lake of the Woods.

81. Richard White, *"It's Your Misfortune and None of My Own": A New History of the American West* (Norman: University of Oklahoma Press, 1991), 77–84. For a detailed analysis of maps of the Louisiana Purchase and of the uncertainty regarding where the northern boundary of this territory lay, see James V. Walker, "Mapping of the Northwest Boundary of the United States, 1800–1846: An Historical Context," *Terrae Incognitae* 31, no. 1 (1999): 72–73.

82. Convention of 1818 between the United States and Great Britain, Arts. I, II, and III (quotation).

83. See, e.g., Thomas Richards Jr., "'Farewell to America': The Expatriation Politics of Overland Migration, 1841–1846," *Pacific Historical Review* 86, no. 1 (2017): 124, stating that the United States and Britain "agreed to possess Oregon by 'joint occupation'" when in fact there was no explicit reference either to Oregon or to "joint occupation" in the 1818 agreement.

84. Haycox, *Alaska*, 117–18.

85. Gibson, *Otter Skins*, 18.

86. Irby C. Nichols Jr., "The Russian Ukase and the Monroe Doctrine: A Re-evaluation," *Pacific Historical Review* 36, no. 1 (February 1967): 13, quoting the translation in Alaska Boundary Tribunal, *Proceedings* (Washington, D.C., 1904), 2:25. See also Victor J. Farrar,

"The Reopening of the Russian-American Convention of 1824," *Washington Historical Quarterly* 11, no. 2 (1920): 83; and Victor J. Farrar, "The Background of the Purchase of Alaska," *Washington Historical Quarterly* 13, no. 2 (1922): 95.

87. See, e.g., Farrar, "Purchase of Alaska," 95–96; and Clive R. Symmons, "An Example from the Past of an Excessive Claim and Adverse International Reaction: The Russian Ukase of 1821 concerning Waters off Alaska," in *Historic Waters in the Law of the Sea: A Modern Re-appraisal* (Leiden: Martinus Nijhoff Publishers, 2008), 71–72.

88. Haycox, *Alaska*, 122. Through 1821, HBC activities were concentrated in Rupert's Land while the NWC, originally formed under French auspices, operated in the coastal regions, with the result that the interests that the HBC acquired as a result of the merger were not immediately clear.

89. Convention Between the United States of America and His Majesty the Emperor of All the Russias, Relative to Navigating, Fishing, Etc., in the Pacific Ocean, signed at St. Petersburg, April 17, 1824, Arts. I and IV.

90. Convention of 1824, Art. II.

91. Convention of 1824, Art. III.

92. Gilbert Malcolm Sproat, handwritten manuscript titled "The Alaska Boundary Dispute," 1, BC Archives, Royal British Columbia Museum, Victoria, B.C., MS-0257. Sproat was sent to the Colony of Vancouver Island by his employer in 1860 and remained there until 1865. He returned to British Columbia in 1876 and served as Indian reserve commissioner in the Kootenay region through 1880. He subsequently served as stipendiary magistrate and gold commissioner in the Revelstoke region through 1889, returning to Victoria in 1898, where he died in 1913. Hamar Foster, "Sproat, Gilbert Malcolm," in *Dictionary of Canadian Biography*, vol. 14, University of Toronto / Université Laval , 2003–, last revised 1998, http://www.biographi.ca/en/bio/sproat_gilbert_malcolm_14E.html.

93. In 1834, a Mr. Wilkins, assigned to negotiate the extension of the 1824 U.S.-Russia convention, noted the problems inherent in "controlling the trade upon a wild and extensive coast, of a great and open ocean, . . . still, with the exception of a few posts, at a vast distance from each other, in the rightful occupancy of the natives, and to which [even in 1834], the sovereignty of Russia has not yet, in any treaty or convention, been admitted." Farrar, "Russian-American Convention of 1824," 86–87.

94. Convention Concerning the Limits of Their Respective Possessions on the Northwest Coast of America and the Navigation of the Pacific Ocean (a.k.a. Anglo-Russian Convention of 1825), Art. III. Art. IV provided that "the island called *Prince of Wales* Island shall belong wholly to Russia" and that "wherever the summit of the mountains which extend in a direction parallel to the Coast . . . shall prove to be at the distance of more than ten marine leagues from the Ocean, the limit between the British Possessions and the line of Coast which is to belong to Russia . . . shall be formed by a line parallel to the windings of the Coast, and which shall never exceed the distance of ten marine leagues therefrom."

95. Anatole G. Mazour, "The Russian-American and Anglo-Russian Conventions, 1824–1825: An Interpretation," *Pacific Historical Review* 14, no. 3 (September 1945): 309.

96. Cruikshank, *Do Glaciers Listen?*, 222.

97. Even in 1834, Farrar argues, Russia's apparent lack of concern regarding the extent of U.S. claims shows that its interests were primarily focused on the fur trade and not on the acquisition of territory. Farrar, "Russian-American Convention of 1824," 88.

98. Convention of 1825, Art. VI; Mazour, "Russian-American and Anglo-Russian Conventions," 310.

99. Convention of 1825, Arts. VIII, X, and XI. Like the 1824 agreement between Russia and the United States, the Anglo-Russian Convention also forbade "trade in spiritous liquors, in firearms, gunpower ... or other warlike stores." Convention of 1825, Art. IX, the wording of which parallels that of Art. V of the 1824 U.S.-Russia convention.

100. Bockstoce, *Furs and Frontiers*, 39; Mazour, "Russian-American and Anglo-Russian Conventions," 309. Although it was initially contemplated that the agreements would remain in force for a period of ten years, both were renewed for an indefinite period when the initial terms expired. Either side, however, was free to abrogate the agreement on a year's notice. Farrar, "Russian-American Convention of 1824," 85.

101. Zavalishin, "[Alta] California in 1824," 275–76. Zavalishin added, "It should be said that [Californios] feared this most of all. In their eyes the Americans were heretics, and the specimens of United States citizens that they had come to know—adventurers and petty traders—had done little to recommend their nation."

102. Gibson, introduction to *California through Russian Eyes*, 19, explaining that Russia was unwilling to expand its settlements on the California coast given that it was "already overextended in Alaska" and California was still more distant.

103. Zavalishin, "[Alta] California in 1824," 274–75.

104. Gibson, introduction to *California through Russian Eyes*, 18–19.

105. "Russian-American Company's Report about a Rebellion in Alta California, 1837," in *California through Russian Eyes, 1806–1848*, comp., trans., and ed. James R. Gibson, with the assistance of Alexie A. Istomin (Norman: University of Oklahoma Press, 2013), 381.

106. Gibson, *Otter Skins*, 80.

107. Gibson, introduction to *California through Russian Eyes*, 18–19; "Mikhail Tebenkov's Report about the Discovery of Gold in California, 1848," *California through Russian Eyes, 1806–1848*, comp., trans., and ed. James R. Gibson, with the assistance of Alexie A. Istomin (Norman: University of Oklahoma Press, 2013), 456n17.

108. Gibson, *Otter Skins*, 14, 63–64, 71, 79, 81. When Fort Stikine was transferred to the United States in 1867, it was renamed Fort Wrangell. Money, "Voyage Up the Stikine," 38.

109. Gibson, *Otter Skins*, 79, 219; Haycox, *Alaska*, 131.

110. Gibson, *Otter Skins*, 82–83.

111. See Jean Barman, *French Canadians, Furs, and Indigenous Women in the Making of the Pacific Northwest* (Vancouver: UBC Press, 2014); and Melinda Marie Jetté, *At the Hearth of the Crossed Races: A French-Indian Community in Nineteenth-Century Oregon, 1812–1859* (Corvallis: Oregon State University Press, 2015).

112. White, *"It's Your Misfortune,"* 69–77.

113. Robert Greenhow, *The History of Oregon and California, and the Other Territories on the Northwest Coast of North America*, 2nd ed. (Boston: Little and Brown, 1845); Thomas Falconer, "The Oregon Question; or, A Statement of the British Claims to the Oregon Territory, in Opposition to the Pretensions of the Government of the United States of America," *North American Review* 62, no. 130 (January 1846): 216–18, 228, 230.

114. Richard White, "Other Wests," in *The West: An Illustrated History*, ed. Geoffrey C. Ward and Dayton Duncan (Boston: Little, Brown, 1996), 49.

115. Gibson, *Otter Skins*, 24–25.

116. Haycox, *Alaska*, 117.

117. Falconer, "Oregon Question," 233, 237.

118. Haycox, *Alaska*, 80, 118; Gibson, *Otter Skins*, 42, noting that the Columbia was known as Gray's River for a time; Falconer, "Oregon Question," 225, 241.

119. Gibson, *Otter Skins*, 38.

120. Falconer, "Oregon Question," 237.

121. Treaty with Great Britain, in regard to Limits Westward of the Rocky Mountains, signed in Washington, D.C., June 14, 1846, Art. III. See also Gertrude Cunningham, "The Significance of 1846 to the Pacific Coast," *Washington Historical Quarterly* 21, no. 1 (January 1930): 45.

122. See Cunningham, "Significance of 1846," 47. Had Polk's supporters prevailed, Smithers would have remained within British territory but only just, rendering it a southern border town, while Prince Rupert, Terrace, and Fort St. James, as well as other Canadian towns down to the forty-ninth parallel, would lie within U.S. borders.

123. As Donald D. Johnson notes, the Opium War between Britain and China, which changed the "basis for relations between China and the West" and led to the establishment of the treaty port system, as well as whaling interests which "increased American presence and investment in Hawaii," also gave the United States a larger stake in the Pacific. Johnson, *United States in the Pacific*, xv–xvi.

124. White, *"It's Your Misfortune,"* 77–84.

125. Barman, *West beyond the West*, 62–71.

126. For a detailed discussion of the colonial history of British Columbia, see Barman, *West beyond the West*, 69–82. See also Haycox, *Alaska*, 150; and Stuart Banner, *Possessing the Pacific: Land, Settlers, and Indigenous People from Australia to Alaska* (Cambridge, Mass.: Harvard University Press, 2007), 198.

127. Stephan, *Kuril Islands*, 61.

128. Kimura, *Kurillian Knot*, 6, 14–17; Haycox, *Alaska*, 104. For a detailed account of the confrontation between Russians and Japanese in the Kuril Islands during the first decades of the nineteenth century, see Stephan, *Kuril Islands*, 73–80.

129. Stephan notes that in 1846, there were some "70,000 men on 736 ships" in the area, roughly one hundred of them in the waters immediately adjacent to the Kuril Islands. Stephan, *Kuril Islands*, 83.

130. Kotzebue, "Russian Colony of Ross," 306–7. Gibson, in including this document in *California through Russian Eyes*, unfortunately omitted "the rest of Kotzebue's digression about whaling and Japan—the fate of the two whalers that landed there" (307n24).

131. Inazo Nitobe, *The Japanese Nation: Its Land, Its People, and Its Life, with Special Consideration to Its Relations with the United States* (New York: Knickerbocker Press, 1912), 268–69.

132. Nitobe, *Japanese Nation*, 73, 270. For an account by one such ship captain, see Henry James Snow, *In Forbidden Seas: Recollections of Sea-Otter Hunting in the Kurils* (London: Edward Arnold, 1910).

133. Nitobe, *Japanese Nation*, 268–69. Commander Biddle reached Uraga Bay near Edo in July 1846 and departed peaceably given his instructions not "to excite hostile feeling, or a distrust of [Japan's] government for the United States." "Translation from the Japanese Explanatory Edict," in U.S. Senate, *Senate Documents*, vol. 9, 32d Cong., 1st Sess., 64–65, quoted

in John E. Van Sant, *Pacific Pioneers: Japanese Journeys to America and Hawaii, 1850–80* (Urbana: University of Illinois Press, 2000), 17, 139n57.

134. Pyle, *Making of Modern Japan*, 60, 63–64. A decade before he arrived in Japan, Perry assumed command of the U.S. African Squadron, tasked with patrolling the west coast of Africa to enforce recent proscriptions against the participation of U.S. vessels in the slave trade. Perry was reportedly a reluctant enforcer of the ban against illegal slaving but was willing to turn his guns on African villagers who did not cooperate with American traders. Douglas R. Egerton, Alison Games, Jane G. Landers, Kris Lane, and Donald R. Wright, *The Atlantic World* (Wheeling, Ill.: Harlan Davidson, 2007), 475.

135. Treaty of Kanagawa, Arts. II, VI.

136. Treaty of Kanagawa, Arts. III, IV.

137. Treaty of Amity and Commerce between the United States and Japan, 1858 (Harris Treaty), Art. III (ports), Art. IV (import and export duties), and VI (extraterritoriality). T. R. Jernigan, "Extraterritoriality and Its Application to Business in China: Defects of Chinese Administration Make Home Protection Necessary," *The Trans-Pacific* 1, no. 1 (September 1919): 37. The Harris Treaty provided for the ports of Edo, Yokohama, Kobe, Niigata, and Nagasaki to be opened to U.S. ships.

138. Pyle, *Making of Modern Japan*, 65.

139. Japanese graves found on the island of Etorofu mark the location of one outpost stationed by Matsumae clan members in the early nineteenth century. "Edo Period Japanese Graves Found on Northern Territories Island in Landmark Discovery," *The Mainichi*, December 3, 2018.

140. Walker, *Conquest of Ainu Lands*, 6; Stephan, *Kuril Islands*, vii, 12, 16; Kimura, *Kurillian Knot*, 1, 3.

141. *The Trans-Pacific*, vol. 4, no. 5 (May 1922), noting that neither Japan nor Russia had an exclusive right to Sakhalin until 1875, after which it became a Russian penal colony. Kimura, *Kurillian Knot*, 1.

142. Stephan, *Kuril Islands*, 2, 61. The Treaty of St. Petersburg was signed in 1875.

143. For a detailed discussion of Japan's reasons for going to war against Russia in 1904 and its consequences, including resistance to the Russo-Japanese War in Japan, see Pyle, *Making of Modern Japan*, 139–47. Given Korea's geographical position in relation to Japan, one advisor to the Meiji government described it as a "dagger" pointing at Japan's heart. Pyle, 137.

144. Japan-Russia Treaty of Peace (Treaty of Portsmouth), Art. IX (Sakhalin), Art. XI (fishery rights), signed September 5, 1905; Stephan, *Kuril Islands*, 94.

145. Nitobe, *Japanese Nation*, 26.

146. Pyle, *Making of Modern Japan*, 78. The Meiji era ended with the death of the Meiji emperor in 1912. It was followed by the Taishō period (1912–1926) and the Shōwa period (1926–1989).

147. For a detailed discussion of Meiji-era reforms eliminating historical status categories and early Japanese emigration, see Andrea Geiger, *Subverting Exclusion: Transpacific Encounters with Race, Caste, and Borders, 1885–1928* (New Haven, Conn.: Yale University Press, 2011), 36–52. See also Pyle, *Making of Modern Japan*, 101–8.

148. Walker, *Conquest of Ainu Lands*, 5, 11, explaining that "the Ainu, once a semi-independent people," in time "became an "ethnic minorit[y] in a Japanese state."

149. Walker, *Conquest of Ainu Lands*, 37, 15, citing David Howell, *Capitalism from Within: Economy, Society, and the State in a Japanese Fishery* (Berkeley: University of California Press, 1995), 27–28. See also Atsuko Okada, "Maritime Adaptations in Hokkaido," *Arctic Anthropology* 35, no. 1 (1992): 340–49. For an early analysis of the emergence of mutually dependent commercial relationships in a North American context, see Richard White, *The Roots of Dependency: Subsistence, Environment, and Social Change among the Choctaws, Pawnees, and Navajos* (Lincoln: University of Nebraska Press, 1983).

150. Hensley, "How the U.S. Purchased Alaska."

151. Gibson, "Russian Dependence on the Natives of Alaska." See also Haycox, *Alaska*, 55–56, noting that "Russians became increasingly and widely dependent on the Aleut people"; Vinkovetsky, *Russian America*, 101, 132–33, noting the mutually dependent nature of the relationship that developed between the RAC and the Indigenous people on whom it relied.

152. Glynn Barratt, *Russian Shadows on the British Northwest Coast of North America, 1810–1890: A Study of Rejection of Defence Responsibilities* (Vancouver: UBC Press, 1983), 116; Vinkovetsky, *Russian America*, 50, 186.

153. Patrick Lane, "The Great Pacific Sealhunt," *Raincoast Chronicles* 1, no. 4 (1974): 44; Victoria Wyatt, "Alaska and Hawaii," in *The Oxford History of the American West*, ed. Clyde A. Milner II, Carol A. O'Connor, and Martha A. Sandweiss (New York: Oxford University Press, 1994), 581.

154. Haycox, *Alaska*, 171, noting that "[U.S. statesman William] Seward also wanted to advance American interests relative to Britain" and reasoned that "the purchase of Alaska would entrap British Columbia in a giant American pincer"; Vinkovetsky, *Russian America*, 3, noting that Seward envisioned the "Alaska purchase . . . as a prelude to an American bid for the entire west coast of North America."

155. Farrar, "Purchase of Alaska," 102, citing F. W. Seward, *Reminiscences* (n.p., n.p.). According to Farrar, this offer was renewed in 1863. Farrar, "Purchase of Alaska," 101, quoting Cassius M. Clay, "minister to Russia at the time of the [Alaska] purchase." See also Haycox, *Alaska*, 128, explaining that Russia did not want American intrusion, but it needed the United States as an ally if Britain moved against Russia, while the United States did not want to see Britain secure an advantage in the Northwest.

156. Vinkovetsky, *Russian America*, 181–82; Haycox, *Alaska*, 152–62.

157. Haycox, *Alaska*, 88, 153.

158. N. N. Bokhovitinov, "The Sale of Alaska in the Context of Russo-American Relations in the Nineteenth Century," in *Imperial Russian Foreign Policy*, ed. Hugh Ragsdale (Cambridge: Cambridge University Press, 1993), 202.

159. Treaty concerning the Cession of the Russian Possessions in North America by His Majesty the Emperor of All the Russias to the United States of America; Concluded March 30, 1867; Ratified by the United States, May 28, 1867; Exchanged June 20, 1867; Proclaimed by the United States, June 20, 1867 (15 Stat. 539) (Treaty of Cession), Art. I. Although U.S government entities suggest "Alaska Purchase Treaty" as the short form for this treaty, I deliberately avoid the use of this term so as not to suggest that Russia had acquired transferrable title from the Indigenous people whose homeland it was.

160. Bockstoce, *Furs and Frontiers*, 221, 241, noting that Indigenous people call the Yukon River the Ekko.

161. Treaty of Cession, Art. V. Bockstoce, *Furs and Frontiers*, 300–301, noting that HBC personnel sent to burn down the fort once the mistake was realized did not arrive before it was occupied by the United States.

162. Treaty of Cession, Art. III.

163. Haycox, *Alaska*, 183, 191–92.

164. Hensley, "How the U.S. Purchased Alaska."

165. British North America Act: An Act for the Union of Canada, Nova Scotia, and New Brunswick, and the Government Thereof, 1867. The Province of Canada, formerly Upper and Lower Canada, became the provinces of Ontario and Quebec.

166. Doug Owram, *Promise of Eden: The Canadian Expansionist Movement and the Idea of the West, 1856–1900* (1980; repr., Toronto: University of Toronto Press, 1992), 37, 39, 49–55. The area once known as Rupert's Land constitutes roughly one third of Canada today.

167. Lane, "Great Pacific Sealhunt," 44; Barman, *West beyond the West*, 93–94.

168. Jinshiro Nakayama, *Canada and the Japanese* [Kanada to nihonjin], trans. Tsuneharu Gonnami (Vancouver, B.C.: Kanada Nihonjinkai, 1940), 251, University of British Columbia Library, Special Collections and Archives, Vancouver, 1999.

169. See, e.g., Canadian Pacific Railway Company, *The Canadian Pacific: The New Highway to the Orient across the Mountains, Prairies and Rivers of Canada* (Montreal, 1891); *Japan and China: The New Short Route from Europe to the Far East* (Liverpool, England: Turner and Dunnett, 1892); and *East to the West: . . . the Great Railway Route across the American Continent* (1898), University of British Columbia Library, Chung Collection, box 223.

170. Owram, *Promise of Eden*, 57–58.

171. *Canada. . . . . . from Ocean to Ocean: An Illustrated Volume Setting Forth the Richness of Canadian Resources and the Monuments of Canadian Enterprise* (Toronto: Dominion Publishing, 1897), 10, also noting that traveling on Canadian railroads cut the distance from Liverpool to Yokohama by over a thousand miles compared to travel through either New York or the Suez Canal.

172. Owram, *Promise of Eden*, 83–94, noting that the impending transfer of Rupert's Land to Canada led, in 1869 and 1870, to the Red River Rebellion by the Métis.

173. Owram, *Promise of Eden*, 50.

174. *The Emigrant's Manual: British America and United States of America* (Edinburgh: William and Robert Chambers, 1851), 73–74.

175. Cruikshank, *Do Glaciers Listen?*, 225–27.

176. Lewis Green, *The Boundary Hunters: Surveying the 141st Meridian and the Alaska Panhandle* (Vancouver: University of British Columbia Press, 1982), 76.

177. C. L. Andrews, *The Story of Alaska* (Seattle: Lowman & Hanford, 1931), 179, 245.

178. Haycox, *Alaska*, 196.

179. Green, *Boundary Hunters*, 76.

180. Green, *Boundary Hunters*, 69–71.

181. William H. Dall, "Memorandum on the Alaskan Boundary," and "Message from the President of the United States Transmitting Report on the Boundary Line between Alaska and British Columbia," U.S. Senate, 50th Cong., 2d Sess., 1889, Ex. Doc. No. 146, Inclosure No. 5. See also Scidmore, *Appleton's Guide-Book*, 34.

182. William Ogilvie, *Early Days on the Yukon* (Ottawa: Thorburn & Abbott, 1913), 31–33, noting that one marine league is equal to 34.5 English miles or 56 kilometers. Ogilvie sur-

veyed the 141st meridian that demarcates the boundary between Alaska and the Yukon in 1887 and was later appointed governor of the Yukon Territory and had lived there for over two decades in 1908. *Douglas Island News* (Alaska), November 18, 1908.

183. Sproat, "Alaska Boundary Dispute," 5–6.

184. Sproat, "Alaska Boundary Dispute," 7, noting that "no Briton" wanted to be denied access to the salt sea.

185. For a detailed summary of the decisions of each of the three entities charged with resolving one or another aspect of the Alaska boundary issue, the Alaska Boundary Commission (1892), the Alaska Boundary Tribunal (1903), and the international Boundary Commission (1904), see Cruikshank, *Do Glaciers Listen?*, 225–30.

186. Ogilvie, *Early Days on the Yukon*, 33–34.

187. Sproat, "Alaska Boundary Dispute," 7. For a detailed account of what is known as the San Juan Island boundary dispute, see James O. McCabe, *The San Juan Water Boundary Question* (Toronto: University of Toronto Press, 1964). The 1872 dispute concerned the question of what channel the U.S.-Canada boundary was to follow to avoid cutting across Vancouver Island and divided the San Juan Islands that lie south of the border from the Gulf Islands to the north, even though they are part of the same archipelago.

188. Geraldo Cadava, "Historians Explore the Borderlands: A Rapidly-Developing Field," *Immigration and Ethnic History Newsletter* 45, no. 1 (May 2013): 1.

189. Quoted in Cruikshank et al., *Life Lived like a Story*, 169, 366n5.

190. I use "contingent" in the same sense that Richard White uses it. As he explains, "Contingency . . . simply means that something that happens is dependent on something else happening, and that the something else is neither inevitable nor even predictable." Richard White, "The Gold Rush: Consequences and Contingencies," *California History* 77, no. 1 (Spring 1998): 46.

191. Gibson, introduction to *California through Russian Eyes*, 16, editor's introduction to "Excerpt from Andrey Lazarev's Journal of a Visit to Alta California, 1823–1824," *California through Russian Eyes, 1806–1848*, comp., trans., and ed. James R. Gibson, with the assistance of Alexie A. Istomin (Norman: University of Oklahoma Press, 2013), 219, also noting the role of Chinese and Japanese isolationism in allowing Russia to establish itself in Siberia.

192. See, e.g., Haycox, *Alaska*, 118, noting that the joint agreement regarding the Oregon Country was "one part of a larger territorial settlement [tying up] loose ends in a new balance of power after the Napoleonic Wars." The 1763 Treaty of Paris served in part to bring what is known in the United States as the French and Indian War to an end. The 1783 Treaty of Paris between Britain and the United States brought the Revolutionary War to an end.

193. The exception is Newfoundland, which became part of Canada only in 1949.

194. "The Alaskan Purchase Scheme: We Should Have All Territory North of the U.S.," *The Province* (Vancouver, B.C.), July 19, 1971.

195. Morgan Hite, "Fifty-Four Forty or Fight: How a U.S. Border Crossing Almost Wound Up in the Bulkley Valley," *Northword Magazine*, December/January 2013.

196. See, e.g., William Pitman Lett, *Annexation and British Connection: Address to Brother Jonathan* (Ottawa: Mason & Jones, 1889); an ex-member of the Canadian Parliament, "The Political Reunion of the United States and Canada," *American Journal of Politics*, December 1893.

197. David Martin, "The Rising Sun over Canada," *Asia*, April 1941, 189.

Chapter Two

1. Ikeda Arichika, *Arasuka hyōzan ryokō* (Journey to Alaska's Icebergs) (Tokyo: Unteisha, Meiji 36 [1903]), i. The publishers of Ikeda's journal use the word *hyōzan* (iceberg) in the title although *hyōga* (glacier) was the more apt term since many of the adventures that Ikeda describes occurred as he traversed Alaska's glaciers. The publishers explain that they worked from a manuscript written by Ikeda in cursive script with the result that it was sometimes difficult to determine just where a sentence ended or just what character Ikeda meant to use, rendering his intended meaning unclear. Ikeda, *Arasuka hyōzan ryokō*, ii. Ikeda was born in 1864, four years before the end of the Tokugawa period, what would become Niigata Prefecture. My thanks to Masaki Watanabe for preparing a translation of this document.

2. Julie Cruikshank in collaboration with Angela Sidney, Kitty Smith, and Annie Ned, *Life Lived like a Story: Life Stories of Three Yukon Native Elders* (Lincoln: University of Nebraska Press, 1990), 8, 186–89; Julie Cruikshank, "Images of Society in Klondike Gold Rush Narratives: Skookum Jim and the Discovery of Gold," *Ethnohistory* 39, no. 1 (Winter 1992): 27–32. Keish was also known as Skookum Jim. At the time he found gold, Keish was traveling with his sister Shaaw Tláa, also known as Kate Carmack, and her husband, George Carmack, a non-Native man from California who claimed credit for discovery. Cruikshank, "Gold Rush Narratives"; Deb Vanasse, *Wealth Woman: Kate Carmack and the Klondike Race for Gold* (Fairbanks: University of Alaska Press, 2016). For a detailed history of the Klondike gold rush, see Kathryn Morse, *The Nature of Gold: An Environmental History of the Klondike Gold Rush* (Seattle: University of Washington Press, 2003).

3. Ikeda, *Arasuka hyōzan ryokō*, i. The Copper River is known as Atna'tuu ("river of the Ahtnas") to the Athapaskan people of the region and as Eekhéeni ("river of copper") to the Tlingit people of the region. John Smelcer, James Kari, and Millie Buck, eds., *Ahtna Noun Dictionary and Pronunciation Guide*, 2nd ed. (Copper Center, Alaska: Ahtna Heritage Foundation, 1998), 31; Thomas F. Thornton, *Being and Place among the Tlingit* (Seattle: University of Washington Press in association with the Sealaska Heritage Institute, Juneau, Alaska, 2008), 64.

4. Ikeda, *Arasuka hyōzan ryokō*, i.

5. Ikeda, *Arasuka hyōzan ryokō*, 2–3; Jutaro Tokunaga, "The Exploits of a Pioneer Issei," *Charlottes: A Journal of the Queen Charlotte Islands* 3 (1973): 22 (for the information about Ikeda's background). Tokunaga met Ikeda's daughter in 1919 on Moresby Island in British Columbia and subsequently became Ikeda's son-in-law. Tokunaga, "Pioneer Issei," 19.

6. Ikeda, *Arasuka hyōzan ryokō*, 4.

7. Nitta Jiro, *Phantom Immigrants*, trans. David Sulz (n.p., 1998), 47, 114; originally published as *Mikkōsen Suian Maru* (Tokyo: Kodansha, 1979).

8. Ikeda, *Arasuka hyōzan ryokō*, 4.

9. Ikeda, *Arasuka hyōzan ryokō*, 5–7. The name of the bay is rendered *a-re-su-to* in katakana in the published book. Given the difficulties that its editors encountered in reading Ikeda's handwriting, however, it may be that he meant to write *aretto*, which is one way "Alert" might be rendered in Japanese. Ikeda may also have spotted orcas and Dall's porpoises.

10. Ikeda, *Arasuka hyōzan ryokō*, 7.

11. Ikeda, *Arasuka hyōzan ryokō*, 8–9. The Haida canoes that they spotted, Ikeda wrote, were so beautifully crafted that they could have been displayed in a museum.

12. Long before the international border cut through what was already an intricately structured borderlands region, the Tsimshian were a quintessential borderlands people who had intermarried, traded, and at times engaged in conflict with other coastal peoples over the course of millennia. Variously spelled as Tsimshean, Tsimpshean, or Chimmesyan in historical documents, "Tsimshian" is the preferred spelling used today by the descendants of those who settled in Metlakatla, Alaska.

13. "Mr. Duncan's Address before the Board of Indian Commissioners, and the Conference of Missionary Boards, and Indian Rights Associations," Washington, D.C., January 6, 1886, U.S. National Archives and Records Administration (NARA), record group (RG) 200, box 92, folder 84, document 6. Fort Simpson was later renamed Port Simpson and is now known as Lax Kw'alaams.

14. The place-name is sometimes spelled Metlakahtla or Metlakatlah in historical documents. I use the spelling preferred today except in titles, quotations, or names where another spelling is employed. There is an extensive literature on Metlakatla. See, e.g., Susan Neylan, "'Choose Your Flag': Perspectives on the Tsimshian Migration from Metlakatla, British Columbia, to New Metlakatla, Alaska, 1887," in *New Histories for Old: Changing Perspectives on Canada's Native Pasts,* ed. Theodore Binnema and Susan Neylan (Vancouver: UBC Press, 2008), 198–219, comparing U.S. and Canadian newspaper accounts; and Jean Usher [Friesen], *William Duncan of Metlakatla: A Victorian Missionary in British Columbia,* Publications in History 5 (Ottawa: National Museum of Man, 1974). "Metlakatla" means both "calm channel" and "a passage between two bodies of saltwater" in Tsimshian. See Ellen Ryan, *History of the Metlakatla Indian Community (Alaska)* (Metlakatla, Alaska: Metlakatla Indian Community, 2007), 2; and John T. Walbran, *British Columbia Coast Names, 1592–1906: Their Origin and History* (Ottawa: Government Printing Bureau, 1909), 336, quoting an elderly Tsimshian former resident of Metlakatla who in 1906 described it as a very old word.

15. William Duncan, "Comments on the Report Rendered to the Indian Department, Ottawa, by the Superintendent of Indian Affairs, British Columbia, for Year 1886," NARA, RG 200, box 96, folder 136-8, document 1. Duncan later reported that the site was chosen by the Tsimshian and that he did not see the site prior to their move. "Compilation of Papers relating to the Affairs of British Columbia, 1860–1870," NARA, RG 200, box 92, folder 84.

16. Excerpts, *Report of the Secretary of the Interior for the Fiscal Year Ending June 30, 1887* (Washington, D.C.: Government Printing Office, 1887), 19, NARA, RG 200, box 92, folder 84, document 8.

17. "List of Magazines and Pamphlets Dealing with the History of the Metlakahtla People," including "Extracts from Letters and Journals of the Missionaries of the Church Missionary Society Labouring in Central Africa, 1877–1884," NARA, RG 200, box 243. Even though they were often at odds with one another, missionaries and fur traders each played an important part in colonial expansion across the Pacific world. Donald D. Johnson, *The United States in the Pacific: Private Interests and Public Policies, 1784–1899,* with Gary Dean Best (Westport, Conn.: Praeger, 1995), 38, 89.

18. See Henry S. Wellcome, *The Story of Metlakahtla* (London: Saxon, 1887). The publication of this book was also a fund-raising effort. A. E. Green, Port Simpson, B.C., to William Duncan, October 10, 1889, NARA, RG 200, box 116, folder 381, document 49. For a detailed account of the rift between Duncan and the Church Missionary Society, including

William Ridley, the Anglican bishop assigned to Metlakatla, see Neylan, "'Choose Your Flag,'" 202–3. Although Wellcome's book credited Duncan with Metlakatla's success, others acknowledged that the Tsimshian were key to the community's success. See, e.g., James G. Swan, quoted by Lieutenant Colonel Robert N. Scott, in *Seal and Salmon Fisheries and General Resources of Alaska* (Washington, D.C.: Government Printing Office, 1898), vol. 4, being a part of the report of William G. Morris, November 25, 1878, NARA, RG 200, box 92, folder 85, document 26.

19. Henry S. Wellcome, Port Simpson, B.C., to William Duncan, October 10, 1889, NARA, RG 200, box 116, folder 381, document 49, reporting that he had sent the Japanese consul his last copy. The Japanese consul at the time was Sugimura Fukashi, the first to be posted to Vancouver, B.C. Zaibei Nihonjinkai (Japanese Association of America, History Preservation Committee), *Zaibeinihonjinshi* (History of Japanese in America), trans. Seizo Oka (San Francisco: Zaibei Nihonjinkai, 1940), 1016, 1040; Kazuo Ito, *Issei: A History of Japanese Immigrants in North America*, trans. Shinichiro Nakamura and Jean S. Gerard (Seattle, 1973), 965. Sugimura is the Japanese consul's family name; the English-language translations of the two histories referred to above list the given names of the authors and translators first.

20. Fumiko Fujita, *American Pioneers and the Japanese Frontier: American Experts in Nineteenth-Century Japan* (Westport, Conn.: Greenwood Press, 1994); Yujin Yaguchi, "Remembering a More Layered Past in Hokkaido: Americans, Japanese and the Ainu," *Japanese Journal of American Studies* 11 (2000), 109–28.

21. "Compilation of Papers relating to the Affairs of British Columbia." James Douglas, who was himself of mixed European and African ancestry, served as the first governor of the Colony of British Columbia from 1858 to 1864.

22. For a detailed examination of the B.C. government's reasons for refusing to recognize Aboriginal title and of Indigenous resistance related to this, see Hamar Foster, "Letting Go the Bone: The Idea of Indian Title in British Columbia, 1849–1927," in *Essays in the History of Canadian Law*, vol. 6, ed. Hamar Foster and John McLaren (Toronto: University of Toronto Press, 1995), 28–86; and Hamar Foster, "'We Want a Strong Promise': The Opposition to Indian Treaties in British Columbia, 1850–1990," *Native Studies Review* 18, no. 1 (2009): 113–37. For a description of Indigenous resistance to colonial intrusion along the Skeena River in the 1880s, see R. M. Galois, "Gitxsan Law and Settler Disorder: The Skeena 'Uprising' of 1888," in *New Histories for Old: Changing Perspectives on Canada's Native Pasts*, ed. Theodore Binnema and Susan Neylan (Vancouver: UBC Press, 2008), 220–41.

23. Marquis of Lansdowne, Government House, Ottawa, to Sir Henry Holland, enclosing a report by the Committee of the Privy Council for Canada, approved June 13, 1887, NARA, RG 200, box 96, folder 136-12.

24. Duncan, "Comments on the Report Rendered to the Indian Department"; "Statement with regard to Mr. Duncan's Work among the Tsimpsheean Indians of British Columbia and Alaska," Sheldon Jackson, U.S. General Agent of Education for Alaska, to Charles F. Manderson, U.S. Senate, April 10, 1894, Senate, 53d Cong., 2d Sess., Misc. Doc. No. 144, NARA, RG 200, box 92, folder 85, document 8-B.

25. The principle long embraced by both Canada and the United States that Indigenous land could only be acquired by treaty stemmed from the common origins of both bodies of law in British colonial law and policy and particularly the Royal Proclamation of 1763. B.C.

government officials reasoned in the alternative that the Royal Proclamation did not apply in British Columbia and that therefore Aboriginal title did not exist; if Aboriginal title did exist, it was extinguished by subsequent inconsistent uses.

26. "Indian Land. The Indian's View of the Land Question. Letter from Chief Mountain and Others," n.d., NARA, RG 200, box 243. Although statements of this kind are often criticized on the basis that they could only have been written with the assistance of non-Indigenous missionaries or others, the direct testimony of Indigenous witnesses before the Metlakatla and other commissions makes clear that such statements are accurate reflections of their own positions.

27. "Letter from Chief Mountain and Others."

28. "Evidence," xlvi, in British Columbia, *Metlakatlah Inquiry, 1884: Report of the Commissioners, Together with the Evidence* (Victoria, B.C.: Government Printing Office, 1885), 48 Vict. 131. Paul Legaic, who "belonged to a line of powerful coastal Tsimshian chiefs who bore the Legaic title . . . meaning 'chief of the mountains,'" maintained ties both with Lax Kw'alaams and New Metlakatla and with traditional culture as well as Christianity. I. V. B. Johnson, "Legaic, Paul," in *Dictionary of Canadian Biography*, vol. 12, University of Toronto/Université Laval, 2003-, accessed October 25, 2021, http://www.biographi.ca/en/bio/legaic_paul_12E.html.

29. Sarah Nashumachken, Lucy Spencer, Barbarre Lachteethsl, and 264 others, November 19, 1884, "Evidence," lxxxii, in British Columbia, *Metlakatlah Inquiry*.

30. Report, December 9, 1884, in British Columbia, *Metlakatlah Inquiry*, 134.

31. Duncan, "Comments on the Report Rendered by the Indian Department." The Supreme Court of Canada ruled that Aboriginal title exists in British Columbia in *Calder v. British Columbia* [1973] S.C.R. 313.

32. British Columbia, *Report of Conferences between the Provincial Government and Indian Delegates from Fort Simpson and Naas River*, February 3 and 8, 1887, 256, appended to British Columbia, *Papers relating to the Commission Appointed to Enquire into the State and Condition of the Indians of the North-West Coast of British Columbia*, appendix B, February 22, 1888, 51 Vict. 415, 460.

33. Report, December 9, 1884, in British Columbia, *Metlakatlah Inquiry*, 133–34.

34. Report, December 9, 1884, in British Columbia, *Metlakatlah Inquiry*, 136. Canada's Indian Act was passed in 1876 to define Indian status and to set up the framework according to which federally recognized Indian bands were to operate; although it has been amended numerous times, it remains in force.

35. "Mr. Duncan's Address," January 6, 1886.

36. "Metlakahtla Indians," in *Report of the Secretary of the Interior for the Fiscal Year Ending June 30, 1887* (Washington, D.C.: Government Printing Office, 1887), 46, NARA, RG 200, box 92, folder 84, document 7-C.

37. For a discussion of Congress's reasons for ending treaty making with tribal nations in the United States, see Francis Paul Prucha, *The Great Father: The United States Government and the American Indians*, abridged ed. (Lincoln: University of Nebraska Press, 1984), 164–66.

38. I use "Indigene" in this context to highlight the racialized thinking of the time grounded, as it was, in pseudoscience.

39. Henry S. Wellcome, Washington, D.C., to William Duncan, March 3, 1887, NARA, RG 200, box 116, folder 381, document 16 (emphasis in the original). Insisting that there

were no "Indians" in Alaska was one element of a larger argument against the extension of the treaty system to Alaska. See, e.g., "Proceedings of the Board of Indian Commissioners at the Thirteenth Lake Mohonk Indian Conference, First Session," October 9, 1895, in *Twenty-Seventh Annual Report of the Board of Indian Commissioners, 1895* (Washington, D.C.: Government Printing Office, 1896), 25–26, NARA, RG 200, box 92, folder 85, document 8, declaring, "We have no Indians in Alaska; we have natives."

40. Henry S. Wellcome, New York, to Editor, *New York Herald*, June 18, 1887, NARA, RG 200, box 116, folder 381, document 19. See also Act to Provide for the Allotment of Lands in Severalty to Indians of the Various Reservations, approved February 8, 1887, 25 U.S.C. §§ 331–334, 339, 341–342, 348–349, 354, 381, also referred to as the Dawes Act and as the General Allotment Act.

41. A. H. Garland, February 28, 1887, excerpt from *Opinions of the Attorney General* (1887), 18: 557, NARA, RG 200, box 92, folder 84, document 7-A. See also "Metlakahtla Indians," in *Report of the Secretary of the Interior*.

42. As Canadian legal scholar Hamar Foster explains, Canadian authorities assumed that "Indians became British subjects when their territory was brought under British jurisdiction," but how they "became British subjects has never been adequately explained." Hamar Foster, "Forgotten Arguments: Aboriginal Title and Sovereignty in *Canada Jurisdiction Act* Cases," *Manitoba Law Journal / Revue de droit manitobaine* 21 (1992): 345, 345n9.

43. Garland, excerpt from *Opinions of the Attorney General*, 18:557. See also "Metlakahtla Indians," in *Report of the Secretary of the Interior*.

44. Brendan W. Resnick notes the existence of similar contradictions along the U.S.-Mexico border and the forty-ninth parallel, although he does not frame them in quite the same way. Brendan W. Resnick, *Native but Foreign: Indigenous Immigrants and Refugees in the North American Borderlands* (College Station: Texas A&M University Press, 2019).

45. See, e.g., *Report of the Commissioner of Education to the Secretary of the Interior, for the Year Ending June 30, 1887* (1887), 17, NARA, RG 200, box 92, folder 84, document 7-B, declaring, "Native Alaskans, it should be understood, are not Indians. Their appearance, habits, language, complexion, and even their anatomy mark them as a race wholly different and distinct from the Indian tribes inhabiting other portions of the United States."

46. "Alaska and Indian Territory," from "Report of the Board of Indian Commissioners, Sixth Session," October 4, 1889, in *Twenty-First Annual Report of the Board of Indian Commissioners, 1889* (Washington, D.C.: Government Printing Office, 1890), 113, NARA, RG 200, box 243.

47. Duncan reported in 1918 that U.S. Supreme Court Justice Miller, who later visited New Metlakatla, assured him that all who settled in Alaska had squatters rights. William Duncan, "Statement of the Metlakahtla Mission," circa 1918, 132, NARA, RG 200, box 96, folder 136-9.

48. "Alaska and Indian Territory," 113.

49. W. F. Macdonald, Victoria, B.C., to Henry S. Wellcome, August 28, 1887, enclosing part of a letter received from an unidentified resident of "Matlakahtla," B.C., NARA, RG 200, box 116, folder 381, document 22.

50. O. H. Tittman, Superintendent, U.S. Coast Pilot, Pacific Coast Alaska, *U.S. Coast & Geodetic Survey*, 4th ed. (Washington, D.C.: Government Printing Office, 1901), pt. 1.

51. Neylan, "'Choose Your Flag,'" 212, 214. William Duncan, Metlakahtla, to Franklin K. Lane, Secretary of the Interior, Washington, D.C., June 11, 1914, in "Statement of the Met-

lakahtla Mission," 156, recalling that the Tsimshian had "found some remains of habitations which had been deserted some fifty years before by a tribe of Tlinget Indians who had resided here from time immemorial but who being at war with other Indians had found it expedient to quit."

52. Report of Assistant Inspector M. E. Fagan, in George R. Tingle, Inspector of Salmon Fisheries, Washington, "Report on the Salmon Fisheries of Alaska, 1896," 4–8, NARA, RG 200, box 92, folder 85, document 14.

53. Tittman, *U.S. Coast & Geodetic Survey*; "Proceedings of the Board of Indian Commissioners at the Twelfth Lake Mohonk Indian Conference, Fourth Session," October 11, 1894, in *Twenty-Sixth Annual Report of the Board of Indian Commissioners, 1894* (Washington, D.C.: Government Printing Office, 1895), 127–28, NARA, RG 200, box 92, folder 85, document 8, describing the island as a lonely place.

54. James D. Bluett, New Metlakatla, Alaska, to Henry S. Wellcome, May 18, 1888, NARA, RG 200, box 116, folder 381, document 36; "Journal of the Nineteenth Annual Conference with Representatives of Missionary Boards and Indian Rights Associations," included in *Twenty-First Annual Report of the Board of Indian Commissioners, 1889* (Washington, D.C.: Government Printing Office, 1890), 137, NARA, RG 200, box 92, folder 84, document 16.

55. See, e.g., Patrick Russ, Speaker, to William Duncan, Victoria, B.C., January 6, 1887, NARA, RG 200, box 108, folder 285, document 4. Although newspapers of the time cited the falling-out between Duncan and the Church Missionary Society as the reason for the move, Neylan concludes that title to land and resources was an equally, if not more, important factor. See, e.g., Neylan, "'Choose Your Flag,'" 202–4, 206, 212, 214.

56. Van F. Toppan, Washington, D.C., to William Duncan, October 6, 1887, NARA, RG 200, box 116, folder 381, document 25.

57. William Duncan, New Metlakahtla, Alaska, to Thomas N. Strong, Attorney at Law, Portland, Oregon, December 9, 1887, NARA, RG 200, box 96, folder 137, document 5, naming the Indian agent as C. Todd, assigned to what was then known as the North West Agency.

58. Transcript of testimony taken in 1887 regarding damage to property at old Metlakatla by "five Indians from Port Chester," NARA, RG 200, box 92, folder 84, document 15-H. Duncan denied the bishop's claim that there was any violence involved on the part of the Tsimshian, insisting that the only person who had a gun or fired any shots was the bishop himself. Duncan to Strong, December 9, 1887.

59. According to Duncan, George Vancouver, when he came upon it many years earlier, thought that the site where Metlakatla was located was an abandoned village because the houses had no roofs, not realizing that the Tsimshian took their roofs, made of wide strips of bark, with them to their summer villages. William Duncan, "Legendary Statements," September 1916–April 1917, 197, NARA, RG 200, box 96, folder 136-12.

60. See, e.g., John A. Yogis, Catherine A. Cotter, and Steven H. Gifis, *Canadian Law Dictionary*, 6th ed. (Hauppauge, N.Y.: Barron's Educational Series, 2009).

61. Thomas N. Strong, Attorney at Law, Portland, Oregon, to William Duncan, New Metlakahtla, Alaska, April 18, 1888, NARA, RG 200, box 96, folder 138, document 6.

62. David Leask for the people of Metlakahtla, New Metlakahtla, Alaska, to George C. Thomas, Esq., Philadelphia, October 26, 1887, NARA, RG 200, box 108, folder 285, document 4.

63. C. Todd, Indian Agent and Commissioner of Police, Metlakatla, B.C., to William Duncan, New Metlakatla, Port Chester, Alaska, March 28, 1888, NARA, RG 200, box 116, folder 381, document 35.

64. Todd to Duncan, March 28, 1888.

65. *Indians of the North-West Coast of British Columbia*, 458, stating that as many as "thirty or forty canoes, ten persons at most in each canoe—men, women and children" that the witness recognized as Tsimshian who had moved to New Metlakatla, continued to access traditional fishing sites now on the Canadian side of the border.

66. Bluett to Wellcome, May 18, 1888. See also "Speech of Benjamin Ahspoo at the Feast Given in Honor of Bishop Cridge and Senator Macdonald's Visit," NARA, RG 200, box 116, folder 381, document 40, declaring that Canada "robbed us of our land and our houses."

67. Neylan, "'Choose Your Flag,'" 207, citing W. White, Superintendent General of Indian Affairs, letter to Privy Council of Canada, January 5, 1888, Library and Archives Canada, RG 10, vol. 3606, file 2959, pt. 2. U.S. and Canadian officials also sought to restrict the movement of Indigenous peoples across the forty-ninth parallel. See, e.g., Andrea Geiger, "'Crossed by the Border': The U.S.-Canada Border and Canada's 'Extinction' of the Arrow Lakes [Sinixt] Band, 1890–1956," *Western Legal History* 23, no. 2 (Summer/Fall 2010): 136, quoting A. Megraw, inspector of Indian agencies, as declaring, "British Columbia Indians should not be living in Washington state."

68. Report, December 9, 1884, in British Columbia, *Metlakatlah Inquiry*, 133.

69. *Indians of the North-West Coast of British Columbia*, 432–33. "Naas" is a spelling used in colonial records for both the river and the Indigenous people who lived near it; "Nass" is the spelling used for the river today. The people whose territories lie along the Nass River in British Columbia are the Nisga'a.

70. *Indians of the North-West Coast of British Columbia*, 451. One missionary reported, for example, "The Kincolith Indians have found themselves in a very humiliating position in asserting their claim to lands disputed by the other Indians, in not being able to show a written authoritative document setting forth their title to their lands and the extent of them." James B. McCullagh, Missionary C.M.S., to Lieutenant Colonel Powell, Indian Commissioner, July 22, 1887, in *Indians of the North-West Coast of British Columbia*, 460.

71. *Indians of the North-West Coast of British Columbia*, 432–34. Russ's talk was interrupted by an elder, Neis Puck, who declared: "I am the oldest man here and can't sit still any longer and hear that it is not our fathers' land. Who is the chief that gave this land to the Queen? Give us his name, we have never heard it." The Laxgalts'ap people were called Greenville Indians by colonial administrators. The Greenville Indian Band was one of the plaintiffs in *Calder v. British Columbia* [1973] S.C.R. 313 who prevailed in 1973 when the Supreme Court of Canada upheld the existence of Aboriginal title in British Columbia.

72. *Indians of the North-West Coast of British Columbia*, 439.

73. "Alaska and Indian Territory," 113.

74. Frank Wood, in *Twenty-Sixth Annual Report of the Board of Indian Commissioners, 1894*, 127–28.

75. Wellcome, *Story of Metlakahtla*, title page, quoting the *New York World* and the *New York Tribune*. See also N. H. R. Dawson, U.S. Commissioner of Education, "Proceedings of the Department of Superintendence of the National Educational Association at Its Meeting in Washington, February 14–16, 1888," excerpt from U.S. Bureau of Education, Circular

of Information No. 6 (comparing the B.C. village of Metlakatla with an Acadian village). For a detailed account of the expulsion of the Acadians from Canada's maritime provinces, see, e.g., John Mack Faragher, *A Great and Noble Scheme: The Tragic Story of the Expulsion of the French Acadians from Their American Homeland* (New York: W. W. Norton, 2005).

76. Wellcome, *Story of Metlakahtla*, title page, quoting the *Providence Journal*. There was also some sympathy for the Tsimshian in Victoria, B.C., where a number of Americans lived. In the words of one B.C. resident in a letter sent to the *Chicago Tribune*, they had "moved from British Columbia to escape the rapacity of greedy whites. When they had built up old Metlakahtla, turning that lonely spot into a thriving village, making the valueless region worth something, the land grabbers of Victoria saw a splendid chance to get something for nothing and worked on the provincial government to sell them the Indians' lands. They accomplished their purpose, and these Tsimsheans fled from that unjust Government to the shelter of the Stars and Stripes." Joseph D. Wilson, Victoria, B.C., to Editor, *Chicago Tribune*, September 4, 1897, NARA, RG 200, box 92, folder 85, document 19.

77. Wellcome to Editor, *New York Herald*, June 18, 1887.

78. C. B. Stowell, Hudson, Michigan, to George Spalding, Member of Congress, Second District, Michigan, April 25, 1898, letter forwarded by Binger Hermann, Commissioner of General Land Office, to the Secretary of the Interior, Washington, D.C., May 1898, NARA, RG 200, box 92, folder 85, document 19.

79. As Charles Manderson, the chair of the Senate Committee on the Territories, which was considering whether to set aside a reserve for the Metlakatlans, observed in 1890: "They are of course not natives of this country as the native Indians of Alaska are under our treaty of purchase from Russia, and they must become in the end, before they can acquire this property, naturalized citizens of the United States." Excerpt from *Congressional Record*, 51st Cong., 1st Sess., September 18, 1890, 10092–93, NARA, RG 200, box 92, folder 85, document 3-B.

80. John S. Bugbee, U.S. District Judge, District of Alaska, Sitka, Alaska, to William Duncan, Metlakatla, Alaska, September 28, 1890, citing *In re* Ah Yup, 5 Sawy. 155 (1878), and *In re* Camille, 6 Sawy. 541 (1880), NARA, RG 200, box 92, folder 85, document 8-B. Although race was not a barrier to Duncan's ability to become a U.S. citizen, he did not file the then required notice of his intention to become a citizen until May 5, 1895. Tingle, "Salmon Fisheries of Alaska," 4–8.

81. *In re* Camille, 6 Sawy. 541 (1880), citing *In re* Ah Yup, 5 Sawy. 155 (1878), holding that "a native of China, of the Mongolian race, is not entitled to become a citizen of the United States" because "a Mongolian is not a 'white person.'"

82. Bugbee to Duncan, September 28, 1890.

83. Fagan report, in Tingle, "Salmon Fisheries of Alaska," 4–8.

84. For a detailed discussion of the factors considered in determining the location of the U.S.-Canada border, see chapter 1.

85. The draft bill contemplated "that until otherwise provided by law, the . . . Annette Islands, situated in Alexander Archipelago in Southeastern Alaska, on the north side of Dixon's Entrance, be . . . set apart as a reservation for the use of the Metlakahtla Indians, and those native people who have recently emigrated from British Columbia to Alaska, and such other Alaskan natives as may join them, to be held and used by them in common, under such rules and regulations and subject to such restrictions, as may be prescribed

from time to time by the Secretary of the Interior." "An act providing for the acquisition of land for town sites and commercial purposes in Alaska, and for other purposes," Draft Bill S. 1859, House of Representatives, 51st Cong., 1st Sess., February 17, 1890, NARA, RG 200, box 92, folder 85, document 3-B.

86. Excerpts from *Congressional Record*, 51st Cong., 1st Sess., September 18, 1890, 10092–93.

87. Excerpt from *Congressional Record*, 51st Cong., 1st Sess., September 18, 1890, 10092–93.

88. Charles F. Manderson, a senator from Nebraska who supported setting aside Annette Island for the exclusive use of the Tsimshian, explained in 1890: "[The New Metlakatlans] are of course not natives of the country as the native Indians of Alaska are under our treaty of purchase from Russia, and they must become in the end, before they can acquire this property, naturalized citizens of the United States. The proposition . . . is simply to allow this band of Indians to remain there under such rules and regulations as the Secretary of the Interior may impose and give them some recognized footing at that place." *Congressional Record*, 51st Cong., 1st Sess., September 18, 1890, 10092–93. See also An Act to Repeal Timber Culture Laws and for Other Purposes, §15, ch. 561, 26 Stat. 1095, 1101 (1891), NARA, RG 200, box 92, folder 85, document 3-B. H.R. 4209, S. 2833, 55th Cong., 2d Sess. (1898).

89. O. H. Platt, Houghton, Mifflin, while in Washington, D.C., to H. O. Houghton, Boston Office, December 22, 1894, NARA, RG 200, box 116, folder 382, document 20.

90. See Andrea Geiger, *Subverting Exclusion: Transpacific Encounters with Race, Caste, and Borders, 1885–1928* (New Haven, Conn.: Yale University Press, 2011), 147, citing D. M. Eberts, B.C. Attorney General, to Christopher Robinson, Esq., K.C., London, June 29, 1901, published in the *Victoria Daily Colonist*, January 3, 1903. Chapter 3 offers a detailed discussion of the denial of the right to vote to both Asian immigrants and those identified as Indians under the terms of Canada's Indian Act in British Columbia.

91. As Frank Wood noted when he appeared before the Board of Indian Commissioners in 1894, "'exclusive use' is not a legal title." Excerpt from *Twenty-Sixth Annual Report of the Board of Indian Commissioners, 1894*, 127–28. It was only in 1923 that the Annette Island Reserve was acknowledged to be Indian Country and that Metlakatlans were given the right to vote. E. C. Hudson, Metlakatla, Alaska, to the Secretary of the Interior, Washington, D.C., September 1, 1934, NARA, RG 200, box 211, October–December 1934.

92. Franklin K. Lane, Secretary of the Interior, "Memorandum regarding Annette Island Reserve, Alaska," 1915, Department Legal Decisions, included in Duncan, "Statement of the Metlakahtla Mission," 132.

93. Excerpt from a letter from James G. Swan, in *Seal and Salmon Fisheries*, 2–3. Swan's concerns about the treaty system were based in part on his conviction that treaties gave those he called "thieving Indian agents" and men of "weak moral stamina" a free hand. Swan, in *Seal and Salmon Fisheries*, 3.

94. "A Definite Policy Needed," excerpt from the Annual Report of the Governor of Alaska (L. E. Knapp) to the Secretary of the Interior, 1891, 36, NARA, RG 200, box 92, folder 85, document 3-B.

95. Excerpt from *Congressional Record*, 51st Cong., 1st Sess., September 18, 1890, 10092–93.

96. "Annette Island," in John G. Brady, Report from the Governor of Alaska to the Secretary of the Interior, 1901, 30, NARA, RG 200, box 96, folder 86, document 6.

97. See, e.g., reports of "numerous murmurs of discontent and jealousy expressed by native Alaska Indians at the fact of the Government having given British Columbia Indians a large island home, when they are not granted the same benefits." Tingle, "Salmon Fisheries of Alaska," 4–8. It was not until 1971 that Congress acknowledged the need to resolve the well-founded claims of Aboriginal title in Alaska.

98. "An act providing for the acquisition of land for town sites and commercial purposes in Alaska, and for other purposes," Draft Bill S. 1859. "Dahl" is now spelled Dall.

99. Report to accompany Draft Bill S. 1859, H.R. 2450, House of Representatives, 51st Cong., 1st Sess., February 17, 1890, 6, NARA, RG 200, box 176, folder: American Government Documents. See also James Wickersham, "Japanese Art on Puget Sound," *American Antiquarian and Oriental Journal* 16, no. 2 (March 1894): 81, stating that "there is no finer boat built than the Haidah canoe . . . its lines are perfect and it is made so large, strong, sea-worthy, and yet light, that they fearlessly go far into the open ocean to attack the whale. As fishermen they excel all races . . . they had located the halibut and seal fisheries and frequented them from ancient times. They have names for each fish and each kind of animal life in the waters."

100. Report from Special Agent W. G. Morris, San Francisco, California, July 28, 1876, NARA, RG 200, box 92, folder 84, document 44.

101. M. P. Berry, Collector, to B. H. Bristow, Secretary of the Treasury, Washington, D.C., May 28 and July 28, 1876, NARA, RG 200, box 92, folder 85, document 14, adding that he suspected that Duncan had been "smuggling goods in Chilcat and other places in Alaska Territory for a great number of years," notwithstanding that the eight canoes he had spotted were Haida canoes.

102. See British Columbia, *Report of the Royal Commission on Indian Affairs for British Columbia* (Victoria, B.C.: Acme Press, 1916) (McKenna-McBride Report), Testimony of Skidegate Indian Council members, Skidegate, B.C., September 13, 1913. The testimony of the Indian Agent for the Queen Charlotte Agency likewise reveals that the Haida had been constant in their insistence that they retained title to their land. Testimony of Thomas Deasy, S.S. *Queen City*, September 15, 1913, 50. Some Haida fiercely resisted British intrusion during the colonial period. See, e.g., *Provincial Museum of Natural History and Anthropology Report for the Year 1957*, 54–59.

103. For a detailed discussion of Meiji emigration policy and emigrants' reasons for going abroad, see, e.g., Geiger, *Subverting Exclusion*, 26, 29, 40–43, 72–75.

104. Robert Tomlinson, Meanskinisht, Skeena River, to William Duncan, October 27, 1897, NARA, RG 200, box 116, folder 382, document 37, reporting that a number of Indigenous people along the Skeena River were "proposing to start for Skagway in the Spring." Sidney L. Harring notes that Indigenous people participated in all aspects of the gold rush. Sidney L. Harring, *White Man's Law: Native People in Nineteenth-Century Canadian Jurisprudence* (Toronto: University of Toronto Press for the Osgood Society for Canadian Legal History, 1998), 202–3.

105. See Geiger, *Subverting Exclusion*, 73; and see, generally, Kenneth B. Pyle, *The Making of Modern Japan*, 2nd ed. (Lexington, Mass.: D. C. Heath, 1996).

106. See, e.g., Pyle, *Making of Modern Japan*, 77–78.

107. Canada, Census, 1891, for Metlakatla, B.C. Although the name of the young Japanese man is written as Salamoto, it was almost certainly Sakamoto. There is no "l" in the Japanese

language, and Sakamoto is a fairly common family name. The census reflects that both of Mary's parents were also born in British Columbia. This, taken together with their residence in the Tsimshian community, suggests that she had deep ancestral ties to the region.

108. In 1891, the U.S. Department of Education estimated the population of Alaska as a whole at 33,000, including, in southeastern Alaska, 1,900 whites, half of them foreign-born and not U.S. citizens, "327 Chinamen, 2 Japanese, and 4 colored persons, making a total, with the 5,834 natives" of just over 8,000 people. Excerpt from bound volume of Reports of Governor of Alaska, 1884–1900 [1891 Report], re Education, 35, NARA, RG 200, box 92, folder 85, document 5-B.

109. Ikeda, *Arasuka hyōzan ryokō*, 11. For a detailed description of the routes used by gold seekers to reach the Klondike goldfields, see Morse, *Nature of Gold*, 4–5.

110. John J. Stephan, *The Kuril Islands: Russo-Japanese Frontier in the Pacific* (Oxford, U.K.: Clarendon Press, 1974), 1, 35. On Kobayashi, see Denbei Kobayashi, "Biographical History," Denbei Kobayashi Fonds (1878–1968), University of British Columbia Library, Rare Books and Special Collections, Vancouver.

111. For a detailed discussion of efforts to encourage "*eta*," a disparaging term historically used to refer to former outcastes in Japan, to emigrate to Hokkaido during the late Tokugawa and early Meiji eras, see Noah McCormack, "*Buraku* Emigration in the Meiji Era—Other Ways to Become 'Japanese,'" *East Asian History* 23 (June 2002): 90–100. See also John A. Harrison, *Japan's Northern Frontier: A Preliminary Study in Colonization and Expansion with Special Reference to the Relations of Japan and Russia* (Gainesville: University of Florida, Press, 1953), 74, noting the presence of settlers of the "poorest class." For a detailed description of historical caste and status categories and their significance, see Geiger, *Subverting Exclusion*, 16–24. Although outcaste status was abolished in 1871, prejudice directed at former members of outcaste groups and their descendants persisted.

112. For the appeal of the open vistas of the North American West in this context, see Geiger, *Subverting Exclusion*, 72–74. See also Yasuo Okada, "The Japanese Image of the American West," *Western Historical Quarterly* 19, no. 2 (May 1988): 143, noting that Meiji-era geography texts described the North American West as "still undeveloped wilderness" in the 1850s.

113. W. M. Rice, "Report of the United States Commissioner Appointed to Inquire into Japanese Emigration," May 2, 1899, in Canada, *Report of the Royal Commission on Chinese and Japanese Immigration, 1902*, 2 Edward VII, Sessional Paper No. 54 (Ottawa: S. E. Dawson, printer to the King's Most Excellent Majesty, 1902), 424. See also Inazo Nitobe, *Japan: Some Phases of Her Problems and Development* (London: Ernest Benn, 1931), 277, describing "extensive plains of virgin land in Hokkaido." Other works by Nitobe are discussed in chapters 1, 3, and 5.

114. Ikeda, *Arasuka hyōzan ryokō*, 1.

115. Emiko Ohnuki-Tierney translates *dojin* as "dirt or earth people" and observes that the term was also used to refer to people from Africa and the Philippines. Emiko Ohnuki-Tierney, "A Conceptual Model for the Historical Relationship between the Self and the Internal and External Others," in *Making Majorities: Constituting the Nation in Japan, Korea, China, Malaysia, Fiji, Turkey, and the United States*, ed. Dru C. Gladney (Stanford, Calif.: Stanford University Press, 1998), 46. Ohnuki-Tierney argues that use of the "label *dojin* (the dirt or earth people)" to refer to Ainu people is important to understanding Japanese

attitudes to Japan's Indigenous people. Also telling is the fact that the Hokkaido Kyūdojin Hogo Hō ([Hokkaido Former Natives Protection Act], Law No. 27, March 1, 1899) referred to the Ainu as *kyūdojin*, or former *dojin*; if the term *dojin* was simply a generic term used to refer to Japan's Indigenous people, there would be no need to refer to the Ainu as "former *dojin*." The Hokkaido Kyūdojin Hogo Hō remained in force through July 1997, when it was rescinded and replaced by the Ainu Cultural Promotion Law. The preferred term used to refer to Indigenous people today is *genjūmin* (original/living/people) or, for North America, simply *"indeien."* Contemporary dictionaries no longer list *dojin* as a word, but English-Japanese dictionaries published before 1920 cite it as the equivalent of "aborigine." See, e.g., Ernest Mason Satow and Ishibashi Masakata, *An English-Japanese Dictionary of the Spoken Language*, 4th ed. (Tokyo: Sanseidō, 1919). Parts of this discussion regarding the use and meaning of the term *dojin* were originally published in Andrea Geiger, "Reframing Race and Place: Locating Japanese Immigrants in Relation to Indigenous Peoples in the North American West, 1880–1940," *Southern California Quarterly* 96, no. 3 (2014): 253–70, and are republished here with permission.

116. Francis Brinkley, *Japan: Its History, Arts, and Literature* (Boston: J. B. Millet, 1920), 1:35; originally published circa 1896.

117. For the assumption that the displacement of Indigenous people by Euro-Americans was inevitable, see Okada, "Japanese Image of the American West," 148. For perceptions of the Ainu as primitive, backward, and an uncivilized or dying race, see William W. Fitzhugh, "Ainu Ethnicity: A History," in *Ainu: Spirit of a Northern People*, ed. William W. Fitzhugh and Chisato O. Dubreuil (Washington, D.C.: Arctic Studies Center, National Museum of Natural History, Smithsonian Institution in association with University of Washington Press, 1999), 15; Emiko Ohnuki-Tierney, "The Ainu Colonization and the Development of 'Agrarian Japan'—a Symbolic Interpretation," in *New Directions in the Study of Meiji Japan*, ed. Helen Hardacre and Adam L. Kern (Leiden: Brill, 1997), 668; and Katarina Sjöberg, "Redefining the Past, Taking Charge of the Present, Appropriating the Future: The Hokkaido Ainu Case," in *Cultural Genocide and Asian State Peripheries*, ed. Barry Sautman (New York: Palgrave Macmillan, 2006), 39, 42.

118. Nakayama Jinshiro, ed., *Kanada dōhō hatten taikan: Zen* (Encyclopedia of Japanese in Canada: Complete) (Tokyo: Japan Times, 1921), 1876. This edition is a compilation of several previous histories of Japanese in Canada edited by Nakayama. Although this compilation was published in Tokyo, the earlier histories incorporated into it were originally published in Vancouver, B.C. References in *Kanada dōhō hatten taikan: Zen* to Native people in Canada as *dojin* are too numerous to cite, but see, for example, pages 477–78, where *dojin* is used several times in the context of discussing the role of Indigenous people in the canneries. For a detailed description of the journey of the group of nine Ainu individuals (members of four families) who made the trip to St. Louis to participate in the 1904 Louisiana Purchase Exposition with University of Chicago anthropology professor Frederick Starr, see James W. Vanstone, "The Ainu Group at the Louisiana Purchase Exposition, 1904," *Arctic Anthropology* 30, no. 2 (1993): 77–91. Anthropologists described the Ainu who attended the exposition as "the most kindly and cleanly, the most courteous and confiding, the most peaceful and gentle of all the peoples—brown, yellow, red, black, or white—assembled in St. Louis." J. W. Buel, ed., *Louisiana and the Fair* (St. Louis: World's Progress Publishing, 1904), 5:vii (anthropology).

119. Okada, "Japanese Image of the American West," 148. For further information about Fukuzawa Yukichi, see Pyle, *Making of Modern Japan*, 80–82. Fukuzawa played an important role in shaping Japanese perceptions of the West during the Meiji period.

120. Hisamatsu Yoshinori, *Shokumin Iseki* (The great achievements of our colonists) (Tokyo: Keiseisha, Meiji 35 [1902]), 37–38. See also Yujin Yaguchi, "Japan's 'Savage': The Significance of the Ainu in the Intercultural History of Japan and the United States," *Proceedings of the Kyoto American Studies Summer Seminar* (Ritsumeikan University), 1998, 107–17, analyzing the autobiography of Jenichiro Oyabe, *A Japanese Robinson Crusoe* (Boston: Pilgrim Press, 1898). For a discussion of negative connotations associated with the notion of rootlessness, see Geiger, *Subverting Exclusion*, 46.

121. *Yomiuri Shimbun*, 28th day of 10th month, Meiji 20 (1887). This appears to have been a belated report about Geronimo's surrender to General Crook at Skeleton Canyon, Arizona, on September 4, 1886.

122. Okada, "Japanese Image of the American West," 148, citing Nakai Hiroshi, *Manyu Kitei* (Travels) (1877), 335–36.

123. Yamazaki Yasushi et al., *Sokuseki* (Footprint) (n.p., 1942), chap. 21, 189–91. Translations by Masaki Watanabe.

124. See Ito, *Issei*, 361; and Kazuo Ito, *Hokubei hyakunen zakura* (Tokyo: Hokubei Hyakunenzakura Jikkō Inkai, 1969), 440.

125. *The Alaskan*, November 19 and 26, 1887, and January 21, 1888, and the *North Star*, March 1888, quoted in Ted C. Hinckley, *The Canoe Rocks: Alaska's Tlingit and the Euramerican Frontier, 1800–1912* (Lanham: University Press of America, 1996), 372.

126. Ikeda, *Arasuka hyōzan ryokō*, 156. The Chinook word *siwash* stems from the French word *sauvage*. Alexandra Harmon, ed., *The Power of Promises: Rethinking Indian Treaties in the Pacific Northwest* (Seattle: University of Washington Press, 2008), 3, 27n2. There is evidence that white settlers were aware that the term was offensive. "The Northland: Information for Everybody," *Douglas Island News* (Alaska), May 8, 1907, noting that "Sitka Indians . . . object to being called Siwashes."

127. Nakayama Jinshiro, ed., *Kanada dōhō hatten taikan: Furoku* (Encyclopedia of Japanese in Canada: Supplement) (Vancouver, B.C., 1921), 116–17, 161–62. Writing in the 1970s, Rintaro Hayashi also imagined that Japanese had a special "blood" connection to the Indigenous people who lived along these western shores and in Alaska. Hayashi Rintaro, *Kuroshio no hate ni* (At the end of the black current) (Tokyo: Nichibo Shuppansha, 1971), 15, 17–18. Although Hayashi wrote in Japanese, he was a Japanese Canadian who had generally adopted the Western custom of listing his given name first. The notion that the Indigenous people of Alaska were descended from Japanese to at least some degree was also shared by U.S. government officials, who reported, for example, "All are strongly built, rather short and by their habits of living inured to hardship and endurance. . . . They have an Asiatic cast of features and coast people are generally thought to have originated from Japanese stock." Reports of Governor of Alaska, 1884–1900 [1890 Report], re Education, 22–23, NARA, RG 200, box 92, folder 85, document 3-C. See also Horace Davis, *Record of Japanese Vessels Driven upon the North-West Coast of America and Its Outlying Islands* (Worcester, Mass.: Charles Hamilton, 1872), 5, 21, concluding that there existed "the possibility of an admixture of Japanese blood on the northwest coast of America" based on the number of vessels known to have drifted ashore—nine in 1872.

128. Nakayama, *Kanada dōhō hatten taikan: Furoku*, 161–62, stating that some Haida people so closely resembled Japanese that they could have been mistaken for one another. Ikeda also commented that Native Alaskans looked like Japanese. Ikeda, *Arasuka hyōzan ryokō*, 12. Jujiro Wada, in turn, is said to have felt at home in Alaska in part because he felt that the Indigenous people he encountered looked like him. Fumi Torigai and Taeko Torigai, "The Life of Jujiro Wada" (Whitehorse, Yukon: Torigai Translation Services, August 30, 2006), 1–2 (summary of Yūji Tani, *Ōrora ni kakeru samurai* [Tokyo: Yama to Keikokusha, 1995]). Copy available through the Yukon Archives, Whitehorse, Yukon, Asian History of the Yukon Display Collection, 2006/146, file 21.

129. Joshua L. Reid, *The Sea Is My Country: The Maritime World of the Makahs* (New Haven, Conn.: Yale University Press, 2015), 103. Other accounts include Kawada Shoryo, *Drifting toward the Southeast: The Story of Five Japanese Castaways*, trans. Junya Nagakuni and Junji Kitadai (New Bedford, Mass.: Spinner Publications, 2003); John E. Van Sant, *Pacific Pioneers: Japanese Journeys to America and Hawaii, 1850–80* (Urbana: University of Illinois Press, 2000); and Frederik Schodt, *Native American in the Land of the Shogun: Ranald MacDonald and the Opening of Japan* (Berkeley, Calif.: Stone Bridge Press, 2003).

130. Ito, *Issei*, 782–83, 785, citing Zaibei Nihonjinkai, *Zaibeinihonjinshi*. Curiously, Ito gives the names of the three survivors as Suzuki Kinzo, Gan, and Kyodo, although others give their names as Iwakichi (age 28), Kyūkichi (age 15), and Otokichi (age 14). See Stephen W. Kohl, "Strangers in a Strange Land: Japanese Castaways and the Opening of Japan," *Pacific Northwest Quarterly* 73, no. 1 (January 1982): 21, citing Akira Haruna, *Nippon Otokichi hyōryūki* [An account of the Otokichi of Japan] (Tokyo, 1979), 29, 38.

131. Kohl, "Strangers in a Strange Land," 21, quoting E. E. Rich, ed., *The Letters of John McLoughlin from Fort Vancouver to the Governor and Committee*, vol. 1, *First Series, 1825–38* (Toronto, 1941), 128 (letter of November 18, 1834).

132. Donald Orth, *Dictionary of Alaska Place Names*, Geological Survey Professional Paper 567 (Washington, D.C.: Government Printing Office, 1967), 470; Katherine Plummer, *A Japanese Glimpse at the Outside World, 1839–1843* (Fairbanks, Alaska: Limestone Press, 1991), n.p., cited in *Alaska's Japanese Pioneers: Faces, Voices, Stories*, by Ronald K. Inouye, Carol Hoshiko, and Kazumi Heshiki (Fairbanks: Alaska's Japanese Pioneers Research Project, 1994), 7–8. See also Eliza Ruhamah Scidmore, *Appleton's Guide-Book to Alaska and the Northwest Coast* (New York: D. Appleton, 1899), 123, noting that "Japonski" means "Japan" and that it was so named because a Japanese fishing vessel washed ashore there in 1805.

133. Zaibei Nihonjinkai, *Zaibeinihonjinshi*, 6–8. See also "Gohei: The Castaway," *Japan Magazine* 3 (April 1910): 225–27, describing the adventures of Zeniya Gohei, who defied the shogunate's bar against vessels larger than five hundred *koku* in size to trade with foreign ships in and around the Kuril Islands, only to be caught in a storm and to be cast ashore on the California coast.

134. Ito, *Issei*, 371–72.

135. In his autobiographical novel, Tooru J. Kanazawa reports that Wada was also known as James Wada and that his given name was sometimes shortened to Ju or misspelled as Jujuiro or Jujira. See Tooru J. Kanazawa, *Sushi and Sourdough: A Novel* (Seattle: University of Washington Press, 1989), 61. See also Ed Ferrell, comp. and ed., *Biographies of Alaska-Yukon Pioneers, 1850–1950* (Bowie, Md.: Heritage Books, 1997), 3:310.

136. Although some aspects of Wada's story are shrouded by myth and conflicting accounts of certain events, his is the most well-documented record of an early Japanese settler in the Alaska-Yukon region. This is due in part to the efforts of Yūji Tani, author of *Ōrora ni kakeru samurai* [The samurai dog-musher under the northern lights] (Tokyo: Yama to Kei-kokusha, 1995), but it is also a function of the fact that Wada's story captured the imagination of many newspaper reporters in Alaska and the Yukon during his lifetime.

137. Torigai and Torigai, "Life of Jujiro Wada," 1–2; Tani, *Ōrora ni kakeru samurai*. The whaling ship Wada joined was the *Balaena* and its captain was H. H. Norwood, who was made an inspector of mines in the Klondike River region of the Yukon in the summer of 1897 based on his experience navigating along the Arctic coast as the captain of a whaling vessel. *The Register* (Berwick, Nova Scotia), August 25, 1897.

138. Torigai and Torigai, "Life of Jujiro Wada," 1–2; Tani, *Ōrora ni kakeru samurai*.

139. For a detailed discussion of the Japanese status system (*mibunsei*), including ways in which former samurai were affected by the social changes that followed the Meiji Restoration and efforts to persuade both former samurai and members of what had been designated outcaste groups to emigrate to Hokkaido, see David L. Howell, *Geographies of Identity in Nineteenth Century Japan* (Berkeley: University of California Press, 2005), 75, 146; Noah McCormack, "Buraku Emigration in the Meiji Era—Other Ways to Become 'Japanese,'" East Asian History 23 (June 2002): 87–108; Geiger, *Subverting Exclusion*, 23–24, 93.

140. The Skagway arrival record misspells both Jujiro (as Jupura) and Hakodate (Haka-date), but the intended meaning is clear. United States, Lists of Aliens Arriving at Skagway (White Pass), Alaska, October 1906–1934, M2017, NARA. Another arrival record reflects that Wada arrived in Ketchikan, Alaska, on the *Princess Mary* on May 3, 1923. United States, Alphabetical Index of Alien Arrivals at Eagle, Hyder, Ketchikan, Nome, and Skagway, Alaska, June 1906-August 1946, M2016, NARA. Also possible is that Hakodate was the ship's port of embarkation and that Wada joined it when it stopped at Seattle or Victoria. While some sources say that Wada did not return to Japan after 1898, when he visited his mother for the last time, his family reportedly lost contact with him during the 1920s and might not have known if he did make a trip to Hokkaido during this period.

141. "List of persons arriving and passing through Forty Mile during the month of April 1908," Yukon Archives, Asian History of the Yukon Display Collection, 2006/146, file 21.

142. Ferrell, *Biographies of Alaska-Yukon Pioneers*, 3:310.

143. Charles Frederick Stansbury, *Klondike: The Land of Gold (Containing All Available Practical Information of Every Description concerning the New Gold Fields . . . [Including] a Digest of the Mining Laws of the United States and Canada)* (New York: F. Tennyson Neely, 1897), 121–22. Mining law was the only body of U.S. law extended to Alaska for over two decades after the United States acquired Russia's interests in the region. Report, Draft Bill S. 1859, H.R. 2450, House of Representatives, 51st Cong., 1st Sess., February 17, 1890, 1, NARA, RG 200, box 176.

144. Frank Cotter, "Ju Wada as I Knew Him," pt. 3, *The Japanese American Courier* (San Francisco), 1937, reporting that he saw Wada's citizenship application. See also Torigai and Torigai, "Life of Jujiro Wada," 3, citing *Nome News*, May 8, 1901, reporting that a Japanese prospector had arrived in Nome to apply for U.S. citizenship but was refused.

145. See, e.g., Cotter, "Ju Wada as I Knew Him"; "Rich Strike Is Made in the Tanana," *Yukon Sun*, January 17, 1903; "Wada Is Champion," *Dawson Daily News*, June 25, 1907; "Gold Is

Located," *Dawson Daily News*, March 16, 1908; and "Wada the Jap at Fairbanks," *Dawson Daily News*, January 12, 1909.

146. "Wada, Famous Jap Musher, Comes into His Own in North: After Spending Nearly Twenty Years in Alaska and Making Many Extraordinary Journeys, He Strikes Gold," *Seattle Daily Times*, July 21, 1912.

147. Canada, Department of the Interior, Yukon Territory, Office of the Gold Commissioner, Application for Grant of Placer Mining No. 188, April 29, 1908. Copy in the possession of the Yukon Archives.

148. "Discovery Located: Wada Applies for Claims on High Cache Creek, in Arctic," *Dawson Daily News*, April 29, 1908. See also Stansbury, *Klondike*, 136–48.

149. United States, Alaska Alien Arrivals, 1906–1949, M2016.

150. Library and Archives Canada, Corporations Branch, Department of the Secretary of State, Annual Returns under the Companies Act, vol. 2020, no. 21862. Copy in the possession of the Yukon Archives.

151. A woman who claimed to be his daughter would later try to track him down; Wada reportedly acknowledged her as such. "Wada Is Forerunner," *Dawson Daily News*, November 20, 1909.

152. In 1908, for example, the *Dawson Daily News* reported that Wada "had undergone a metamorphosis, and instead of fur trimmed parka and cap, he stood forth a fashion plate in a neat clay worsted suit, pressed to a chappie's taste, and to finish his appearance was a brown derby, fancy socks, rivaling those of Dad's Boy in baseball days and a fine pair of shoes." "Discovery Located," *Dawson Daily News*.

153. As discussed in chapter 5, Wada was accused of being a spy following the First World War, an accusation that continued to haunt him as the Second World War approached. See, e.g., "America Warned of Japanese Move for Grip on Alaska: Treasure Must Be Guarded; Mining Man from Interior Says Japan Is Casting Covetous Eyes on Defenseless Territory, Jap Wada Declared to Be Agent of Tokio Government Making Maps of Harbors and Mines," *Cordova Daily Times*, 1923. Publication of a claim that Wada was a spy is also reported in R. N. DeArmond, "This Is My Country," *Alaska Magazine*, March 1988, 74. The accuser reportedly later rescinded the claim.

154. See, e.g., "Wada Is on Yukon: Dawson's Phenomenal Empire Builder in a New Contest," *Dawson Daily News*, May 19, 1908; Helen Hegener, "Jujiro Wada: Co-founder of Fairbanks and Iditarod Trailblazer," *Alaska Dispatch*, April 13, 2010. In the 1930s, Wada would also be embraced in Japan, itself an expanding imperial power, as someone who typified the Japanese spirit given his success in contending both with the harsh climate and with racial animus.

155. See, e.g., "Wada Is King of Esquimos," *Yukon World*, March 24, 1907. Tani reports the complaints about Wada being identified as "king" of an Inuit group. Torigai and Torigai, "Life of Jujiro Wada," 4, citing Tani, *Ōrora ni kakeru samurai*. For Frank Yasuda, see interview with Hana Yasuda Kangas, interview by Ronald K. Inouye, Palmer, Alaska, December 2, 1990, Alaska's Japanese Pioneers Research Project Records, 1990–1991 (HMC-0374) (AJPRP), Archives and Special Collections, Consortium Library, University of Anchorage, Anchorage, Alaska, transcript, 12–13, 15, 17; Inouye, Hoshiko, and Heshiki, *Alaska's Japanese Pioneers*, 50–51, interview with Hana Yasuda Kangas, noting that Frank (Kyōsuke) Yasuda was from Ishinomaki in Miyagi-ken on the northeastern coast of Japan and that Hana's mother's name was Nevalo. Hana was born on November 24, 1914, in Beaver, Alaska, and

had three sisters. Beaver was "a community of Inupiat Eskimos and Gwichin Athapaskan Indians on the Yukon River near the Chandalar mining country and a trading post . . . which served local and regional trappers and miners."

156. Shimada Saburō and Ariiso Toshirō, *Kaigai katsudō no nihonjin* (Japanese who are active overseas) (Tokyo: Shokado, Meiji 39 [1906]), 42–45. My thanks to Masaki Watanabe for his translation of this source. For a brief English-language biography of Frank Yasuda, see Charles C. Hawley and Thomas K. Bundtzen, "Frank Yasuda (1868–1958) and Nevelo Yasuda (1879–1966)," Alaska Mining Hall of Fame Foundation, Fairbanks, Alaska, alaska-mininghalloffame.org/inductees/Yasuda.php. For his forced removal from Alaska in 1942 and his forced confinement in the contiguous states, see chapter 5.

157. Records show, for example, that Wada was in San Pedro working in California at a fish processing plant in the 1920s. See, e.g., J. Wada, Van Camp Sea Food Company, San Pedro, California, to Sunada [no first name given], April 26, 1916. Copy in the possession of the Yukon Archives, file 21. Sunada was a cousin who reportedly lived in Wyoming and whom Wada visited at times. In 1921, Wada also guided a group of investors to an area where oil had been found near Great Slave Lake in the Northwest Territories. "Wada the Jap Is Taking Party to Northern Fields: Prospector and Fur Trader Is Making Overland Trip after Oil," *Edmonton Journal*, December 24, 1920; "Vancouver Group of Capitalists Will Profit by Wada's Fast Run: Japanese Prospector and Adventurer Has Returned from Dash to the Oil Fields; Staked Claims for Prominent Men on Pacific Coast," *Edmonton Journal*, April 11, 1921. In the 1930s, Jujiro Wada's exploits would also be celebrated in Japan as representative of the courageous and intrepid nature of Japanese who ventured abroad. Wada died in San Diego on March 5, 1937, at the age of sixty-two. State of California, County of San Diego, Certificate of Death No. 37-023109. Copy in the possession of the Yukon Archives.

158. For a detailed description of Ikeda Mine based on the diaries of the German American mining supervisor that Ikeda hired, see Andrea Geiger, "Haida Gwaii as North Pacific Borderland, Ikeda Mine as Alternative West: 1906–1910," *Pacific Northwest Quarterly* 108, no. 4 (Fall 2017): 119–33. See also the discussion of Ikeda Mine in chapter 4.

159. See Julie Cruikshank, *Do Glaciers Listen? Local Knowledge, Colonial Encounters, and Social Imagination* (Vancouver: UBC Press, 2005), 3, noting that in "Athapaskan and Tlingit oral tradition, glaciers take action and respond to their surroundings. They are sensitive to smells and they listen. They make moral judgments and they punish infractions." Cruikshank also explains that glaciers make "thunderous cracking and explosive noises" and notes that Aboriginal elders emphasize the importance of being quiet and humble while on a glacier. Cruikshank, *Do Glaciers Listen?*, 19, 69. One early Euro-American traveler in Alaska reported that Tlingit oral histories described glaciers as "children of the mountains" whose "parents hold them in their arms, dip their feet in the sea, [and] cover them with deep snows in winter." Hair seals, in turn, were regarded as "children of the glacier." Scidmore, *Appleton's Guide-Book*, 75–76. Scidmore was also told that one must "speak softly, tread lightly, and neither defile nor offend [a glacier] with crumb or odour of their food" lest the spirit of the glacier throw down icebergs that release great waves and cause great damage.

Chapter Three

1. Andrei Val'terovich Grinev, *The Tlingit Indians in Russian America, 1741–1867*, trans. Richard L. Bland and Katerina G. Solovjova (Lincoln: University of Nebraska Press, 2005), 26, noting the presence of Tlingit ḵwáan (villages) both in Atlin, B.C., and in Teslin, Yukon, just north of the B.C.-Yukon border, by the second half of the nineteenth century.

2. Christine Frances Dickinson and Diane Solie Smith, *Atlin: The Story of British Columbia's Last Gold Rush* (Atlin, B.C.: Atlin Historical Society, 1995), x, 17, 36, 41, also noting that the name of Atlin Lake is from the Tlingit word for "great water" or "tlen." See also *Atlin Claim*, March 20, 1902. Caribou Crossing, renamed Carcross in 1904, is a hunting and fishing site the Tlingit and Tagish people have occupied for as long as forty-five hundred years. Mike MacEacheran, "The Unlikely Home of the World's Smallest Desert," *BBC Travel*, June 22, 2018, https://www.bbc.com/travel/article/20180621-the-unlikely-home-of-the-worlds-smallest-desert.

3. In 1899, the lieutenant governor of British Columbia described his journey across Bennett and Atlin Lakes as "indescribably lovely." *Vancouver Daily Province*, July 31, 1899. For a detailed description of the journey, see W. D. MacBride and Barbara Kalen, "The Taku Tram," in *Pioneer Days in British Columbia* (Surrey, B.C.: Heritage House, 1973), 125. In 1901, a traveler explained that the journey to Atlin entailed a short trip on the White Pass & Yukon Railway over the pass to Bennett on the Yukon side of the provincial border, where travelers boarded a steamboat for the twenty-hour trip across Bennett and Tagish Lake to Taku. There another small train made the two-and-a-half-mile crossing to Atlin Lake, where they boarded a steamer to travel the last eight miles to Atlin, "beautiful for situation, the joy of the whole north." *Saturday Globe* (Toronto), April 27, 1901.

4. Dickinson and Smith, *Atlin*, x. See also *Atlin Claim*, March 8, 1902; *Vancouver Daily Province*, April 1, 1902; *Victoria Colonist*, April 2, 1902.

5. *Atlin Claim*, March 29, 1902; Guy Lawrence, "When the Riot Act Was Read at Atlin," *Shoulder Strap*, December 1949, 11–12; *Vancouver Daily Province*, May 14, 1902.

6. D. M. Eberts, Attorney General, to James Stables, [MLA], Victoria, B.C., March 17, 1902, British Columbia, Sessional Papers, 1902, 2 Ed. 7, 843–44. Atlin was connected to other parts of British Columbia by telegraph in September 1901. Dickinson and Smith, *Atlin*, 189–90.

7. *Vancouver Daily Province*, April 1, 1902, noting that "old man Ward," the leader of the miners, was reportedly "well known in Skagway," an observation that may have been intended to imply that he was American and not a British subject. Skagway was established in 1897, just one year before Atlin.

8. *Victoria Colonist*, April 2, 1902. The number of miners cited by various reporters range from 90 to 300. The figure of 150, taken from the account published in the *Victoria Colonist*, is described by Guy Lawrence, one of the special constables hired to monitor the miners, as among the most accurate, although details in his own later accounts also vary. See, e.g., Guy Lawrence, "Atlin Placer Camp," *Cariboo & Northwest Digest*, December 1950, 38, reporting that 300 miners marched to McKee Creek to intimidate thirty-eight Japanese.

9. Lawrence, "Altin Placer Camp," 39. If the rifles were intended as a bluff, the Atlin Mining Company had clearly miscalculated. The sight of the rifles reportedly triggered "a thrill of rage and disgust" among the miners who had gathered to watch their arrival. *Victoria Daily Colonist*, April 2, 1902.

10. *Atlin Claim*, March 29, 1902, noting that the miners warned that "there might be some trouble." See also *Victoria Colonist*, April 2, 1902, reporting that Thaine himself was "fearful of bloodshed."

11. *Atlin Claim*, March 29, 1902.

12. *Vancouver Daily Province*, May 14, 1907, stating that the miners had told the Japanese that "if they [did] not leave the camp forthwith," "they would be forcibly ejected" and that miners had "forcibly chased them down the trail."

13. *Vancouver Daily Province*, April 1, 1902. No record of their names appears to have been preserved.

14. *Atlin Claim*, March 29, 1902; April 5, 1902. See also, Dickinson and Smith, *Atlin*, 124.

15. *Atlin Claim*, March 29, 1902. See also *Atlin Claim*, April 5, 1902, describing the dispute surrounding the hiring of Japanese labor as having been "tranqually [*sic*] settled." For a description of Soapy Smith's activities in Skagway and his death, see William R. Hunt, *Distant Justice: Policing the Alaskan Frontier* (Norman: University of Oklahoma Press, 1987), 52–64. Ironically, Smith's death resulted from a confrontation with a group of local residents who organized in an effort to put an end to his activities themselves in the absence of effective law enforcement; in taking the law into their own hands, they were not unlike the Atlin miners who organized to drive the hired Japanese out of town. The *Atlin Claim* reported in 1902 that the *Alaska Travelers Guide* dated March 17, 1900, had disparaged Atlin as "a hoodoo of a mining camp": "first, the Canadians drove out all the white men with their Exclusion Act, and now they are taking in Japanese to work in the mines[.]" *Atlin Claim*, March 29, 1902. Note that the Alaska Boundary Tribunal had yet to determine whether Skagway was located on the U.S. or the Canadian side of the international border. See chapter 1.

16. "Alaskans Bar All Asiatics: Will Permit No More Coolies to Land at Skagway; Anti-Chinese Association Organizes Branches at Various Points," *San Francisco Call*, April 29, 1902.

17. Advertisement placed by A. C. Hirschfeld, *Atlin Claim*, August 30, 1902.

18. Dickinson and Smith, *Atlin*, 122, citing *Atlin Claim*, October 1, 1901.

19. "Japs for Manitoba," *Atlin Claim*, August 11, 1900. There is no indication that the plan succeeded. Doukhobors are a Christian sect, originally from Russia, whose members immigrated to Canada, where many settled in the west.

20. *Vancouver Daily Province*, May 14, 1907; "May Remove Japs by Force: Agitation against Orientals in Atlin," *Victoria Daily Times*, May 14, 1907, stating that the miners had declared that they would "driv[e] [the Japanese] out by force" if Ruffner did not "send out the Japs"; the white miners secured the cooperation of local businesspeople by threatening to boycott those who "would not sign a petition to send out the Japs." The miners had reportedly done the same in 1902, boycotting "storekeepers of the town [who] had served the Japanese while they were in the camp." *Vancouver Daily Province*, May 14, 1907. Although the *Vancouver Daily Province* reported that Ruffner had hired thirty-six Japanese, Dickinson and Smith report that just twenty-one arrived. Compare *Vancouver Daily Province*, April 5, 1907, with Dickinson and Smith, *Atlin*, 126, citing the *Atlin Claim*, April 20 and 27, 1907, and May 4, 1907.

21. *Vancouver Daily Province*, April 5, 1907. Ruffner's claim regarding the wages he paid to white laborers was disputed in a letter to the editor dated May 4, 1907, from someone in Atlin who referred to himself only as "Truth" and insisted that actual wages amounted to

$80.00 per month and that the going rate in the area was $3.50 an hour and board. *Vancouver Daily Province*, June 8, 1907.

22. *Victoria Daily Times*, May 14, 1907; *Atlin Claim*, October 26, 1907.

23. *Vancouver Daily Province*, April 19, 1907.

24. The *Yukon Sun* first reported that Asian migrants were required to post a bond to transit U.S. territory at Skagway in 1902. *Yukon Sun*, July 3, 1902. See also "Aliens Must Pay Tax at White Pass: Charge Made to Enter the Territory of Alaska from Yukon," *Fairbanks Daily Times*, September 25, 1908, explaining that "only Americans, Mexicans, Filipinos and Canadians [were] allowed to enter free" but that "Chinamen and Japan[ese] must show their papers." See also Nakayama Jinshiro, ed., *Kanada dōhō hatten taikan: Zen* (Encyclopedia of Japanese in Canada: Complete) (Tokyo: Japan Times, 1921), 1902, stating that Japanese entering the United States at Skagway were required to post a bond. For a detailed discussion of the transit privilege and efforts to burden it, see Andrea Geiger, "Caught in the Gap: The Transit Privilege and North America's Ambiguous Borders," in *Bridging National Borders in North America: Transnational and Comparative Histories*, ed. Benjamin H. Johnson and Andrew R. Graybill (Durham, N.C.: Duke University Press, 2010), 199–202.

25. Diane S. Smith, letter dated April 23, 2001, Atlin Historical Society, Atlin, B.C. Ruffner was reportedly on his way to the Klondike in 1898 when he learned about the gold strike on Pine Creek near Atlin and traveled there instead. Although he and his wife spent most of their lives in Atlin, they remained U.S. citizens. He had also invested in an apple orchard venture in Washington State that failed. Charles Hallam to Melissa Ruffner, November 18, 1998, Atlin Historical Society; *Daily Courier* (Yavapai County, Arizona), July 28, 1998.

26. Nakayama, *Kanada dōhō hatten taikan: Zen*, 1902. For a discussion of the importance of the family registration, or *koseki*, system in identifying an individual, see Andrea Geiger, *Subverting Exclusion: Transpacific Encounters with Race, Caste, and Borders, 1885–1928* (New Haven, Conn.: Yale University Press, 2011), 163.

27. For a more detailed discussion of the Alaska Boundary Tribunal, see chapter 1.

28. *The Globe* (Toronto), May 28, 1900; April 27, 1901.

29. William Sloan, "Driving White Labor from the North," *Atlin Claim*, August 31, 1907. For a detailed discussion of Japanese participation in the coastal fisheries, see chapter 4.

30. *Victoria Daily Times*, September 21, 1907; World's Outlook section, *Sydney Mail*, September 25, 1907.

31. *Vancouver Daily Province*, September 21, 1907; *Victoria Daily Times*, September 21, 1907; *Atlin Claim*, October 26, 1907. For a discussion of Japanese diplomats' concerns that Japanese not be conflated with Chinese "coolies," see Geiger, *Subverting Exclusion*, 57–62.

32. World's Outlook section, *Sydney Mail*, September 25, 1907; "Chinese Buy Revolvers for Defence in Case of Riots," *Vancouver Daily Province*, September 9, 1907. The latter article reported that although "few Japanese were seen buying arms," "hundreds of bottles . . . stones, clubs and bricks" had been stored on the roofs of Japanese businesses in Vancouver to "be hurled at whites in the streets below should any further trouble occur." The article added that hundreds of Japanese had "rushed the attacking force, armed with "sticks, clubs, iron bars, revolvers, knives and broken glass bottles" and that "many a white man was badly gashed about the arms, face, and neck." For Japanese perspectives on the riot and its aftermath, see Kazuo Ito, *Issei: A History of Japanese Immigrants in North America*, trans. Shinichiro Nakamura and Jean S. Gerard (Seattle, 1973), 101–9.

33. For another reference to Japanese as coolies, see Sloan, "Driving White Labor from the North." For a detailed discussion of efforts by Japanese diplomats to distinguish Japanese from Chinese labor based on presumed racial characteristics, see Geiger, *Subverting Exclusion*, 57–61.

34. *Atlin Claim*, October 26, 1907. Ishii Kikujiro, then imperial Japanese commissioner and vice minister for foreign affairs from 1908 to 1912, was appointed to the House of Peers in the Japanese Diet in 1916 and negotiated the Lansing-Ishii Agreement with the United States in 1917 and 1918. He also participated in the Paris Peace Conference. He is assumed to have died during a bombing raid on Tokyo in May 1945. The *Ottawa Free Press* suggested that the Vancouver Riot was timed to coincide with Ishii's visit. "Attack Was Planned to Impress Jap Official," *Ottawa Free Press*, September 10, 1907.

35. *Vancouver Daily Province*, September 11, 1907. The Japanese press avoided reporting news of the Vancouver Riot. *Vancouver Daily Province*, September 10, 1907. The consul's equating those who had attacked Japanese with "dogs" (*inu*) demonstrates his profound disdain for these individuals. See, e.g., Geiger, *Subverting Exclusion*, 78–79.

36. The article, filed by the Tokyo correspondent for the *London Times* after Japanese children were expelled from San Francisco's public schools, was republished in *The Globe* on October 22, 1906.

37. W. W. Bilsland reports that over time "almost every major mining company in Canada, Great Britain, and the United States conducted hydraulic mining operations in the Atlin area." W. W. Bilsland, "Atlin, 1898–1910: The Story of a Gold Boom," *British Columbia Historical Quarterly*, vol. 16 (1952): 135.

38. Guy Lawrence, "Atlin Miners Ignored Riot Act," *Vancouver Sun Magazine Supplement*, July 31, 1948. See also Rosalind Watson Young, "Mining in Atlin, British Columbia, 1898–1908," *The Journal of the Canadian Mining Institute*, vol. XII (1909), explaining that placer claims in British Columbia were originally limited to one hundred feet on each side, whereas those in the Yukon and the Northwest Territories were 250 feet.

39. According to *The Globe*, "Most of the men who went [to Atlin] were poor men and soon became 'dead broke.'" "A few men strike it rich where the gravel is not deep and there is gold, but as a rule, the gravel is too deep on bed rock to permit of individual miners doing much." *The Globe*, May 28, 1900.

40. *The Globe*, May 28, 1900. Although the Vancouver Riot was initially blamed on American agitators who had purportedly crossed into British Columbia from Washington State, Americans were less likely to have been a factor in Atlin because they and other foreigners had been barred from staking mining claims in British Columbia. The legislation passed in response to the initial rush of gold miners to northern British Columbia after the discovery of gold there in 1898 did not bar U.S. citizens who were prepared to become naturalized British subjects and "to acknowledge their obligations as citizens of the British Empire" from staking claims, nor did it bar them and other foreigners from working on claims staked by British subjects. C. A. Semlin, Provincial Secretary, to British Columbia's Lieutenant Governor in Council, June 6, 1899, "Report in regard to Petition of United States Residents of Atlin Complaining of Recent Mining Legislation of This Province, Chap. 50, 'An Act to Amend the Placer Mining Act,'" British Columbia, Sessional Papers, 1900, 63 Vict. 485–86. See also *Atlin Claim*, March 29, 1902; May 11, 1907. See also Lawrence, "Atlin Placer Camp," 39, reporting that after passage of the "Alien Law, several hundred men found

themselves stranded in the camp without means of support or the price of the fare to take them to other parts" in the "winter of 1900–1901." Patricia Roy notes that even in Vancouver, B.C., "the evidence for the thesis that American agitators caused the riot [there] was thin." Patricia E. Roy, *A White Man's Province: British Columbia Politicians and Chinese and Japanese Immigrants, 1858–1914* (Vancouver: UBC Press, 1989), 196.

41. Treaty of Commerce and Navigation between Great Britain and Japan, signed at London on July 16, 1894, Dominion of Canada, 5–6 Edward VII, Sessional Paper No. 117. Canada allowed the adhesion period to expire, but the fact that Great Britain was one of the parties to the agreement meant that the clauses that pertained to the rights afforded the subjects of each party to the agreement in the territory of the other were binding on all British subjects including those resident in Canada. J. Chamberlain, Downing Street, to the Officer Administering the Government of Canada, December 2, 1899, 5–6 Edward VII, Sessional Paper No. 117.

42. For a discussion of British Columbia's repeated efforts to pass a Natal Act that would have allowed immigration inspectors to impose a language test requiring Japanese immigrants to respond in some European language, see Geiger, *Subverting Exclusion*, 100–104. See also Adam M. McKeown, *Melancholy Order: Asian Migration and the Globalization of Borders* (New York: Columbia University Press), 185–195.

43. Anglo-Japanese Alliance, signed January 30, 1902. See also J. E. Thomas, *Modern Japan: A Social History since 1868* (London: Longman, 1996), 133.

44. *Atlin Claim*, March 29, 1902. In fact, King Edward VII—who became king when Queen Victoria died in 1901—may well have been aggrieved by those of his subjects whose actions violated principles not just of international law but also of criminal law, for example, the provisions of the Riot Act. For other examples of the resentment felt in B.C. in response to the Dominion government's disallowance of the Natal Acts, see, e.g., "Ottawa Holds the Jap Sacred: Imperial Edict Establishes That They Must Not Be Given the Chinese Medicine," *Daily Columbian*, December 19, 1902; William Hemmingway, "A Japanese Hornet's-Nest for John Bull," *Harper's Weekly*, October 5, 1907.

45. *Vancouver Daily Province*, April 4, 1907, explaining that this Natal Act was intended not just to target the Japanese but also to give British Columbia "the power to turn back to Hongkong the hordes of Hindus who are as undesired by the people of the oriental colony from which they come as they are to the citizens of this province" based on the assumption that "not one in a hundred Hindus reaching Vancouver from the Orient is capable of passing the test."

46. *Atlin Claim*, May 11, 1907.

47. "Japanese Invasion of B.C.," *Atlin Claim*, July 27, 1907, originally published in the *B.C. Saturday Sunset*.

48. Jean Pfaelzer, *Driven Out: The Forgotten War against Chinese Americans* (New York: Random House, 2007), xx–xxi, 115, 261–62, reporting that Indigenous farmworkers joined with white farmworkers in the attack on Chinese hop pickers in Squak Valley (now Issaquah), which caused the death of three Chinese who were shot in their tents. See also Benjamin Mountford and Stephen Tuffnell, eds., *A Global History of Gold Rushes* (Oakland: University of California Press, 2018), 115.

49. Jules Alexander Karlin, "The Anti-Chinese Outbreaks in Seattle, 1885–1886," *Pacific Northwest Quarterly* 39, no. 2 (April 1948): 104, 111; Phil Dougherty, "Mobs Forcibly Expel

Most of Seattle's Chinese Residents Beginning on February 7, 1886," *HistoryLink*, November 17, 2013, http://historylink.org/File/2745. Kornel Chang reports that Indigenous boat-owners sometimes transported Chinese and Japanese migrants across the ocean boundary that divided Canada and the United States in the Puget Sound region early in the twentieth century "for as little as three dollars," not withstanding the testimony of immigration officials that Chinese were willing to pay as much as a thousand dollars. Kornel Chang, *Pacific Connections: The Making of the U.S.-Canadian Borderlands* (Berkeley: University of California Press, 2012), 164, citing Fumiko Uyeda Groves interview, June 16, 1998. Densho: The Japanese American Legacy Project; letter from Immigrant Inspector P.L. Prentis to the Commissioner General of Immigration Frank P. Sargent, August 22, 1907, NARA, RG 85, Entry 9, 51686, Folder 17-A.

50. Anjuli Grantham, "Expulsion of Chinese from Oregon City, 1886," *Oregon Encyclopedia*, 2019, https://www.oregonencyclopedia.org/articles/expulsion_of_chinese_from_oregon _city_1886/#.YUzXf2LMLIU; Greg Nokes, "Chinese Massacre at Deep Creek," *Oregon Encyclopedia*, 2018, https://www.oregonencyclopedia.org/articles/chinese_massacre_at_deep _creek/#.YUzX5GLMLIU. Pfaelzer notes, however, that "the term *expulsion* doesn't fully represent the rage and violence of these purges." Pfaelzer, *Driven Out*, xxix.

51. John McKenna, Deputy U.S. Marshal, Douglas Island, Alaska, to Governor A. P. Swineford, Sitka, Alaska, in *Report of the Governor of Alaska to the Secretary of the Interior, 1885* (Washington, D.C.: Government Printing Office, 1885), 38–46.

52. Curtiss Takada Rooks, "Asian Americans in Subarctic America: A Multicultural, Multivariate Comparative Analysis" (Ph.D. diss., University of California, Irvine, 1996), 73–74; Pfaelzer, *Driven Out*, 270. In contrast to the residents of Seattle and Tacoma, residents of Olympia, Washington, adopted a resolution in November 1885, declaring that although they believed they had "too much of the Chinese element in [their] midst," they "as clearly recognize[d]" that they were there "in and by the virtue of law and treaty stipulations" and that they were "decidedly opposed to their expulsion by force or by intimidation, or by any other unlawful means." Quoted in Gwen Perkins, "Exclusion in Washington," Washington State History Museum, 2007, https://www.washingtonhistory.org/wp-content/uploads /2020/04/WAExclusion.pdf.

53. Patricia E. Roy, "The Preservation of the Peace in Vancouver: The Aftermath of the Anti-Chinese Riot of 1887," *BC Studies*, no. 31 (Autumn 1976): 47–48, noting that the story of the first anti-Chinese riot in Vancouver, B.C., in 1887 is not as well known as the anti-Asian riot that occurred in September 1907. Maps in two otherwise informative books on patterns of anti-Asian violence in North America fail to include Canada, arguably leaving a critical hole in the larger story by seeming to suggest that such events did not occur outside the boundaries of the United States. See Pfaelzer, *Driven Out*; and Beth Lew-Williams, *The Chinese Must Go: Violence, Exclusion, and the Making of the Alien in America* (Cambridge, Mass.: Harvard University Press, 2018).

54. See Roy, "Preservation of the Peace," 48, 51.

55. Roy, "Preservation of the Peace," 49, citing *Victoria Daily Times*, January 14, 1887; *Vancouver News*, January 21, 1887; and *The Colonist*, January 21, 1887. See also Jules Alexander Karlin, "The Anti-Chinese Outbreak in Tacoma, 1885," *Pacific Historical Review* 23, no. 3 (August 1954): 280, noting that the *Tacoma News* described the expulsion of Chinese as "this glorious victory—this peaceful and successful culmination."

56. Stefan Tanaka, "The Toledo Incident: The Deportation of the Nikkei from an Oregon Mill Town," *Pacific Northwest Quarterly* 69, no. 3 (July 1978): 117–18, 121. According to a 1948 U.S. Department of Labor report, "green chain work" is particularly hazardous due to the heavy weight of green wood. U.S. Department of Labor, Wage and Hour and Public Contracts Divisions, *Supplementary Investigation of the Logging and Sawmilling Industries* (Washington, D.C.: U.S. Department of Labor, 1948), 28.

57. Tanaka, "Toledo Incident," 122–23. Also see Ted W. Cox, *The Toledo Incident of 1925* (Corvallis, Ore.: Old World Publications, 2005); Ito, *Issei*, 214–15.

58. See Geiger, *Subverting Exclusion*, 40–43.

59. R. N. DeArmond, comp., "This Month in Northland History," *Alaska Sportsman*, April 1969, 16.

60. "No Chinese Wanted Here," *White Horse Star* (semi-weekly edition) (Whitehorse, Yukon), June 28, 1902; "Driven from the Territory; Five Chinese Appear at White Horse," *Yukon Sun*, July 3, 1902. Although these men were reported by Whitehorse papers as being Chinese, Nakayama includes this incident, or one much like it, in his discussion of hostility directed against Japanese. Nakayama, *Kanada dōhō hatten taikai: Zen*, 1066.

61. *White Horse Star* (semi-weekly edition), July 2, 1902; *Klondike Nugget*, September 2, 1901.

62. Nakayama, *Kanada dōhō hatten taikan: Zen*, 1067, reporting that white workers in Salmo also approached the Japanese consulate in Vancouver to demand that Japanese workers leave their area.

63. See, e.g., "Night Raid on Hindoos, Hundreds Driven into the Woods," *Dawson Daily News*, September 9, 1907. "Everette, WA—The police place one hundred and fifty Hindu mill laborers under arrest to save them from assault by a white mob," as recorded in the *Daily Alaskan*, November 8, 1907. "Another horde of Hindus, numbering 200, are due to arrive on the steamer Mount Eagin in a few days. The provincial government is expected to apply the new Natal Act to them, to test if they can speak the English language," as reported by the *Yukon World*, February 22, 1908.

64. Nakayama, *Kanada dōhō hatten taikan: Zen*, 1942. The continuous passage rule was intended primarily as a bar against immigration from India, something that had been difficult to accomplish because Indian immigrants were also British subjects. Canadian authorities were aware, however, that there were no vessels that traveled directly from India to North America and that it was necessary for immigrants from India to change ships at one port or another along the way, making them vulnerable to a continuous passage rule. See Hugh Johnston, *The Voyage of the Komagata Maru: The Sikh Challenge to Canada's Colour Bar* (Vancouver: UBC Press, 1989). Although its primary target was Indian immigration, the continuous passage rule was also invoked to bar Japanese immigrants on occasion. See, e.g., Geiger, *Subverting Exclusion*, 120, 135.

65. Kaori Mizukami, "The *Komagata Maru* Incident as Described in Two Japanese Works," in Rita Kaur Dhamoon, Davina Bhandar, Renisa Mawani, and Satwinder Kaur Bains, *Unmooring the Komagata Maru: Charting Colonial Trajectories* (Vancouver: UBC Press, 2019), 175, quoting Yoshida Sadao, *Komagata Maru Jiken* (The Komagata Maru Incident) (1936). 160–61.

66. "Hindus Leave Vancouver for Distant Home: . . . British Subjects, but Cannot Land," *Fairbanks Daily Times*, July 24, 1914. Immigrants from the Indian subcontinent were often

referred to as "Hindu" in the popular press even if they were Muslim or Sikh, as a majority of the passengers aboard the *Komagata Maru* were, because the region was also known as "Hindustan." For two compelling accounts that locate the voyage of the *Komagata Maru* within the framework of empire, see Seema Sohi, *Echoes of Mutiny; Race, Surveillance, and Indian Anticolonialism in North America* (New York: Oxford University Press, 2014); and Renisa Mawani, *Across Oceans of Law: The* Komagata Maru *and Jurisdiction in the Time of Empire* (Durham, N.C.: Duke University Press, 2018). For an examination of cross-border ties to riots in Bellingham, Washington, and San Francisco, see Erika Lee, "Hemispheric Orientalism and the 1907 Pacific Coast Race Riots," *Amerasia Journal* 33, no. 2 (2007): 19–47. But see Roy, *A White Man's Province*, 196.

67. Kiyoshi Karl Kawakami, *Asia at the Door: A Study of the Japanese Question in Continental United States, Hawaii and Canada* (New York: Fleming H. Revell, 1914), 254 (original source not named). For more about Kawakami's arguments and ways in which they sometimes worked against the Japanese immigrant community, see Ian Haney López, *White by Law: The Legal Construction of Race* (revised ed.) (New York: New York University Press, 2006), 106–07, arguing that "we are *all* implicated in the legal construction of race to the extent we uncritically accept the racial categories employed by law."

68. As Keith Thor Carlson and Colin Murray Osmond observe, "Violence, and the threat of violence, nests at the heart of all colonial projections of power and works to facilitate the displacement of indigenous people from their lands and resources in ways that range from the subtle to the overt." Keith Thor Carlson and Colin Murray Osmond, "Clash at Clayoquot: Manifestations of Colonial and Indigenous Power in Pre-Settler Colonial Canada," *Western Historical Quarterly* 48 (Summer 2017): 160.

69. Claus-M. Naske and Herman E. Slotnick, *Alaska: A History*, 3rd ed. (Norman: University of Oklahoma Press, 2011), 109–11; Stephen Haycox, *Alaska: An American Colony* (Seattle: University of Washington Press, 2002), 183–84; John R. Bockstoce, *Furs and Frontiers in the Far North: The Contest among Native and Foreign Nations for the Bering Strait Fur Trade* (New Haven, Conn.: Yale University Press, 2009), 326. The fact that the United States initially made the army responsible for the governance of Alaska is itself indicative of its willingness to resort to violence to coerce the cooperation of its Indigenous people. First under the control of the army and then the navy, Alaska was reorganized as a district in 1884 under the auspices of the Department of the Interior. A year later, the Department of the Interior assigned responsibility for matters related to Alaska's Indigenous people to the Bureau of Education and not the Bureau of Indian Affairs as elsewhere in the United States. Stephen Haycox, "'Races of a Questionable Ethnical Type': Origins of the Jurisdiction of the U.S. Bureau of Education in Alaska, 1867–1885," *Pacific Northwest Quarterly* 75 (October 1984): 155–63.

70. See, e.g., David A. Chang, "Borderlands in a World at Sea: Concow Indians, Native Hawaiians, and South Chinese in Indigenous, Global, and National Spaces," *Journal of American History* 98, no. 2 (September 2011): 385, noting that "reservation policy . . . was at the leading edge of the federal effort to build restrictive borders to defund the settler nation from unwanted and racialized others." As early as 1850, Archibald Barclay, secretary of the Hudson's Bay Company (HBC), instructed James Douglas that "You are to consider the natives as the rightful possessors of such lands only as they occupied by cultivation, or had houses built on, at the time when the Island came under the undivided sovereignty of

Great Britain in 1846. . . . All other land is to be regarded as waste [unoccupied and un-owned] and applicable to the purposes of colonization." Quoted in Stuart Banner, *Possessing the Pacific: Land, Settlers, and Indigenous People from Australia to Alaska* (Cambridge, Mass.: Harvard University Press, 2007), 206. Both nations set up systems to facilitate the administrative assimilation of indigenous people, to limit obligations of government to them, notwithstanding that in both countries, that obligation was owed in substantial part as a consequence of the wholesale absorption of their territories and resources into the nation-state.

71. *Taku River Tlingit First Nation: Wenah Specific Claim Inquiry* (Ottawa, March 2006), reported (2008) 21 I.C.C.P. 97, Rev. Father Jules Le Chevallier, O.M.I., "La croix dans les Rocheueses," undated, Deschâtelets Archives, Ottawa, HPK 5006.B86C, Indian Claims Commission (ICC) Exhibit 13h, p. 415 (translation). In 1916, the Atlin band comprised 150 individuals. British Columbia, *Royal Commission on Indian Affairs for British Columbia* (Victoria, B.C.: Acme Press, 1916) (McKenna-McBride Report), January 18, 1916, Meeting with W. Scott Simpson, Indian Agent for the Stikine Agency, Victoria, B.C., 41, 77.

72. A. B. Taylor, Secretary, Atlin Board of Trade, to J. Bergeron, Secretary, Royal Commission on Indian Affairs for British Columbia, McKenna-McBride Report, February 17, 1915, in BC Archives, Royal British Columbia Museum, Victoria, B.C., file 8313/12, ICC Exhibit 1a, 51.

73. McKenna-McBride Report, June 16, 1915, Testimony of Chairman Neville, Atlin Board of Trade, 13–14, also asserting that the Atlin Board of Trade "practically represents the citizens of Atlin."

74. Taylor to Bergeron, McKenna-McBride Report, February 17, 1915. For a detailed description of Indigenous resistance to colonial settlement in British Columbia, see Cole Harris, *Making Native Space: Colonialism, Resistance, and Reserves in British Columbia* (Vancouver: UBC Press, 2002).

75. McKenna-McBride Report, Testimony of Chairman Neville, 15.

76. McKenna-McBride Report, June 16, 1915, Testimony of Mr. Egert, Atlin Board of Trade, 14.

77. McKenna-McBride Report, June 16, 1915, Testimony of Indian Agent W. Scott Simpson, Stikine Agency, and Captain Hawthorn, 16.

78. McKenna-McBride Report, Meeting with the Atlin Band or Tribe of Indians at Atlin, B.C., June 16, 1915, Testimony of Chief Taku Jack, 19–22. Chief Taku Jack also testified that he thought that whites understood that he belonged to the area around the Taku River because they called him Taku Jack even though Taku was not his name. Testimony of Chief Taku Jack, 26.

79. McKenna-McBride Report, Testimony of Chief Taku Jack, 19–22.

80. *Wenah Specific Claim Inquiry*, transcript, May 12–13, 2004, ICC Exhibit 5a, 41, Testimony of Antonia Jack. See also Bilsland, "Atlin, 1898–1910," 128, 157, reporting that the miners who arrived in 1898, and who would number 3,000 before the year was out, "pitched their tents indiscriminately along the creeks and began their feverish scrambling for claims and gold."

81. McKenna-McBride Report, Testimony of Chief Taku Jack, 22. During later years, Chief Taku Jack would also take advantage of a thriving tourist industry to supplement his income, as did the Tsimshian who had settled at Metlakatla and others. See photograph of

Chief Taku Jack with "Tourist Lady," Fig. 3.3; Frank Norris, "Touring Alaska," *Alaska History* 2, no. 2 (Fall 1987): 1–18, republished in *An Alaska Anthology: Interpreting the Past*, eds. Stephen Haycox and Mary Childers Mangusso (Seattle: University of Washington Press, 1996), 274–75.

82. McKenna-McBride Report, Meeting with the Atlin Band or Tribe of Indians at Atlin, B.C., June 16, 1915, Comment of Commissioner MacDowell, 27. The governor-general was the King's representative in Canada.

83. McKenna-McBride Report, 1916, Final Report—Stikine Agency, Minutes of Decision—Nelson River Tribe and Atlin-Teslin Lake Tribe, 761–63.

84. McKenna-McBride Report, Testimony of Chief Taku Jack, 28. Bilsland reports that Father F. J. Allard, O.M.I., "opened a religious school and home for the children of Atlin's Indian village" in 1907. Bilsland, "Atlin, 1898–1910," 167.

85. See *Wenah Specific Claim Inquiry* ruling.

86. For an example of one Indigenous group whose traditional territories were transected by the U.S.-Canada border and who were pressured to identify themselves as either American or Canadian Indians, see Andrea Geiger, "'Crossed by the Border': The U.S.-Canada Border and Canada's 'Extinction' of the Arrow Lakes [Sinixt] Band, 1890–1956," *Western Legal History* 23, no. 2 (Summer/Fall 2010): 121–53.

87. The Taku River Tlingit First Nation was formerly Atlin Band of Indians. For a description of the transboundary claim, see Taku River Tlingit First Nation v. Canada (Attorney General), 2016 Y.K.S.C. 7, 8, Schedule A, a map of the claimed area. The western boundary of the claimed area runs along the Canada-U.S. border given that the Taku River Tlingit First Nation was in negotiations with Canada, which has the power to resolve such land claims within the boundaries of Canada alone. The Tlingit Nation in Canada comprises three separate bands: the Taku River Tlingit First Nation, the Carcross-Tagish Band, and the Teslin Band. *Taku River Tlingit First Nation*, Y.K.S.C. 7, 5 (original typescript). "The Tlingits in Alaska have entered into a land claim treaty with the United States government on at least two separate occasions." *Taku River Tlingit First Nation*, Y.K.S.C. 7, 8–9 (original typescript), quoting the testimony of Jennie Jack, Taku River Tlingit Chief Negotiator before Standing Committee on Aboriginal Affairs and Northern Development for treaty negotiations.

88. *Wenah Specific Claim Inquiry*, 167, quoting W. Scott Simpson, Indian Agent, to Frank Pedley, March 31, 1913, in Canada, *Annual Report of the Department of Indian Affairs for the Year Ended March 31, 1912* (Ottawa: printed by C. H. Parmelee, 1912), 253 (I.C.C. Exhibit 12, 16). The route described was one of three that led from Juneau, Alaska, to the B.C. interior, the other two ending at Teslin and Tagish Lakes. Eliza Ruhamah Scidmore, *Appleton's Guide-Book to Alaska and the Northwest Coast* (New York: D. Appleton, 1899), 157–58. Scidmore also notes the presence of a "village of Taku Indians [that] adjoins [Juneau] on the E. below the wharf." Scidmore, *Appleton's Guide-Book*, 82.

89. McKenna-McBride Report, Meeting with W. Scott Simpson, 77. As Bilsland notes, various routes for both a railway and a roadway that would link Atlin to the coast were considered. Bilsland, "Atlin, 1898–1910," 142–44, 149–51.

90. Article III of the Treaty of Amity, Commerce, and Navigation, between His Britannic Majesty and the United States of America (Jay Treaty), signed 1794, proclaimed 1796, provides that "Indians dwelling on either side" of the boundary line that the U.S. and Great Britain had established as between themselves are entitled "freely to pass and repass . . .

into the respective territories and countries of the two parties on the continent of America." While the United States continues to recognize certain rights under the treaty, Canada takes the position that it has no obligations under the treaty because it has not legislated it.

91. For a comprehensive summary of race-based exclusion laws in the United States, see Roger Daniels, *Guarding the Golden Door: American Immigration Policy and Immigrants since 1882* (New York: Hill and Wang, 2004). For a detailed overview of anti-Asian exclusion law and policy in British Columbia, see Roy, *A White Man's Province*, and its sequel, *The Oriental Question: Consolidating a White Province, 1914–1941* (Vancouver: UBC Press, 2003). Both the United States and Canada passed deportation laws early in the twentieth century that provided for deportation on a wide variety of grounds, including illness and political persuasion. Both laws also included the very vague and subjective category "likely to become a public charge" that could be broadly applied by immigration inspectors on a variety of grounds. See United States, Law of February 20, 1907, sec. 2, as amended by act of March 26, 1910; Canada, Immigration Acts, 1906, 1911.

92. See, e.g., "Japs and Coreans [*sic*] Are Opposed: San Francisco League Objects to Mongolian Children in Schools," *Fairbanks Daily Times*, October 11, 1906; and "Japan and America May Have Trouble: Order of San Francisco School Board Relegating Japanese to Negro Schools, the Cause," *Fairbanks Daily Times*, October 19, 1906.

93. For a detailed description of the Gentlemen's Agreements, each of which was recorded in a series of confidential diplomatic notes and memoranda that made enforcement of the agreements difficult for border officials, see Geiger, *Subverting Exclusion*, 118–21. For a detailed account of the 1907 Vancouver Riot and the diplomatic negotiations that followed between Canada and Japan, see also Julie F. Gilmour, *Trouble on Main Street: Mackenzie King, Reason, Race, and the 1907 Vancouver Riots* (Toronto: Allen Lane, 2014).

94. Joan M. Jensen, *Passage from India: Asian Indian Immigrants in North America* (New Haven, Conn.: Yale University Press, 1988), 73; Geiger, *Subverting Exclusion*, 118–19. Mackenzie King later served as prime minister of Canada during the Second World War.

95. For the Meiji government's concerns, see K. T. Takahashi, *The Anti-Japanese Petition: Appeal in Protest against a Threatened Persecution* (Montreal: Gazette Printing Company, 1897), 15. The Chinese Exclusion Act passed by the United States in 1882 was renewed in 1892 and again in 1902. Daniels, *Guarding the Golden Door*, 19–21. Canada imposed a head tax of $50 on Chinese immigrants in 1885, raising it to $100 in 1900 and to $500 in 1903 before banning further Chinese immigration in 1923. Both sets of restrictions remained in place through World War II. See, e.g., Peter S. Li, *The Chinese in Canada* (Toronto: Oxford University Press, 1998), 7, 34.

96. Memorandum from Vice Minister of Foreign Affairs [Ishii], Tokyo, Japan, July 1, 1908, U.S. National Archives and Records Administration (NARA), record group (RG) 85. See also Harry A. Millis, *The Japanese Problem in the United States* (New York: Macmillan, 1915), 109, citing *Annual Report of the Commissioner-General of Immigration for the Fiscal Year Ended June 30, 1908* (Washington, D.C.: Government Printing Office, 1908), 125–26. Canada, *Report of the Royal Commission Appointed to Inquire into the Methods by Which Oriental Labourers Have Been Induced to Come to Canada*, W. L. Mackenzie King, C.M.G., Commissioner (Ottawa: Government Printing Bureau, 1908), 66. Also see Ken Adachi, *The Enemy That Never Was: A History of the Japanese Canadians* (Toronto: McClelland and Stewart, 1976), 81.

97. Canada, *Debates of the House of Commons, 1912–1913*, cited in Charles H. Young and Helen R. Y. Reid, *The Japanese Canadians* (Toronto: University of Toronto Press, 1938), 11.

98. The Fourteenth Amendment, ratified in 1866, provides that "all persons born or naturalized in the United States, and subject to the jurisdiction thereof, are citizens of the United States and of the State wherein they reside." The Fifteenth Amendment, ratified in 1870, provides that the "right of citizens of the United States to vote shall not be denied or abridged by the United States or by any state on account of race, color, or previous condition of servitude." Ratified on February 3, 1870.

99. Patricia E. Roy, J. L. Granatstein, Masako Iino, and Hiroko Takamura, *Mutual Hostages: Canadians and Japanese during the Second World War* (Toronto: University of Toronto Press, 1990), 7.

100. James Baker, Clerk, Executive Council, British Columbia, to Secretary of State, Ottawa, May 6, 1897, B.C. Sessional Paper No. 74b. B.C. officials also complained that Australia was allowed to deny Japanese immigrants the ability to apply to become naturalized British subjects.

101. An Act to Amend the "Provincial Voters Act," S.B.C. 1895, c. 20; *Vancouver Daily Province*, December 1, 1900, citing numbers provided by the Collector of Voters for Vancouver, B.C. The Provincial Voters Act was amended in 1907 to add "Hindus" to the list of those excluded from the franchise in British Columbia.

102. Cunningham v. Homma, [1903] A.C. 151, 156 (P.C.).

103. Provincial Elections Act, S.B.C. 1897, c. 67, s. 3; Canada, Indian Act, 1876, c. 18, s. 86(1). Because being listed on the provincial voters list was a precondition to voting in federal elections, those excluded from the provincial franchise were also denied the ability to vote in federal elections.

104. D. M. Eberts, B.C. Attorney General, to Christopher Robinson, Esq., K.C., London, June 29, 1901, published in the *Victoria Daily Colonist*, January 3, 1903 (quoting Gibb v. White, 5 Ontario Practice Reports, 315, affirmed in Johnson v. Jones, 26 Ontario Reports 109). For a general discussion of Canadian law pertaining to Indian access to the franchise, see R. H. Bartlett, "Citizens Minus: Indians and the Right to Vote," *Saskatchewan Law Review* 44 (1980): 163.

105. Eberts, to Robinson, June 29, 1901 (quoting Gibb v. White, 5 Ont. Practice Reports, 315, affirmed in Johnson v. Jones, 26 Ontario Reports 109). Canadian legal scholar Hamar Foster explains that Canadians simply assumed "Indians became British subjects when their territory was brought under British jurisdiction" but that how they "became British subjects has never been adequately explained." Hamar Foster, "Forgotten Arguments: Aboriginal Title and Sovereignty in Canada Jurisdiction Act Cases," *Manitoba Law Journal / Revue de droit manitobaine* 21 (1992): 345, 345n9.

106. Case for the Respondent, Intervenant the Attorney-General of Canada, In the Privy Council on Appeal from the Supreme Court of British Columbia, Cunningham and the Attorney-General for British Columbia (Intervenant), Appellants, and Tomey Homma and the Attorney-General for the Dominion of Canada (Intervenant), No. 45 of 1901, para. 15, 17. See also "No Japanese Need Apply to Be Voters," *Vancouver Daily Province*, December 17, 1902.

107. *In re* Provincial Elections Act and *In re* Tomey Homma, a Japanese (1900), 7 B.C.R. 368, 369 (Co. Ct.).

108. *Homma*, A.C. 151, 156. Although B.C. law was generally extended to the Yukon, Patricia E. Roy reports that "the Yukon Territory did not disenfranchise Japanese. In 1902, some of the approximately 100 Japanese in Dawson nominated Y. Kawakami for the Territorial Council. Amidst protests . . . Kawakami withdrew." Roy, *White Man's Province*, 285n64, citing *Yukon Sun*, December 9–31, 1902; *The Colonist*, January 18, 1903. Even if not formally written into Yukon law, in short, prejudices similar to those that motivated the discriminatory provisions of British Columbia's Provincial Voters Act discouraged Japanese willing to serve in local government in the Yukon from doing so.

109. *Homma*, A.C. 151, citing Henry Wheaton, *Elements of International Law*, 2nd annot. ed., ed. William Beach Lawrence, 1863 (London, 1864) ("Lawrence's Wheaton"). In the context of Aboriginal law cases, Canadian courts have at times looked to decisions of U.S. courts, reasoning that federal Indian law doctrine in both Canada and the United States has its origins in pre–Revolutionary War British colonial Indian policy, and particularly the Royal Proclamation of 1763, which established the basic tenets of federal Indian law in both the United States and Canada. No similar rationale exists, however, for invoking U.S. law in this context, particularly because the language that the Privy Council borrowed arises out of a discussion of Article IV of the U.S. Constitution, which, by definition, has no application in Canada. For a more detailed discussion of the Privy Council's reasoning, see Andrea Geiger, "Writing Racial Barriers into Law: Upholding B.C.'s Denial of the Vote to Its Japanese Canadian Citizens, *Homma v. Cunningham*, 1902," in *Nikkei in the Pacific Northwest: Japanese Americans and Japanese Canadians in the Twentieth Century*, ed. Louis Fiset and Gail M. Nomura (Seattle: University of Washington Press, 2006), 20–43. Because being listed on the provincial voters list was a prerequisite to voting in federal elections, people of Asian ancestry, "even unto the *n*th Canadian-born generation," were also denied this right. A range of occupations was closed to them as a result, including careers in law and pharmacy, as well as "positions in the provincial or municipal services," jobs as schoolteachers, nor could they be employed "by government contractors," "on timber leases," or as hand loggers. David Martin, "The Rising Sun over Canada," *Asia*, April 1941, 191.

110. See, e.g., John Chesterman, "Natural-Born Subjects? Race and British Subjecthood in Australia," *Australian Journal of Politics and History* 51, no. 1 (2005): 30–39.

111. Francis Paul Prucha, *The Great Father: The United States Government and the American Indians*, abridged ed. (Lincoln: University of Nebraska Press, 1984), 231; General Allotment (Dawes) Act of 1887, ch. 199, 24 Stat. 119, codified as amended at 25 U.S.C. §§ 331–334, 339, 341–342, 348–349, 354, 381. Russia had likewise assumed that the Indigenous people of the territories it colonized were Russian subjects. See, e.g., Ilya Vinkovetsky, *Russian America: An Overseas Colony of a Continental Empire, 1804–1867* (New York: Oxford University Press, 2011), 137.

112. Dawes Act of 1887, 25 U.S.C. §§ 331–334, 339, 341–342, 348–349, 354, 381; Canada, Indian Act, 1876, s. 86(1).

113. Treaty concerning the Cession of the Russian Possessions in North America by His Majesty the Emperor of All the Russias to the United States of America; Concluded March 30, 1867; Ratified by the United States, May 28, 1867; Exchanged June 20, 1867; Proclaimed by the United States, June 20, 1867 (15 Stat. 539) (Treaty of Cession). Also unclear was whether this exception also applied to Creoles or whether they were eligible to apply for U.S. citizenship, an ambiguity that Sonja Luehrmann notes was resolved in different

ways in different places. Sonja Luehrmann, *Alutiiq Villages under Russian and U.S. Rule* (Fairbanks: University of Alaska Press, 2008), 118.

114. U.S. uncertainty as to Alaska's role—as a hinterland valued primarily for its resources or as a settlement frontier—was reflected in its changing governance structure. In effect a "colony" in its own right, Alaska was first organized as a department (1867–84), then as a district (1884–1912), and, only in 1912, as a territory in the absence of any intention, until then, that it became a state. Naske and Slotnick, *Alaska*, 101, 219; Mary Alice Cook, "Manifest Opportunity: The Alaska Purchase as a Bridge between United States Expansion and Imperialism," *Alaska History* 26, no. 1 (Spring 2011): 1–10.

115. Although it is often pointed out that white U.S. citizens who were residents of Alaska were also denied formal representation in Congress and unable to obtain title to land outside organized townsites, the governing structures that were put in place, limited and unwieldy though they were, supported their way of life. See, e.g., "An act providing for the acquisition of land for town sites and commercial purposes in Alaska, and for other purposes," Draft Bill S. 1859, House of Representatives, 51st Cong., 1st Sess., February 17, 1890, NARA, RG 200, box 92, folder 85, document 3-B.

116. Prucha, *Great Father*, 273; Act of June 2, 1924, ch. 233, 43 Stat. 253 ("Indian Citizenship Act"), codified as amended at 8 U.S.C. § 1401(b). Eric Sandberg et al., *A History of Alaska Population Settlement* ([Juneau]: Alaska Department of Labor and Workforce Development, April 2013), 7–8. For a detailed discussion of the consequences of unilaterally imposing U.S. citizenship on Indigenous peoples within the borders of the United States, see Robert B. Porter, "The Demise of the Ongwehoweh and the Rise of the Native Americans: Redressing the Genocidal Act of Forcing American Citizenship upon Indigenous Peoples," *Harvard BlackLetter Law Journal* 15 (Spring 1999): 107–84.

117. Immigration Act of 1924, 68th Cong., Sess. 1, ch. 190, 153–69. The effect was to restrict Japanese immigration to roughly 250 non-quota immigrants a year. For a detailed discussion of the debates surrounding passage of the act, see Mae M. Ngai, *Impossible Subjects: Illegal Aliens and the Making of Modern America* (Princeton, N.J.: Princeton University Press, 2004).

118. In 1928, Canada amended the Hayashi-Lemieux Agreement again to include wives and children among the 150 labor immigrants admissible to Canada each year. For a discussion of these amendments to the Hayashi-Lemieux Agreement, see, e.g., Roy et al., *Mutual Hostages*, 11.

119. Zaibei Nihonjinkai [Japanese Association of America, History Preservation Committee], *Zaibeinihonjinshi* (History of Japanese in America), trans. Seizo Oka (San Francisco: Zaibei Nihonjinkai, 1940), 973.

120. Ozawa v. United States, 260 U.S. 178 (1922); U.S. Congress, *Congressional Record: Proceedings and Debates of the First Session of the Sixty-Eighth Congress*, vol. 65, pt. 6, April 1–April 14, 1924 (Washington, D.C.: Government Printing Office, 1924), 5692, 6317.

121. The key issue when the *Ozawa* case reached the U.S. Supreme Court was whether, in 1790, the reference to "free white person" in the Naturalization Act, which states that "any alien, being a free white person, . . . may be admitted to become a citizen," was meant to be broadly read to exclude only persons of Native and African descent, or narrowly read to include only "whites." *Ozawa*, 260 U.S. at 192, quoting "An Act to Establish an Uniform Rule of Naturalization," March 26, 1790, ch. 3 (1 Stat. 103). In 1875, the Naturalization Act

was amended to limit the ability to apply for naturalization to "free white persons" and to aliens "of African descent." *In the Matter of the Petition for Naturalization of Sakharam Ganesh Pandit*, Los Angeles County Superior Court, May 7, 1914 (Judge Willis I. Morrison). For additional elements of Ozawa's argument, see Ian Haney López, *White by Law: The Legal Construction of Race* (revised ed.) (New York: New York University Press, 2006), 56–61; Geiger, *Subverting Exclusion*, 150–52.

122. Ototaka Yamaoka of the Pacific Coast Japanese Association Deliberative Council, for example, stated at the time: "We might be unlearned, but we never made an argument that Japanese are of the white race, which is akin to child's play [*jigi*]." Quoted in Taro Iwata, "Race and Citizenship as American Geopolitics: Japanese and Native Hawaiians in Hawai'i, 1900–1941" (Ph.D. diss., University of Oregon, 2003), 30. For an earlier example, see the comment of the Japanese consul in Vancouver, B.C., in chapter 2.

123. Shiga Shigetaka, *Shiga Shigetaka Zenshu* (Collected works of Shigetaka Shiga) (Tokyo, 1927), 1:75, as quoted in and translated by Yasuo Wakatsuki, "Japanese Emigration to the United States, 1866–1924: A Monograph," *Perspectives in American History* 12 (1979), 442.

124. "Nosse in Montreal: Japanese Consul Gives His Opinion on British Columbia and Oriental Immigration," *Victoria Daily Colonist*, March 28, 1897.

125. Takahashi, *Anti-Japanese Petition*, 11. Japan's population, which had been estimated at 33 million in 1872, had nearly doubled to 64 million just half a century later. Yamato Ichihashi, *Japanese in the United States: A Critical Study of the Problems of the Japanese Immigrants and Their Children* (Stanford, Calif.: Stanford University Press, 1932), 380. In contrast, the population of British Columbia was estimated by its attorney general to be just 125,000 in 1901 (only 12,000 of whom were Japanese or Chinese immigrants) in an area some two and a half times larger than that of Japan. Eberts to Robinson, June 29, 1901, published in *Victoria Daily Colonist*, January 3, 1903.

126. Takahashi, *Anti-Japanese Petition*, 13. For a detailed discussion of status as a British subject and fishing rights in Canada, see chapter 4.

127. Testimony of Colin B. Sword, Dominion Government Inspector of Fisheries, British Columbia, *Report of the Royal Commission on Chinese and Japanese Immigration*, 2 Edward VII, Sessional Paper No. 54 (Ottawa: S.E. Dawson, 1902), 349.

128. Osada Shohei, ed., *Kanada no Makutsu* (Brothels of Canada) (Vancouver, B.C.: Tairiku Nippō-sha [Continental News Company], 1909), 4–5.

129. Nakayama Jinshiro, *Canada and the Japanese* (*Kanada to nihonjin*), trans. Tsuneharu Gonnami (Vancouver, B.C.: Kanada Nihonjinkai, 1940), 251, University of British Columbia Library, Rare Books and Special Collections, Vancouver, B.C., 1999. Canada, the authors of the *Zaibeinihonjinshi* observed, is forty-three times larger than Japan and British Columbia alone is several times larger than Japan. Zaibei Nihonjinkai, *Zaibeinihonjinshi*, 50.

130. Takeo Ujo Nakano, *Within the Barbed Wire Fence: A Japanese Man's Account of His Internment in Canada*, with Leatrice M. Willson Chan (Toronto: James Lorimer, 2012), 53.

131. Rempei Kondo, "Japan Harbors No Ill Feeling toward America," in *Japan's Message to America: A Symposium by Representative Japanese on Japan and American-Japanese Relations*, ed. Naoichi Masaoka (Tokyo, 1914), 38–40. See also Shimpei Goto, "The Real Character of the Japanese Race," in Masaoka, *Japan's Message to America*, 23, noting that it was "natural" that Japanese should have "migrated toward the . . . Pacific coast of America," where "the unbroken land was waiting for the hands of men."

132. In 1913, California became the first state to pass an alien land law, a still more restrictive version of which was passed in 1920. Arizona, Washington, Texas, Louisiana, New Mexico, Idaho, Montana, Oregon, and Kansas had all passed alien land laws of their own by 1925. Masao Suzuki, "Important or Impotent? Taking Another Look at the 1920 California Alien Land Law," *Journal of Economic History* 64, no. 1 (March 2004): 125–43, 130.

133. Seiichiro Terashima, "Exclusionists Not True to the Principles of America's Founders," in *Japan's Message to America: A Symposium by Representative Japanese on Japan and American-Japanese Relations*, ed. Naoichi Masaoka (Tokyo, 1914), 73–78.

134. Statement of Professor Nagai of Waseda University as quoted in Montaville Flowers, *The Japanese Conquest of American Opinion* (New York: George H. Doran, 1917), 47. Although Flowers refers to him only as Professor Nagai, this is almost certainly a reference to Ryutaro Nagai, who became a professor of "social policy and colonial policy" at Waseda University after he returned from three years' study in England in 1909. *Kodansha Encyclopedia of Japan* (Tokyo: Kodansha, 1983), 5:301.

135. Horace Capron, U.S. Commissioner of Agriculture, served as primary adviser. Katarina Sjöberg, Richard Siddle, and Yujin Yaguchi have all demonstrated that certain elements of the colonial system established by the Kaitakushi (Colonization Board) were modeled on colonial structures first established in the U.S. West. Katarina Sjöberg, *The Return of the Ainu: Cultural Mobilization and the Practice of Ethnicity in Japan* (Chur, Switzerland: Harwood Academic Publishers, 1993), 117. See also Richard Siddle, *Race, Resistance and the Ainu of Japan* (London: Routledge, 1996); and Yujin Yaguchi, "Japan's 'Savage': The Significance of the Ainu in the Intercultural History of Japan and the United States," *Proceedings of the Kyoto American Studies Summer Seminar* (Ritsumeikan University), 1998, 107–17.

136. Inazo Nitobe cited the "English colonies as models" for Japan's colonial development but (without explanation) described the "French colonies as examples not to be followed." Inazo Nitobe, "Japan as Colonizer," *Journal of Race Development* 2, no. 1 (April 1912): 358.

137. See, e.g., Siddle, *Race, Resistance and the Ainu*, 56, observing that Japan treated Ainu land as *terra nullius* and looked to U.S. policy as one model; and Sjöberg, *Return of the Ainu*, 117, 125. See also Yujin Yaguchi, "Remembering a More Layered Past in Hokkaido: Americans, Japanese and the Ainu," *Japanese Journal of American Studies* 11 (2000): 109–28.

138. The Hokkaido Former Natives Protection Act (Law No. 27, March 1, 1899), remained in force through July 1997, when it was rescinded and replaced by the Ainu Cultural Promotion Law.

139. For a detailed discussion of the term *dojin* and its negative implications, see chapter 2.

140. Sjöberg, *Return of the Ainu*, 117, 125.

141. Meiji officials were certainly aware of and may well have been influenced by the 1871 decision of the U.S. Congress to declare an end to treaty making with tribal nations in the United States. For a discussion of Congress's reasons for ending treaty making with tribal nations in the United States, see Prucha, *Great Father*, 164–66. The executive branch retained the authority, in its discretion, to establish reservations it deemed necessary or desirable on their behalf. Prucha, *Great Father*.

142. Japanese administrators distinguished the Indigenous people of Taiwan from the Chinese settler population that had settled parts of the island during the two centuries that

preceded Japan's acquisition of Taiwan. See, e.g., Nitobe, "Japan as Colonizer," 349, contrasting the "peaceful Chinese" with Taiwan's indigenous people, described as "brigands and bandits" whom the Japanese had "nearly eradicated" by 1912 (despite the fact that they still numbered more than one hundred thousand).

143. For an essay describing the pass system implemented in Canadian prairies, see Laurie Barron, "The Indian Pass System in the Canadian West, 1882–1935," *Prairie Forum* 13, no. 1 (Spring 1988): 27–29. See also Sarah Carter, *Lost Harvests: Prairie Indian Reserve Farmers and Government Policy* (Montreal: McGill-Queen's University Press, 1990), 151–56.

144. Nitobe, "Japan as Colonizer," 357–358. Nitobe studied in the United States between 1884 and 1887, became a Quaker, and married an American woman. After becoming a professor at Kyoto Imperial University, he served as director of the Bureau of Industries on behalf of the Japanese colonial administration from 1901 to 1904. See also Ronald G. Knapp and Laurence M. Hauptman, "'Civilization over Savagery': The Japanese, the Formosan Frontier, and United States Indian Policy, 1895–1915," *Pacific Historical Review* 49, no. 4 (1980): 649, 651, who state that the Japanese set aside reservations for Taiwan's Indigenous people as the United States had done for American Indians, in an asserted attempt "to deal with these savage tribes peacefully" but that it had also engaged in "punitive expeditions . . . based on the American model" in the face of their continued resistance to colonial rule.

145. Nitobe, "Japan as Colonizer," 358, 347. See also Robert Eskildsen, "Of Civilization and Savages: The Mimetic Imperialism of Japan's 1874 Expedition to Taiwan," *American Historical Review* 107, no. 2 (April 2002): 389, noting that Japan's rationale for colonizing Taiwan was premised in part on the "colonial logic of bringing civilization to [its] 'savages.'"

146. Eskildsen, "Of Civilization and Savages," 389.

Chapter Four

1. Early participants in the commercial sealing industry also included Makah sealers, whose territories were centered on the Olympic Peninsula just south of the U.S.-Canada border. Some purchased and captained their own sealing vessels and argued against the 1897 constraints that limited their access to a resource they had relied on historically for what these governments defined as "subsistence purposes" and required them to hunt only with spears and from canoes. Joshua L. Reid, "Articulating a Traditional Future: Makah Sealers and Whalers, 1880–1999," in *Tribal Worlds: Critical Studies in American Indian Nation Building*, ed. Brian Hosmer and Larry Nesper (New York: State University of New York Press, 2014), 166, 170–73. See also Joshua L. Reid, "Marine Tenure of the Makahs," in *Indigenous Knowledge and the Environment in Africa and North America*, ed. David Gordon and Shepard Krech III (Athens: Ohio University Press, 2012), 246–47.

2. Canada, *Report of the Royal Commission on Chinese and Japanese Immigration, 1902,* 2 Edward VII, Sessional Paper No. 54 (Ottawa: S. E. Dawson, printer to the King's Most Excellent Majesty, 1902), 373–74, testimony of Captain William Munsie, also noting that Japanese were not hired as "overseers or superintendents."

3. Canada, *Report of the Royal Commission on Chinese and Japanese Immigration,* 374.

4. As Marcus Rediker has noted in the context of his work on sealing vessels in the Atlantic world in the eighteenth century, the sailing ship itself became an instrument of colonialism

crucial to the projection of European sovereignty into maritime spaces and to the production of new categories of race; it was on board such vessels, he argues, that Africans became a "negro race." See Marcus Rediker, *Between the Devil and the Deep Blue Sea: Merchant Seamen, Pirates, and the Anglo-American Maritime World, 1700–1750* (Cambridge: Cambridge University Press, 1987).

5. Canada, *Report of the Royal Commission on Chinese and Japanese Immigration*, 373–74. Munsie's support of Japanese exclusion is all the more puzzling given his observation that Japanese were hired only if white sailors could not be found and that the number of Japanese employed on sealing vessels was already declining as compared with the number of those hired five years earlier.

6. For a detailed discussion of the issue of outcaste status and its association with butchering and leatherwork, see Andrea Geiger, *Subverting Exclusion: Transpacific Encounters with Race, Caste, and Borders, 1885–1928* (New Haven, Conn.: Yale University Press, 2011), 17. A number of early twentieth-century observers noted that antiquated attitudes associated with the Meiji period often persisted longer among Japanese living abroad than they did in a rapidly changing Japan.

7. Roy Kiyooka, *Mothertalk: Life Stories of Mary Kiyoshi Kiyooka* (Edmonton, Alberta: NeWest Press, 1997), 96–97. The whaling station at Rose Harbour on Moresby Island was one of three in British Columbia at the time; the other two were located at Naden Harbour on Graham Island, in Haida Gwaii, and Kyuquot on the west coast of Vancouver Island. Deputy Commissioner of Fisheries, Victoria, to W. L. Keate, 441 Seymour Street, Vancouver, B.C., August 5, 1912, BC Archives, Royal British Columbia Museum, Victoria, B.C., GR-435, box 188, file 2. See also Terry Glavin, *The Last Great Sea: A Voyage through the Human and Natural History of the North Pacific Ocean* (Vancouver, Greystone Books, 2000), 152, noting that "at Rose Harbour in the 1930s, the work force consisted of five white men and sixty-three Japanese and Chinese workers."

8. Kazuo Ito, *Issei: A History of Japanese Immigrants in North America*, trans. Shinichiro Nakamura and Jean S. Gerard (Seattle, 1973), 357, poem by Nogiku Itoi. The poem was originally written in Japanese in the form of a tanka, which utilizes lines of five, seven, five, seven, and seven syllables in length. See also Zaibei Nihonjinkai [Japanese Association of America, History Preservation Committee], *Zaibeinihonjinshi* (History of Japanese in America), trans. Seizo Oka (San Francisco: Zaibei Nihonjinkai, 1940), 1015, noting that these early arrivals were often seamen or cooks on sealing vessels.

9. *The Trans-Pacific*, vol. 4, no. 6 (June 1921); James R. Gibson, *Otter Skins, Boston Ships and China Goods: The Maritime Fur Trade of the Northwest Coast, 1785–1841* (Montreal: McGill-Queen's University Press, 1992), 7.

10. See, e.g., David Igler, *The Great Ocean: Pacific Worlds from Captain Cook to the Gold Rush* (New York: Oxford University Press, 2013), 103, 105, 114. Terry Glavin notes the wasteful nature of pelagic seal hunting. Terry Glavin, *The Last Great Sea: A Voyage through the Human and Natural History of the North Pacific Ocean* (Vancouver, Greystone Books, 2000), 158, reporting that "only one in seven seals—some estimates suggest one in ten—was recovered from the sea after being shot," citing Peter Murray, *The Vagabond Fleet: A Chronicle of the North Pacific Sealing Schooner Trade* (Victoria: Sono Nis Press, 1998).

11. Ilya Vinkovetsky, *Russian America: An Overseas Colony of a Continental Empire, 1804–1867* (New York: Oxford University Press, 2011), 29.

12. Patrick Lane, "The Great Pacific Sealhunt," *Raincoast Chronicles* 1, no. 4 (1974): 44.

13. E. W. Wright, ed., *Lewis & Dryden's Marine History of the Pacific Northwest* (ca. 1905; New York: Antiquarian Press, 1961), 432; "Thirty Miles Their Limit," *Fairbanks Daily Times*, September 6, 1908, regarding the seizure of Japanese sealing vessels by Russia.

14. See Henry James Snow, *Notes on the Kuril Islands* (London: John Murray, 1897); and Henry James Snow, *In Forbidden Seas: Recollections of Sea-Otter Hunting in the Kurils* (London: Edward Arnold, 1910).

15. Wright, *Marine History of the Pacific Northwest*, 451.

16. See, e.g., Benedict J. Colombi and James F. Brooks, eds., *Keystone Nations: Indigenous Peoples and Salmon across the North Pacific* (Santa Fe, N. Mex.: School for Advanced Research Press, 2012), noting the importance of various species of fish to Indigenous peoples around the North Pacific Rim, from Sakhalin on the western coast of the Pacific to Kodiak on what is now the southern coast of Alaska, and as far south as the Columbia River in what is now Washington State.

17. Canadian Pacific Railway Company, *Canadian Pacific: The Great Highway across the Continent to and from Europe, Japan, China, Australasia and around the World* (Montreal: Montreal Litho, 1909), 10, Chung Collection, University of British Columbia Library, Vancouver, B.C.

18. Zaibei Nihonjinkai, *Zaibeinihonjinshi*, 971. Regular steamer service to San Francisco began in 1897. Hisashi Tsurutani, *America-Bound: The Japanese and the Opening of the American West*, trans. Betsey Scheiner (Tokyo: Japan Times, 1989), 43; originally published in 1977 as *Amerika Seibu Kaitaku to Nihonjin*.

19. *Canada . . . . . . from Ocean to Ocean: An Illustrated Volume Setting Forth the Richness of Canadian Resources and the Monuments of Canadian Enterprise* (Toronto: Dominion Publishing, 1897), 37.

20. *The Globe* (Toronto), March 2, 1901.

21. *Vancouver Daily Province*, September 16, 1907, 1.

22. Report to accompany Draft Bill S. 1859, H.R. 2450, House of Representatives, 51st Cong., 1st Sess., February 17, 1890, 4, U.S. National Archives and Records Administration (NARA), record group (RG) 200, box 176, folder: American Government Documents. The report further noted Juneau's accessibility to "the large shipping interests, and for the accommodation of the steam whalers cruising in Alaskan waters as well as to the Government vessels in their trips in the North Pacific, Behring Sea, and the waters adjacent." It also pointed out that Juneau was an important point of access to "valuable coal deposits" and "the only point in the Territory from which miners outfit for the great Yukon." Passage of the Jones Act, which "required U.S.-flagged vessels to be built in the United States, owned by U.S. citizens, and documented under the laws of the United States" and also provided that "all goods entering or leaving Alaska had to be transported by American carriers and shipped to Seattle prior to further shipment," bound Alaska more closely still to the U.S. states and particularly Washington State.

23. *The Globe*, March 2, 1901.

24. Nakayama Jinshiro, ed., *Kanada dōhō hatten taikan: Zen* (Encyclopedia of Japanese in Canada: Complete) (Tokyo: Japan Times, 1921), 457; James L. McClain, *Japan: A Modern History* (New York: W. W. Norton, 2002), 432–34.

25. Nakayama, *Kanada dōhō hatten taikan: Zen*, 452; Jinshiro Nakayama, *Canada and the Japanese (Kanada to nihonjin)*, trans. Tsuneharu Gonnami (Vancouver, B.C.: Kanada

Nihonjinkai, 1940), 211, University of British Columbia Library, Rare Books and Special Collections.

26. Frank Leonard, *A Thousand Blunders: The Grand Trunk Pacific Railway and Northern British Columbia* (Vancouver: UBC Press, 1996), 21. Although the Grand Trunk Pacific Railway was completed in 1914, the start of World War I exacerbated other financial problems that undercut Prince Rupert's development as a major port, and Hays himself died in 1912 in the sinking of the *Titanic*. Leonard, *Thousand Blunders*, 5–7.

27. The primary salmon and halibut fishing grounds along the province's northern coastline were located near the mouths of the Skeena and the Nass Rivers, each one of which lay twenty or thirty miles north or south of Prince Rupert. Nakayama, *Kanada dōhō hatten taikan: Zen* 453. While Juneau was also centrally located in relation to the salmon and halibut fishing grounds north of the Dixon Entrance and a frequent port of call for ships making their way north and west, it offered no comparable railway connection into the North American interior.

28. Nakayama, *Kanada dōhō hatten taikan: Zen*, 454, noting Prince Rupert's role in the timber industry; Nakayama, *Canada and the Japanese*, 223, noting the need for water to transport; Zaibei Nihonjinkai, *Zaibeinihonjinshi*, 1017, noting that by 1910, there were 10 sawmills in Vancouver and 152 in British Columbia as a whole.

29. S. R. MacClinton, "Logging Report," January 8, 1909, published in C. Nogero, *Queen Charlotte Islands (Illustrated)* (Jedway: Jedway, B.C. Commercial Association, 1909), 70–74, noting that Japan was already an excellent market for timber produced in British Columbia.

30. Charles R. Menzies, "The Disturbed Environment; The Indigenous Cultivation of Salmon," in *Native Pathways: American Indian Culture and Economic Development in the Twentieth Century*, ed. Brian Hosmer and Colleen O'Neill (Boulder: University Press of Colorado, 2004), 164–65.

31. British Columbia, *Royal Commission on Indian Affairs for British Columbia* (Victoria, B.C.: Acme Press, 1916) (McKenna-McBride Report), Nass Agency, September 29, 1915, Testimony of Stephen A. Allan, 76–77; December 16, 1915, Testimony of C. C. Perry, Indian Agent, 186.

32. Nakayama, *Kanada dōhō hatten taikan: Zen*, 465.

33. Rolf Knight and Maya Koizumi, "Ryuichi Yoshida: An Issei Life," ed. John Skapski, in *Raincoast Chronicles Six/Ten*, ed. Howard White, 2nd collector's ed. (Madeira Park, B.C.: Harbour Publishing, 1983), 60. Born in Chiba Prefecture in 1887 to a family that had opposed the Meiji Restoration, Yoshida arrived on Canada's west coast in 1910 and never returned to Japan even after the Second World War.

34. Referred to as *tokoro no hito*, these networks were rooted in the distinctive cultures of the various domains that were replaced by prefectures when Japan remade itself as a modern nation-state. Where particularly large numbers of individuals came from a single village, as they did from Mio-mura in Wakayama Prefecture, village associations also served as a foundation for interpersonal networks in North America.

35. See, e.g., Dr. Alfred T. Watt, Superintendent of Quarantine for British Columbia, testifying that "the Japanese in Victoria [are] more of a floating population; they come and go away again. They go out to farms and canneries and wherever they can get work in good weather and come back here in the wintertime." Canada, *Report of the Royal Commission on*

Chinese and Japanese Immigration, 337. See also Joseph E. Taylor III, *Persistent Callings: Seasons of Work and Identity on the Oregon Coast* (Corvallis: Oregon State University Press, 2019), describing the emergence of what he calls seasonal identities and how censuses conducted at different times of year reflect different population numbers. In his words, the "economy was dynamic, seasonal, linked to the environment."

36. Takeshe Uyeyama, interview by Kirsten McAllister, May 12, 1990, Japanese Canadian Oral History Collection (JCOHC), Nikkei National Museum, Burnaby, B.C.

37. Ito, *Issei,* 253. Taiji was the focus of the 2009 documentary titled *The Cove,* which describes methods used to hunt dolphins along its coast. See Brian Duignan, "Dolphin Slaughter in Japan," Saving Earth, Encyclopedia Britannica, https://www.britannica.com /explore /savingearth/ (accessed October 28, 2021). For the logging industry on Haida Gwaii, see Nakayama, *Kanada dōhō hatten taikan: Zen,* 454, 951, reporting that there were 110 Japanese working in the logging industry on Haida Gwaii in the 1920s and arguing that their skill was worthy of note and that they were rapidly overtaking whites in terms of productivity.

38. Bill Tatsuda, interview by Tony Nakazawa, Ketchikan, Alaska, December 12, 1990, Alaska's Japanese Pioneers Research Project (AJPRP) Records, 1990–1991 (HMC-0374) (AJPRP), Archives and Special Collections, Consortium Library, University of Anchorage, Anchorage, Alaska, tape 15.

39. Ito, *Issei,* 356.

40. Douglas C. Harris, *Fish, Law, and Colonialism: The Legal Capture of Salmon in British Columbia* (Toronto: University of Toronto Press, 2001), 117.

41. Mack Mori, for example, recounts the joking banter he shared with some of the older Indigenous women in a cannery at which he worked in southeastern Alaska. Mack Mori and Harue Mori, interview by Ronald K. Inouye, Seattle, Washington, October 13, 1991, AJPRP, tapes 18 and 19, transcript, 38–39.

42. Sonja Luehrmann, *Alutiiq Villages under Russian and U.S. Rule* (Fairbanks: University of Alaska Press, 2008), 104–5, 109.

43. McKenna-McBride Report, West Coast Agency, 1915, Testimony of Chief Tyhee Jack, 78.

44. For a map of canneries along the north coast of British Columbia, see Gladys Young Blyth, *Salmon Canneries: British Columbia North Coast* (Lantzville, B.C.: Oolichan Books, 2006), 168. For maps of canneries in Alaska, see David F. Arnold, *The Fishermen's Frontier: People and Salmon in Southeast Alaska* (Seattle: University of Washington Press, 2008), 1; and Chris Friday, *Organizing Asian American Labor: The Pacific Coast Canned-Salmon Industry, 1870–1942* (Philadelphia: Temple University Press, 1994), n.p., inset after 52.

45. Zaibei Nihonjinkai, *Zaibeinihonjinshi,* 36–37. Sugitani contracted with a company called the A. P. Peterson Company, and he himself took the first hundred Japanese cannery workers that he hired north.

46. Zaibei Nihonjinkai, *Zaibeinihonjinshi,* 36–37. See also William Shurtleff and Akiko Aoyagi, *History of Tofu and Tofu Products (965 CE to 2013): Bibliography and Sourcebook* (Lafayette, Calif.: Soyinfo Center, 2013), 2568, citing interview with Seizo Oka, 1989; Ito, *Issei,* 353. Kosuke Sakamaki's name is also sometimes given as Kosa Sakamaki.

47. Shimada Saburō and Ariiso Toshirō, *Kaigai katsudō no nihonjin* (Japanese who are active overseas) (Tokyo: Shokado, Meiji 39 [1906]), 39–40.

48. For a detailed discussion of the Chinese Exclusion Act, its amendments, and its consequences, see Erika Lee, *At America's Gates: Chinese Immigration during the Exclusion Era, 1882–1943* (Chapel Hill: University of North Carolina Press, 2003), 43–46.

49. Friday, *Organizing Asian American Labor*, 94.

50. Friday, *Organizing Asian American Labor*, 94; Mack Mori, interview, 45, noting that large canneries in Bristol Bay hired forty or fifty people; George Yanagimachi, interview by Ronald K. Inouye, Seattle, Washington, October 14, 1991, AJPRP, tape 20, transcript, 10; Isamu Taguchi, interview by Ronald K. Inouye, Juneau, Alaska, October 19 and 20, 1990, AJPRP, tapes 13 and 14, transcript, 11–14.

51. Mack Mori, interview, 33–36. Although canneries became more mechanized over time, butchering and cleaning were the most difficult to mechanize given the variations in the size and shape of the fish, but a "practical butchering machine" had been developed by 1905. Patrick W. O'Bannon, "Waves of Change: Mechanization in the Pacific Coast Canned-Salmon Industry, 1864–1914," *Technology and Culture* 28, no. 3 (July 1987): 560–61. Butchers were among the most-skilled workers with the result that those in such positions, often older Chinese men, did all they could to protect their positions. See Friday, *Organizing Asian American Labor*, 26–37, explaining the canning process and the respective roles of Japanese and Chinese workers.

52. Yanagimachi, interview, 5–6; Mack Mori, interview.

53. Yanagimachi, interview, 15. While Euro-American women sometimes worked alongside Asian and Indigenous women in the canneries, Euro-American men generally served as mechanics or bookkeepers. Taguchi, interview, 14. Indigenous women had initially done most of the work in the northern canneries, but by 1915 canners were actively recruiting white, Japanese, and Chinese women. McKenna-McBride Report, Testimony of C. C. Perry, 194.

54. Irene Takizawa and Helen Nakashima, interview by Carol Hoshiko, Seattle, Washington, October 24, 1990, AJPRP, [no tape], transcript, 8–9.

55. Taguchi, interview, 11–14.

56. Yanagimachi, interview, 7–8, explaining that when no fish had come in, older men might gamble, while younger boys played catch or went down to the beach. Wages from one cannery to another were largely comparable, but, he chuckled, the meals provided by some contractors were better than others; in his opinion, it was "Nagamachi" who provided the best meals and made sure that they always had pie on Saturdays.

57. Taguchi, interview, 11–14.

58. See Masako Fukawa, *Spirit of the Nikkei Fleet: BC's Japanese Canadian Fishermen*, with Stanley Fukawa and the Nikkei Fishermen's History Book Committee (Madeira Park, B.C.: Harbour Publishing, 2009), 47, quoting interview with Allan Okabe.

59. See, e.g., Yamato Ichihashi, *Japanese in the United States: A Critical Study of the Problems of the Japanese Immigrants and Their Children* (Stanford, Calif.: Stanford University Press, 1932), 149, reporting that one year the five Japanese labor contractors in San Francisco hired a total of 1,235 Japanese, 1,166 Chinese, 362 Filipinos, and 53 Koreans.

60. Mack Mori, interview, 28–29, 44. For a detailed discussion of attitudes to Chinese among Meiji-era Japanese diplomats and immigrants, see Geiger, *Subverting Exclusion*, 56–66.

61. Mack Mori, interview, 44. For an in-depth discussion of Japan's colonization of Korea, see Jun Uchida, *Brokers of Empire: Japanese Settler Colonialism in Korea, 1876–1945*

(Cambridge, Mass.: Harvard University Press, 2011); and Peter Duus, *The Abacus and the Sword: The Japanese Penetration of Korea, 1895–1910* (Berkeley: University of California Press, 1995). Japan distinguished between subjects of the Japanese home islands, called *naichi*, and those of territories newly incorporated within the boundaries of the Japanese empire, known as *gaichi*. See, e.g., Michele M. Mason and Helen J. S. Lee, eds., *Reading Colonial Japan: Text, Context, and Culture* (Stanford, Calif.: Stanford University Press, 2012), 126, 159.

62. See, e.g., Friday, *Organizing Asian American Labor*, 101, 125–26, 172.

63. See, e.g., Dorothy Fujita-Rony, "History through a Postcolonial Lens: Reframing Philippine Seattle," *Pacific Northwest Quarterly* 102, no. 1 (Winter 2010/2011): 4–5, 7. The status of Filipinos changed with the passage of the 1934 Tydings-McDuffie Act, which reclassified them as aliens and limited the number of Filipinos admissible to the United States to just fifty a year, although they were categorized as "Malays" and not "Mongoloids." Stephanie Hinnershitz, "'We Ask Not for Mercy, but for Justice': The Cannery Workers and Farm Laborers' Union and Filipino Civil Rights in the United States, 1927–1937," *Journal of Social History* 47, no. 1 (2013): 134, 147.

64. Zaibei Nihonjinkai, *Zaibeinihonjinshi*, 1103–104, noting that Japan had tried in vain to protect the existing rights of the 61,000 Japanese in Hawaii, more than one-third of its total population of 150,000, when it was annexed by the United States. Also a source of bitterness was the failure of the United States to compensate them for their losses, whereas it agreed to pay $20 million for its acquisition of Spanish interests in the Philippines at the end of the Spanish-American War. Zaibei Nihonjinkai, *Zaibeinihonjinshi*, 1103–104.

65. For a detailed account of Japan's response to U.S. annexation of the Philippines, see James K. Eyre Jr., "Japan and the American Annexation of the Philippines," *Pacific Historical Review* 11 (1942): 55–71.

66. Yanagimachi, interview, 13–14. Mack Mori reported that he was hired as part of a group of both Japanese and Filipino laborers by a Japanese labor contractor named Ueminami in 1928 to work at a cannery in Loring, Alaska. Mack Mori, interview, 24–28. But see Donald L. Guimary, *Marumina Trabaho: A History of Labor in Alaska's Salmon Canning Industry* (New York: iUniverse, 2006), 22, quoting Bruno Lasker, *Filipino Immigration* (Chicago: Institute of Pacific Relations, 1931), 11, for the point that although "Japanese are well disposed toward Filipinos where their own status is assured," conflict between Japanese and Filipino workers increased to the point where fights broke out as the number of Filipino cannery workers increased.

67. Zaibei Nihonjinkai, *Zaibeinihonjinshi*, 1040, listing 1,500 fishermen in Steveston, 800 on the Skeena River, 330 at Rivers Inlet, and 140 on the Nass River in 1909.

68. Zaibei Nihonjinkai, *Zaibeinihonjinshi*, 996, listing 320 Japanese settlers in Alaska in 1922, including 210 men, 33 women, and 77 children. The largest group of 70 was based in Ketchikan, and the next largest of 37 at Kennecott, a copper mine in the southwest corner of the Yukon Territory near Mount St. Elias, while Cordova, Juneau, and Petersburg each had about 30 residents. Of the 210 men, the largest number—81—worked in towns, 39 were railway workers, and 29 were fishery workers. There were also 4 grocers, 14 restaurant workers, 13 laundry workers, 4 lumber mill workers, 3 barbers, and 1 fox breeder.

69. Menzies, "Disturbed Environment," 163–64; Courtney Carothers, "Salmon and the Alutiiq/Sugpiaq Peoples of the Kodiak Archipelago, Alaska," in *Keystone Nations: Indigenous*

Peoples and Salmon across the North Pacific, ed. Benedict J. Colombi and James F. Brooks (Santa Fe, N. Mex.: School for Advanced Research Press, 2012), 147. See also Luehrmann, *Alutiiq Villages*, 104.

70. Zaibei Nihonjinkai, *Zaibeinihonjinshi*, 961, for reference to Washington State; Joan S. Wang, "The Double Burdens of Immigrant Nationalism: The Relationship between Chinese and Japanese in the American West, 1880s–1920s," *Journal of American Ethnic History* 27, no. 2 (Winter 2008): 30, noting that Oregonians also protested the extension of fishing rights to Chinese and Japanese fishers, while California succeeded in barring aliens ineligible for citizenship from its fisheries only in 1943. See also Junzo Sasamori, *Facts about Japanese in America: Anti-Japanese Agitation Refuted* (Los Angeles: Central Japanese Association of Southern California, 1921), 10, noting that "in 1910 there were 172 Japanese fishermen in the Far West and soon they had extended their activities all along the coast line from San Diego to Seattle. In 1917 their number had increased to 1,113." And see Tsuyoshi Matsumoto, "The Japanese in California: An Account of Their Contributions to the Growth and Development of the State and of Their Part in Community Life" (unpublished report, distributed by the Welfare Committee of the Central Japanese Association of America, 1941), 32–37.

71. For the reference to Terminal Island as a "Japanese village on American soil, see Lillian Takahashi Hoffecker, "A Village Disappeared," *American Heritage* 52, no. 8 (December 2001): 64–65. By the 1930s, the village of East San Pedro was served by a variety of *issei* and *nisei* businesses, among them "restaurants, groceries, barbershops, beauty shops and poolhalls, in addition to three physicians and two dentists," as well as a Fisherman's Hall and a Shinto shrine. Hoffecker, "Village Disappeared," 64–65, 70–71.

72. Yuko Konno, "Trans-Pacific Localism and the Creation of a Fishing Colony: Pre–World War II Taiji Immigrants on Terminal Island, California," in *Trans-Pacific Japanese American Studies: Conversations on Race and Racializations*, ed. Yasuko Takezawa and Gary Y. Okihiro (Honolulu: University of Hawai'i Press, 2015), 85.

73. Bob Kumamoto, "The Search for Spies: American Counterintelligence and the Japanese American Community, 1931–1942," *Amerasia Journal* 6, no. 2 (1979): 59.

74. Emil Engelcke, Inspector in Charge, San Diego, California, to Commissioner General of Immigration, Washington, D.C., April 27, 1908, in United States, Department of State, *Report of the Honorable S. Morris on Japanese Immigration and Alleged Discriminatory Legislation against Japanese Residents in the United States* (Morris Report) (Washington, D.C.: Government Printing Office, 1921), Exhibit B. Passports began to be used only toward the end of the nineteenth century.

75. Mitsuo Yesaki, *Sutebusuton: A Japanese Village on the British Columbia Coast* (Vancouver, B.C.: Peninsula Publishing, 2003); Mitsuo Yesaki, Harold Steves, and Kathy Steves, *Steveston Cannery Row: An Illustrated History* (Richmond, B.C.: Lulu Island Printing, 1998), 9, for the names of the Coast Salish villages. But see Yesaki, *Sutebusuton*, 9, stating that "there were no permanent settlements, only temporary fishing, hunting and berry-gathering camps." Yesaki was himself a fisherman whose grandfather had immigrated in 1896 from Wakayama Prefecture to Steveston, B.C., where he fished for sockeye and chum salmon. Michelle Hopkins, *Richmond News*, July 28, 2011.

76. Nitta Jiro, *Phantom Immigrants*, trans. David Sulz (n.p., 1998), 19, citing Nakabayashi Kouemon; originally published as *Mikkōsen Suian Maru* (Tokyo: Kodansha, 1979). For a

description of the collapse of the sardine fishing industry in Japan and the subsequent migration of Japanese immigrants from Wakayama Prefecture to Canada, see Yesaki, *Sutebusuton*, 8–9; and Ken Adachi, *The Enemy That Never Was: A History of the Japanese Canadians* (Toronto: McClelland and Stewart, 1976), 18.

77. Nakayama, *Canada and the Japanese*, 210. Friday reports there were nearly a thousand Japanese fishermen and four thousand Japanese cannery workers along the Fraser River by 1896. Friday, *Organizing Asian American Labor*, 116–17. The latter group included women, but there is relatively little information available about them. See Audrey Kobayashi and Peter Jackson, "Japanese Canadians and the Racialization of Labour in the British Columbia Sawmill Industry," *BC Studies*, no. 103 (Fall 1994): 44n50, noting that "because menial work was eschewed with the Japanese patriarchal system, such work is denied in all written accounts."

78. As Ryuichi Yoshida later explained, "Fishing is quite complicated and that's what is interesting. You have to find where to go and when to put in your net, you have to think how best to use it each time and place, for high tide and low tide, when the wind is blowing and when it's calm." Knight and Koizumi, "Ryuichi Yoshida," 59. A fisherman familiar with the waters of the North Pacific who describes the seasons of both ocean and fish adds that the ways in which the ocean changes in the spring are "more subtle but as profound" as those at other times of the year. Mrs. Amor de Cosmos (pseudonym), *Notes from the Netshed* (Vancouver, B.C.: Harbour Publishing, 1997), 19, 142–43. My thanks to Gillian McMillan for drawing my attention to this source.

79. Shimada and Ariiso, *Kaigai katsudō no nihonjin*, 34.

80. Yesaki, *Sutebusuton*, 61.

81. Kazuichi Tasaka, interview by Eric Sokugawa and Carin Holroyd, Richmond, B.C., August 16, 1983, JCOHC.

82. For the term *kusawake*, see, e.g., Tomekichi Homma, "*Kusawake Koromo*: The Early Pioneers," *New Canadian: An Independent Organ for Canadians of Japanese Origin*, June 24, 1977. Japanese pioneers were regarded as heroes. See Andrew Nathaniel Nelson, *The Modern Reader's Japanese-English Character Dictionary*, 2nd ed. (Tokyo, 1974), 936–37, noting that the character 雄—pronounced *osu* or, in combination with other characters, *yū*—implies masculinity, heroism, superiority, excellence, ambition, and strong leadership.

83. Shimada and Ariiso, *Kaigai katsudō no nihonjin*, 41. Japanese settlers, Eiichiro Azuma explains, "consider[ed] the [North] American West as their own frontier," and "many educated Issei considered themselves to be modern settler colonists intent on conquering a wilderness, just like their Anglo-Saxon predecessors, for the sake of advancing civilization." Eiichiro Azuma, "Japanese Immigrant Settler Colonialism in the U.S.-Mexican Borderlands and the U.S. Racial-Imperialist Politics of the Hemispheric 'Yellow Peril,'" in "Conversations on Transpacific History," special issue, *Pacific Historical Review* 83, no. 2 (May 2014): 257–58, 276. See also Eiichiro Azuma, "Remapping a Pre–World War Two Japanese Diaspora: Transpacific Migration as an Articulation of Japan's Colonial Expansionism," in *Connecting Seas and Connected Ocean Rims: Indian, Atlantic, and Pacific Oceans and China Seas Migrations from the 1830s to the 1930s*, ed. Donna R. Gabaccia and Dirk Hoerder, Studies in Global Social History 8 (Leiden: Brill, 2011), 419–20, stating that the frontier myth "first played an important role in the development of hitherto sparsely inhabited Hokkaido in the 1870s and culminated in the conquest of Manchuria in the 1930s."

84. Nakayama Jinshiro, ed., *Kanada dōhō hatten taikan: Furoku* (Encyclopedia of Japanese in Canada: Supplement) (Vancouver, B.C., 1921), 116–17; Nakayama, *Canada and the Japanese,* 210, 275–77. Although the original source is not always acknowledged, authors whose works have drawn on Nakayama's account include Adachi, *Enemy That Never Was,* 28. This founding story is also recounted in *Zaibeinihonjinshi,* which explains that the account vividly describes the hardship that those who embarked on the journey north endured. Zaibei Nihonjinkai, *Zaibeinihonjinshi,* 1015.

85. Nakayama, *Canada and the Japanese,* 276; Homma, "*Kusawake Koromo.*" For a description of the Hastings sawmill and the Indigenous villages nearby, see Joe Simson, "Gastown: Everybody Knew Everybody," in *Raincoast Chronicles Six/Ten,* ed. Howard White, 2nd collector's ed. (Madeira Park, B.C.: Harbour Publishing, 1983), 170–72. While Nakayama does not name the village of Namgis, this is bound to have been the village where they pulled in.

86. The three others on the journey were Kawamura of Kochi Prefecture, Masuda of Echizen Province (which had become part of Fukui Prefecture), and a man who called himself Kichi, of Echizen Province (which had become part of Niigata Prefecture). Because the Buddha had endured all kinds of hardship for the salvation of all people, Yoshizawa later wrote, he set sail on April 8, the Buddha's birthday, in order to aid his fellow Japanese. Nakayama, *Kanada dōhō hatten taikan: Zen,* 112–15; Nakayama, *Kanada dōhō hatten taikan: Furoku,* 116–17, describing them as "pioneers of the northern fisheries"; Nakayama, *Canada and the Japanese,* 210, 277. Where my own account draws on more than one of these sources, in each of which Nakayama provides different sets of details, I cite all on which I draw.

87. Nakayama, *Kanada dōhō hatten taikan: Zen,* 112–15; Nakayama, *Kanada dōhō hatten taikan: Furoku,* 116–17; Nakayama, *Canada and the Japanese,* 210, 277.

88. Nakayama, *Canada and the Japanese,* 276.

89. Scott Byram and David G. Lewis, "Ourigan: Wealth of the Northwest Coast," *Oregon Historical Quarterly* 102, no. 2 (Summer 2001): 143, 155n46 (Tsimshian); Donald Mitchell and Leland Donald, "Sharing Resources on the North Pacific Coast of North America: The Case of the Eulachon Fishery," *Anthropologica* 43, no. 1 (2001): 21–22 (Nisga'a). For a list of the various spellings (including ourigan, oolichan, and eulachon) and a description of the importance of ooligan to northwest coast peoples in particular, see Byram and Lewis, "Ourigan," 130–31, 142–48. The ooligan is a "small smelt-like [delicately flavored] fish which is very rich in oil" that ran "in the largest number to the Nass River," where it had long been "used by the Indians, who extract[ed] for their own uses a considerable amount of oil." It was also an important trade item for the Indigenous peoples along the north Pacific coast. Assistant to the Commissioner, Fisheries, Victoria, B.C., to C. B. Marquis, Clinton, Iowa, January 18, 1928, BC Archives, GR-435, box 146, file 1928(4). Although the range of the ooligan extended from the Pribilof Islands to the Russian River in California, there are just thirty-five spawning streams along the entire coast of North America. Mitchell and Donald, "Sharing Resources," 20. People traveled from Haida Gwaii and deep in the B.C. interior both to trade for and, with the permission of coastal communities, to participate in the ooligan fishery, and groups like the Haida that had no spawning streams were sometimes granted privileges by others to access ooligan along the coast, but it could also trigger conflict. Mitchell and Donald, "Sharing Resources," 23, 27.

90. Shimada and Ariiso, *Kaigai katsudō no nihonjin,* 26–28.

91. Nakayama, *Kanada dōhō hatten taikan: Zen*, 463–64. At the time, Bella Bella had some 870 homes, a school, and a hospital. Shimada and Ariiso, *Kaigai katsudō no nihonjin*, 23–24.

92. Nakayama, *Kanada dōhō hatten taikan: Zen*, 463–64; Toyo Takata, *Nikkei Legacy* (Toronto: New Canada Publications, 1983), 90, referring to "Yasukichi Yoshigawa" as "Indian Yasu." See also, Nakayama, *Canada and the Japanese*, 277, reporting that Yoshizawa and eleven other Japanese fishermen learned English from a missionary stationed on the B.C. coast with the result that "even those whose literacy in Japanese was not very good were able to read and write English." For a discussion of the importance of Chinook jargon in facilitating trade along the north Pacific coast, see Byram and Lewis, "Ourigan," 148–50. As noted in chapter 2, the term *saibashi* was an adaptation of the term *siwash*. While both had derogatory connotations, not all Japanese immigrants were aware of this.

93. Nakayama, *Canada and the Japanese*, 274.

94. For the recruitment of recently arrived Japanese immigrants in Victoria, B.C., by Aikawa and Yoshizawa in 1891, see Nakayama, *Canada and the Japanese*, 277.

95. Nakayama, *Kanada dōhō hatten taikan: Furoku*, 160.

96. Nakayama, *Canada and the Japanese*, 209–10. The waters of Rivers Inlet were reportedly calm enough that even those with little experience could learn to handle small fishing boats there. Nakayama, *Kanada dōhō hatten taikan: Furoku*, 459. According to Fukawa and Yesaki, other fisheries that Japanese fishers helped to develop include the chum salmon fishery and the salt herring fishery. Fukawa, *Spirit of the Nikkei Fleet*, 18; Yesaki, *Sutebusuton*, 25–26. See also Takata, *Nikkei Legacy*, 90–91. Mitsuo Yesaki, who grew up fishing along the B.C. coast, acknowledges that Indigenous "fishermen [had] been trolling salmon off the BC coast" long before others arrived. Yesaki, *Sutebusuton*, 58.

97. Douglas C. Harris, *Landing Native Fisheries: Indian Reserves and Fishing Rights in British Columbia, 1849–1925* (Vancouver: UBC Press, 2008), 135, citing Canada, Order-in-Council, March 29, 1899, *Canada Gazette* 32, p. 1884.

98. In Canada, the Dominion government was responsible both for immigration and for regulating coastal fisheries. Constitution Act, 1867 (British North America Act), sec. 91, 92. Both the Dominion and the provincial governments played a role in enforcing the restrictions.

99. See, e.g., "Fraudulent Naturalization," *Victoria Daily Colonist*, July 27, 1900, and December 1, 1900; *Vancouver Daily Province*, December 2, 1900. Also see D. M. Eberts, Attorney General, *Return of Correspondence relating to Fraudulent Naturalization of Japanese*, 1 Ed. 7, 531, March 14, 1901; Canada, *Report of the Royal Commission on Chinese and Japanese Immigration*, 351, discussing allegations regarding fraudulent naturalization. For a detailed discussion of such claims and ways in which they were deployed, see Geiger, *Subverting Exclusion*, 139–42.

100. See Treaty of Commerce and Navigation between the United Kingdom and Japan, London, April 3, 1911, 104, *British and Foreign State Papers*, 159, VIII Martens, N.R.G. 3d ser., 413, incorporated into Canadian law by the Japanese Treaty Act, 1913, S.C. 1913, c. 27; B.C. Sessional Paper No. 74b. "Shall" is generally interpreted as "must" in law-related contexts.

101. Kiyoshi Karl Kawakami, *Asia at the Door: A Study of the Japanese Question in Continental United States, Hawaii and Canada* (New York: Fleming H. Revell, 1914), 248–50; Kiyoshi Karl Kawakami, *The Real Japanese Question* (New York: Macmillan, 1921), 222.

Harry A. Millis relied on Kawakami for his conclusion that "in British Columbia . . . a few thousand Japanese have become naturalized, the majority of them incidental to obtaining licenses as fishermen." Harry A. Millis, *The Japanese Problem in the United States* (New York: Macmillan, 1915), 47, citing Kawakami, *Asia at the Door*, 68–69. Kawakami was born in Tokyo in 1873 and emigrated to the United States after receiving a degree in law from the University of Tokyo. He later adopted the name Karl because he admired Karl Marx. *Survey of Race Relations*, box 30, "The Anti-Japanese League, Seattle," Hoover Institution Library and Archives, Stanford University.

102. Kunio Hidaka, *Wartime Legal Status of Persons of Japanese Race in Canada; Preliminary Investigation* (Vancouver, B.C., ca. 1940). For the denial of the franchise to Japanese Canadians, see chapter 3.

103. Whereas Indigenous fishermen held 151 and whites 102 of the fishing licenses issued for salmon fisheries along the northern B.C. coast in 1913, *nikkei* fishermen held 624. Canada, Department of Marine and Fisheries, *Forth-Sixth Annual Report of the Fisheries Branch, 1912–1913* (Ottawa: King's Printer, 1913).

104. Nakayama, *Kanada dōhō hatten taikan: Zen*, 87–88, 461; Nakayama, *Kanada dōhō hatten taikan: Furoku*, 160, noting the height of the waves. See also Hayashi Rintaro, *Kuroshio no hate ni* (At the end of the black current) (Tokyo: Nichibo Shuppansha, 1971), 116–18. As noted in chapter 2, although Hayashi wrote in Japanese, he was a Japanese Canadian who had generally adopted the Western custom of listing his given name first. I therefore refer to him as Rintaro Hayashi in the text. See also Dianne Newell, *Tangled Webs of History: Indians and the Law in Canada's Pacific Coast Fisheries* (Toronto: University of Toronto Press, 1993), 84, noting that the Indian agent "Charlie Todd . . . said that unlike the Japanese, Indians and whites would not travel as far out to sea, or on bad days, or at night (in the case of the Indians)." But see James Wickersham, "Japanese Art on Puget Sound," *American Antiquarian and Oriental Journal* 16, no. 2 (March 1894): 81, stating that Haida "fearlessly go far into the open ocean to attack the whale" as well as to seek out other kinds of fish and had done so for centuries.

105. Nakayama, *Canada and the Japanese*, 209.

106. McKenna-McBride Report, Testimony of C. C. Perry, 193, confirming that Indians were not willing to begin work at 6:00 P.M. on Sundays to ensure that the canneries could operate six days a week but also stating that he had encountered a Japanese who overextended his net only once and had never seen Japanese fishing during prohibited hours.

107. Nakayama, *Kanada dōhō hatten taikan: Zen*, 774–75. Nakayama and Rintaro Hayashi both use the term *dojin* to refer to Indigenous people. For a discussion of the term *dojin* and its social and cultural implications, see chapter 2. Although *buraku* simply means "village," use of this term in this context invokes a further negative association with outcaste villages, historically known as *tokushu buraku* (special hamlets). See Geiger, *Subverting Exclusion*, 5.

108. Nakayama, *Kanada dōhō hatten taikan: Zen*, 774–75.

109. McKenna-McBride Report, Testimony of Stephen A. Allan, 78–79.

110. McKenna-McBride Report, Rivers Inlet, Oweekano Tribe, 1915, Testimony of Wilson, 49.

111. M. Johnson, R. Brown, et al., to J. D. Hazen, Minister of Fisheries, August 11, 1913, Canada, Department of Marine and Fisheries, RG 23, file 6, pt. 8, quoted in Harris, *Landing Native Fisheries*, 144.

112. Leslie A. Robertson and the Kwagu'l Gi<u>xs</u>a̱m Clan, *Standing Up with Ga'a̱xsta'las: Jane Constance Cook and the Politics of Memory, Church and Custom* (Vancouver: UBC Press, 2012), 248, 516n20, citing petition presented to D. C. Scott, Ottawa, on behalf of the Kwagutl Agency, February 17, 1919.

113. McKenna-McBride Report, Testimony of Stephen A. Allan, 79–80. Rolf Knight and Maya Koizumi, *A Man of Our Times: The Life History of a Japanese-Canadian Fisherman* (Vancouver, B.C.: New Star Books, 1976), 44.

114. McKenna-McBride Report, Testimony of C. C. Perry, 190–92. Whereas independent fishers got twenty-five cents a fish, attached fishers received roughly half that amount.

115. McKenna-McBride Commission, *Confidential Report*, 17, quoted in Harris, *Landing Native Fisheries*, 145.

116. Harris, *Landing Native Fisheries*, 147.

117. Yesaki, *Sutebusuton*, 51, providing a year-by-year description of annual fisheries regulations during the 1920s.

118. The B.C. Fisheries Commission explained that it was easier to "substitut[e] white fishermen for . . . Orientals in the southern parts of the province" than it was along British Columbia's northern coast. British Columbia Fisheries Commission (1922), *Report and Recommendations* (Ottawa: King's Printer, 1923), 11–12. Although Chinese migrants also worked in the canneries, fishermen were primarily of Japanese origin and thus Japanese fishers were the group primarily affected by the licensing restrictions applied to "Orientals."

119. Canada, Department of Marine and Fisheries, *Fifty-Ninth Annual Report of the Fisheries Branch, 1925–1926* (Ottawa: King's Printer, 1926).

120. Yesaki, *Sutebusuton*, 17–18, 40, reporting that boundary redrawing was also used as part of the larger effort to exclude Japanese from the fishery. See also Hayashi, *Kuroshio no hate ni*, 116; Kanada Nihonjinkai [Japanese Association of Canada], *Zaika dōhō rōdō chōsa* (Labor survey of the Japanese in Canada) (Vancouver, B.C.: Kanada Nihonjinkai, 1923), 4–8. For a Japanese translation of fishery regulations in various districts see Capt. U. Nishikawa, "An Extract of Rules of the Road at Sea: Specially for the Fishing Vessels and Other Small Boats," n.d. [1931], 9, Vancouver Public Library, Special Collections, Vancouver, B.C.

121. Hayashi, *Kuroshio no hate ni*, 117. Although gas engine fishing boats were banned, Nakayama reports that canneries were permitted to provide tugboats to tow groups of fishing boats out to selected fishing sites and back again; if the tugboats did not arrive, fishers used their sails. Nakayama, *Kanada dōhō hatten taikan: Zen*, 479–80.

122. Compare Hayashi, *Kuroshio no hate ni*, 117–19, with Yuko Shibata, Shoji Matsumoto, Rintaro Hayashi, and Shotaro Iida, *The Forgotten History of the Japanese-Canadians*, vol. 1, *The Role of Japanese-Canadians in the Early Fishing Industry in B.C. and an Annotated Bibliography* (Vancouver, B.C.: New Sun Books, 1977), 10–12. It is important to recognize that it was the race-based regulatory framework established by the Fisheries Department in the first instance that set the stage for the strategic calculations Hayashi recounts. But for its persistent policy of limiting the *nikkei* access to the salmon fishery, there would have been no need for any *nikkei* fishermen to engage in the kinds of strategies Hayashi describes, to avoid its impact. To reduce the dynamic along British Columbia's north Pacific coast to nothing more than a race-based contest between undifferentiated racialized groups, however, is to

obscure the far more nuanced and complex negotiations of the race-based divides created under the law of the time by various members of each group.

123. Hayashi, *Kuroshio no hate ni*, 119; Shibata et al., *Forgotten History of the Japanese-Canadians*, 12. Although Shibata et al., Yesaki, Fukawa, and the Japanese Canadian Fishermen's Association all use the spelling "Kisawa," I use "Kizawa" because this is the spelling Kizawa himself used on English-language documents. See Japanese Canadian Research Collection (JCRC), Skeena Fishermen's Association (SFA) Fonds, box 11, University of British Columbia Library, Rare Books and Special Collections. The JCRC includes letters and telegrams written both in Japanese and in English, both of which I draw on.

124. Hayashi, *Kuroshio no hate ni*, 120.

125. Telegram from J. Kizawa, Port Essington, B.C., to S. Tsugimura, International Brokerage, Vancouver, B.C., June 10, 1929, JCRC, SFA; unsigned letter to J. Ringstad, Skeena Packing Company, Port Edward, Skeena River, B.C., May 15, 1929, JCRC, SFA, summarizing the history of the gas boat issue.

126. Telegram from Amalgamated Fishermen Association to Skeena Fishermen Association [*sic*], June 12, 1929, JCRC, SFA. Hayashi reports that Kizawa deliberately bought an old and battered boat for this purpose so that the loss would be minimal if it were confiscated. Hayashi, *Kuroshio no hate ni*, 122.

127. "Fishery Case Is Dismissed," *Evening Empire* (Prince Rupert, B.C.), June 19, 1929. It was clearly for the best that a telegram sent by the Amalgamated Fishermen's Association in Vancouver the same morning urging Kizawa not to proceed with the case because Parliament had just amended the discriminatory section of the Fisheries Act was not delivered in time to stay the proceedings. Telegram from Amalgamated Fishermen Association to Skeena Fishermen Association [*sic*], June 19, 1929, JCRC, SFA. When it became clear that the amendments would take effect only on August 1, however, Kizawa notified supporters of his determination to go out in a gas engine fishing boat a second time in mid-July based on the earlier court decision. Jun Kizawa to T. Takeuchi, Vancouver, B.C., July 2, 1929, JCRC, SFA.

128. In the Matter of a Reference as to the Constitutional Validity of Certain Sections of the Fisheries Act, 1914, [1928] S.C.R. 457.

129. The Attorney-General for Canada, Appellant v. The Attorney-General for British Columbia and Others, Respondents [including fishermen of Japanese origin in the Province of British Columbia], on Appeal from the Supreme Court of Canada (Reference as to the constitutional validity of certain sections of the Fisheries Act, 1914) [1930] A.C. 111, stating that "any British subject resident in the province of British Columbia who is not otherwise legally disqualified, has the right to receive a license, if he submits a proper application and tender the prescribed fee."

130. Dominion Fisheries Act, S.C. 1929, c. 42.

131. Skeena Fishermen's Association, Port Essington, B.C., to J. Roberts (referring to Roberts as "my dear friend"), August 19, 1932, JCRC, SFA.

132. "Attachment of Japanese Salmon Fishing Licenses to Be Taken Up by Local Commerce Chamber" [newspaper article, n.d.]; Jun Kizawa, "Message to All Fishermen regarding the Abolition of Fishing Area II Canneries 'Slave' Licenses," n.d. [1931], JCRC, SFA.

133. "Fishermen to Become Free," *The Province* (Vancouver, B.C.), December 22, 1931.

134. "Protests by Japanese" [newspaper article, n.d.]; Kizawa, "Message to All Fishermen," JCRC, SFA.

135. "Fishermen to Become Free: Attachment of Japanese to Canneries Is Discontinued," *The Province*, December 22, 1931.

136. Skeena Fishermen's Association to Roberts, August 19, 1932. See also M. Sakamoto to J. Kizawa, December 3, 1931; J. Kizawa to S. Obata, Prince Rupert, March 7, 1932; J. Roberts, Secretary, Northern B.C. Fishermen's Association, Prince Rupert, B.C., to S. Obata, Prince Rupert, April 27, 1932, JCRC, SFA. J. Roberts to Editor, *Daily Province*, Vancouver, B.C., April 19, 1932, JCRC, SFA, claiming that "the white fishermen on this coast, realizing that, where there is one section of the working class in bondage they are a menace to the rest of our class, and have always fought to get their Japanese Comrades free."

137. See, e.g., British Columbia Fisheries Commission, *Report and Recommendations*, 13, finding that "flagrant abuses are prevalent among Orientals in the securing of such papers for the purpose of obtaining fishing licenses" and recommending that naturalization papers be recalled and reissued with photographs and fingerprints.

138. J. A. Motherwell, Chief Supervisor of Fisheries, Vancouver, B.C., to J. Kizawa, Secretary, Skeena Fishermen's Association, Port Essington, B.C., April 13, 1932, JCRC, SFA.

139. Konishi [given name not provided], Skeena Fishermen's Association, to unnamed individual, n.d.; letter from Kizawa to *Kanada Shimbunsha* (Canada daily news), n.d., JCRC, SFA.

140. Births were not always registered, which meant that even *nisei* born to naturalized British subjects required naturalization certificates. Shibata et al., *Forgotten History of the Japanese-Canadians*, 3.

141. Knight and Koizumi, *Man of Our Times*, 44. See also *Summons* and *Plaint* [*sic*], *Hakaku Murota v. T. Hattaro*, Vancouver County Court, case no. B746/22, filed March 21, 1922, demanding the return of his naturalization certificate on the ground that it was "required by him to enable him to pursue his calling as a fisherman" or, in the alternative, awarding $500 in damages.

142. Kanada Nihonjinkai, *Zaika dōhō rōdō chōsa*, 3, noting that while there was a time when Japanese fishermen in Fishing Districts No. 1 and No. 3 also borrowed others' naturalization papers to obtain a fishing licence, by the 1920s it was relatively rare in those areas.

143. J. A. Motherwell, Chief Supervisor of Fisheries, Vancouver, B.C., to unnamed recipient, December 20, 1933, JCRC, SFA.

144. According to letters written by "Lex" in *The Columbian* (New Westminster, B.C.) (June 10, 1893) and *The Colonist* (June 15 and 21, 1893), "Many white fishermen were themselves foreigners, chiefly Americans, Austrians, Italians and Swedes, who became naturalized only to get fishery licenses, did not bring their families with them, build homes or develop the land, or pay much in the way of taxes." Patricia E. Roy, *A White Man's Province: British Columbia Politicians and Chinese and Japanese Immigrants, 1858–1914* (Vancouver: UBC Press, 1989), 85, 285n56. Also see comment of K. T. Takahashi in chapter 2 regarding the "dispatch" with which Americans who traveled to British Columbia to participate in seasonal fisheries presented themselves as Canadians.

145. Hidaka, *Wartime Legal Status of Persons of Japanese Race in Canada*, quoting 1927 Fisheries Department report, 78.

146. See, e.g., Commissioner of Fisheries to A. Forsyth, Provincial Police Office, Port Essington, B.C., May 4, 1911; and to C. P. Hickman, Fisheries Overseer, Naas Harbour, B.C., May 16, 1911 (providing instructions for the enforcement of fisheries regulations), BC Archives, GR-435, box 70, file 665.

147. The underlying figures are provided by Hozumi Yonemura, "Japanese Fishermen in British Columbia and British Fair-Play," *Canadian Forum* 10, no. 118 (July 1930): 375, noting that "in 1922, there were 2321 Japanese as against 3683 Whites and Indians. Today there are only 1068 as against 7171 Whites and Indians—or 1 Japanese for every 7 Whites and Indians." As for fisheries around Haida Gwaii, according to Japanese-language reports published early in the 1920s, there were 140 Japanese fishermen working in the waters around Haida Gwaii for eight separate Japanese operators, four of whom were from Wakayama Prefecture, two from Oita Prefecture and one each from Shimane and Hiroshima Prefectures. Nakayama, *Kanada dōhō hatten taikan: Zen*, 951.

148. International Fisheries Commission (IFC), 1939, Hearing Transcript, Testimony of J. A. Motherwell, 899, BC Archives, GR-435, box 222.

149. IFC, Testimony of J. A. Motherwell, 195. Boats and gear represented a major investment for all fishermen, and Aboriginal fishermen, isolated on small reserves along the B.C. coast, did not always have the means to acquire the equipment needed to compete as the technology of fishing changed. Yonemura, "Japanese Fishermen in British Columbia," 375. Harris notes that Indigenous participation was also complicated by competition between different reserves. Harris, *Landing Native Fisheries*, 137–38.

150. Nora Marks Dauenhauer, "Five Slices of Salmon," in *First Fish, First People: Salmon Tales of the North Pacific Rim*, ed. Judith Roche and Meg McHutchison (Seattle: University of Washington Press, 1998), 103.

151. See, e.g., Alisha M. Gauvreau, Dana Lepofsky, Murray Rutherford, and Mike Reid, "'Everything Revolves around Herring': The Heiltsuk-Herring Relationship through Time," *Ecology and Society* 22, no. 2 (2017), https://doi.org/10.5751/ES-09201-220210.

152. Shingo Hamada, "Ainu Geographic Names and an Indigenous History of the Herring in Hokkaido, Japan," *Canadian Journal of Native Studies* 35, no. 2 (2016): 47, 49; Gauvreau et al., "'Everything Revolves around Herring.'" The authors of each article estimate that the Ainu and Heiltsuk have fished for herring for some seven thousand years.

153. Shigeru Kayano, "Traditional Ainu Life: Living off the Interest," trans. Jan Corddry Langill with Rie Taki, in *First Fish, First People: Salmon Tales of the North Pacific Rim*, ed. Judith Roche and Meg McHutchison (Seattle: University of Washington Press, 1998), 24. Born in Nibutani, Hokkaido, in 1926 and of Ainu origin, Kayano was a member of the Japanese Diet (Upper House) from 1994 to 1998 and dedicated to the preservation of Ainu culture. Kayano, "Traditional Ainu Life," 38.

154. Gauvreau et al., "'Everything Revolves around Herring.'"

155. Ito, *Issei*, 118; Yesaki, *Sutebusuton*, 26.

156. Nakayama, *Kanada dōhō hatten taikan: Zen*, 471.

157. Although British Columbia's decision to ban the use of herring for nonfood purposes is also sometimes treated as an act of racial discrimination, British Columbia's policy in this regard was consistent with that of Washington State: whereas "unlimited use of herring and pilchards in reduction plants had long been allowed in Alaska, with the exception of very recent restrictions in an area of Cooke Inlet known as Halibut Cove," Washington State "prohibit[ed] the use of any food fish in reduction plants." "Memo re Herring and Pilchards," 1924, BC Archives, GR-435, box 147, file 1928–29. Ikeda was a principal in the firm of Awaya, Ikeda and Company, Ltd.; his business partner, Shinazo Awaya, was based primarily in Japan but occasionally visited Vancouver.

158. Nakayama, *Canada and the Japanese*, 214; Kawakami, *Asia at the Door*, 239.

159. See, e.g., Walter Prescott, Provincial Constable, Jedway, B.C., to T. G. Wynn, Chief Constable, Provincial Police Office, Prince Rupert, B.C., April 8, 1910, BC Archives, GR-435, box 70, file 660.

160. S. North, Vancouver, B.C., to H. J. Davis, Fishery Department, Victoria, B.C., October 19, 1910, BC Archives, GR-435, box 70, file 661, noting that fishery officers concluded that the problem in Tabata's case was that the licensing fee had been "collected by the Provincial Police of [Nanaimo]." See also Nakayama, *Canada and the Japanese*, 214–15, reporting that Korenaga, Ode, Tabata, and Tsuchiya all ran competing salt herring production companies along the B.C. coast.

161. Kawakami, *Asia at the Door*, 239.

162. Ito, *Issei*, 109, 118; Nakayama, *Kanada dōhō hatten taikan: Zen*, 1095.

163. "Flames Destroy Big Salteries: Morning Blaze Causes Loss of $20,000 on Coast Near Nanaimo," *Spokane Chronicle*, July 23, 1910; "Fires Believed to be Work of Incendiaries: Insurance Companies Investigating Destruction of Salteries at Nanaimo," *Victoria Daily Times*, October 22, 1910, reporting that ten Japanese-run salteries and one non-Japanese-run saltery had been destroyed by fire since 1909.

164. See, e.g., "Fire Destroys Fish Salteries," *Vancouver Sun*, July 19, 1912.

165. Nakayama, *Kanada dōhō hatten taikan: Zen*, 749, noting that Ikeda's most recent trip to Alaska was in 1904 and that he had spent six weeks there on that visit; *Douglas Island News* (Alaska), June 29, 1904.

166. B.C. Fisheries report, "The Fisheries of Rivers Inlet" (1908), 3, BC Archives, GR-435, box 70, file 657.

167. Nakayama, *Kanada dōhō hatten taikan: Zen*, 91.

168. Onodera Kannichi, ed., *Kanada e wattatta tōhoku no mura: Imin hyakunen to kokusai koryū* (Miyagi: Kōfusha, 1996), 107, 116, 288, 358, 372; Nitta, *Phantom Immigrants*, 20, 22, 87, quoting Jinsaburo Oikawa, *Autobiography*, chap. 8.

169. Nitta, *Phantom Immigrants*, 81, quoting Oikawa's friend and partner, Sato Jinuemon, as saying, "We wanted a place of our own, a place for Japanese only," from *The Recollections of Sato Jinuemon*.

170. Nitta, *Phantom Immigrants*, 57. As I explain in *Subverting Exclusion*, "the restrictions on travel within Japan maintained by the Tokugawa shogunate for over two centuries, together with the difficulty inherent in traveling through Japan's mountainous terrain, had led to the evolution of local customs and regional dialects so distinctive that some were virtually incomprehensible to people from other areas" well into the 1930s. "While this did not mean that travelers could not make themselves understood, it fostered the perception that those from other parts of Japan were as foreign as those from outside the country." Geiger, *Subverting Exclusion*, 23, citing Shotaro Frank Miyamoto, *Social Solidarity among the Japanese in Seattle*, University of Washington Publications in the Social Sciences, vol. 2, no. 2 (Seattle: University of Washington, 1939), 11; and Cullen Tadao Hayashida, "Identity, Race and the Blood Ideology of Japan" (Ph.D. diss., University of Washington, 1976), 57, who notes that Japanese from other domains—which later became prefectures—were referred to as *takokumono*, or "outside country persons," in contrast to *kunimono*, or "country persons" from the same domain. The character *kuni* or *koku* is now used to denote "country" or "nation."

171. Nitta, *Phantom Immigrants*, 63, 66, citing Oikawa, *Autobiography*, chap. 8.

172. Lion Island was reportedly used as shorthand for both Lion and Don Islands. When they wanted to differentiate between the two, Japanese residents reportedly referred to Don Island as Oikawa-jima and Lion Island as Sato-jima. Nitta, *Phantom Immigrants*, 84, 91.

173. Nitta, *Phantom Immigrants*, 96, 117. Oikawa visited Kuichi Airan in July 1907 and "discovered that there was a large population of Natives and Whites in the northern town of Masset and in the central town of Queen Charlotte but there was practically nobody in the smaller towns scattered around the island. Furthermore, there was only a handful of Japanese fishermen and nobody at all lived in the southern regions which were covered in luxuriant, virgin forest." Nitta, *Phantom Immigrants*, 148. Note that it was Goro Kaburagi who invited the Ainu group on its way to the Louisiana Purchase Exposition in St. Louis to visit his church as they passed through Vancouver. See chapter 2.

174. Nitta, *Phantom Immigrants*, 154.

175. Nitta, *Phantom Immigrants*, 117–19.

176. Nitta, *Phantom Immigrants*, 155. Oikawa returned to Japan in 1917, following the death of his son Eiji, who in 1912 drowned while taking out a boat on his own on the Fraser River. After Oikawa returned to Japan, Japanese settlers, who reportedly no longer felt unable to live in a white world, began to leave Oikawa Island when their children were old enough to attend school. Oikawa died in Japan on April 4, 1927. Nitta, *Phantom Immigrants*, 162, 189, 192.

177. Jutaro Tokunaga, "The Exploits of a Pioneer Issei," *Charlottes: A Journal of the Queen Charlotte Islands* 3 (1973): 21–22. Tokunaga met Ikeda's daughter when she visited Ikeda Bay for eight months in 1919–20. "A Japanese Gentleman on the Queen Charlottes," *Charlottes: A Journal of the Queen Charlotte Islands* 3 (1973): 19. Tokunaga's account is likely based on stories he was told by Ikeda and other family members. Ikeda's family continued to live in Vancouver but occasionally visited the mine. Like fish, copper ore also provided Japanese entrepreneurs with a way to contribute to the economic development of Japan and thereby to enhance Japan's place in the world as it became an increasingly active participant in the race for a commercial empire. See Lon Kurashige, *Two Faces of Exclusion: The Untold History of Anti-Asian Racism in the United States* (Chapel Hill: University of North Carolina Press, 2016), for discussion of the phrase "race for commercial empire."

178. For a detailed discussion of the copper mine established by Ikeda on Moresby Island, see Andrea Geiger, "Haida Gwaii as North Pacific Borderland, Ikeda Mine as Alternative West: 1906–1910," *Pacific Northwest Quarterly* 108, no. 4 (Fall 2017): 123, citing *B.C. Gazette*, November 28, 1907, 8280; Joseph Marko diary, 1908, Nancy Jo Marko Taylor Fonds, Haida Gwaii Museum at Ḵay Linagaay, Skidegate, B.C., May 2, 1908; and *Map Shewing the Property of the Ikeda Mines Limited, Ikeda Bay, Queen Charlotte Islands, B.C.*, Phillips/Dalzell Fonds, Haida Gwaii Museum at Ḵay Linagaay, Skidegate, B.C.

179. Ikeda is credited with starting what has been called the "copper rush" or "copper boom" on Moresby Island in 1906. While white settlers also sought out copper mining opportunities in the area, Ikeda's mine was the only one that proved to be economically viable. Kathleen E. Dalzell, *The Queen Charlotte Islands, Volume 2: Places and Names* (Madeira Park, B.C., 1973), 117, for use of the term "copper rush"; "Japanese Gentleman on the Queen Charlottes," 19.

180. Tokunaga, "Pioneer Issei," 22; Nogero, *Queen Charlotte Islands*, 36, referring to "little Japan."

181. *Prince Rupert Optimist*, December 10, 1909. See also Nogero, *Queen Charlotte Islands*, 37.

182. Geiger, "Haida Gwaii as North Pacific Borderland," 125–26.

183. *The Empire* (Prince Rupert, B.C.), July 18, 1908, noting that "visitors from Jedway were welcomed, treated handsomely and sent home on Ikeda's launch." The stipendiary magistrate at the time was E. M. Sandilands, and the provincial constable was Walter Prescott. The phrase "hi no maru" literally means "circle of the sun."

184. Geiger, "Haida Gwaii as North Pacific Borderland," 120.

185. *The Empire*, March 14, 1908. In 1910, following the death of two Japanese miners and the mine engineer Joseph Marko in mining accidents, the mine was recapitalized and sold, although Ikeda would remain on the board. Geiger, "Haida Gwaii as North Pacific Borderland," 128.

186. Geiger, "Haida Gwaii as North Pacific Borderland," 129–30.

187. Adachi, *Enemy That Never Was*, 99. See also Yesaki, Steves, and Steves, *Steveston Cannery Row*, 66, for photographs of "Japanese Imperial Navy training vessels off Steveston surrounded by a flotilla of gillnetters" and a fish packer boat flying Japanese flags to honor its visit. As Juneau's *Alaska Daily Empire* noted, a thousand naturalized Japanese Canadians enlisted in the Canadian Army in 1916. *Alaska Daily Empire*, January 13, 1916.

188. Nakayama, *Canada and the Japanese*, 283.

189. Nakayama, *Canada and the Japanese*, 285; Knight and Koizumi, "Ryuichi Yoshida," 62, reporting Yoshida's comment that "the Anti-Asiatic League blamed the Japanese for unemployment, for low pay . . . they blamed us for everything. It became very strong after the First World War."

190. Geiger, "Haida Gwaii as North Pacific Borderland," 128.

191. A. H. Sonsthagen, Petersburg, Alaska, to B.C. Fisheries Department, Victoria, January 2, 1935, BC Archives, GR-435, box 148, file 1934(2); Harry E. Hoffman, Kyuquot P.O., B.C., to George S. Pearson, Minister, Commissioner of Fisheries Office, May 1, 1934, BC Archives, GR-435, box 147, file 1934–37, reporting that pilchards (a species of herring) were disappearing.

192. Carothers, "Salmon and the Alutiiq/Sugpiaq Peoples," 143–44.

193. McKenna-McBride Report, Nass Agency, September 29, 1915, Testimony of Moses Johnson, 42–43, 45.

194. "Canneries carried on their operations as if the salmon were indestructible . . . and waste abounded." David F. Arnold, "Work and Culture in Southeastern Alaska: Tlingit Indians and the Industrial Fisheries, 1880s-1940s," in *Native Pathways: American Indian Culture and Economic Development in the Twentieth Century*, eds. Brian C. Hosmer and Colleen O-Neill (Boulder, Colo.: University Press of Colorado, 2004), 168, noting that thousands of pink and dog salmon simply were discarded.

195. McKenna-McBride Report, Nass Agency, September 29, 1915, Testimony of William Moody, 41. As noted later in this chapter, *nikkei* fishermen were often referred to as "Japanese" even though they could not have obtained a fishing license if they were not British subjects by naturalization or by birth. I use "Japanese" here in paraphrasing the material under discussion, however, to accurately reflect the way in which they were characterized by those referring to them.

196. McKenna-McBride Report, Testimony of Moses Johnson, 42–43.

197. McKenna-McBride Report, Testimony of C. C. Perry, 196–97, explaining that the Tsimshian spread branches of trees held down by rocks on the beach; when the tide came in the herring spawned all over the branches, which they would then take home and dry for food. It was one of their most important food items, and they did the "best they [could] to avoid waste." Heiltsuk people, Dianne Newall reports, "traded dried herring spawn with Japanese Canadians for supplies of soya sauce." Dianne Newall, *Tangled Webs of History: Indians and the Law in Canada's Pacific Coast Fisheries* (Toronto: UTP Press, 1993), 191.

198. Nakayama, *Kanada dōhō hatten taikan: Zen*, 474.

199. "Memo re Herring and Pilchards," 1924.

200. Miss M. S. Caldwell, Ganges, B.C., to Hon. S. L. Howe, Victoria, B.C., November 30, 1929, BC Archives, GR-435, box 147, file 1928(3). During the 1920s, roughly forty thousand tons of salt herring were shipped to Asia each year. Charlotte Gordon, "Little Brown Men Have Developed Huge Trade out of the Pacific's Silver Schools Which They Export to the Orient," *Victoria Times Colonist*, August 1, 1925.

201. George G. Bushby, Rupert Marine Products, Ltd., Prince Rupert, B.C., Report regarding "Herring in District #2," BC Archives, GR-435, box 149, file 1929–30.

202. "Cabinet Hears Views on Fisheries Problem," *The Province*, December 7, 1929.

203. "Herring in District #2," in Memorandum to the Commissioner of Fisheries from Assistant GJA, March 5, 1934, titled "Dry-Salt Herring versus Reduction of Herring," BC Archives, GR-435, box 149, file 1931–33, reporting that "the trans-Pacific transportation is handled very largely by Japanese vessels and the sales end of the business is in the hands of Orientals."

204. V. J. Creeden, Vancouver, B.C., to Hon George S. Pearson, Commissioner of Fisheries, Victoria, B.C., February 5, 1934, BC Archives, GR-435, box 149, file 1934; "Dry-Salt Herring versus Reduction of Herring." British Columbia passed regulations to force Japanese out of the salt herring business in 1924. "British Columbia Seeks Exclusion of Japanese," *Santa Fe New Mexican*, March 20, 1925. By 1938, "more than 50 per cent of the workers [at salmon and herring salteries were] whites or native Indians." "White Control for Salteries: Orientals Are Being Replaced in B.C. Industry," *The Province*, January 13, 1938.

205. Harry E. Hoffman, Kyuquot P.O., B.C., to George S. Pearson, Minister, Office of the Commissioner of Fisheries, May 1, 1934, BC Archives, GR-435, box 147, file 1934–37.

206. "Chinese Boycott Putting Stop to Herring Industry," newspaper clipping, January 13, 1932, BC Archives, GR-435, box 146, file 1932.

207. Memorandum, Acting Assistant to the Commissioner of Fisheries, August 2, 1933, enclosing a letter from M. J. Q. Dunsford, BC Archives, GR-435, box 148, file 1933. See also "B.C. Herring Salteries at Bargain Prices," *The Province*, February 26, 1932; and "Japanese Lead in B.C. Fishing: Gradual Elimination from Industry Urged," *The Province*, February 25, 1938, reporting that all "Japanese" applying for saltery licenses were required to "produce papers to prove citizenship."

208. Nakayama, *Kanada dōhō hatten taikan: Zen*, 475–76; Fukawa, *Spirit of the Nikkei Fleet*, 113.

209. Although their children born in the United States were citizens by birth, the second generation would not come of age until the 1920s or 1930s.

210. "Immediate Action Needed," *Fairbanks Daily Times*, March 26, 1912, reprinting article originally published in the *Ketchikan Miner*.

211. "The Yellow Peril," *Fairbanks Daily Times*, May 2, 1913. In a separate article, the *Fairbanks Daily Times* noted that Canada had decided not to bar the "Jap landowners" that it anticipated would choose to immigrate to Canada after California passed an alien land law. "Canada Will Not Put Ban on Japs: Anglo-Japanese Treaty Assures Open Door for Brown Men," April 22, 1913.

212. Reid, "Marine Tenure of the Makahs," 246.

213. C. P. Hickman, Fishery Overseer, Prince Rupert, B.C., to D. M. McIntyre, Deputy Commissioner of Fisheries, Victoria, B.C., May 30, 1913, BC Archives, GR-435, box 71, file 677.

214. John P. Babcock, "The Halibut Fishery—Its Investigation and Condition," August 2, 1933, BC Archives, GR-435, box 148, file 1933.

215. IFC, Testimony of W. S. Thompson, Director of Investigations, 16. International Fisheries Commission (IFC), Hearing Transcript, Testimony of W. S. Thompson, Director of Investigations, comment by R. Kearly, November 29, 1927, 16. See also Testimony of W. S. Thompson, 25, reporting that he had been told that "halibut are not greatly used in Japan."

216. Babcock, "The Halibut Fishery." In 1923, a halibut treaty, "the first treaty signed by Canada as an independent member of the Empire," provided for a closed season and established an international fisheries commission to continue the investigation by B.C. fisheries officials, which had been interrupted by the First World War. Under the terms of the 1930 treaty, "[Halibut] 'nursery' areas where fishing is forbidden [include] one at Masset Inlet in the Queen Charlotte Islands, . . . [where the] current joins the great eddy that carries eggs and larvae along the shore of the Gulf of Alaska and southwestward along the Alaska Peninsula." "International Commission Finds Out Life Secrets of Pacific Halibut," *Fisheries News Bulletin* (Department of Fisheries), vol. 3, no. 28 (February 1932).

217. See, e.g., "Japan Diplomat Goes to Valdez," *Fairbanks Daily Times*, September 8, 1906, noting the distinction between a charge of piracy and a statutory charge; "Japan to Investigate Killing of Poachers," *Fairbanks Daily Times*, August 25, 1906, noting that piracy was punishable by death, whereas more minor charges might result in a fine or a few years imprisonment.

218. *Daily Gateway* (Seward), August 16, 1905.

219. Ruth Hamaguchi, interviews by Miyoshi Tanaka, June 27, 1996, and July 1, 1996, JCOHC.

220. "Redfield Asks for Boats for Alaska Waters: Foreign Fishermen Will Be Kept Out," *Fairbanks Daily Times*, November 29, 1913.

221. "Japanese Fish Boats Are under Canada Registry," *Fairbanks Daily News-Miner*, June 15, 1939.

222. See, e.g., "Seal Poachers Captured," *Alaska Prospector* (Valdez), August 9, 1906; "Killed Five Japanese for Raiding Rookery: Was Done by Order of Lampke, Agent on Island for Department of Labor and Commerce," *Fairbanks Daily Times*, August 9, 1906; "To Be Given Speedy Trial," *Fairbanks Daily Times*, August 10, 1908 (giving number of Japanese sealers killed as seven).

223. See "Jap Poachers Active," *Daily Prospector Bulletin* (Valdez), September 1, 1907; "Jap Sealer in Forbidden Water: Men Are Landed near Sitka and Schooner Reported to Be off Yakutat," *Alaska Prospector*, May 7, 1908. See also "Japanese Poachers Seized by the *Bear*," *Fairbanks Daily Times*, August 16, 1908; and "The Northland," *Douglas Island News*, May 5,

1909, reporting that thirty Japanese seal poachers were captured near Sitka; November 15, 1911, reporting that twenty-two Japanese poachers were to go on trial in Ketchikan.

224. *Douglas Island News*, May 5, 1909.

225. "Japanese Sealers Approaching Coast," *Fairbanks Daily Times*, May 7, 1911; "Japs Poaching Again," *Alaska Citizen*, May 8, 1911.

226. Convention for the Preservation and Protection of the Fur Seals and Sea Otter, between the United States, Great Britain, Russia, and Japan, signed July 7, 1911, in effect December 15, 1911 (North Pacific Fur Seal Convention). The United States, Russia, and Britain each agreed that 30 percent of the skins taken each year would be equally divided among the other three parties. See also "Notes on the Fur-Seal," BC Archives, GR-435, box 189, file 1925; and "Alaska Seals Protected," *Fairbanks Daily Times*, August 2, 1911. As Patrick Lane notes, "The slaughter [of seals] was paralleled only by that of the buffalo during America's railroad heyday some hundred years later." Lane, "Great Pacific Seal-hunt," 45.

227. "Review of the North Pacific Sealing Convention of July 7, 1911," BC Archives, GR-435, box 189, file 1925; "Protecting the Seal," *Fairbanks Daily Times*, November 13, 1912. No rookeries were located in British territory. See also "Sealers Would Have Ottawa Government Reopen Claims Case," *The Colonist*, December 11, 1929, reporting that "the Japanese sealers, who did not pay any attention to the regulations and disregarded the three-mile limit from shore, have been compensated by their government when prohibited from carrying on."

228. North Pacific Fur Seal Convention, Art. IV. See also O.D. Skelton, Under-Secretary of State for External Affairs, Canada, Ottawa, to John Oliver, Prime Minister, Province of British Columbia, Victoria, B.C., 5 March 1927, BC Archives, GR-435, box 187, citing "Annual Seal Patrol Will Commence Soon: Vancouver and Armentieres to Guard Seal Herds in Canadian Waters May 1-June 10: Indians Only Ones Who Can Kill Seals and Then Only in Canoes and With Spears," *Times*, March 17, 1932.

229. "Caught Poaching," *Fairbanks Daily Times*, September 18, 1911; "Many Seal Skins Taken by Japanese Poachers: British Cutter Reports Having Captured Five of Outlaws," *Fairbanks Daily Times*, September 22, 1911.

230. A. Ikeda, Special Commissioner for Canada, Department of Agriculture and Commerce [Japan], 615 Hastings Street West, Vancouver, B.C., to John P. Babcock, Bureau of Fisheries, Victoria, B.C., December 1, 1926, BC Archives, GR-435, box 189, file 1929.

231. Memorandum for the Honourable the Premier from Assistant to the [Fisheries] Commissioner, December 22, 1926; B.C. Fisheries Commission, Victoria, B.C., to Dr. B. W. Evermann, Director, California Academy of Sciences, San Francisco, California, December 28, 1926, BC Archives, GR-435, box 189, file 1929. See also John P. Babcock, Provincial Fisheries Department, Victoria, B.C., to Dennis Winn, Department of Commerce, Bureau of Fisheries, Seattle, Washington, January 2, 1924, BC Archives, GR-435, box 89, file 866, noting that "our Indians on the west coast of Vancouver [Island] and off the Skeena's mouth and Goose Island took over 3,000 [fur] seals last year."

232. Capt. Charles Spring, Vancouver, B.C., to William Sloan, Commissioner of Fisheries for British Columbia, Victoria, B.C., February 9, 1927. BC Archives, GR-435, box 89, file 870. All parties understood that Britain would no longer represent Canada in renegotiating the treaty but that Canada would represent itself.

233. Memorandum from [Fisheries] Commissioner to the Premier, December 22, 1926; Barton W. Evermann, California Academy of Sciences, San Francisco, California, to John P. Babcock, IFC, March 12, 1925, BC Archives, GR-435, box 89, file 869.

234. "U.S. Seal Herds Depleting Supply of Japanese Fish: Tokyo Government Urging Revision [of] International Seal Convention—Claims $10,000,000 Annual Loss," *Fairbanks Daly News-Miner*, May 27, 1930.

235. "Sea Lion and Seal Blamed without Cause: Plea for Their Preservation Voiced at Meeting of Prominent Naturalists in Victoria; Stomach Analysis Acquits Accused," July 28, 1929, BC Archives, GR-435, box 187, file 2; Joseph Mandy, "Is the Sea-Lion a Menace? Thousands Killed on B.C. Cost by Machine Guns Each Year," *Vancouver Sunday Province*, July 10, 1927.

236. See, e.g., "Jap Vessels Are Fishing near Alaska," *Fairbanks Daily News-Miner*, July 8, 1930, noting the cutter *Chelan* had spotted the *Myogi Maru* along with twenty smaller boats all engaged in fishing off the Alaska coast.

237. "Aliens Are Destroying U.S. Fishing," *Fairbanks Daily News-Miner*, November 5, 1938; "[Anthony J.] Dimond Sees Fish War Ahead: Japan's Abrogation of Seal Treaty Means Will Invade Fish Runs," *Fairbanks Daily News-Miner*, November 13, 1940.

238. Senkichi Awaya, *Japan's Fisheries Industry—1939* (Tokyo: Japan Times and Mail, 1939), quoted in "Japanese Writers on Aims of Nipponese in North Pacific Fishing," *Fairbanks Daily News-Miner*, May 22, 1940. See also "Jap Fish Boats Operating Again in Bristol Bay," *Fairbanks Daily News-Miner*, noting that "two Japanese mother ships with fishing gear" had been sighted "in the water operating off Amak Island."

239. "Driven from Anchorage," *Vancouver Daily Province*, 1938. Seals had once been abundant along the west coast of Vancouver Island, but by 1915, Chief Tyhee Jack told the McKenna-McBride Commission, the canoes that went out from the village of It-att-soo to hunt for seals saw none. McKenna-McBride Report, Testimony of Chief Tyhee Jack, 76.

240. "Japs Toss Warning to Soviet Union: Siberian Fishing Rights Dispute Appears to Be Headed for a Showdown," *Fairbanks Daily News-Miner*, March 15, 1939.

241. "Dangers of Japs Fishing Alaska Area," *Fairbanks Daily News-Miner*, March 23, 1939; "Japs Fishing, Sounding near Sitka," *Fairbanks Daily News-Miner*, June 13, 1939.

242. "These Jap 'Fish' Boats," *Alaska Miner* (Fairbanks), August 20, 1940; "Alaska Fishing War," *Alaska Miner*, December 3, 1940.

243. Nakayama, *Canada and the Japanese*, 285.

Chapter Five

1. Jim Sinnett and Anthony Nakazawa, "Prospector Jujiro Wada Blazed the Iditarod Trail," *Seward Phoenix Log*, September 1, 2011. For a detailed discussion of Jujiro Wada's early exploits in Alaska and the Yukon, see chapter 2.

2. "America Warned of Japanese Move for Grip on Alaska: Treasure Must Be Guarded; Mining Man from Interior Says Japan Is Casting Covetous Eyes on Defenseless Territory, Jap Wada Declared to Be Agent of Tokio Government Making Maps of Harbors and Mines," *Cordova Daily Times*, 1923. See also Fumi Torigai and Taeko Torigai, "The Life of Jujiro Wada" (Whitehorse, Yukon: Torigai Translation Services, August 30, 2006), 7–8 (summary of Yūji Tani, *Ōrora ni kakeru samurai* [Tokyo: Yamato Keikokusha, 1995]),

Yukon Archives, Whitehorse, Yukon, Asian History of the Yukon Display Collection, 2006/146, file 21. R. N. DeArmond reports that such claims date back to 1910. R. N. DeArmond, "This Is My Country," *Alaska Magazine*, March 1988, 75, 80.

3. See, e.g., David Martin, "The Rising Sun over Canada," *Asia*, April 1941, 189, arguing that "the large number of Japanese fishermen, with their intimate knowledge of Canada's western waters, could be particularly helpful [to Japan if war broke out]."

4. International Fisheries Commission (IFC), 1939, Hearing Transcript, Testimony of J. A. Motherwell, 195, BC Archives, Royal British Columbia Museum, Victoria, B.C., GR-435, box 222.

5. Ken Adachi, *The Enemy That Never Was: A History of the Japanese Canadians* (Toronto: McClelland and Stewart, 1976), 100.

6. Patricia E. Roy, *The Oriental Question: Consolidating a White Province, 1914–41* (Vancouver: UBC Press, 2003), 161. Anthony J. Dimond, Alaska's delegate in the U.S. House of Representatives, reportedly said much the same about Japanese fishermen operating off the Alaska coast. Claus-M. Naske, "The Relocation of Alaska's Japanese Residents," *Pacific Northwest Quarterly* 74, no. 3 (July 1983): 127, citing *Congressional Record*, 73d Cong., 2d Sess. (1934).

7. See, e.g., Richard White, *"It's Your Misfortune and None of My Own": A New History of the American West* (Norman: University of Oklahoma Press, 1991), 328–29; and Robert V. Hine and John Mack Faragher, *The American West: A New Interpretive History* (New Haven, Conn.: Yale University Press, 2000), 474–75.

8. For a discussion of Yoshizawa's journey, see chapter 4.

9. Gordon G. Nakayama, *Issei: Stories of Japanese Canadian Pioneers* (Toronto: Britannia Printers, 1983), 160.

10. Kazuo Ito, *Issei: A History of Japanese Immigrants in North America*, trans. Shinichiro Nakamura and Jean S. Gerard (Seattle, 1973), 103. See also Zaibei Nihonjinkai [Japanese Association of America, History Preservation Committee], *Zaibeinihonjinshi* (History of Japanese in America), trans. Seizo Oka (San Francisco: Zaibei Nihonjinkai, 1940), 1070–71.

11. For a detailed discussion of historical status categories in Japan, see Andrea Geiger, *Subverting Exclusion: Transpacific Encounters with Race, Caste, and Borders, 1885–1928* (New Haven, Conn.: Yale University Press, 2011).

12. Quoted in Eiichiro Azuma, "Japanese Immigrant Settler Colonialism in the U.S.-Mexican Borderlands and the U.S. Racial-Imperialist Politics of the Hemispheric 'Yellow Peril,'" in "Conversations on Transpacific History," special issue, *Pacific Historical Review* 83, no. 2 (May 2014): 274. See also "Japanese Located on Mexican Coast: Los Angeles Times Correspondent Says Japs Have Acquired Base," *Fairbanks Daily Times*, April 23, 1915.

13. "Japan Knows Every Inch of Shore Lines: Nippon's Fishing Boats Should Be Restricted Operating out of U.S. Ports," *Fairbanks Daily News-Miner*, March 17, 1939, emphasis in the original.

14. Martin, "Rising Sun over Canada," 189; Bob Kumamoto, "The Search for Spies: American Counterintelligence and the Japanese American Community, 1931–1942," *Amerasia Journal* 6, no. 2 (1979): 45–75.

15. "Jap Fish Boats Seized at Hawaii," *Victoria Daily Times*, July 30, 1941. As Max Everest-Phillips notes, reports that Japan was actively engaged in espionage were ubiquitous throughout Asia and all around the Pacific Rim. Max Everest-Phillips, "The Pre-war Fear of Japanese Espionage: Its Impact and Legacy," *Journal of Contemporary History* 42, no. 2 (2007): 243–65.

16. *Halifax Herald* (Nova Scotia), November 20, 1937, depicted in Roy, *Oriental Question*, 167.

17. *Toronto Star Weekly*, April 9, 1938. In fact, the number of Japanese Canadians was just half that figure. See also Adachi, *Enemy That Never Was*, 183, 390n15, citing *The Province* (Vancouver, B.C.), November 17, 1937.

18. Hal Griffin, "Japan Spy Ring in B.C. Exposed: Bases Established by Fascist Agents Here; Linked with Nazis," *People's Advocate*, July 29, 1938. Japan, it is worth noting, was not without its own suspicions regarding foreign visitors in Japan whom they suspected of spying on behalf of Britain and the United States. A. Carly Buxton, "The Enemies among Us: Race, Trust, and Allied Internment in World War II Japan," in *Defamiliarizing Japan's Asia-Pacific War*, ed. W. Puck Brecher and Michael W. Meyers (Honolulu: University of Hawai'i Press, 2019), 196.

19. See, e.g., *Nicola Valley News* (Merritt, B.C.), March 11, 1910 (Haida Gwaii); and Griffin, "Japan Spy Ring in B.C. Exposed."

20. See, e.g., *Victoria Daily Colonist*, February 26, 1901; *Victoria Daily Colonist*, October 24, 1906, 5.

21. *Nicola Valley News*, March 11, 1910.

22. *The Review* (Courtenay, B.C.), July 31, 1913, 3, reporting that eleven Japanese had been landed in Bella Coola; *Evening Empire* (Prince Rupert, B.C.), August 8, 1913. "Nine Japs landed from junk which is being sought in Bella Bella area."

23. Ito, *Issei*, 63. Nakayama Jinshiro, *Canada and the Japanese (Kanada to nihonjin)*, trans. Tsuneharu Gonnami (Vancouver, B.C.: Kanada Nihonjinkai, 1940), 274, University of British Columbia Library, Special Collections and Archives, Vancouver, B.C., 1999.

24. Onodera Kannichi, ed., *Kanada e wattatta tōhoku no mura: Imin hyakunen to kokusai koryū* (Miyagi: Kōfusha, 1996), 107, 116, 288, 358, 372. Nitta Jiro, *Phantom Immigrants*, trans. David Sulz (n.p., 1998); originally published as *Mikkōsen Suian Maru* (Tokyo: Kodansha, 1979). W. D. Scott, Superintendent of Immigration, Department of the Interior, Ottawa, Canada, to Mr. Mitchell, July 26, 1913. Library and Archives Canada, Immigration Branch Files, record group 76, vol. 83. See also *Victoria Daily Colonist*, October 21, 1906.

25. Quoted in Roy, *Oriental Question*, 168.

26. Adachi, *Enemy That Never Was*, 53, 180–81; Ito, *Issei*, 81. Another smuggling ring, identified in the 1930s, relied not on surreptitious landings but on visa-related irregularities and was organized in part by Yoshie Saburo (Fred Yoshi), an employee of the Japanese consulate in Vancouver. At the conclusion of this investigation, however, just 145 Japanese determined to have entered the country illegally were deported from Canada. Ito, *Issei*, 86, 88.

27. *Douglas Island News* (Alaska), May 6, 1908; see also "Deserters Fare Badly along Alaska's Cost," *Fairbanks Daily Times*, August 10, 1911, reporting that "four Japs" who had deserted their ship reported that it had been wrecked, only to have it turn up in port. "Jap Sealer in Forbidden Water: Men Are Landed near Sitka and Schooner Reported to Be off Yakutat," *Alaska Prospector* (Valdez), May 7, 1908.

28. *Fairbanks Daily Times*, September 6, 1914.

29. Kahei Otani, "America and Japan Always Friends," in *Japan's Message to America: A Symposium by Representative Japanese on Japan and American-Japanese Relations*, ed. Naoichi Masaoka (Tokyo, 1914), 67.

30. T. Iyenaga and Kenosuke Sato, *Japan and the California Problem* (New York: G. P. Putnam's Sons, 1921), 108. For a detailed discussion of Japanese emigration across

the U.S.-Mexico border during the early twentieth century, see Andrea Geiger, "Caught in the Gap: The Transit Privilege and North America's Ambiguous Borders," in *Bridging National Borders in North America: Transnational and Comparative Histories*, ed. Benjamin H. Johnson and Andrew R. Graybill (Durham, N.C.: Duke University Press, 2010), 199–222.

31. Zaibei Nihonjinkai [Japanese Association of America, History Preservation Committee], *Zaibeinihonjinshi* (History of Japanese in America), trans. Seizo Oka (San Francisco: Zaibei Nihonjinkai, 1940), 971–72.

32. *The Globe* (Toronto), October 22, 1906, reporting on the survey originally published in the London *Times*.

33. "Diplomatic Relations between Japan and America," in *Japan and America: In Commemoration of the Visit of Japanese Representative Businessmen to America at the Invitation of the American Chambers of Commerce on the Pacific Slope*, ed. Kotaro Mochizuki (August 19, 1909), 21.

34. Yosaburo Takekoshi, *Japanese Rule in Formosa*, trans. George Braithwaite (London: Longmans, Green, 1907), vii. Note that the translation of Takekoshi's work lists his given name first.

35. Yosaburo Takekoshi, "Japan's Colonial Policy," in *Japan's Message to America: A Symposium by Representative Japanese on Japan and American-Japanese Relations*, ed. Naoichi Masaoka (Tokyo, 1914), 110.

36. See, e.g., Kenneth B. Pyle, *The Making of Modern Japan*, 2nd ed. (Lexington, Mass.: D. C. Heath, 1996), 184–85. British historians identify Britain's withdrawal from the Anglo-Japanese Alliance in 1921 at the Washington Conference as one of the leading causes of the Second World War. See, e.g., Ian H. Nish, *Alliance in Decline: A Study in Anglo Japanese Relations, 1908–1923* (London: Athlone Press, 1972), 381–83; Malcolm D. Kennedy, *The Estrangement of Great Britain and Japan* (Los Angeles: University of California Press, 1969), 54; and Charles N. Spinks, "The Termination of the Anglo-Japanese Alliance," *Pacific Historical Review* 6, no. 4 (1937): 337.

37. Nakayama Jinshiro, *Kanada dōhō hatten taikan: Zen* (Encyclopedia of Japanese in Canada: Complete) (Tokyo: Japan Times, 1921), 1105.

38. *Fairbanks Daily Times*, January 29, 1914.

39. See, e.g., Pyle, *Making of Modern Japan*, 183.

40. See, e.g., *Fairbanks Daily News-Miner*, March 8, 1932, admitting that "Japan did . . . take her lessons in empire building from the Western powers, America included, but the Western powers are not teaching those lessons any more."

41. Konoe Fumimaro, "Against a Pacifism Centered on England and America," *Japan Echo* 22 (1995): 12–14, a translation of "Ei Bei hon'i no heiwashugi o haisu," *Nihon oyobi Nihonjin*, December 15, 1918, 23–26. Konoe stepped down as prime minister in October 1945 and was replaced by Tōjō Hideki.

42. Eleanor Tupper and George E. McReynolds, *Japan in American Public Opinion* (New York: Macmillan, 1937), 2–3. In the Agreement between Japan and the United Kingdom, signed at London, August 12, 1905, Britain likewise assured Japan that it would not interfere with its interests in "Corea" and Japan assured Britain that it would not interfere in its interests in India.

43. *The Trans-Pacific*, vol. 1, no. 1 (September 1919).

44. See Geiger, *Subverting Exclusion*, 186–88.

45. Hugh H. and Mabel M. Smythe, "Race, Culture, and Politics in Japan," *Phylon* 13, no. 3 (1952): 192–98.

46. Izumi Hirobe, *Japanese Pride, American Prejudice: Modifying the Exclusion Clause of the 1924 Immigration Act* (Stanford, Calif.: Stanford University Press, 2001), 1.

47. As quoted in and translated by Yusuke Tsurumi, *Present Day Japan* (New York: Columbia University Press, 1926), 105.

48. Ito, *Issei*, 785–86.

49. "Japan's Umbrage [at] America Is Told [to] New Ambassador," *Fairbanks Daily News-Miner*, May 24, 1930.

50. Pyle, *Making of Modern Japan*, 185–86, 191.

51. Pyle, *Making of Modern Japan*, 141, 143. See also Sakada Yasuo, "The Enactment of the 1891 Immigration Law of the United States and Conflicting American and Japanese Perceptions: The 'Undesirable' and the 'Undesired,'" *Kokusaigau Ronshū* 9, no. 1 (June 1998): 81–82, noting that there were some in Japan who argued in the 1890s that, like Africans, Japanese in the United States also "suffered from white racism, and that the Japanese government should send the Imperial Navy to defeat the white Americans in retaliation for such humiliations."

52. Kiyoshi Karl Kawakami, *Asia at the Door: A Study of the Japanese Question in Continental United States, Hawaii and Canada* (New York: Fleming H. Revell, 1914), 10. Admiral Togo also spoke in British Columbia, and news of his tour across the United States reached Alaska. See, e.g., *Admiral Togo Visit to Kokumin Language School, Vancouver, B.C.*, 1911, photograph, Nikkei National Museum, Burnaby, B.C., Japanese Canadian Cultural Centre Photographic Collection, 2001.11.53; and "Admiral Togo Is Kept Busy," *Fairbanks Daily Times*, August 10, 1911, reporting that thousands had turned out to greet the admiral and had hoped to shake his hand. The Treaty of Portsmouth, mediated by Theodore Roosevelt and negotiated at the Portsmouth Naval Shipyard in Maine, formally recognized Japan's "interests" in Korea and divided Sakhalin between Russia and Japan. See chapter 1.

53. Inazo Nitobe, *The Japanese Nation: Its Land, Its People, and Its Life, with Special Consideration to Its Relations with the United States* (New York: Knickerbocker Press, 1912), 16–19.

54. Nitobe, *Japanese Nation*, 329–30. See also Ito, *Issei*, 214.

55. Rempei Kondo, "Japan Harbors No Ill Feeling toward America," in *Japan's Message to America: A Symposium by Representative Japanese on Japan and American-Japanese Relations*, ed. Naoichi Masaoka (Tokyo, 1914), 40.

56. Ryusaku Tsunoda, William Theodore de Bary, and Donald Keene, comps., *Sources of Japanese Tradition* (New York: Columbia University Press, 1958), 714–17.

57. Konoe, "Pacifism Centered on England and America," 12–14.

58. Brief filed by Takao Ozawa. U.S. District Court, District of Hawaii, Honolulu, Naturalization Case Files, 1927–1959, Ozawa Case File. RG 21, NARA. *Ozawa v. United States*, 260 U.S. 178 (1922) is discussed in chapter 3.

59. *Alaska Daily Empire* (Juneau), February 12, 1916. See also "Japs Displeased: Many Urging War [in Reaction to California's Passage of an Alien Land Law]," *Fairbanks Daily Times*, May 21, 1913. The *Fairbanks Daily Times* regarded the Panama Canal as the "chief obstacle in the way of a Japanese invasion of the Pacific coast," given how quickly the U.S. Navy, which was concentrated on the east coast of the United States, could meet an

invading force on the west coast. "Panama Canal Prevents Jap War Movement: Nipponese Realize That the Canal Will Render American Navy Doubly Effective in Case of Trouble," *Fairbanks Daily Times*, June 15, 1913.

60. "Japan Plans Alaska Raid with Salmon," *Fairbanks Daily News-Miner*, April 26, 1934.

61. *Alaska Miner* (Fairbanks), December 3, 1940. For a detailed discussion of the consequences of the Great Kanto earthquake, see Joshua Hammer, *Yokohama Burning: The Deadly 1923 Earthquake and Fire That Helped Forge the Path to World War II* (New York: Free Press, 2006). Some 92 percent of the buildings in Yokohama were destroyed, as were over 440,000 buildings in Tokyo, leaving 67 percent of Tokyo's population homeless. Hammer, *Yokohama Burning*, 244.

62. Azuma, "Japanese Immigrant Settler Colonialism," 276.

63. Azuma, "Japanese Immigrant Settler Colonialism," 266, 268, quoting "Japan and Mexico," *New York Times*, April 4, 1923.

64. Culver Jones, "Rising Sun over B.C.," *Toronto Star Weekly*, October 1, 1938, citing timber and mining interests in the Queen Charlotte Islands; "Japs Invade B.C.," clipping, December 30, 1942, BC Archives, H. D. Wilson Fonds, box 3.

65. Charles E. Hope and W. K. Earle, "The Oriental Threat," *Maclean's*, May 1, 1933, 12, 54–55.

66. Elmore Philpott, quoted in Roy, *Oriental Question*, 184.

67. Hope and Earle, "Oriental Threat," 12, 54–55. F. Leighton Thomas, a self-described veteran of the British Imperial Army, made similar claims in his *Japan: The Octopus of the East and Its Menace to Canada* (n.p., 1932).

68. Yamazaki Yasushi et al., *Sokuseki* (Footprint) (n.p., 1942), chap. 4. See also chap. 13, by Kodama Genichi, in *Sokuseki*.

69. Zach Jones, "Seiki Kayamori and His Place in Alaska History," Alaska Historical Society, January 10, 2013, https://alaskahistoricalsociety.org/seiki-kayamori-and-his-place-in-alaska-history/; Juliana Hu Pegues, "'Picture Man': Shoki Kayamori and the Photography of Colonial Encounter in Alaska, 1912–1941," *College Literature: A Journal of Critical Literary Studies*, 41, no. 1 (Winter 2014): 90–118. Kayamori is sometimes referred to as "Fhoki" Kayamori, a mistransliteration of this name; Jones states that his family reports that his name was Seiki but Pegues explains that he preferred the name Shoki, an alternate reading of the character that constituted his name.

70. Eileen Sunada Sarasohn, ed., *The Issei, Portrait of a Pioneer: An Oral History* (Palo Alto, Calif.: Pacific Books, 1983), 131. For a detailed discussion of Japanese emigration to Manchuria, see, e.g., Greg P. Guelcher, "Paradise Lost: Japan's Agricultural Colonists in Manchukuo," in *Japanese Diasporas: Unsung Pasts, Conflicting Presents, and Uncertain Futures*, ed. Nobuko Adachi (London: Routledge, 2006), 71–84; and Sandra Wilson, "The 'New Paradise': Japanese Emigration to Manchuria in the 1930s and 1940s," *International History Review* 17, no. 2 (May 1995): 249–86. See also John J. Stephan, "Hijacked by Utopia: American Nikkei in Manchuria," *Amerasia Journal* 23, no. 3 (1997): 1–42.

71. *Japanese American Courier*, March 11, 1939, quoting Naoki Hoshino. For a discussion of historical status categories, see Geiger, *Subverting Exclusion*. The *Japanese American Courier* was the first English-language newspaper published by *nikkeijin* in North America that had no Japanese-language component.

72. *Japanese American Courier*, January 25, 1941.

73. *Japanese American Courier*, February 1, 1941. Russia had ceded Karafuto (southern Sakhalin) to Japan under the terms of the Treaty of Portsmouth in 1905.

74. See, e.g., Henry Walsworth Kinney, "The Other Side of Japan's Emigration Story: Official Figures Show More Japanese Returning from America than Are Going There," *The Trans-Pacific*, February 1921, 76–78, noting that return migration had begun to exceed new immigration in both Canada and the United States. See also Kazuhiro Ono, "The Problem of Japanese Emigration," *Kyoto University Economic Review* 28, no. 1 (April 1958): 46, noting that "increasing momentum attached to the popular opinion that Japanese migration should be concentrated on Manchuria and Korea. Japan's migration westward, [which replaced] the eastward movement, persisted up to the time of the Pacific War of 1941–45."

75. Eiichiro Azuma, "Remapping a Pre–World War Two Japanese Diaspora: Transpacific Migration as an Articulation of Japan's Colonial Expansionism," in *Connecting Seas and Connected Ocean Rims: Indian, Atlantic, and Pacific Oceans and China Seas Migrations from the 1830s to the 1930s*, ed. Donna R. Gabaccia and Dirk Hoerder, Studies in Global Social History 8 (Leiden: Brill, 2011), 431–33. See also James L. Tigner, "Japanese Immigration into Latin America: A Survey," *Journal of Interamerican Studies and World Affairs* 23, no. 4 (November 1981): 457–82; Donald Hastings, "Japanese Emigration and Assimilation in Brazil," *International Migration Review* 3, no. 2 (Spring 1969): 32–53; J. F. Normano, "Japanese Emigration to Brazil," *Pacific Affairs* 7, no. 1 (March 1934): 42–61. For population figures after 1910, see An Authority [pseud.], "The Japanese Immigrant in Brazil," *The Trans-Pacific*, January 1921, 88–91.

76. Zaibei Nihonjinkai, *Zaibeinihonjinshi*, 972; 1066–68, also opining that even the French had been a target of U.S. racism because of their "slightly darker skin-color."

77. See, e.g., Martin, "Rising Sun over Canada," 189, suggesting that "the fact that the major part of the British Columbia coast is virtually uninhabited would make secrecy at least temporarily possible." The entire convoy comprised thirty vessels. Iturup or Etorofu is the same island that, together with Urup, marked the initial division of the Kuril Islands between Russia and Japan in 1855, before Russia relinquished its claims to the Kuril Islands in 1875 in exchange for Japan's relinquishment of its claims to Sakhalin. See chapter 1.

78. Muriel Kitagawa, *This Is My Own: Letters to Wes & Other Writings on Japanese Canadians, 1941–1948*, ed. Roy Miki (Vancouver, B.C.: Talonbooks, 1985), 230.

79. Kitagawa, *This Is My Own*, 78. See also Jean-Pierre Antonio, "Japanese-Canadian Diary Provides Rare Insights into War Years," *British Columbia History* 48, no. 3 (Fall 2015): 25, quoting Japanese Canadian Masayuki Yano's entry for the days following Japan's attack on Pearl Harbor: "I can't express the disastrous feeling I have about the treatment we will receive in the future." For the connection that some elderly *issei* continued to feel to Japan, see, e.g., Mitsuru Shimpo, *Ishi o mote owaruru gotoku: Nikkei Kanadajin Shakaishi* (Like being chased away by thrown stones: A social history of Japanese Canadians) (Toronto: Tairiku Jiho, 1975), 3–4.

80. *Japanese American Courier*, March 27, 1942.

81. See, e.g., Jeanne Wakatsuki Houston and James D. Houston, *Farewell to Manzanar: A True Story of Japanese American Experience during and after the World War II Internment* (Boston: Houghton Mifflin, 1973), 66–67, 144, expressing concerns about being perceived as disloyal to Japan or as a "traitor" by Japanese.

82. See, e.g., Ito, *Issei*, pt. 15, "Pro-Japanese," 647–98; and Mitsuo Yesaki, *Sutebusuton: A Japanese Village on the British Columbia Coast* (Vancouver, B.C.: Peninsula Publishing, 2003), 100–107, listing "supporters of the Japanese."

83. Anthony J. Dimond, the Territory of Alaska's delegate in Congress, warned in March 1934 that any attack on the contiguous states would come through Alaska, which would be used as a based to attack Seattle and San Francisco. Martin, "Rising Sun over Canada," 189.

84. Ronald K. Inouye, Carol Hoshiko, and Kazumi Heshiki, *Alaska's Japanese Pioneers: Faces, Voices, Stories* (Fairbanks: Alaska's Japanese Pioneers Research Project, 1994), 24, interview with Walter Tsuneo Fukuyama.

85. Isamu Taguchi, interview by Ronald K. Inouye, Juneau, Alaska, October 19 and 20, 1990, Alaska's Japanese Pioneers Research Project (AJPRP) Records, 1990–1991 (HMC-0374) (AJPRP), Archives and Special Collections, Consortium Library, University of Anchorage, Anchorage, Alaska, tapes 13 and 14, transcript, 17–18, 61. Mack Mori and Harue Mori, interview by Ronald K. Inouye, Seattle, Washington, October 13, 1991, AJPRP, tapes 18 and 19, transcript, 10, 13. The Fukuyama children were older, but the Tanaka children were small and one was a baby. See also Inouye, Hoshiko, and Heshiki, *Alaska's Japanese Pioneers*, 28–29.

86. Jerry D. Lewis, "5th Column in California: Will the Japanese Blitzkrieg Strike at the U.S.A.?," clipping, H. D. Wilson Fonds; Lloyd Wendt, "Another Phase of Japanese Espionage," clipping (circa 1940), H. D. Wilson Fonds, alleging that the tuna boats never brought in a catch. See also *Fairbanks Daily News-Miner*, August 7, 1940.

87. Martin, "Rising Sun over Canada," 189, refuting the notion that "'British Columbia may become the Belgium of a Pacific war.'" The archdeacon in question was Frederick George Scott, who was appointed as archdeacon of Quebec in 1925. See also Adachi, *Enemy That Never Was*, 183, 390n15.

88. "Three Men and Fish Boat in Alaska Could Paralyze National Defense Program," *Alaska Miner*, September 3, 1940.

89. "Alderman Wants Jap Fish Boats Confined"; "Ald. Wilson Urges Further Curb on Japanese: Fears Fishing Fleet Menace," clippings (circa 1940), H. D. Wilson Fonds.

90. "The Japan Hazard in B.C.," *Financial News*, October 11, 1940, also including trucks used to transport berries in its warning.

91. Yesaki, *Sutebusuton*, 114. On learning of the Canadian Navy's seizure of Japanese Canadian fishing vessels, Masayuki Yano wrote: "The bear that has been sleeping until now has awoken. The bear is roaring and is shocked and is lost. They even took the rowboats, and at night there is blackout. Police with guns patrol the town. A curfew has begun." Antonio, "Japanese-Canadian Diary," 26, quoting Yano's entry for the days following Japan's attack on Pearl Harbor.

92. Randy Enomoto, ed., *Honouring Our People: Breaking the Silence* (Burnaby, B.C.: Japanese Canadian Citizen's Association, 2016), 135, interview with Ellen Crowe-Swords née Kimoto, whose father fished in the Tofino and Stubbs Island area.

93. Thomas Madokoro, "Good Old Days in Tofino," in *Changing Tides: Vanishing Voices of Nikkei Fishermen and Their Families*, ed. Kotaro Hayashi, Fumio "Frank" Kanno, Henry Tanaka, and Jim Tanaka (Burnaby, B.C.: Nikkei National Museum & Cultural Centre, 2017), 30.

94. Toshio Murao, "Weathering the Storm," in *Changing Tides: Vanishing Voices of Nikkei Fishermen and Their Families*, ed. Kotaro Hayashi, Fumio "Frank" Kanno, Henry Tanaka, and Jim Tanaka (Burnaby, B.C.: Nikkei National Museum & Cultural Centre, 2017), 52, regarding Tsunetaro Oye. See also Yesaki, *Sutebusuton*, 115; and Masako Fukawa, *Spirit of the*

Nikkei Fleet: BC's Japanese Canadian Fishermen, with Stanley Fukawa and the Nikkei Fishermen's History Book Committee (Madeira Park, B.C.: Harbour Publishing, 2009), 120. Oye's widow later reported that his tongue had been slit and shared a coroner's report with Grace Eiko Thomson that states that he died of asphyxiation after disconnecting his life support. Grace Eiko Thomson, *Chiru Sakura—Falling Cherry Blossoms: A Mother & Daughter's Journey through Racism, Internment and Oppression* (Halfmoon Bay, B.C.: Caitlin Press, 2021), 84.

95. Kazuo Nakagawa, "Twelve Terrifying Days," in *Changing Tides: Vanishing Voices of Nikkei Fishermen and Their Families*, ed. Kotaro Hayashi, Fumio "Frank" Kanno, Henry Tanaka, and Jim Tanaka (Burnaby, B.C.: Nikkei National Museum & Cultural Centre, 2017), 42–43, 52.

96. See Yesaki, *Sutebusuton*, 115–16, and Fukawa, *Spirit of the Nikkei Fleet*, 125–30, for a detailed analysis of the fishing boats and associated gear that was sold. See also Hayashi et al., *Changing Tides*, 37. Order-in-Council P.C. 251 (January 13, 1942) provided that Japanese Canadians were "prohibited from fishing for the duration of the war"; Order-in-Council P.C. 288 (January 13, 1942) established the Japanese Fishing Vessel Disposal Committee and provided for the sale of all impounded vessels to non-Japanese. Fukawa, *Spirit of the Nikkei Fleet*, 176.

97. Rolf Knight, *Indians at Work: An Informal History of Native Labour in British Columbia, 1858–1930* (1978; Vancouver, B.C.: New Star Books, 1996), 325; Geoff Meggs, *Salmon: The Decline of the British Columbia Fishery* (Vancouver, B.C.: Douglas and McIntyre, 1991), 159; Fukawa, *Spirit of the Nikkei Fleet*, 128–30 (chart).

98. Yesaki, *Sutebusuton*, 115–16; Fukawa, *Spirit of the Nikkei Fleet*, 125, 127–28; Hayashi et al., *Changing Tides*, 37.

99. Enomoto, *Honouring Our People*, 135–36, interview with Ellen Crowe-Swords, explaining that "there was a lot of activism" among Japanese fishermen and that "they didn't take what was happening to them lying down." One former fisherman estimated that two-thirds of the members of the Nisei Mass Evacuation Group, who refused to cooperate with removal orders that broke up families, were fishermen. Harry Yonekura, cited in Masako Fukawa, *Spirit of the Nikkei Fleet: BC's Japanese Canadian Fishermen*, with Stanley Fukawa and the Nikkei Fishermen's History Book Committee (Madeira Park, B.C.: Harbour Publishing, 2009), 149.

100. *Japanese American Courier*, January 9 and 16, 1942.

101. "News-Herald Editorial," reprinted in *Tairiku Nippō* (Vancouver, B.C.), H. D. Wilson Fonds.

102. Adachi, *Enemy That Never Was*, 203, citing Maurice Pope, *Soldiers and Politicians* (Toronto: University of Toronto Press, 1962), 177.

103. Royal Canadian Mounted Police (RCMP), Notice to Male Enemy Aliens, February 7, 1942, describing the perimeter of the protected area as following the line of the "Cascade Mountains" from "boundary point No. 7 on the International Boundary between the Dominion of Canada and Alaska" to B.C.'s southernmost boundary, and including all of the islands along the B.C. coast; *Japanese American Courier*, February 6, 1942. As along the U.S.-Mexico border, the protected area extended further inland along the international border to include the area surrounding the town of Trail, where there was a well-established Italian immigrant community. The Yukon was not included in the protected area: Alaska was seemingly regarded as a sufficient buffer, such that it was not deemed to be in danger.

104. Rolf Knight and Maya Koizumi, *A Man of Our Times: The Life History of a Japanese-Canadian Fisherman* (Vancouver, B.C.: New Star Books, 1976), 48–50. Yoshida was a labor leader who had studied law in Japan at Hosei University; he candidly admitted that he immigrated after failing his exams. He would be rearrested and incarcerated for a time at Hastings Park after being denounced by Etsuji Morii, who was working with the RCMP. Knight and Koizumi, *Man of Our Times*, 51. See also Rolf Knight and Maya Koizumi, "Ryuichi Yoshida: An Issei Life," ed. John Skapski, in *Raincoast Chronicles Six/Ten*, ed. Howard White, 2nd collector's ed. (Madeira Park, B.C.: Harbour Publishing, 1983), 59–67. Muriel Kitagawa, a *nisei* who lived in Vancouver, also feared that a riot might occur. Kitagawa, *This Is My Own*, 83. For more on Etsuji Morii, see Adachi, *Enemy That Never Was*, 237–39.

105. Knight and Koizumi, *Man of Our Times*, 52. For a description of the Rogers Pass avalanche, see Adachi, *Enemy That Never Was*, 93; and Nakayama, *Kanada dōhō hatten taikan: Zen*, 1915.

106. Canada, Order-in-Council P.C. 1486 (February 23, 1942); Order-in-Council P.C. 1665 (March 4, 1942).

107. Wm. Stapleton, G. A. Rushton, and G. Bruce Burpee, to Major Austin C. Taylor, British Columbia Security Commission, March 13, 1942, Vancouver, B.C., Union Steamship Company Collection, box 1, file 8, Vancouver Maritime Museum Archives, Vancouver, B.C. The proposal was based on the understanding that those being removed would carry no more than "blankets and hand luggage" and that they would be required to pay their own passage unless they were able to prove to the RCMP that they lacked the funds to do so.

108. Yesaki, *Sutebusuton*, 116; Fukawa, *Spirit of the Nikkei Fleet*, 142, listing *nikkei* coastal settlements.

109. Stapleton, Rushton, and Burpee to Taylor, March 13, 1942.

110. Yesaki, *Sutebusuton*, 116; Fukawa, *Spirit of the Nikkei Fleet*, 142.

111. *Japanese American Courier*, April 17, 1942.

112. Enomoto, *Honouring Our People*, 40, interview with Ray Iwasaki.

113. *Japanese American Courier*, April 24, 1942.

114. "'Nazi' Button Found in Steveston Jap Shack," *Vancouver Sun*, June 8, 1942, Nikkei National Museum, Kishizo Kimura Fonds, 2010.4.4.13.66; Don Mason, "No More Japanese at Steveston, B.C.: White and Indian Families Move in as Warfare Move[s] out the Little Yellow Fishermen," newspaper clipping dated June 22, 1942, Kishizo Kimura Fonds, 2010.4.4.13.80. See also "Once-Thriving Jap Village Now Deserted," May 1, 1942, newspaper clipping dated July 2, 1942, Kishizo Kimura Fonds, 2010.4.4.13.53.

115. Enomoto, *Honouring Our People*, 41, interview with Ray Iwasaki, noting that mattresses were bags of straw and sanitary conditions were primitive.

116. Enomoto, *Honouring Our People*, 98–99, interview with Henry Shimizu, born in 1928 in Prince Rupert, B.C.

117. Knight and Koizumi, *Man of Our Times*, 51.

118. Fukawa, *Spirit of the Nikkei Fleet*, 153.

119. Linda Kawamoto Reid and Beth Carter, *Karizumai* (Temporary dwelling places) (Burnaby, B.C.: Nikkei National Museum, 2012), 37. Sandon, which had a population of fewer than twenty before Japanese Canadians arrived, was the site of an abandoned silver mine and reportedly in shadow much of each day. Reid and Carter, *Karizumai*.

120. Knight and Koizumi, *Man of Our Times*, 92. For those who had owned their own fishing boats, their seizure had already cut deep, a loss compounded by the seizure of their homes and real property in 1943. Fukawa, *Spirit of the Nikkei Fleet*, 148, quoting Harry Yonekura, a Steveston-based fisherman interviewed in 2006: "To the fisherman his boat is second only to his life."

121. Fukawa, *Spirit of the Nikkei Fleet*, 153.

122. Knight and Koizumi, *Man of Our Times*, 53.

123. Zaibei Nihonjinkai, *Zaibeinihonjinshi*, 304–6; *Personal Justice Denied: Report of the Commission on Wartime Relocation and Internment of Civilians* (Washington, D.C.: Civil Liberties Public Education Fund; Seattle: University of Washington Press, 1997), 69, 108–9. See also Yuko Konno, "Trans-Pacific Localism and the Creation of a Fishing Colony: Pre–World War II Taiji Immigrants on Terminal Island, California," in *Trans-Pacific Japanese American Studies: Conversations on Race and Racializations*, ed. Yasuko Takezawa and Gary Y. Okihiro (Honolulu: University of Hawai'i Press, 2015), 85. Konno reports that Japanese fishermen based on Terminal Island sometimes assisted other villagers from Taiji to enter the United States from Mexico illegally. Village ties, she notes, had a stronger claim on their sense of obligation than nation-based ties. Konno, "Trans-Pacific Localism," 91.

124. Fuki Endow Kawaguchi, "On the Brink of Evacuation: The Diary of an Issei Woman," *Prospects: An Annual of American Cultural Studies* 28 (2004): 359–82, 362 (December 8 diary entry), 379n14; *Personal Justice Denied*, 108.

125. *Personal Justice Denied*, 69, 108–9. Terminal Island, one writer alleged, was one of several colonies established by Japan at strategic locations in the United States. Lewis, "5th Column in California."

126. Kumamoto, "Search for Spies," 59–60. Similar status-based distinctions existed among Japanese Canadians. As Ellen Crowe-Swords, whose own father was a fisherman who fished the west coast of Vancouver Island, explained: "Fishermen were sort of considered— not the dregs of the world, you know, pretty close." Enomoto, *Honouring Our People*, 136, interview with Ellen Crowe-Swords.

127. *Personal Justice Denied*, 108.

128. *Japanese American Courier*, March 20, 1942.

129. *Japanese American Courier*, January 30, 1942.

130. *Japanese American Courier*, March 30, 1942.

131. *Japanese American Courier*, February 13 and 27, 1942. On February 19 and 20, 1942, Franklin D. Roosevelt issued two executive orders. The first established designated military zones and the second, Executive Order 9066, identified those who were to be excluded from them.

132. *Japanese American Courier*, February 27, 1942.

133. *Japanese American Courier*, March 6, 1942; *Pacific Citizen*, November 12, 1942, referring to "Mexican Japanese." All of California was later included in the barred zone.

134. *Japanese American Courier*, April 24, 1942, reporting in the last issue it would publish before it was shut down that all Alaska had been designated a military area and that plans to remove "all Nipponese" were underway.

135. *Japanese American Courier*, April 3, 1942. The Japanese Canadian Citizens Council and the Japanese American Citizens League both urged cooperation with the removal orders; however, there were also those who resisted, including some who regarded resistance itself as an expression of loyalty. Although some have attributed cooperation with the

removal orders to a sense of fatalism they say is encompassed in the expression *shigata ga nai* (there is nothing to be done), my own understanding of this phrase, given the contexts in which I heard it used in Japan as a child, speaks to courage and a quiet determination to carry on. But see, e.g., Adachi, *Enemy That Never Was*, 225–26, saying Japanese Canadians cooperated with a "docility that was almost wholly in line with their background and their particular development as a minority group."

136. Memorandum, Ernest Gruening, Governor of Alaska, to Secretary, Department of the Interior, Division of Territories and Island Possessions, Washington, D.C., February 19, 1942, U.S. National Archives and Records Administration (NARA), record group (RG) 101, file 77, Alaska State Archives, box VS 571, folder 4 (Evacuation, 1942–1947). Gruening had arrived in Alaska just two years earlier in December 1939 after being appointed governor by President Roosevelt. Claus-M. Naske, "Dr. Alaska: Ernest Gruening," *Journal of the West* 20, no. 1 (January 1981): 32–40, republished in *An Alaska Anthology: Interpreting the Past*, eds. Stephen Haycox and Mary Childers Mangusso (Seattle: University of Washington Press, 1996), 378–79.

137. Office of the Commanding General, Fort Richardson, Alaska, Public Proclamation No. 1, April 7, 1942, Alaska State Library, Juneau, Historical Collections, U.S. War Relocation Authority, RG 210, MS 51, box 3, folder 3-1. See also *Japanese American Courier*, April 24, 1942.

138. E. L. Bartlett, Acting Governor, Juneau, Alaska, to General S. B. Buckner Jr., Fort Richardson, Alaska, April 10, 1942, NARA, RG 101, file 77-1, Alaska State Archives, box VS 571, folder 5 (Japanese Evacuation, 1942–1945).

139. Earl N. Ohmer, President and General Manager, Alaskan Glacier Sea Food Company, Petersburg, Alaska, to Mr. Bob Bartlett [sic], Acting Governor, Juneau, Alaska, April 14, 1942, NARA, RG 101, file 77-1, Alaska State Archives, box VS 571, folder 5 (Japanese Evacuation, 1942–1945).

140. Ito, *Issei*, 371–72; Otis Hays Jr., *Alaska's Hidden Wars: Secret Campaigns on the North Pacific Rim* (Fairbanks: University of Alaska Press, 2004), 6, for biographical details. Some older men left for Japan before the war. Mack Mori, interview, 12.

141. E. L. Bartlett, Acting Governor, Juneau, Alaska, to Leonard C. Allen, Indian Service, Ketchikan, Alaska, April 14, 1942; Schick, AG, ADC, Fort Richardson, Alaska, to CO U.S. Troops, Juneau, Alaska, April 2, 1942, NARA, RG 101, file 77-1, Alaska State Archives, box VS 571, folder 5 (Japanese Evacuation, 1942–1945).

142. Bartlett to Buckner, April 10, 1942. Although the War Relocation Authority initially disapproved of Indigenous wives being allowed to accompany their husbands, it later relented.

143. Simon Bolivar Buckner, HQ, ADC, Ft. Richardson, Alaska, to E. L. Bartlett, Acting Governor, Juneau, Alaska, April 9, 1942; Bartlett to Buckner, April 10, 1942. General Buckner was responsible for operations in Alaska during the early years of World War II.

144. Russell G. Maynard, Director, Department of Public Welfare, Territory of Alaska, Juneau, Alaska, to E. L. Bartlett, Acting Governor of Alaska, Juneau, Alaska, April 22, 1942, NARA, RG 101, file 77-1, Alaska State Archives, box VS 571, folder 5 (Japanese Evacuation, 1942–1945).

145. Alice Stuart, Fairbanks, Alaska, to Governor Ernest H. Gruening, Juneau, Alaska, April 24, 1942, NARA, RG 101, file 77-1, Alaska State Archives, box VS 571, folder 5 (Japanese Evacuation, 1942–1945).

146. E. L. Bartlett, Interior Department, Governor's Office, Juneau, Alaska, to Governor Ernest Gruening, San Francisco, California, April 27, 1942, NARA, RG 101, file 77-1, Alaska State Archives, box VS 571, folder 5 (Japanese Evacuation, 1942–1945).

147. E. L. Bartlett, Acting Governor, Juneau, Alaska, to Alice Stuart, Fairbanks, Alaska, April 29, 1942, NARA, RG 101, file 77-1, Alaska State Archives, box VS 571, folder 5 (Japanese Evacuation, 1942–1945).

148. Mamie Attunga Moto Karmun, interview by Ronald K. Inouye, Carol Hoshiko, and Kazumi Heshiki, Anchorage, February 22, 1991, AJPRP, tape 6, transcript, 21–22.

149. Karmun, interview, 22–24, 43.

150. Hana Elavgak Yasuda Kangas, interview by Ronald K. Inouye, Palmer, Alaska, December 2, 1990, AJPRP, transcript, 12–13, 15, 17. See also Inouye, Hoshiko, and Heshiki, *Alaska's Japanese Pioneers*, 50–51.

151. Irene Takizawa and Helen Nakashima, interview by Carol Hoshiko, Seattle, October 24, 1990, AJPRP, transcript, 15–16; Patrick Hagiwara, interview by Carol Hoshiko, Bellevue, Washington, May 17, 1991, AJPRP, tape 2, transcript, 31.

152. The circumstances of Kayamori's death are not entirely clear. While local reports that he was beaten by U.S. soldiers may well be accurate, most *issei* were arrested immediately, not beaten and then allowed to return home. For examples of his photographs and for more detailed accounts of his life and interaction with the community in which he lived, see, e.g., India Spartz and Ronald K. Inouye, "Fhoki Kayamori: Amateur Photographer of Yakutat, 1912–1941," *Alaska History* 6, no. 2 (Fall 1991): 30–36; Margaret Thomas, *Picture Man: The Legacy of Southeast Alaska Photographer Shoki Kayamori* (Fairbanks: University of Alaska Press, 2015); Pegues, "'Picture Man,'" 90–118.; and Jones, "Seiki Kayamori." Kayamori's suicide, together with his reported attempt to burn some papers in his possession, ironically, served to perpetuate suspicions that he was a spy. See Margaret Thomas, "Was Kayamori a Spy?," *Alaska Magazine*, November 1995, 48–54.

153. *Japanese American Courier*, March 13, 1942.

154. *Japanese American Courier*, April 3, 1942.

155. Inouye, Hoshiko, and Heshiki, *Alaska's Japanese Pioneers*, 26–27. See also Robert Teruo Ohashi, interview by Carol Hoshiko, Seattle, October 23, 1990, AJPRP, tape 11, transcript, 15–16, reporting the false allegation regarding Patrick Hagiwara.

156. Inouye, Hoshiko, and Heshiki, *Alaska's Japanese Pioneers*, 26–27.

157. Mack Mori, interview, 11, 14–15, 21; Inouye, Hoshiko, and Heshiki, *Alaska's Japanese Pioneers*, 26–27.

158. Inouye, Hoshiko, and Heshiki, *Alaska's Japanese Pioneers*, 10; Taguchi, interview, 20–21. The 218 people forcibly removed from Alaska included some forty families with some degree of Japanese ancestry. The largest number—8—were from Ketchikan and 6 from Petersburg. Four families had lived in Killisnoo and three in Anchorage; two in each of Cordova, Fairbanks, and Wrangell; and one in each of Beaver, Nome, Seward, Deering, Bristol Bay, and Kodiak. Minutes, Meeting with the Evacuees from the Territory of Alaska, Minidoka Relocation Center, April 30, 1943, Alaska State Library, Historical Collections, War Relocation Authority files, MS 51, box 3, folder 3-2.

159. Komatsu Ohashi and Hope Ohashi, interview by Ronald K. Inouye and Kazumi Heshiki, Ketchikan, Alaska, December 8, 1990, AJPRP, tape 10, transcript, 26–28; Mack Mori, interview, 19–21.

160. Hope Ohashi, interview, transcript, 27–28, 39; Inouye, Hoshiko, and Heshiki, *Alaska's Japanese Pioneers*, 33, 36–37, 40–41, noting that most Japanese-run businesses in Ketchikan were located on Stedman Street. See Jeffery F. Burton, Mary M. Farrell, Florence B. Lord, and Richard W. Lord, *Confinement and Ethnicity: An Overview of World War II Japanese American Relocation Sites*, revised ed., Publications in Anthropology 74 ([Tucson, Ariz.]: Western Archeological and Conservation Center, National Park Service, 2000), chap. 17, for a description of the Lordsburg Detention Facility.

161. Tad Fujioka and Cherry Tsuruko Tatsuda Fujioka, interview by Kazumi Heshiki and Ronald K. Inouye, Juneau, December 9, 1990, AJPRP, tape 1, transcript, 28; Inouye, Hoshiko, and Heshiki, *Alaska's Japanese Pioneers*, 8.

162. Ronald K. Inouye, Carol Hoshiko, Kazumi Heshiki, and Stephen Haycox, *Guide to Collection*, AJPRP, 11.

163. Hope Ohashi, interview, 27–28, 39.

164. Hope Ohashi, interview, 30.

165. In Ryuichi Yoshida's words, "Various troubles and factions divided the Issei." Knight and Koizumi, *Man of Our Times*, 48. Crowe-Swords, in turn, described the social structure at the self-supporting community at Bridge River: "The very rich Japanese lived on top, then there was the middle group the merchants, and then the fisherman [in] the bottom group . . . had the smallest shacks." Enomoto, *Honouring Our People*, 137. Even fishing families did not constitute a single, undifferentiated group: there was the "'Saimoto clan, the Gulf of Georgia group . . . the Prince Rupert people, the Skeena people, the Chemainus people, [as well as] the Cumberland people. A keen ear could detect the different experiences by the dialect or proficiency of either language.'" Enomoto, *Honouring Our People*, 148, quoting Peter Nimi, "Recollections of Minto Days," *Sentimental Journey*, 49.

166. Enomoto, *Honouring Our People*, 252–53, interview with Ed Suguro: *chibi* is a disparaging term for small people; "lily" may well be adapted from the phrase "lily white."

167. Nakashima, interview, 18. The name "Foode" is an adaptation of "Fuji" or "Fujii."

168. Taguchi, interview, 23.

169. George Yanagimachi, interview by Ronald K. Inouye, Seattle, Washington, October 14, 1991, AJPRP, transcript, 24.

170. Hagiwara, interview, transcript, 19. See also Dianne Newell, *Tangled Webs of History: Indians and the Law in Canada's Pacific Coast Fisheries* (Toronto: University of Toronto Press, 1993), quoting Buck Suzuki as saying: "[Indian people] were looked down [on] as being, well I'll tell you the truth, even by the Japanese themselves, who were being persecuted, they were looked down [on] as being inferior"; Ito, *Issei*, 366, quoting Kibun Miyazaki as saying, "[some] Indian houses remind me of something to be found at the back of tenement houses in Japan."

171. Cherry Tsuruko Tatsuda Fujioka, interview, 14.

172. Hagiwara, interview, 12. For similar attitudes among Japanese immigrants in Canada, see Kitagawa, *This Is My Own*, 283.

173. War Relocation Authority records show that most Alaska families were sent to Minidoka, in Hunt, Idaho; one person was sent to Manzanar, where residents of Bainbridge Island were also sent, and seven to Tule Lake, California, which would be used to house those identified as resisters. Inouye, Hoshiko, and Heshiki, *Alaska's Japanese Pioneers*, 10.

174. Komatsu Ohashi, interview, 31. *Kuronbo* is a disparaging word for African Americans, but the use of the suffix "san" is clearly intended to make it more polite. Alaskans who

joined 442nd included the Tatsuda boys, the Hagiwara boys, Akagi Urata, and Kenny Oyama (from Petersburg). Cherry Tsuruko Tatsuda Fujioka interview, 34.

175. Takizawa, interview, 17.

176. Mack Mori, interview, 49.

177. Taguchi, interview, 24. For an environmental history of camps run by the War Relocation Authority, see Connie Y. Chiang, *Nature behind Barbed Wire: An Environmental History of the Japanese American Incarceration* (New York: Oxford University Press, 2018).

178. Hope Ohashi, interview, 31–32.

179. Kangas, interview, 24–25.

180. Taguchi, interview, 25–26.

181. Handwritten notes on Memorandum, Carl V. Sandoz, Counselor, Minidoka War Relocation Project, Hunt, Idaho, to Dillon Myer, National Director, War Relocation Authority, October 17, 1942, Alaska State Library, Historical Collections, War Relocation Authority files, MS 51, box 3, folder 3-2.

182. Memorandum, Carl V. Sandoz, Counselor, Minidoka War Relocation Project, Hunt, Idaho, to Dillon S. Myer, National Director, War Relocation Authority, October 17, 1942, Alaska State Library, Historical Collections, War Relocation Authority files, MS 51, box 3, folder 3-2, enclosing a list of those incarcerated at Minidoka who hailed from Alaska, noting the degree of "Japanese blood" in each instance. See also John H. Provinse, Chief, Community Management Division, to Joseph C. McCaskill, Planning Branch, Office of Indian Affairs, Washington, D.C., Alaska State Library, Historical Collections, War Relocation Authority files, MS 51, box 3, folder 3-2.

183. James H. Condit, Pasadena, California, to Anthony J. Dimond, Delegate from Alaska, Washington, D.C., December 31, 1942, Alaska State Library, Historical Collections, MS 51, box 3, folder 3-3.

184. Dillon S. Myer, Director, War Relocation Authority, to Anthony J. Dimond, Delegate from Alaska, Washington, D.C., December 31, 1942, citing Title 32, National Defense, Chapter I, War Relocation Authority, Part V, "Issuance for Leave for Departure from a Relocation Area (September 26, 1942), Alaska State Library, Historical Collections, MS 51, box 3, folder 3-3. Both the Gila River and the Poston detention camps were located on Indian reservations, the Poston Relocation Center on the Colorado River Indian Reservation and the Gila River War Relocation Center on the Gila River Indian Reservation. Karen J. Leong and Myla Vicenti Carpio, "Carceral Subjugations: Gila River Indian Community and Incarceration of Japanese Americans on Its Lands," *Amerasia Journal* 4, vol. 1 (2016), 103–20. See also Eric L. Muller, "'A Penny for Their Thoughts': Draft Resistance at the Poston Relocation Center," *Law & Contemporary Problems* 68 (2005): 135, noting that War Relocation Authority and Office of Indian Affairs personnel also moved from one agency to the other.

185. James H. Condit, Pasadena, California, to Dillon S. Myer, Director, War Relocation Authority, May 15, 1943, Alaska State Library, Historical Collections, MS 51, box 3, folder 3-3.

186. Dillon S. Myer, Director, War Relocation Authority, to James H. Condit, Pasadena, California, May 21, 1943, Alaska State Library, Historical Collections, MS 51, box 3, folder 3-3. Among those released from Minidoka were Hope Ohashi, who studied music at the University of Rochester; Alice Togo, who attended Vassar; and Isamu Taguchi, who worked at a hospital in Rochester, Minnesota, where there were about "50 Japanese student nurses," and

later moved to Chicago to work in a pinball machine factory. Ohashi, interview; Taguchi, interview.

187. Charles Foode, Rexburg, Idaho, to E. N. Gruening, Governor, Alaska, November 24, 1943, NARA, RG 101, file 77-1, Alaska State Archives, box VS 571, folder 5 (Japanese Evacuation, 1942–1945).

188. E. L. Bartlett, Acting Governor, Juneau, Alaska, to Charles Foode, Rexburg, Idaho, December 7, 1943, NARA, RG 101, file 77-1, Alaska State Archives, box VS 571, folder 5 (Japanese Evacuation, 1942–1945).

189. Ralph C. Parker, Captain, U.S. Navy, Commander, Alaskan Sector, Passage Seward, Alaska, to Ernest Gruening, Governor, Juneau, Alaska, August 5, 1941, NARA, RG 101, file 77, Alaska State Archives, box VS 571, folder 4 (Evacuation, 1942–1947).

190. Naval Air Station, Dutch Harbor, Alaska, to Superintendent, Bureau of Indian Affairs, Juneau, Alaska, December 8, 1941, NARA, RG 101, file 77, Alaska State Archives, box VS 571, folder 4 (Evacuation, 1942–1947).

191. V. R. Farrell, Director of Education, Office of Indian Affairs, Interior Department, Juneau, Alaska, to Homer I. Stockdale, Unalaska, Alaska, December 12, 1941; Claude M. Hirst, General Superintendent, Alaska Indian Service, Interior Department, Juneau, Alaska, to Corthell, Unalaska, December 26, 1941; see also Hugh J. Wade, Territorial Director, Social Security Board, Juneau, Alaska, to Red Cross, Alaska Defense Command, Fort Richardson, Anchorage, Alaska, June 14, 1942, making clear that lack of funds was a continuing issue; Fred R. Geeslin, Acting General Superintendent, Interior Department, Alaska Indian Service, Juneau, Alaska, to Commanding Officer, Naval Air Station, Dutch Harbor, Alaska, December 8, 1941, NARA, RG 101, file 77, Alaska State Archives, box VS 571, folder 4 (Evacuation, 1942–1947).

192. George Sundborg, Report re Evacuation Meeting, March 18, 1942, NARA, RG 101, file 77, Alaska State Archives, box VS 571, folder 4 (Evacuation, 1942–1947). Copies of the report were sent to Admiral Freeman, Captain Parker, and General Buckner in April. George Sundborg, Senior Planning Technician, Region X, National Resources Planning Board, Field Office, Juneau, Alaska, to E. L. Bartlett, Acting Governor, Juneau, Alaska, April 17, 1942. Those attending the meeting along with Bartlett included Clade M. Hirst, superintendent, and Virgil Farrell, director of education, both of the Office of Indian Affairs; Edna Wright and Hugh J. Wade of the Federal Security Agency (Social Security Board); and Russell G. Maynard, director, and Kenneth R. Forsman, Child Welfare supervisor, Territorial Department of Public Welfare. Memorandum, E. L. Bartlett, Acting Governor, Juneau, Alaska, March 18, 1942, NARA, RG 101, file 77, Alaska State Archives, box VS 571, folder 4 (Evacuation, 1942–1947).

193. General Buckner, Fort Richardson, Alaska, to Ernest Gruening, Governor, Juneau, Alaska, June 3, 1942, Alaska State Archives, Alaska at War Materials, Sites file. Brendan Coyle explains that Japan's primary goal in launching the attack on Dutch Harbor was "drawing the American carrier fleet north" at a time when it was preparing to launch an attack on Midway Island far to the south. Because the U.S. was aware of the imminent attack on Midway Island, the attack on Dutch Harbor did not have the intended effect. Brendan Coyle, *Kiska: The Japanese Occupation of an Alaska Island* (Fairbanks: University of Alaska Press, 2014), 27.

194. John J. Stephan, *The Kuril Islands: Russo-Japanese Frontier in the Pacific* (Oxford, U.K.: Clarendon Press, 1974), 3.

195. "Indian Schools Secured for Japs: 6000 More to Be Moved at Once," newspaper clipping dated June 5, 1942, Kishizo Kimura Fonds, 2010.4.4.13.65; "Last Nipponese to Be Gone in August," newspaper clipping dated July 6, 1942, Kishizo Kimura Fonds, 2010.4.4.13.104, noting that "50 families [were] to be quartered into Indian Schools in Edmonton, [Alberta]."

196. Stephen Haycox, *Alaska: An American Colony* (Seattle: University of Washington Press, 2002), 8, noting that fifteen hundred miles is the same distance as that between Anchorage and Seattle.

197. Samantha Seiple, *Ghosts in the Fog: The Untold Story of Alaska's WWII Invasion* (New York: Scholastic Press, 2011), 7, noting that reports regarding the attack were marked "classified."

198. Susan Marks, Hoonah, Alaska, to Ernest Gruening, Governor, Juneau, Alaska, June 13, 1942; Senior Planning Technician, Region X, National Resources Planning Board, Field Office, Juneau, Alaska, to E. L. Bartlett, Acting Governor, Juneau, Alaska, April 17, 1942, NARA, RG 101, file 77, Alaska State Archives, box VS 571, folder 4 (Evacuation, 1942–1947).

199. See, e.g., Robert Schoettler, Juneau, Alaska, to Commander, Alaskan Sector, Kodiak, Alaska, June 14, 1942; Commander, Alaskan Sector, Kodiak, Alaska, to Lieutenant Schoettler, Juneau, Alaska, June 15, 1942 [note states "taken over the telephone from Lieutenant Schoettler, Navy Department, June 15, 1942," and "paraphrased"], NARA, RG 101, file 77, Alaska State Archives, box VS 571, folder 4 (Evacuation, 1942–1947).

200. Ernest Gruening, Governor, Juneau, Alaska, to Harold L. Ickes, Secretary of the Interior (through the Division of Territories and Island Possessions), Interior Department, Washington, D.C., June 4, 1942, NARA, RG 101, file 77, Alaska State Archives, box VS 571, folder 4 (Evacuation, 1942–1947). Gruening stated that Superintendent Hirst of Indian Affairs agreed with General Buckner. Residents of Atka numbered "eighty Natives and four whites," while "445 Natives [and] twenty whites" resided in the Pribilof Islands. Navy Command, Kodiak, Alaska, to Navy Department, Seattle, Washington, June 15, 1942; J. W. Wark, Capt., C.E., Adjutant, Headquarters U.S. Troops, Juneau, Alaska, to Bureau of Indian Affairs, Juneau, Alaska, June 16, 1942, NARA, RG 101, file 77, Alaska State Archives, box VS 571, folder 4 (Evacuation, 1942–1947).

201. R. C. Parker, Captain, U.S. Navy, Commander, Alaskan Sector, Thirteenth Naval District, Naval Air Station, Kodiak, Alaska, to H. J. Thompson, Weather Bureau, U.S. Department of Commerce, Anchorage, Alaska, June 17, 1942, NARA, RG 101, file 77, Alaska State Archives, box VS 571, folder 4 (Evacuation, 1942–1947).

202. Ernest Gruening, Governor, Juneau, Alaska, to Harold L. Ickes, Secretary of the Interior (through the Division of Territories and Island Possessions), Interior Department, Washington, D.C., June 20, 1942, NARA, RG 101, file 77, Alaska State Archives, box VS 571, folder 4 (Evacuation, 1942–1947). Native Alaskans evacuated from the western Aleutian islands included 72 from Unmak, 41 from Akutan, 20 from Kashega, 18 from Biorka, 8 from Makushi (as well as a sixty-two-year-old man described as "white"), and 1 from Unalaska. List of Individuals Evacuated from Nikolski, Akutan, Kashega, Biorka, Makushi, and Unalaska, n.d., NARA, RG 101, file 77, Alaska State Archives, box VS 571, folder 4 (Evacuation, 1942–1947).

203. Gruening to Ickes, June 20, 1942.

204. Gruening to Ickes, June 20, 1942.

205. William Zimmerman, Office of Indian Affairs, Washington, D.C., to Claude M. Hirst, [Superintendent], Bureau of Indian Affairs, Juneau, Alaska, June 15, 1942, NARA, RG 101, file 77, Alaska State Archives, box VS 571, folder 4 (Evacuation, 1942–1947). See also Dean Kohlhoff, *When the Wind Was a River: Aleut Evacuation in World War II* (Seattle: University of Washington Press, 1995), insert, map 2, showing Aleut evacuation sites in Alaska.

206. Schwartzman, for the Commanding Officer, J. W. Wark, Captain, C.E. Adjutant, Headquarters U.S. Troops, Juneau, Alaska, to Bureau of Indian Affairs, Federal Building, Juneau, Alaska, June 18, 1942; Baish, Juneau, Alaska, to Commanding Officer, U.S. Troops, Nikolski, Alaska, June 19, 1942, NARA, RG 101, file 77, Alaska State Archives, box VS 571, folder 4 (Evacuation, 1942–1947). The removal of the Aleut from Atka and the Pribilof Islands was itself a difficult journey: they traveled in the hold of a vessel designed to carry half their number that charted an uneven course to avoid the Japanese submarines that they feared might be lurking in the waters below before being transferred to a "freight barge that stunk of rotting fish" for the remainder of a journey almost two thousand miles in length. Seiple, *Ghosts in the Fog*, 159–61.

207. Mary Breu, *Last Letters from Attu: The True Story of Etta Jones, Alaska Pioneer and Japanese P.O.W.* (Portland, Ore.: Alaska Northwest Books, 2009), 143, 149, 151–53. According to Breu, Etta Jones's grand-niece, Etta Jones was born in 1880 and had lived in Alaska since 1922. Charles Foster Jones was born in 1879 and had been employed by the Alaska Indian Service since 1930. The two married in 1923 and were both sixty-two in June 1942. Breu, *Last Letters from Attu*, 15, 17, 29, 37. Breu explains that her book is based on "descriptive letters [Etta Jones] penned, her unpublished manuscript, historical documents and personal interviews."

208. Donald Q. Palmer, Chief Information Officer, Office of Indian Affairs, Chicago, Alaska State Library, Historical Collections, MS 51-01, Alaska File: A Selection of Letters and a Report on Upper Tanana Indians, 1930–1932, folder 3; Breu, *Last Letters from Attu*, 154.

209. Nick Golodoff, *Attu Boy: A Young Alaskan's WWII Memoir* (Fairbanks: University of Alaska Press, 2915), 11–12. Golodoff likewise recalled that when "some trappers from the village [were] found shot on Attu[,] the old-timers thought it was the Japanese who shot them." Golodoff, who was born on December 19, 1935, notes that their Russian family names reflect the influence of Russian colonizers during an earlier period. Golodoff, *Attu Boy*, 7.

210. Golodoff, *Attu Boy*, 12, 51.

211. Breu, *Last Letters from Attu*, 174. See also Seiple, *Ghosts in the Fog*, for information about Karl Kasukabe.

212. Translation of Fukuzawa Mikizo, *Arushan Shugeki Senki* (Attack on the Aleutians) (Tokyo, 1943), included in John C. Kirtland and David F. Coffin Jr., *The Relocation and Internment of the Aleuts during World War II* (Anchorage: Aleutian/Pribilof Islands Association, [1981]), reprinted in Breu, *Last Letters from Attu*, 293–94. Attu is rendered both Attsu and Atta in Japanese.

213. Golodoff, *Attu Boy*, 63–64, 84, stating that the Aleut prisoners were moved to Shimizu-cho, where they were housed in "Shinto priests' quarters." See also Kohlhoff, *When the Wind Was a River*, 85–86, 106–7, 131–34.

214. Shimada Saburō and Ariiso Toshirō, *Kaigai katsudō no nihonjin* (Japanese who are active overseas) (Tokyo: Shokado, Meiji 39 [1906]), 38.

215. Golodoff, *Attu Boy*, 65, citing Henry Stewart, "Aleuts in Japan, 1942–1945," in *Alaska at War, 1941–1945: The Forgotten War Remembered*, ed. Fern Chandonnet (Fairbanks: University of Alaska Press, 2008), 303.

216. Golodoff, *Attu Boy*, 2, 17–18, 82–83, reporting that Golodoff's maternal grandmother had died on the journey to Japan. See also Donald Q. Palmer, Chief Information Officer, Office of Indian Affairs, Chicago, Alaska State Library, Historical Collections, MS 51-01, Alaska File: A Selection of Letters and a Report on Upper Tanana Indians, 1930–1932, folder 3.

217. Breu, *Last Letters from Attu*, 181, 195, 203, 227, 239, and see, generally, chap. 19 for Etta Jones's life postwar.

218. For a detailed account of the battle of Attu and the retaking of Kiska, see Stetson Conn, Rose C. Engelman, and Byron Fairchild, *Guarding the United States and Its Outposts* (Washington, D.C.: Center of Military History, United States Army, 2000), 284–97, 294 (numbers of casualties).

219. Other *nisei* had to take Japanese-language courses at army intelligence schools such as that at Fort Snelling to brush up their Japanese-language skills, and, in some cases, even that was not enough. Although his older brother served as an interpreter in the U.S. Army, Bill Tatsuda, born in Ketchikan in 1916, later told an interviewer with a chuckle, when he himself was transferred to Fort Snelling to begin his language training, they discovered that "I couldn't speak or read Japanese worth a darn. I guess I flunked!" Bill Tatsuda, interview by Tony Nakazawa, Ketchikan, Alaska, December 12, 1990, AJPRP, tape 15, transcript, 17–18. All three Tatsuda brothers served in the U.S. military during the Second World War. For a description of the language program and of the *nisei* who participated in the battle of Attu, see Hays, *Alaska's Hidden Wars*, 15–29. The word *kibei* refers to youngsters born in the United States but educated in Japan who later returned to the United States; the term *kika* refers to Canadian-born youngsters educated in Japan who later returned to Canada.

220. Conn, Engelman, and Fairchild, *Guarding the United States*, 297. For a discussion of the various considerations surrounding the joint U.S. and Canadian operations in the Aleutians, see Galen Roger Perras, *Stepping Stones to Nowhere: The Aleutian Islands, Alaska, and American Military Strategy, 1867–1945* (Vancouver: UBC Press, 2003), 139–45, 192–93.

221. Colonel A. M. Tollefson, Assistant Director, Prisoner of War Division, Office of the Provost Marshal General, Headquarters Army Service Forces, Washington, D.C., to B. M. Stauber, War Relocation Authority, Department of the Interior, Washington, D.C., December 5, 1944, Alaska State Library, Historical Collections, MS 51, box 3, folder 3-4. While Yasuda had made the best of his time at various detention or relocation camps, he was reportedly the first of the *issei* to apply to return to Alaska. The use of the phrase "former homes" serves to distance the reader from the fact that they did not leave those homes voluntarily.

222. Lucy W. Brown to Marie D. Lane, c/o R. B. Cozzens, San Francisco, California. Alaska State Library, Historical Collections, MS 51, box 3, folder 3-4.

223. Harry L. Stafford, Director, Minidoka Project, War Relocation Authority, Hunt, Idaho, to Dillon S. Myer, Director, War Relocation Authority, Washington, D.C., February 1, 1945, Alaska State Library, Historical Collections, MS 51, box 3, folder 3-4; Dillon S. Myer, Director, War Relocation Authority, to Colonel Harrison A. Gerhardt, War Department, Washington, D.C., Alaska State Library, Historical Collections, War Relocation Authority files, MS 51, box 3, folder 3-3. Among those whose request to return to Alaska was

twice denied was Harry Sotaro Kawabe, who had lived in Seward. Hays, *Alaska's Hidden Wars*, 6–7, citing Alaska Defense Command, G-2 Weekly Periodic Reports & Annexes, G-2 Report No. 146, Annex (counterintelligence) 4, March 10, 1945, NARA, RG 338.

224. Harrison A. Gerhardt, Colonel, General Staff Corps, Exec to Ass't Secretary of War, War Department, Washington, D.C., to Dillon S. Myer, Director, War Relocation Authority, Washington, D.C., May 7, 1945; H. Rex Lee, Acting Chief, Relocation Division, to Harold Fisters, Area Supervisor, War Relocation Authority, Seattle, Washington, Alaska State Library, Historical Collections, War Relocation Authority files, MS 51, box 3, folder 3-3.

225. Naske, "Relocation of Alaska's Japanese Residents," 124.

226. Some U.S. officials claimed that the Attuans preferred to settle on Atka, but the Attuans insisted that was not the case. Contrast Golodoff, *Attu Boy*, 79–80, with Donald Q. Palmer, Chief Information Officer, Office of Indian Affairs, Chicago. Alaska State Library, Historical Collections, MS 51-01, Alaska File: A Selection of Letters and a Report on Upper Tanana Indians, 1930–1932, folder 3, stating that they chose to settle on Atka "where they had friends and relatives." See also Kohlhoff, *When the Wind Was a River*, 175.

227. See Dean Kohlhoff, "Matters of Death and Life," in *When the Wind Was a River*, 108–34. Diseases included pneumonia, flu, tuberculosis, and measles, exacerbated by the lack of available medical treatment. As a petition signed by forty-nine Aleut women confined at one facility explained, "This place is no place for a living creature." There was no running water, inadequate clothing, impure water that caused "the children [to] get skin disease," and no bathing or laundry facilities. Petition (Aleut Women), U.S. Fish and Wildlife Service, NARA, RG 22, [identifier 2641505].

228. Kangas, interview, 14. Five evacuees were listed as having died in a hospital. Handwritten note on list, "Japanese Alaskan Internees," forwarded by Calvert L. Dedrick, Chief, Statistical Division, Wartime Civil Control Administration, San Francisco, California, to Major M. H. Astrup, Western Defense Command and Fourth Army, January 30, 1943, Alaska State Library, Historical Collections, War Relocation Authority files, MS 51, box 3, folder 3-2.

229. Karmun, interview, 21–22.

230. Masako Fukawa, ed., *Nikkei Fishermen on the BC Coast: Their Biographies and Photographs* (Madeira Park, B.C.: Harbour Publishing, 2007), 43.

231. Mack Mori, interview, 11; Roy Kiyooka, *Mothertalk: Life Stories of Mary Kiyoshi Kiyooka* (Edmonton, Alberta: NeWest Press, 1997), 140.

232. Enomoto, *Honouring Our People*, 210–12 (interview with Shig Kuwabara), 214–19 (interview with Roy Uyeda). Uyeda would return to Canada only in 1958 and to British Columbia only in 1977, after living in Montreal for eighteen years. For a detailed discussion of Canada's postwar expatriation policy, see Ann Gomer Sunahara, "Deportation: The Final Solution to Canada's 'Japanese Problem,'" in *Ethnicity, Power and Politics in Canada*, eds. Jorgen Dahlie and Tissa Fernando (Toronto: Methune, 1981), 254–78; and Greg Robinson, *A Tragedy of Democracy: Japanese Confinement in North America* (New York: Columbia University Press, 2010), 262–83.

233. Fukawa, *Spirit of the Nikkei Fleet*, 148.

234. Inouye, Hoshiko, and Heshiki, *Alaska's Japanese Pioneers*, 26–27, interview with Patrick Hagiwara. Kichirobei Tatsuda, known as Jimmy, who had run a boardinghouse and grocery store in Ketchikan for many years, was likewise sent to New Mexico, where he was

separated from his family in Minidoka for the duration of the war. Bill Tatsuda, interview, 12; Inouye, Hoshiko, and Heshiki, *Alaska's Japanese Pioneers*, 20–21.

235. Leonard C. Allen, Indian Office, Ketchikan, Alaska, to Indian Office, Juneau, Alaska, April 8, 1942, NARA, RG 101, file 77-1, Alaska State Archives, box VS 571, folder 5 (Japanese Evacuation, 1942–1945). Harvey's given name is sometimes recorded as Harry and his family name is sometimes misspelled as Sharai.

236. List, "Japanese Alaskan Internees," forwarded by Dedrick to Astrup, January 30, 1943.

237. Robert A. Lefler, Assistant Solicitor, to Helen Shippe, Medical Department, Room 501, March 9, 1944, Alaska State Library, Historical Collections, War Relocation Authority files, MS 51, box 3, folder 3-2, citing memorandum of July 16, 1942, from Major Herman P. Goebel to Captain Astrup, laying out the mixed marriage policy of the Western Defense Command. The rule in question also applied to children in Oregon and California.

238. For a detailed discussion of Canadian policy regarding Japanese Canadians after the Second World War, see Patricia E. Roy, "Lessons in Citizenship, 1945–1949: The Delayed Return of the Japanese to Canada's Pacific Coast," *Pacific Northwest Quarterly* 93, no. 2 (Spring 2002): 69–80.

239. K. T. Homma and C. G. Isaksson, *Tomekichi Homma: The Story of a Canadian* (Surrey, B.C.: Hancock House, 2008), 56–57.

240. Andrea Geiger, "Writing Racial Barriers into Law: Upholding B.C.'s Denial of the Vote to Its Japanese Canadian Citizens, *Homma v. Cunningham*, 1902," in *Nikkei in the Pacific Northwest: Japanese Americans and Japanese Canadians in the Twentieth Century*, ed. Louis Fiset and Gail M. Nomura (Seattle: University of Washington Press, 2006), 32, citing conversation with Keay Homma, Surrey, B.C., January 19, 1998.

241. Fukawa, *Spirit of the Nikkei Fleet*, 117.

242. Keibo Oiwa, ed., *Stone Voices: Wartime Writings of Japanese Canadian Issei* (Montreal: Véhicule Press, 1991), 117–19. Kaoru Ikeda was born in 1875 in Niigata-ken, the same prefecture where Arichika Ikeda was born, and immigrated to Canada in 1914 after they married. Oiwa, *Stone Voices*.

243. One Japanese immigrant family in British Columbia who already lived in a remote area was also reportedly not removed. Stapleton, Rushton, and Burpee to Taylor, March 13, 1942.

244. Taguchi, interview, transcript, 1–3. Kazuo Ito also recounts the stories of two *nikkeijin* who told others they were Chinese when they were confronted with anti-Japanese hostility after the outbreak of war. Ito, *Issei*, 156, quoting Kano Furukawa and James M. Unosawa, both of Seattle. Similar strategies were employed in Canada, where Grace Eiko Thomson's mother, Sawae Nishikihama, recalled that Chinese Canadians took to wearing buttons to ensure that they were not mistakenly identified as Japanese. Thomson, *Chiru Sakura—Falling Cherry Blossoms*, 40.

245. Sarasohn, *Issei, Portrait of a Pioneer*, 139.

246. Fukawa, *Spirit of the Nikkei Fleet*, 159.

247. Information provided by Linda Kawamoto Reid, Archivist, Nikkei National Museum, Burnaby, B.C., citing RG 31, folder 18, Census of Canada 1921, Skeena District, Bella Coola Agency; British Columbia, Canada, Marriage Index, 1872–1935, Death Index, 1872–1990. On July 29, 1907, Vickers married Cecilia Carpenter, born in Bella Bella, B.C.,

in 1886. While Joe Vickers himself died in Vancouver in 1926, he was buried in Namu, B.C., about twenty miles south of Bella Bella.

248. Nakayama, *Kanada dōhō hatten taikan: Zen*, 774.

249. For the claim that the Japanese government secretly funded Japanese fishers who were willing to serve as spies, also discussed in chapter 4, see Nakayama, *Kanada dōhō hatten taikan: Zen*, 774–75. For an example of a instance where a Japanese figure was incorporated into a dance performed at a potlatch held, in this case, at the Gitksan village of Gitsegukla, see Margaret Anderson and Marjorie Halpin, eds., *Potlatch at Gitsegukla: William Beynon's 1945 Field Notebooks* (Vancouver: UBC Press, 2000), 97–98, 259n5, describing the emergence of a "Japanese Warrior naxnox" that likely had "reference to the Second World War." A "naxnox" is a powerful and often dangerous spirit that poses a potential danger to the community.

250. Knight, *Indians at Work*, 325, noting that some confiscated fishing boats were sold and some rented. See also Newell, *Tangled Webs of History*, 106, 115, stating that "some Indian fishers obtained confiscated boats at low prices" and that the "expulsion of the Japanese from the coast [and the subsequent auction of their entire fishing fleet] proved to be windfalls that temporarily boosted [Indigenous] participation in both fishing and fish-processing."

251. Leslie A. Robertson and the Kwagu'l Gixsam Clan, *Standing Up with Ga'axsta'las: Jane Constance Cook and the Politics of Memory, Church and Custom* (Vancouver: UBC Press, 2012), 265, 354–56. Regarding Jane Cook's use of the word "Japs," Robertson observes: "While jarring, this use of the Anglo-Canadian label for Japanese immigrants suggests aboriginal participation in the mainstream discourse of the 1920s. Just as the epithet *Indian* is deemed pejorative when used by particular speakers today, the term *Jap* had not yet accumulated the stigma associated with it during the Second World War." Robertson and the Kwagu'l Gixsam Clan, *Standing Up with Ga'axsta'las*, 520n80.

252. Knight and Koizumi, *Man of Our Times*, 61. Yoshida notes that only about a third of the Japanese Canadian fishers who fished the coastal waters of British Columbia returned to fishing after the war. Knight and Koizumi, *Man of Our Times*, 95.

253. Knight and Koizumi, *Man of Our Times*, 61. Newell notes that "in 1949 and 1950, Skeena chiefs and the local northern branches of the Native Brotherhood had spoken out against the return of Japanese Canadians to the North Coast." Newell, *Tangled Webs of History*, 134. See also Rolf Knight, *Indians at Work*, 325, 364n9. For a discussion of Canada's postwar expatriation policy, see Sunahara, "Deportation"; and Robinson, *Tragedy of Democracy*, 262–83. For a discussion of Canada's refusal to allow Japanese Canadians to return to the coast until 1949, see Roy, "Lessons in Citizenship."

254. Yesaki, *Sutebusuton*, 134.

255. Co-operative Committee on Japanese Canadians, "Brief re Repatriation of Japanese Canadians," Toronto, Ontario, July 25, 1945, Nikkei National Museum, file 90-10.

256. Co-operative Committee on Japanese Canadians, "Brief re Repatriation of Japanese Canadians." Although Canada's prime minister, William Lyon Mackenzie King, declared in the House of Commons in August 1944, that "It is a fact no person of Japanese race born in Canada has been charged with any act of sabotage or disloyalty during the years of war," he also went on to state that "[his] government is of the view that persons of Japanese race, whether Japanese nationals or British subjects by nationalization or birth, who have shown disloyalty to Canada during the war, should not have the privilege of remaining in Canada

after the struggle is terminated." Statement by W. L. Mackenzie King before the House of Commons, August 4, 1944, in *Report of the Department of Labour on the Re-Establishment of Japanese in Canada, 1944–1946* (January 1947), 6, published in Department of Labour of Canada, *Two Reports on Japanese Canadians in World War II* (New York: Arno Press, 1978). Note, however, that those who were expatriated to Japan were not necessarily individuals found—or even suspected of having been—disloyal. Roger Daniels notes that "not one single case of espionage or sabotage by an ethnic Japanese was ever detected in the United States after war came." Roger Daniels, "Incarcerating Japanese Americans: An Atrocity Revisited," *Peace & Change* 23, no. 2 (April 1998): 117–34, 120.

257. "[Returnees] to Seek Kin in Atom-Bombed City," *Vancouver Daily Province*, May 23, 1946.

258. The total number of those exiled from Canada was 3,964: 34 percent remained Japanese subjects, 15 percent were naturalized British subjects, and 51 percent were Canadians by birth. HomeComing Panel, "Exiled to Japan," October 10–11, 1992, Nikkei National Museum, IF/95.055.

259. William E. Conklin, "The Transformation of Meaning: Legal Discourse and Canadian Internment Camps," *International Journal for the Semiotics of Law* 9, no. 27 (1996): 230.

260. *New Canadian*, March 12, 1949, noting that British Columbia's legislation was introduced in March 1949, just three weeks before the federal government's restoration of the franchise was to take effect on March 31, 1949. British Columbia had already acted to restore the franchise to Chinese, South Asians, and Indigenous people living off-reserve.

261. For a description of the coast watchers on Haida Gwaii, see Lucien J. Kemble, Port Alberni, B.C., to Neil and Betty Carey, Sandspit, B.C., November 19, 1976, "Wartime Coast Watchers," Neil and Betty Carey Collection, Prince Rupert City and Regional Archives, Prince Rupert, B.C. North of the international border in Alaska, travel along some parts of the Pacific coast was also restricted. See, e.g., Norah Marks Dauenhauer, "Five Slices of Salmon," in Judith Roche and Meg McHutchison, eds., *First Fish, First People; Salmon Tales of the North Pacific Rim* (Seattle: University of Washington Press, 1998), 103–04, 106, recalling that before the war, her Tlingit family often "wintered in tents at Graves Harbor and other sites on the outer Pacific Coast of what is now Glacier Bay National Park" but that after World War II began, "travel to the Pacific Ocean end of Icy Strait was restricted."

262. As John J. Stephan writes of the Kuril Islands, "When the tide reversed in 1943, the archipelago suddenly emerged in Japanese eyes as the empire's first line of defence and in American eyes as stepping stones to the enemy's heartland." Stephan, *Kuril Islands*, 3. As Breu notes, "The main purpose of the Aleutians operations by Japanese task forces was threefold: (1) to defend the Japanese homeland from an attack by United States naval carrier task forces through the Northern Pacific Ocean, (2) to protect Japan from an attack by the United States land-based bombers using air bases in the Aleutian Islands, and (3) to create a diversion from the Battle at Midway." Breu, *Last Letters from Attu*, 177.

263. Although it did launch a few bombing missions on the two northernmost of the Kuril Islands, the United States reportedly decided by 1944 not to invade Paramushiro and Shumushu Islands or to advance on Japan through the Kuril Islands, in part because it would have left any U.S. troops posted there as isolated and devoid of support as the Japanese troops on Attu and Kiska had been. Perras, *Stepping Stones to Nowhere*, 160, 162. See also Conn, Engelman, and Fairchild, *Guarding the United States*, 298.

264. Keiichi Takeuchi, "How Japan Learned about the Outside World: The Views of Other Countries Incorporated in Japanese School Textbooks, 1868–1986," *Hitotsubashi Journal of Social Studies* 19 (1987): 11. The term "sea of islands" is borrowed from Epeli Hau'ofa, "Our Sea of Islands," *Contemporary Pacific* 6, no. 1 (Spring 1994): 147–61. Brett L. Walker also discusses Japan's interest in establishing a "pelagic empire." Brett L. Walker, *A Concise History of Japan* (Cambridge: Cambridge University Press, 2015), 224–27.

265. Takeuchi, "Outside World," 11.

266. "Japs Getting Worst of It: Declare That Their Rights [in Hawaii] Are Being Discriminated against by Americans and They Desire that They Shall Be Recognized," *Fairbanks Daily Times*, September 19, 1906. See also Toyama Yoshifumi, *Nihon to Hawaii, ichimei, kakumei zengo no Hawaii,* 1–2, 17–25, published by the Japan Patriot League in 1893, arguing that "Japan should secure its interest in Hawaii to fight a race war against the U.S.," quoted in Sakada, "Enactment of the 1891 Immigration Law," 81–82.

267. "Why Japanese Are Coming," *British Columbian Weekly*, January 7, 1908.

268. Fewer than 2,000 of 158,000 Hawaiians of Japanese descent were incarcerated during the war. Although those regarded as "dangerous enemy aliens"—a category that included commercial fishermen—were detained within the hours following the attack on Pearl Harbor, many were released following investigation. Note, however, that martial law was declared right after the attack and not lifted until October 24, 1944. For a detailed discussion of wartime policy in Hawaii, see *Personal Justice Denied*, 261, 268, 278.

Afterword

1. Max Everest-Phillips, "The Pre-war Fear of Japanese Espionage: Its Impact and Legacy," *Journal of Contemporary History* 42, no. 2 (2007): 244, 251. As Everest-Phillips explains, "The history of espionage is often a history of ignorance, xenophobia, racial prejudice and stereotyping. Allegations of foreign subversion often play an important part for political leadership in promoting a sense of national unity, clarifying national values and providing a high moral sanction and sense of righteousness. Emphasizing the 'falsehoods' of a foreign country helps a government underline the legitimacy and just authority of its own institutions." Everest-Phillips, "Pre-war Fear of Japanese Espionage," 263.

2. Ryuichi Yoshida later reported, for example, that in his observation, there was a direct link between resentment of race-based discrimination and attraction to Japanese militarism. Rolf Knight and Maya Koizumi, *A Man of Our Times: The Life History of a Japanese-Canadian Fisherman* (Vancouver, B.C.: New Star Books, 1976), 41. Although he himself was opposed to Japanese militarism, Yoshida admits that he nevertheless hoped that "Japan wouldn't be defeated or destroyed." Knight and Koizumi, *Man of Our Times*, 55.

3. As persons who remained Japanese subjects, ironically, the *issei* men arrested during the days immediately following the war were afforded a level of due process denied those born in the United States. See, e.g., Claus-M. Naske, "The Relocation of Alaska's Japanese Residents," *Pacific Northwest Quarterly* 74, no. 3 (July 1983): 127, citing *Congressional Record*, 73d Cong., 2d Sess. (1934), 128.

4. "Indian Schools Secured for Japs: 6000 More to Be Moved at Once," newspaper clipping dated June 5, 1942, Nikkei National Museum, Burnaby, B.C., Kishizo Kimura Fonds, 2010.4.4.13.65; As noted in chapter 5, Japanese American detention facilities located on

Indian reservations included the Poston War Relocation Center on the Colorado River Indian Reservation and the Gila River War Relocation Center on the Gila River Indian Reservation.

5. For a detailed discussion of blood degree in relation to Japanese Americans in Alaska, see chapter 5.

6. See, e.g., "Why Japs Are Unwelcome," *The British Columbian*, March 2, 1909, declaring that "the wish of the people of the west is that the [frontier of American civilization] shall be the water line of the Pacific ocean." See also chapter 4.

7. James Baker, Clerk, Executive Council, British Columbia, to Secretary of State, Ottawa, May 6, 1897, B.C. Sessional Paper No. 74b, complaining that British Columbia's "geographical contiguity to Japan" rendered it more vulnerable to "unchecked immigration" from Asia than other Canadian provinces.

8. Kazuo Ito, *Issei: A History of Japanese Immigrants in North America*, trans. Shinichiro Nakamura and Jean S. Gerard (Seattle, 1973), 280–81.

Index

Adachi, Ken, 183, 308n135

Adams-Onis Treaty of 1819, 38

Aikawa, Shiga, 133–36

Ainu Cultural Promotion Law, 253n115, 274n138

Ainu Moshir. *See* Ezo, Hokkaido

Ainu people: assimilation of, 117; avoidance of Russian subjugation, 22; and boundary with Japanese areas, 230n32; as "Caucasoid race," 113; as colonized minority, 43, 238n148; and herring, 145, 290n152; Hokkaido as traditional homeland of, xv, 13, 19–20, 22, 76, 77, 117–18, 229n12, 274n137; and Indigenous trading networks, 19–20, 23, 26, 43, 228n8; Japanese perceptions of, 77, 118, 252–53n115; Japanese relations with, 22–23, 41, 43, 58, 82; Kuril Islands territory of, 22, 23, 40, 41; legal status of, 117; at Louisiana Purchase Exposition in St. Louis, Missouri, 77, 253n118, 292n173; and Manchuria, 176; as maritime people, 229n12; and Matsumae clan, 43; Meiji government's policy toward, 117; resistance to Russian encroachment, 24; seal hunting of, 157–58; trade in pelts of sea otters, 230n31

Alaska: and Aboriginal title, 72, 73, 118, 251n97; access to resources of, 72; boundaries of, 11, 45, 260n16; and British Columbia boundary, 9, 16, 48, 50, 51, 53, 156, 241n184; British Columbia's proposal for acquisition of, 53; census figures for, 76, 252n108; Creole population of, 25, 79, 231n41, 233n72, 271–72n113; as derivation of Aliaska, 24, 230–31n37; as designated military area, 187, 189; exclusion of Japanese labor migrants in, 14; fishing license regulation in, 154, 156; forced removal in, 187, 189–200, 215, 217, 219, 307n134, 309n152, 309n158, 311n182; gold strike attracting miners to, 43; governance structure of, 272n114; Indigenous peoples of, 45, 47, 54, 101–2, 112–13, 239n159, 245–46n39, 266n69; integration into political and economic structures, 7, 11; Japanese castaways on island near, 80; Japanese immigrants in, 131, 154, 156, 159, 178, 281n68; and Japanese poaching claims, 156–61; Japan's attack on, 202–7, 208, 214, 313n197, 319n262; Japan's proximity to, 132, 147, 162; panhandle of, 1, 9, 17, 18, 34, 48, 50, 178, 233n72; peninsula of, 1, 17, 24, 28, 160, 201, 202; population at European contact, 30; as possible base of Japanese attack on U.S., 178–79, 200–202, 304n83; racialized violence in, 98; representation in Congress, 272n115; rumors of Japanese invasion of, 162, 177; Russian colonization of, 24–25, 43; sea otter population of, 43; settler communities of, 8; as state, 221n4, 272n114; as territory, xv, 272n114; Treaty of Cession, 43–46, 48, 239n159; Tsimshian attempts to secure reservation in, 62–63, 65–66, 72–73, 86, 246–47n51, 247n55; understanding the borderlands of, 16; U.S. acquisition of Russian interests in, 13, 42, 43–46, 47, 52, 53, 54, 83, 112, 122, 157, 179, 239n154, 239n155, 239n159, 249n79; U.S. census of, 233n72; U.S. geopolitical considerations in, 44, 219; U.S. influence over, 6; U.S. military rounding up Japanese men in, 81; Jujiro Wada in, 81–83, 85, 86, 87, 162, 255n128, 256n136; white residents

Tule Lake War Relocation Center
(detention camp), California, 196, 198,
310n173
Tydings-McDuffie Act (1934) (U.S.),
281n63
Tyhee Jack (chief), 297n239

Unalaska, 30, 160, 201–2, 204, 205
Unangan (Unangax̂) people, 20, 205,
206–7, 208, 233n72
Union Steamship Company, 184
United States: and Aboriginal title, 118;
anti-Japanese sentiment in, 168, 173,
176–77, 187, 217; boundary drawing and
law used by, 7, 219; as colonial power, 16,
43, 117, 119, 168–69, 219, 274n137, 300n40;
Convention of 1818 with Britain, 31–34,
37, 40, 52, 234n83; Convention of 1824
with Russia, 33–35, 235n93, 235n97,
236n99, 236n100; defining of, 8;
deportation laws of, 269n91; erasure of
Indigenous presence in, 14; federal
Indian law doctrine in, 271n109; federal
Indian law in, 221n1; fishing license
regulation, 154; founding principles of,
69, 177, 219; Gentlemen's Agreement
with Japan, 108–9, 113, 131, 167; imperialism of, 1, 4, 5, 8, 11, 13, 16, 20, 29–31, 36, 38,
43, 101, 117, 119, 168–69, 218, 219, 274n137,
300n40; Indigenous citizenship rights
in, 67, 70, 87, 110, 177; Indigenous land
rights in, 62–63, 69–73, 118, 244–45n25;
Japanese immigration to, 174, 176; and
Japanese return migration, 219–20, 303n74;
and land-based access to Pacific Ocean,
31, 38, 52; and Oregon Country, 32, 34,
35, 36, 41, 52, 234n83, 241n192; racialized
immigration laws of, 113, 116, 130, 170–73,
176, 186, 209, 272n117, 301n51; racism of,
177, 303n76; relations with Japan, 95, 157,
162, 164, 168–70, 172, 262n34; reservation
policy of, 64, 71–73, 102, 116, 250n88,
266n70; and Russian empire, 33;
settlement in West, 76; territorial claims
in north Pacific coast, 1, 4, 13, 14, 31–34;

trade with Japan, 38, 40–41, 42, 53, 75,
168, 237n133, 238n137; treaty agreements
of, 14; and Treaty of Paris (1783), 31,
234n80, 241n192; violence used in
displacement of Indigenous people,
101–2, 266n69. *See also* U.S.-Canada
border, U.S.-Mexico border
U.S. Board of Indian Commissioners,
62–63, 69, 250n91
U.S.-Canada border: border crossings of,
51, 86, 225–26n27, 248n67; and cession
treaty between Russia and U.S., 48; and
Coast Mountains, 9, 49, 88; evolving
bodies of law on, 7–8, 13, 102; and
forty-ninth parallel, 9, 31–32, 38–39, 53,
225n20, 225–26n27, 248n67; and
Indigenous fisheries, 67, 248n65; and
Indigenous peoples, 9, 13, 51; and
Indigenous territories, xvi, 51, 63, 73–75,
106–7, 218; and Indigenous trading
networks, 74; and Jay Treaty, 23, 107,
268–69n90; maritime border of, 48, 74,
156, 264n49; and 141st meridian, 9, 48,
49–50; racialized legal framework of, 8,
57, 84, 86–87, 217; role of nonhuman
actors on, 9–10; and Salish Sea, 225n25;
San Juan Island boundary dispute,
241n187; state-sanctioned crossing
points along, 10; survey of, 48–51; U.S.
regulation of, 14; World War II defense
of, 213. *See also* Canada-U.S. border
U.S. Civil War, 44, 46
U.S. Congress: on Alaska as base of attack
from Japan, 304n83; on citizenship for
Indigenous people, 87; on immigration,
113; moratorium on seal hunting on
Pribilof Islands, 157; reservations for
Indigenous peoples, 64, 71–73, 250n88;
on treaty making with tribal nations,
274n141; on tribes recognized as
independent nations, 63, 73
U.S. Department of Education, 65, 252n108,
266n69
U.S. Department of Interior, 63, 189,
266n69

CPSIA information can be obtained
at www.ICGtesting.com
Printed in the USA
LVHW111919021122
732204LV00003B/64